GEORGE CLINTON

& THE COSMIC ODYSSEY OF THE P-FUNK EMPIRE

GEORGE CLINTON

& THE COSMIC ODYSSEY OF THE P-FUNK EMPIRE

KRIS NEEDS

OMNIBUS PRESS

London / New York / Paris / Sydney / Copenhagen / Berlin / Madrid / Tokyo

Exclusive Distributors
Music Sales Limited,
14/15 Berners Street,
London, W1T 3LJ.

Music Sales Corporation
180 Madison Avenue, 24th Floor,
New York,
NY 10016,
USA.

Macmillan Distribution Services
56 Parkwest Drive
Derrimut, Vic 3030,
Australia.

Every effort has been made to trace the copyright holders of the photographs in this book but one or
two were unreachable. We would be grateful if the photographers concerned would contact us.

Typeset by Phoenix Photosetting, Chatham, Kent
Printed in the EU

A catalogue record for this book is available from the British Library.

Visit Omnibus Press on the web at www.omnibuspress.com

Contents

Introduction	7
Chapter 1: Pre–Funk	9
Chapter 2: Nothing Before Me But Thang	31
Chapter 3: There's A Riot Going On With Laughing Sam's Dice	56
Chapter 4: Motor City Madness	77
Chapter 5: Mommy, What's A Funkadelic?	97
Chapter 6: Looney Tunes And Scary Melodies	122
Chapter 7: America Eats Its Young	142
Chapter 8: Standing On The Verge Of Getting It On	163
Chapter 9: Space Is The Place	188
Chapter 10: The Awesome Power Of A Fully Operational Mothership	213
Chapter 11: Don't Fake The Funk Or Your Nose Will Grow	234
Chapter 12: The Empire Strikes Black	250
Chapter 13: Invasion Of The Booty Snatchers	267
Chapter 14: Old Dog New Tricks	284
Chapter 15: Give Out But Don't Give Up	304
Epilogue	323
Where Are They Now?	327
Acknowledgements	338
Bibliography	341
Index	345

For Helen

Introduction

November 1989, Apollo Theatre, Harlem

For the last two hours George Clinton and his faithful Mothership crew members have been giving up The Funk on the legendary boards which probably figure higher in Dr Funkenstein's history than any other stage in the world.

An extraterrestrial Biblical vision in long white robes and multi-coloured hair, this last great figure from black music's seminal sixties and revolutionary seventies is showing he can still trump anything from the eighties as he conducts both band and rabid audience through immortal P-Funk classics such as 'Cosmic Slop', 'Maggot Brain' and 'Flash Light' for over two hours.

A few months earlier I'd realised the lifelong ambition to interview George, followed by subsequent meetings where he relived and recounted what it had meant to be the planet's loudest and most innovative exponent of The Funk and its nasty essence. A quarter century later, here's my chance to tell the astonishing tale of this towering figure of 20th century music and the stellar musicians who flew with him during his incredible journey, along the way creating the most gloriously crazy (and most sampled) catalogue in music.

You will hear about the self-described blackest, funkiest and filthiest band of all time that would materialise from a pyramid onstage in America's biggest arenas while a giant skull puffed a six-foot spliff; the landing of a full-blown Mothership obtained from their record company at a cost of half a million dollars to disgorge Dr Funkenstein in all his space pimp finery; 'Starchild' Garry Shider wielding his stroboscopic Bop Gun while flying over disbelieving crowds; a lineage of guitarists clad only in oversized diapers; the cartoon space-bass funk onslaughts of Bootsy Collins; the horrific drug guzzling contest which nearly sent Tawl Ross – furthest out Funkadelic of all – beyond the point of no return; Eddie Hazel – the only guitarist to ever carry Hendrix's incendiary mantle before tragically losing his own inner battle; epoch-making powerhouse drummers such as Jerome 'Bigfoot' Brailey; oddball satellite bands such as Sparky & the Pimpadelics and spin-offs such as the Brides Of Funkenstein; how an artist called Pedro Bell defined a new cartoon world of doo doo chasers and hardcore jollies; old-school music business skullduggery sparking full-blown mutiny and the subsequent fall of an empire; trailblazing masterpieces arising from hard, high or triumphant times set against a backdrop of Black Power, barbershops, socio-cultural revolutions and vast quantities of mind-expanding drugs.

It's hard to imagine what life would have been like without P-Funk or how music might have ended up today. This is a story about famous dogs told through the eyes of a lifelong 'maggot'.

Let's take it to the stage...

Chapter One

Pre-Funk

"That guy has great commercial potential. He's also clean cut, soft spoken, with a beautiful smile. Tailored pin-stripes and a briefcase."
Raynoma Gordy on George Clinton, circa 1963

Whether indulging in expert myth-stoking or extreme barbershop ribaldry, George Edward Clinton always says he dropped into the world in the outside toilet of the family home in Kannapolis, North Carolina on July 22, 1941.

He maintains that this was where he entered the world simply because his mother, Julia Keaton, told him, recounting at different times, "My mother thought she was just going to the bathroom" or, "She was on her way to the bathroom. I almost got wiped out." This may not be as glamorous as Dr Funkenstein ascending from the hatch of the Mothership but George has always been a master of the grand entrance.

George liked to describe Kannapolis as "out in the sticks behind the pigpen", painting a picture of a rural backwoods, although the town was known for its household linens and textiles industries and now enjoys small city status. It's also the home of stock-car racing, which sprang out of night-time bootlegging runs during the twenties.

Brendan Greaves runs the Paradise Of Bachelors obscure Americana label from a nearby address and knows the area well. He told me, "Kannapolis spans two counties, bearing the odd distinction of being named for Cannon Mills; a rather bittersweet association given the rapid decline of the textile economy here in the mid-South in the last few decades.

"The Western Piedmont of North Carolina demonstrates a rich warp and weft of culture and landscape. Situated on the edge of the Piedmont's rolling hills, near the Appalachian foothills, it's beautiful country – known as one of the state's centres of textile production (the Piedmont was once one of the foremost producers of denim).

"One of the notable cultural contributions of textile mill towns is the development of the string band and bluegrass music fostered in these and surrounding communities, black and white alike. It was perhaps sonically influenced in part by the rapid, mechanised pace of the textile machinery in the factories, in addition of course by mountain ballads, old-time string band music, minstrelsy, parlour guitar music, and African American Piedmont blues and banjo styles. Earl Scruggs and Don Gibson, as well as David Lee Roth, hail from Cleveland County.

"Twenty-five miles to the south west, Charlotte is the closest major city and, in its heyday, preceded and rivalled Nashville as a major recording nexus for 'hillbilly music'. The Carter Family, Uncle Dave Macon and Bill Monroe all made early recordings there, but ultimately the city couldn't compete with Nashville's WSM (Radio) and Grand Ole Opry. However, Charlotte remained a recording hotbed on a smaller scale, with Arthur 'Guitar Boogie' Smith's studios hosting sessions by James Brown and legions of soul and country stars and aspirants. Kannapolis plays a vital role in the soul and gospel music history of the Carolinas. Even in his short time there, George Clinton would have been exposed to a wealth of music, both sacred and secular, black and white."

Like many African-American families, the Clinton clan lived in extreme poverty. George found responsibilities thrust upon him at an early age, being the eldest of nine children born to Julia, who tried to support her family through cleaning and baby-sitting work, but times were hard.

George told John Corbett, author of *Extended Play: Sounding Off From John Cage To Dr. Funkenstein,* "The first thing I can remember I was about five years old. My father had just come back from the service. The war was over; everybody was talking about the atomic bomb. I can remember the blackouts, big searchlights all over the sky at night. And in the daytime you couldn't see the sky for rows and rows and rows of planes. I mean, it literally had a *top* on it, all day, every day."

George's first memory of music having any kind of impact on his soul was as a seven year old, hearing his mother and sister playing Louis Jordan and Charlie Brown records when they were getting ready to go out. His father wasn't around much of the time.

Starting during World War One, large numbers of rural black families migrated to cities along the northeastern seaboard, west coast and industrial belt running from New York and Philadelphia through Cleveland to Chicago. Looking for work and a better standard of living, the Clinton family headed north, first taking in Virginia and Washington DC. In 1952, they settled in New Jersey; the 'Garden State', birthplace of FM radio, drive-in movies, the zipper, the phonograph, the motion picture camera and ice-cream cone, along with Dionne Warwick, Faye Adams, Frank Sinatra, Count Basie, jazz pianist Bill Evans and the Four Seasons.

Like many, the Clintons gravitated to Newark, New Jersey's 'Gateway City'. During the 19th and early 20th century, the state's largest metropolis had been a vital centre of the Industrial Revolution as one of America's major air, shipping and rail hubs and centre for the pharmaceutical and chemical industries. However, Newark was in decline by the time George and his family arrived, and was among America's most impoverished cities.

George attended the recently opened Clinton Place Junior High School (off the main Clinton Avenue thoroughfare) in downtown Newark. By all accounts it was a brand new facility with several cool teachers. The school song reflected the optimism of its educational ideals; 'Nestled in Newark on a busy street, stands a school that can't be beat, Clinton Place, oh Clinton Place, your banners raised on high, we sing to you as song of praise your name never will never die' – George

11

was singing his name at a young age. While still attending school, he proved he could work with people when he made it to foreman during his first holiday job, at the Wham-O hula hoop factory. The company led the market in blockbuster fads, following the hula hoop with the frisbee to huge success, accompanied by suitably zany advertising.

Having made the long trip from North Carolina, Newark would have been the first vibrant black community the young George spent any amount of time in, with new social patterns, entertainment outlets and a cultural legacy for him to explore. In the early fifties, black music was pretty divided between songs of religious devotion and the rhythm and blues that would soon magnetise George. The term 'rhythm and blues' was originally coined by *Billboard* in 1949 as a means of describing 'race' music in a less offensive way to blacks and make it palatable to white audiences. R&B quickly began to evolve into something approaching the sound and meaning of its name, in much the same way as would subsequently happen with rock'n'roll, doo-wop, or punk.

As theatrical rocker Screamin' Jay Hawkins, an early perpetrator of sinister onstage props and theatrical shock tactics, later observed, "Can't get to soul without rhythm 'n' blues. And gospel. And what they call rock'n'roll, which ain't nothing but R&B. Labels are bullshit. You wanna get to the sixties, you gotta start with the forties and the beginning of rhythm and blues … Somewhere along the mid-fifties, people started doing gospel and blues, too. You can't make a clean separation anywhere."

In rural areas, rhythm and blues encompassed gospel, hillbilly and country blues as dominating influences, eventually morphing into deep soul and the rockabilly which spawned Elvis and magnetised white teenagers. Iconic vocalist Isaac Hayes recalls being instructed as a youngster that the blues was 'plantation darkie stuff'. The cities produced their own sleeker, harder model, incorporating urban blues, gospel, big band modern jazz and the harmonies of black vocal groups such as the Inkspots and Mills Brothers. There were two different styles for vastly different environments – country and the ever-growing but already rotting ghettos emerging in the cities. R&B provided momentary escape, whereas church music promoted eternal joy and salvation through devotional celebration.

For many families, the church provided most of their direct musical exposure. Many of the black singers I've interviewed over the last 40 years credit the local gospel choir as their initial musical outlet, the church a vital part of growing up. Rather than running the streets, getting into the kind of trouble which would magnify as they got older, the church gave the most deprived neighbourhoods a sense of unity, equality and inspiration in early years, families out on a Sunday morning in their best clothes, relishing their week's spiritual and cultural highlight. The power of the preacher and euphoric eruptions of the gospel music which drove the congregations to noisy heights of speaking-in-tongues catharsis would later make its presence felt in George's devotional funk gatherings.

Although Newark's church music would find a global audience at Whitney Houston's funeral in 2012, it had thrived, largely unnoticed by outsiders, for around a century before that. Decorum and etiquette went out the window as the singers let their emotions fly, jettisoning their inhibitions and sometimes discovering unforeseen vocal talents. In the fifties, gospel was a heart-lifting release for participants. It would all be going on inside the warm sanctity of the church, no matter how harsh the environment outside was.

George's musical enlightenment was enhanced by his cousin Ruth in Passaic, who gave him popular records of the day. Ruth lived next door to one of the Shirelles, long before the girl group goddesses led by Shirley Owens hit big later in the decade with such lustrous outings as 'Will You Love Me Tomorrow', 'Dedicated To The One I Love' and 'Soldier Boy'. Their first single, 'I Met Him On A Sunday', came about after a schoolmate at New Jersey's Passaic High School mentioned the group to her mother, Florence Greenberg, who just happened to be president of the Scepter record company.

The wide-eyed, teetering-on-teenage George was allowed to watch the Shirelles rehearse and later witnessed them at Harlem's legendary Apollo Theatre at 253 W 125th Street. It would become a key venue in his musical development. Occupied by Minsky's Burlesque until

1932, the Apollo was taken over by theatre-owner Sydney Cohen, who refurbished the 20-year-old building, reopening it in 1934 as the 125th Street Apollo Theatre – a black variety entertainment centre which admitted black customers. After Cohen was edged out by established local promoter Leo Becher, the Apollo started presenting all-day bills mixing variety acts with jazz giants of the day at Depression-friendly admission prices. Operating as a black-run community epicentre, the Apollo established its legend over the next few years, with Wednesday's Amateur Nights (which unearthed stars such as Ella Fitzgerald and Sarah Vaughan).

The Theatre got through the World War Two, surviving the 1943 Harlem riot which raged for two days after a black army private was shot by a white cop on 126th Street. It left six dead, looted stores and increased the isolation of what was turning into New York's black city within a city. White audiences stopped coming up to the Apollo as the neighbourhood gained its 'no go' reputation for non-blacks, but the venue continued operating as one of the key spots for black artists to play in the US, along with Washington's Howard Theatre.

I'll admit to being a little nervous when my mate Steve and I took a cab up to the Apollo to witness the P-Funk All Stars in late 1989 but the gig was electric and the place carried an aura of venerability and tangible history in the old staircases. Just thinking whose feet had trodden them is hard to grasp. When George was a regular, the Apollo was a madhouse, the crowd either embracing an act they liked or mercilessly vociferous if they didn't, resulting in the famous hook being brought on to get them off. The cheap seats on the second balcony were named the Buzzard's Roost, source of much rowdy behaviour (best cleared between houses by the projectionist showing a 30 minute film called *The River*, the running water performing its bladder voodoo to clear the place).

George's first time at the Apollo with the Shirelles in 1953 turned into something of a doo-wop epiphany as noted vocal group the Spaniels were also on the bill. He noticed the girls screaming and going crazy at the group, which made more of an impression on him than the music at that time.

After being smitten by one of the great singing groups at this early age, the young George enthusiastically pursued the doo-wop singing being sent out over urban rooftops by poor black teenagers. Like other tough neighbourhoods at that time, downtown Newark was awash with gangs, a product of the new independence and self-awareness which motivated post-war teenagers to create their own codes of dress, music and slang. This new world of music ended George's flirtation with a neighbourhood gang called the Outlaws, replacing criminal kicks with a burning ambition to perform. This was typical of the kind of street-spawned motivation which contributed more to the evolution of R&B than is commonly recognised, as each group brought their different styles and the music evolved organically. In George's case, he'd got out of gang life after his friend Leroy was murdered right in front of him, recalling on his VH1 Legends series documentary *George Clinton: Biography,* "This car drove up and boom!.. Blood and everything spattered all over everything, and nobody knew what had happened. We realised that somebody was hit and it was like… Leroy was shot, and the car pulled off. Then it went blank on me."

As one of the most basic musical genres, doo-wop was an early form of teenage punk rock; the sound of disaffected or under-privileged kids making music the only way their circumstances would allow – with the human voice. Initially a black movement, it was an expression of post-war urban blues defined by the poetry of inner city life. Most ghetto teenagers were unemployed and living in poverty, with no interest in school. A lifetime's gospel services had ingrained call-and-response vocal patterns and group harmonies on many, but R&B's swagger, subject matter and sense of discovery was far more exciting. From tenor leads to booming bass, it didn't cost anything to gather in a stairwell, on a corner or subway station and unleash the one instrument they didn't have to buy, hoping they might make it out of the ghetto by imitating singers who already had. It also got them out of their overcrowded houses and away from controlling parents – an escape from daily despair and drudgery, even a way to be heard by the world. By the mid-fifties street singing had become a way of life.

The excellent *Doo-Wop: The Forgotten Third Of Rock 'N' Roll* by Dr

Anthony J Gribin and Dr Mathew M Schiff (one of the few in-depth books about this music) exhaustively validates doo-wop as a vital (and distinct) entity in music's evolution; often overlooked and ham-fistedly misrepresented when it was shown to the masses in movies such as *Grease* – where it was portrayed as some brief craze which grabbed innocent teenagers as they gambolled through puberty. Rather than being a mere fleeting substrata of rock'n'roll trampled by the Beatles, doo-wop actually commanded an entire department of the notional R&B superstore.

Failing to see how a major new wave was crashing into America's cultural mainstream, record labels tried to brush it off as a fad. Meanwhile, the music was performing an enormous service to post-war integration, as audiences became increasingly mixed. George has always cited doo-wop as his biggest influence and its multi-tiered harmonies resonated through P-Funk into the most extreme Mothership outings; from obvious elements such as Ray Davis' bass ruminations and Garry Shider's imploring lead vocals to more subliminal structural traits. While it provided foundations for George's later sonic skyscrapers, barbershop group singing was led by group harmony rather than backing a lead vocal. George would be referencing an earlier style on the Funkadelic and Parliament chorales of 'Biological Speculation' or 'Give Up The Funk (Tear The Roof Off The Sucker)'. It speaks volumes about his natural aptitude for assimilating trends and the inherent progressive essence of cutting-edge black music that George would subsequently master happening forms such as funk and hip-hop (itself a continuation of the DIY doo-wop spirit).

Groups such as the Spaniels and the Fiestas defined an *a capella* style possessed of an angelic beauty which now sounds like some kind of alien transmission from a distant, innocent time. Listening to the interplay and passion sparking and intertwining can be a startling, moving experience; evoking a time before the human voice was abused and castrated by studio manipulation and edge-sanding gadgetry. Doo-wop was romantic in an idealised way, its love songs born from gospel bordering on pure prayer, but placing the subject of the singer's affections (rather than the Lord) on a pedestal. As well as aspiring to the celestial, singing was also a good way to get girls.

"The fifties in New York were an incredibly romantic time to be brought up hearing that stuff," George later affirmed. "That was the music of your day. It was the music you fell in love to. I imagine it's like that for every generation, but here you had the soundtrack to incredibly in-depth emotions of love. You combine that with being a teenager."

Doo-wop's roots as an urban vocal style go back to 19th century barbershop singing, which subsequently gave rise to black vocal outfits such as the Ink Spots and the Mills Brothers, who influenced the first pioneering wave of R&B groups. Baltimore's unearthly Orioles, who took the music into the charts in 1948 with 'It's Too Soon To Know', are widely credited as the most innovative of the R&B groups, originating four-part ballad harmony with tenors, baritone and bass, a major influence on both the R&B groups of the fifties and early rock'n'roll.

The Ravens first appeared in 1946 with 'Honey' before releasing a further 42 sides for National; being the first 'race' group to achieve international fame and also push forward a lead bass vocal. No group had done that before and group co-founder Jimmy Ricks can be viewed as the godfather of the ba-boom vocal style, although the Robins and the Coasters were quick to follow as the bass voice became the rumbling foundation of doo-wop. The animated voices, high and low, on 'Be I Bumble Bee Or Not' could be a flying insect portent of the areas where George would be cavorting some years hence, by which time he would have developed one of the best bass voices in the business.

By 1950, the success of the Ink Spots, Ravens and Orioles opened the door for street-corner groups to hear themselves on record. As the decade progressed, the Moonglows from Cleveland sprang to prominence through Alan Freed, the radio DJ who exposed white teenagers to R&B and put on huge stage shows featuring artists of the day. Just as George would take black music to mixed stadium crowds, Freed was breaking down barriers, taking the Moonglows with him as their hits on Chicago's Chance and Chess labels set a template for group harmonies in years to come. Led by Harvey Fuqua, they pioneered the bass voice intro and pleading tenor leads as later used by Parliament. With their unique method of 'blow-singing' into the microphone, the

Moonglows were perhaps the most influential of all the groups who came up in the fifties.

Other prominent fifties doo-wop ensembles included the Clovers, Drifters, Five Keys, Spaniels, and Larks. Alongside these, upcoming groups such as the Teenagers, Flamingos, Penguins, Crows, Cadillacs, Solitaires, Five Satins, Keynotes and Harptones emerged. Many of these lasted through the decade's golden age until the style's demise in the early sixties. All were far removed from the sanitised fifties rock'n'roll archetypes that the media would project through rose-tinted lenses across subsequent decades. The Larks' 'Eyesight To The Blind'* is a gutbucket blues sing-along, voices spontaneously buzzing and bubbling behind the impassioned lead. The Crows' million-selling 'Gee' was the first doo-wop 45 to be recognised by the white media – thus blasting the style's sperm across the purity of white pop, arguably creating the first rock'n'roll record in the process.

The progression from street corner into the studio brought about changes in the vocal styles, with different groups adapting the flavours they'd discovered – Harlem's the Solitaires' rooftop magic presaging the Temptations, or blues interpretations of the Clovers' rousing soul music. George particularly liked the Spaniels, the group he'd first seen at the Apollo. Hailing from Gary, Indiana, the Spaniels were doo-wop innovators, being the first vocal group to give the lead singer his own mic. Led by James 'Pookie' Hudson's smooth, quavering tenor, the group uncurled rich, ethereal harmonies, underpinned by Gerald Gregory's subterranean bass utterances. They were the first to sign to Vee-Jay Records, the first large, independent black music record label, debuting in 1953 with 'Baby, It's You' and becoming its biggest sellers. While gliding through finger-snappers such as 'People Will Say We're In Love', the group were masters of heart-soaring ballads such as 'Here Is Why I Love You' and their big 1954 hit, 'Goodnight Sweetheart Goodnight' (as heard in *American Graffiti* and even *Three Men And A Baby*).

---

* Respectfully revamped by the Who in Pete Townshend's rock opera *Tommy*.

The Heartbeats were a Jamaica, Queens high-school quartet who recorded three slow grinds for Bea Casalin's Hull Records before adding James 'Shep' Sheppard as lead vocalist and scoring a hit with 'A Thousand Miles Away', a pivotal monster record in the winter of 1956. Only the Dells, who first appeared on Chess in 1956 as the El-Rays, could lay claim to being their successors or replicating their sound in the sixties and into the seventies, having honed their harmonies hanging out outside the Chess building on South Michigan Avenue. Songs such as 'Tell The World' and 'Oh What A Night' showed how a street-corner group could succeed by following their own sound.

Newark winters were harsh and sub-zero but the hot, muggy summers encouraged hanging out and singing on the corner. In *George Clinton And P-Funk: An Oral History* George recalls, "I used to skip school and go to the Apollo Theatre. I left out of the eleventh grade. Cocky as hell. 'I'm not even going back to school.' That's how much I knew I was going to sing."

Doo-wop groups often started young, while still at school, like the Parliaments, formed by the 14-year-old George in 1955. He maintains that the group was called the Parliaments from the start, after the brand of cigarettes. This was happening all over the country, as street-corner groups coalesced as an outward manifestation of the intertwining personal relationships of kids at school or on the street. George's pals harmonising in the boys' room included Gene Boykins, Charles 'Butch' Davis, Herbie Jenkins and George's brother Robert.

Like many groups formed in 1955, the Parliaments were motivated by the meteoric success of Frankie Lymon & the Teenagers, who had a similar effect in motivating teenagers to form groups as the Sex Pistols would 20 years later. Lymon was actually a year younger than George. "Then Frankie Lymon popped up with his little hit record 'Why Do Fools Fall In Love?' and that was it. Frankie Lymon and them had the girls, man … The doo-woppers had girls running across the stage," he says in *An Oral History*.

Although now a well-known golden oldie, 'Why Do Fools Fall In Love?' is still one of the most vibrant, universal encapsulations of this era, exploding with the joys of young love with its spring-enforced rhythm and Lymon's soaring soprano. The group's own story was not so innocent. Lymon was born in a Washington Heights tenement in 1942, to a truck driver father, who sang in a gospel group called the Harlemaires, and a mother who worked as a maid. The neighbourhood was a hotbed of prostitutes, junkies and dealers (one of his brothers died from drugs). Frankie grew up fighting and getting into trouble. To help his family, he started working as a grocery boy at the age of 10, began smoking marijuana and supplementing his paltry wages by hustling prostitutes by the age of 13, and was enjoying relationships with women twice his age.

He also sang on street corners with a group of mid-teenage boys from school who decided to call themselves the Premiers – with lead tenor Herman Santiago, second tenor Jimmy Merchant, baritone Joe Negron and bass-voice Sherman Garnes. The Premiers changed their name to the Teenagers, impressing Valentines singer Richard Barrett, who arranged an audition with New York record producer George Goldner. On the big day, Santiago had a cold, so Frankie stepped up, declaring he co-wrote the song before unleashing his supernatural falsetto. Goldner signed them to his Rama Records, releasing 'Why Do Fools Fall In Love?' in January, 1956.* It stayed on top of the R&B chart for weeks, peaking at number six on the pop chart and number one in the UK. Almost overnight, the group shot from poverty to earning thousands of dollars a week. In 1956, the Teenagers were part of the first integrated rock'n'roll tour, along with gospel-soul sensation Clyde McPhatter, Bill Haley & the Comets, the Platters and the Flamingos, encountering Ku Klux Klan opposition and bomb scares along the way.

The group enjoyed further hits, including 'I'm Not A Juvenile Delinquent', but broke up in mid-1957 after Goldner tried to push Frankie as a solo artist. He failed to get off the ground and was shunned after daring to dance with a white girl when he appeared on Alan Freed's *The Big Beat* live TV show promoting his single, 'My

---

* The group had adapted the song from a poem called 'Why Do Birds Sing So Gay', written by a woman in their building.

Girl', the perceived outrage resulting in Southern uproar and shows being cancelled. More disaster loomed when Frankie's voice broke, although he tried straining for the high notes across a few singles. As his popularity shrank, his addiction to heroin grew. The sixties saw failed drug cures and solo records before he reformed the Teenagers. He married an already-married woman, relocated to LA, married twice more without divorce and got drafted into the army. After getting a promising new record deal with the Big Apple label, Lymon returned to New York in February 1968 but was found dead from an overdose in his grandmother's Harlem bathroom the next morning. However, his work had long been done, paving the way for early teen pop stars such as Stevie Wonder and Michael Jackson, while Berry Gordy used Teenagers songs as a style template.

George and friends initially concentrated on the lady-killing ahead of the music. "We got girls before we got records," he crowed in *An Oral History*. "I mean, we were the baddest group around the town, 'cause love songs was the shit anyway. Matter of fact, that's why I still love doo-wop, because doo-wop was all about grinding and getting pussy."

George claims he couldn't sing for shit, but was handling falsetto and bass, while the group honed their harmonies on the subway and in the hallways of the projects. The first line-up of the group consisted of George, Charles 'Fat Butch' Davis, Herbie Johnson and Gene Boykins.

The Parliaments' first gigs were school dances, talent shows and YMCA hops. He told *MOJO*'s Lloyd Bradley in 2006: "Instantly, we became the favourite group in the area. I don't know why, maybe because we were the youngest and our audience was very young. Or it might have been the showmanship and shit, because right from back then we put on a show. We had the Newark area sewn up, through the high schools and that. Amateur nights we'd always win, Battle of the Groups we'd always win. We did shows with Joey Dee & the Starlighters … the Four Seasons, Monotones… all of them were in the Battle of the Groups in New Jersey with us and we'd usually win. We won Amateur Night at the Apollo so many times we had to go on under different names."

George's first adult job was sweeping the floor then styling hair at Newark's Uptown Tonsorial Parlor, a typically funky barbershop of the time. "First I started out singing, you know, at 14 or 15 years old. Everybody had a group in Newark, Brooklyn, [or] Harlem. When I came out in the era of doo-wop, everybody sang and when you sang you had to get your hair done. So we started out doing each other's hair. And I immediately got a job in the barbershop doing processes, which was the big money maker in the fifties and through the sixties."

Black barbershops had been influential in helping to develop African American culture at the turn of the 18th century. By the fifties, the barbershop was a vital cog of the local community, an African-American cultural institution where news and sport were savoured and chewed, along with a large amount of fat, by fathers, sons, relatives and friends. Along with the shit being shot, plans were made, which inevitably led to bands being formed by the younger customers. From George's reminiscences, it always struck me as the ghetto equivalent of the old local British pub, an escape from home strife and outside pressure for older patrons, while younger elements were risking a beating by sneaking into this occasionally shady adult world.

This writer lived in downtown Newark in the late eighties, and mention of this sparked a stream of reminiscences from George – in a New York dressing room during his filming for MTV's coverage of his 1993 team-up with Primal Scream – who sat regaling the rapt group with anecdotes about the Parliaments and those early days. He remembered the barbershop with much affection as a local hangout hated by parents but loved by budding local musicians and juvenile delinquents, some as young as eight. "It was the place to be," he laughed, while adding that it was also the birthplace of hip-hop. At one point, he put on a cassette of a doo-wop album he had put together, featuring the original songs being sung by his old comrades. It was magical, but was sadly never released.

Notwithstanding the crazed exotic stacks which adorned George's noggin over the years, hair was the first thing he excelled at, specialising in finger waves and conking (straightening wavy hair with toxic chemicals). While financing his earliest musical endeavours, George's musical foundations were laid in the barbershop. "After you've done other people's hair for so long you know the concept of doin' hair," he explained to John Corbett. "The garbage man looked just as cool as the pimp and the singer when they left the barbershop."

At its peak George's barbershop boasted up to 10 barbers working 13 chairs charging five dollars a do. The place was so successful George rarely had time to do his own barnet but used this as an ad slogan under his photo – 'Come and get your hair done or you could end up looking like me.' "We was making so much money we had Cadillacs at 16," he once told me.

George's growing clientele included visiting luminaries such as Jackie Wilson and the Temptations as well as local pimps and players. "Really, style is just a bunch of bullshit, it's just how you carry it. If you is safe with that concept, then you can be as ugly as you wanna be or as cool as you wanna be and know that neither of 'em mean shit! No matter how cool you are, you can go some place where you look corny as hell to somebody. They thought that to have your do was the corniest stuff in the world when you got around hippies. And then a few years later, the afros came out and then the black people started looking silly. So it means that styles just go round and round and ain't nothing permanently cool or corny."

The Parliaments line-up was constantly changing, and by the start of 1956 it comprised George, Herbie Jenkins, Robert Lambert, Danny Mitchell and baritone/bass Grady Thomas – the first of the P-Funk's renowned vocal group nucleus to appear. Born on January 5, 1941, in Newark, Grady worked at the same salon as George and became the first long-term P-Funker to join, staying until the 1977 walk-out. The first known Parliaments recording is an acetate carrying their renditions of the Diablos' 'The Wind' and 'Sunday Kind Of Love', captured in a Newark recording booth in 1956.*

Nolan Strong & the Diablos were one of the hottest vocal groups during the mid-to-late fifties, thanks to a string of hits including 'The Way You Dog Me Around', released on Detroit's Fortune label. I've never heard the Parliaments take but, listening to the sweet, haunted

---

* The one existing copy is now owned by a record collector in Philadelphia.

cry of the Diablos' original now it's not hard to imagine that P-Funk chorale unleashing its rich tones.

By 1958, the line-up had changed again, seeing George, Grady, Lambert and a returning Charles Davis joined by Calvin Simon from Beckley, West Virginia, who had been in a group called the Crystals and knew Grady at school. Calvin's falsetto convinced George to offer him a place in the group, ironically firing Grady to make room for him. This line-up made the Parliaments' first venture into a studio to record two songs, 'Poor Willie' and 'Party Boys', released on Hull. Casalin licensed the single to ABC-Paramount's recently launched APT subsidiary (its name derived from American Broadcasting Paramount Theatres), who issued it in June, 1959 to scant reaction.

Compared to other vocal group records of the time, the Parliaments already carried an edge under their rich harmonies, weaving and soaring through a hefty wedge of doo-wop and gospel-charged stylings over minimal instrumentation. They sound much older than a bunch of teenagers, especially on the flip's 'Party Boys', George managing to dip a 'glory hallelujah' hook into rolling sleaze blues.

This Parliaments line-up originally recorded the lustrous, church organ-backed ballad swoon of 'Lonely Island' for Newark's New Records but, instead, it was released the following year on future Rolling Stones producer Jimmy Miller's Patterson-based Flipp label, backed with the uptempo gospel-pumping steam-whoop of '(You Make Me Wanna) Cry' and its astounding progressive harmony introduction. Local singer Johnny Murray guested on lead vocals for the A-side. Listening to these songs now, it is apparent that the full-throated vocals have formed into a rich rooftop chorale which compares well with the big groups of the day – maybe they're a bit more ragged, belting raw emotion with young energy rather than spinning silkier tones.

These singles show how the fledgling independent label system functioned at that time. Initially, major labels hadn't been interested in releasing rock'n'roll or doo-wop, only climbing on the bandwagon once it took off, but still ignoring a vast area of black music. While major labels mainly stuck to white mainstream artists, independent imprints had started springing up by the end of World War Two, funnelling the different strains of black music into independent stores such as Bobby Robinson's Bobby's Record Shop, the first black-owned music store, on Harlem's 125th Street. Independent labels filled the gap, establishing a pattern that would continue to act as a means for the underdogs to have their say on record. Such enterprises included Chicago's Chess and Vee Jay, New York's Atlantic, Jubilee, Apollo, Ember, Laurie and Winley; Modern, Kenty, Aladdin, Dootone in LA and Syd Nathan's King operation in Cincinnati.

As many of these labels operated locally, owners would have their fingers on the pulse of what was going on at street level, living in the culture they were furthering through making it heard, but encountering cash flow and distribution problems in the process. Some labels sold the rights to a record to a major, such as happened with the first Parliaments release going through Paramount. Groups were invariably ripped off, deprived of writing credits and royalties while playing thankless, gruelling tours.

It's interesting to see how George was getting his name on the record labels from the start, being blessed with the same business savvy which was turning his hair-processing exploits into an in-demand outlet for his tonsorial talents. By now, he had picked up a second hairdressing gig at George White's Silk Palace barbershop. This was at the site of the former Capitol Bakery on West Third Street in the 'Queen City' of Plainfield, 18 miles South West of Newark in central New Jersey's Raritan Valley. Here, in the back room, the P-Funk empire was born, partly because Plainfield was more of a concentrated, close-knit scene than Newark and the number of kids risking their parents' wrath to sneak in escalated.

Throughout the Plainfield years, the Parliaments became inextricably linked with another young local group called the Del-Larks, led by Sammy Campbell and Ron Taylor. Although their styles were totally different, the two groups were barbershop regulars, played on the same bills and sometimes loaned each other members. Sammy Campbell was born in Plainfield on May 6, 1941, the seventh of 10 children after his parents migrated from Virginia in 1938 in search of work. Like many,

Sammy started off singing gospel at Lovelace Watkins' small Church of God in Christ on Liberty St. and 2nd (before Watkins went on to Las Vegas fame).

The original Del-Larks formed in Plainfield around 1953, lining up as Sammy singing lead vocals, his brother David (first tenor), Allen Walker (baritone), Louie Dickerson (second tenor) and Harold Erby (bass). The quintet began appearing around northern New Jersey performing sets comprising mostly covers. They split after opening for the Moonglows at Newark's Wideaway Ballroom, with a new line-up (the first to record) rising out of the pivotal local hotbed of Plainfield's Washington School. This incarnation featured Sammy, Mert Matthews (baritone), Ron Taylor (second tenor), the multi-ranged Jimmy Anderson, and James Jeffers (first tenor).

Ron Taylor was born in Plainfield on July 6, 1939, his parents originally from Virginia. He started singing baritone with a gospel group called the Male Quartet in his mother's church at 13, which also included Donald Walker (first tenor), James Boyd (bass) and Albert Brown (second tenor), performing songs such as 'The Little Brown Church In The Wildwoods' and 'I'll Never Touch It (Smoking And Drinking)'.

In the early fifties, Plainfield hosted a lively vocal quartet scene. During a seventh grade assembly in Washington School in 1953, students entertained their classmates, including a young prodigy called Bernie Worrell on piano. Shows run at the school brought in top R&B acts of the day to preview and promote their upcoming shows, ensuring that the fortunate pupils got to see the likes of the Heartbeats, the Dells and many more. The future Del-Larks decided to form a group outside such a show, sometimes rehearsing at the home of jazz organist Nat Kimble, but more often in tunnels, on street corners and even bathrooms – wherever the echo was good.

Before they recorded, the teenage Del-Larks appeared all over New Jersey, becoming ambassadors of Plainfield's vibrant vocal group scene, which also included United Soul, Nonchalants, Wonders, Cor-Wrens, Bel-airs and the invading Parliaments from Newark, who they befriended.

The Del-Larks' recording break came when they won a marathon talent show held at Seidler Field in the East End of Plainfield in summer 1957, triumphing over local groups including the Parliaments, United Soul, the Nonchalants and the Admirations. Their performance impressed a well-connected lady named Yolanda Gregory, the wife of artist Waylande Gregory, best known for his ceramic sculptures. She took the group into New York to cut demos, which clinched a deal with Ahmet Ertegun and Jerry Wexler at Atlantic Records in March, 1958. Hitting the studio, the Del-Larks recorded 'Lady Love', 'Remember The Night', 'Bubble Gum Doll' and 'Can't Believe You're Mine Tonight' with the Atlantic house band, which included saxophone titan King Curtis. Yolanda secured bookings for the Del-Larks and scored a coveted appearance on *The Ed Sullivan Show*, but the group blew it when an argument about her percentage erupted into a foul-mouthed row, which was unfortunately beamed to a shocked Sullivan over an open microphone. The record was released but Atlantic got cold feet, ending the relationship, and sending the Del-Larks back to Plainfield.

Despite this setback, the Del-Larks continued with their bespoke-suited smart image, contrasting with the Parliaments' inexorably disintegrating wardrobe as they continued to funk up. "In the fifties, groups had routines and rich harmonies and dressed," recalled Sammy on the website *Classic Urban Harmony*. "We had our own suits made. We designed most of our own clothes. We had this tailor, Luigi, down on Washington Ave and 2nd Street. We told him what we wanted and gave him an idea of the style. He made the suits for us. Back then when you compared the two groups with the songs we were singing, the styles were good because George and them were wild … They had a lot of steps. We were more Temptations-ish. But I give George credit, their style was different then. Our style was smooth and pretty; theirs was gutsy and funky."

The Del-Larks continued to play any clubs and dances that Sammy could book them into around New Jersey, Pennsylvania and New York. Then Sammy brought Ray Davis, a new bass singer who had just moved into the neighbourhood, along to a rehearsal. His booming presence moved Jimmy up to baritone.

The future 'Sting Ray' Davis was born in Sumter, South Carolina, on March 29, 1940 but had moved up to Brooklyn by the time he hooked up with the Del-Larks. "I had a sister in Plainfield," he recalled in *An Oral History*. "I used to come over from Brooklyn every Friday. I had moved there from down south. Being that I'm from down the way, Plainfield was a lot like what I was used to, it was a little bit country, so I felt at home there. That's when I met Sammy Campbell and them, the Del-Larks. This would have been around '59."

Ray gravitated to the Silk Palace. "Every Friday, that's where I would be. When I'd hit town, the barbershop was the first place I'd go. That's where I met George and the Parliaments. We were always harmonising, either in the barbershop or on the street corner. I wasn't looking to get with a group, I was just the new guy around. Sammy and them were getting their group together and asked me if I wanted to join. I said, 'Sure, why not?'"

By now, doo-wop was undergoing something of a revival as the sound became ingrained in rock'n'roll and new practitioners sprang up. During the fifties, the New Jersey doo-wop scene was ruled by producer Hy Weiss's Old Town label, which released records by the Solitaires, the Valentines, the Cleftones, the Capris and Newark's the Fiestas (the latter rehearsing in George's barbershop). The Fiestas lined up as lead Tommy Bullock, his brother George, Eddie Morris, Sam Ingalls and Preston Lane. According to legend, Weiss discovered them when he overheard them singing in a bathroom at the Triboro Theatre, next door to his office. Their first single, a cover of the Sheikhs' 'So Fine', made the US Top 20 in April 1959, followed by a string of sublime misses, including 'Our Anniversary' and 'You Could Be My Girlfriend', before 'Broken Heart' made the Hot 100 in 1962.

The Del-Larks released their second single to local acclaim around 1961. 'I Never Will Forget' was a fifties-style soul ballad led by Sammy, while 'Baby Come On' was more uptempo. The 45 was released on George Eastman's Ea-Jay label (connected to Flipp, which recorded the Parliaments). Another single called 'Out In The Crowd', featuring Ray Davis on lead vocal, and which appeared on the Jet label in the early sixties, is thought to have provided a blueprint for Dobie Gray's 1965 hit 'The In Crowd'. The Del-Larks were unaware that the song had been released, but it's possible it was developed into Dobie's hit a few years later.

Further line-up changes saw Jerry Cunningham replaced by Boobie Meyers, and Ron Taylor leave in 1961. He was replaced by Leroy 'Brother' Wheeler Jr., also from Sumter, South Carolina, whose family moved to Linden, New Jersey, when he was in high school. He was at a Del-Larks gig in Newark when they appealed for a first tenor from the stage, and swiftly stepped up.

Now lining up as Sam, Ray, Jimmy Anderson, Boobie Meyers and Brother, the Del-Larks continued singing locally. After a year, Brother left the group, bringing in Jerry Timmons as his replacement. He was followed in 1963 by Ray, who departed to join the Parliaments.

"A Parliament quit and I said, 'Here's my chance'," he recounted. "Grady Thomas and Calvin Simon came over to talk to me one afternoon and I said, 'Do you want me to join the group?' The Del-Larks were always going down to four guys. The Parliaments had five guys. I like singing five-part harmony. I told Sammy I was going to go. He said, 'No problem. If you think it's going to be good for you, go on'."

Ray brought one of the most crucial doo-wop elements to the Parliaments, remaining the loudest link to the music as his unmistakable caramel throat rumble cut through the funk a few years hence on 'Tear The Roof Off The Sucker'. In doo-wop the bass was used under the lead voice or to punctuate the song between choruses, or as a voice separate from lead and harmony – and also as the 'talking bridge', which Ray employed several times with P-Funk. It could also be used as a percussive instrument – the first human beatbox. As Sammy Campbell observed, "Every time Ray opened his mouth the girls was peeing on themselves."

The Parliaments line-up now included Clarence 'Fuzzy' Haskins, who had joined the group from the Bel-Airs in 1960 after auditioning in the barbershop and quickly became an integral part of P-Funk operations until his departure in 1977. Born in Elkins, West Virginia on June 8,

1941, he was another West Third Street regular who now took many of the lead vocals.

With their line-up solidified as George, Fuzzy, Calvin, Grady and Ray, the Parliaments were ready for the next step up the ladder and onto the roof – although the footing would turn out not to be as firm as it looked from down below.

Chapter Two

Nothing Before Me But Thang

"Plainfield is a weird kind of place. We were all in love with Motown but we were there in Jersey, you know, waiting to be discovered. So, the barbershop's the best place to do it."

George Clinton

The tumultuous sixties reshaped America, spawning major social, cultural and economic upheavals against a backdrop of conflict between old guard and new radicals. As the decade dawned, George was a fiercely ambitious 19 year old with a thriving career in hairdressing and the burning desire to make his mark in the music business by any means necessary. Although he would later create works of surreally incisive social comment and reality-troubling defiance, George and the Parliaments were still singing doo-wop-derived R&B with no protest or insurrectionary agenda. In some ways, it's even remarkable that, after spending the first half of the decade as a struggling songwriter/producer geared to the mainstream, George ended up leading the most outrageous, taboo-shattering band to come out of that whole riotous decade.

Inevitably, he picked up on current socio-cultural developments each day in the barbershop, but they were yet to be processed into any grand plans. While many of his contemporaries were reflecting the increasingly desperate plight of his people and country, George was serving his apprenticeship in the art of songwriting and dealing with old-school music-biz machinations. His productions in the first half of the sixties reflected contemporary black mainstream styles – particularly Motown, which could essentially be viewed as preoccupying his ambitions during that period.

The psychedelic anarchy of Funkadelic wouldn't start appearing until after George had fully explored traditional music industry routes to achieving his dreams and been stop-searched during the 1967 riots. By then, Black Power was on its way to becoming one of the most radical, effective and demonised movements of the 20th century – instilling conscious black identity, unity and decisive action in the face of savage racism. Ultimately, George's personal solution would be to morph into one of the loudest embodiments of black empowerment through the very presence of his unfettered cosmic pimp self and the extraterrestrial ghetto army which rode beside him. With 'freedom' becoming the buzzword of the day, George would take his lysergically minted 'free your mind and your ass will follow' ethos to further extremes than anyone before or since. But, although he could make himself at home among hippie chicks at an acid-fried love-in, he never lost his seminal grounding in ghetto life and his mission to give it a cutting-edge party soundtrack.

As the sixties progressed, a new consciousness was making its presence felt in social conditions and daily life, manifesting in music through self-expression and increasing the demand for unifying anthems. The civil rights movement's establishment of a new identity through exploring its cultural heritage also provided an activist template for women's and gay liberation, Native American rights and other disenfranchised causes. But although it had been striving to dispel discrimination and establish voting rights since the mid-fifties, with giant steps taken to remove the more overtly racist inequities imposed on African-Americans, bigotry and ignorance continued to rage at the dawn of this embattled decade.

Artists such as Paul Robeson, Josh White, Odetta and Harry Belafonte had been soundtracking the quest for freedom for decades, braving all kinds of opposition, but had also gradually seen their messages become a vital part of the sea-changes in US society. The civil rights movement sent major reverberations across the decade, creating a huge impact on the arts, as black music rose as a major force from New York's Brill Building to Berry Gordy's Motown in Detroit.

No matter what was happening in the wider social circus, gospel music and the church remained a constant, vital presence in black communities. During the sixties, the church continued to provide the prime emotional lifeline and an arena for soul-affirming spiritual catharsis, harnessing the sense of unity and collective defiance that had maintained it through previous crises. More than ever, churchgoers plunged into fevered musical celebrations to rise above and protect themselves from the unimaginable danger and brutality of modern America. The concept of Black Power welded these souls together with a siege mentality, sparking superhuman courage and spreading healing balm when the going got tough.

This passionate devotion underpinned the black revolution of the sixties, manifesting as soul music for a secular world. Pioneering blues-turned-gospel composer Thomas Dorsey wasn't entirely happy with gospelised R&B being called soul, telling Gerri Hirshey, author of *Nowhere To Run: The Story Of Soul Music*, "It was first in the Negro church. When I was a little boy, the churches couldn't afford an organ and the sisters sat in the amen corner and kept rhythm by clapping their hands. There is no need for some fellow born yesterday to come up and tell me now that soul is something new. At church, they do more foot tapping and hand clapping than they ever did. Some people go to church for the rhythm. And white people like the same kind of rhythm."

Obviously, the question, 'what is soul' remains hotly debated – indeed, George would go on to pose that very question on the first Funkadelic album. Gospel stoked the soul to unleash its music in its purest form, providing song templates to be adapted by the civil rights movement and Black Power activists, who changed lyrics and titles to suit their respective manifestos. If the black revolution's mission to confront and overturn existing social and economic systems failed to have much lasting physical effect, its impact on the arts and culture was manifestly epoch-making. This was particularly true of the music broadly termed soul, which went on to reach a peak during the sixties through its churning mix of steaming funk, conscious messages, Blaxploitation cool, unfettered jazz sensibility and popular accessibility. Soul was further galvanised by the new sense of identity gained by singers and players who voiced support for the common cause, including James Brown, Curtis Mayfield, John Coltrane, Nina Simone, Jimi Hendrix, Aretha Franklin, Sly Stone and, in the fullness of time, George Clinton.

James Brown once neatly summed it up, "The word soul meant a lot of things, in music and out. It was about the roots of black music, and it was kind of a pride thing too, being proud of yourself and your people. Soul music and the civil rights music went hand in hand, sort of grew up together."

Civil rights strode defiantly into the new decade in February, 1960, when four smartly-dressed students from the all-black North Carolina Agricultural and Technical College sat down politely on the white side of the segregated lunch counter at Greensboro's Woolworth's store to protest at being refused service, leaving stools available for white sympathisers to join in. The move sparked similar sit-ins in Virginia, Tennessee and Georgia, and quickly spread to parks, theatres and public places in northern states such as Illinois and Ohio. That April, the Student Nonviolent Co-ordinating Committee and James Farmer's Congress of Racial Equality (CORE) increased activities to include the Freedom Rides, facing firebombing as they tried to use segregated toilets and water fountains at bus terminals along the way. After several riders were jailed and beaten, public outrage led to Kennedy's newly elected administration overseeing a new desegregation order, allowing people of any skin colour to use all facilities and be served at lunch counters. Unsurprisingly, redneck cops were blowing their pointy little heads, extending their basket of vile tactics to include encouraging police dogs to attack peaceful protesters.

In 1960 revered jazz drummer Max Roach released *We Insist! Max Roach's Freedom Now Suite*; the single most shatteringly powerfully emotional statement of the whole era. Brave and all-consuming, it was recorded at a time when the Civil Rights Bill of 1964 seemed a distant utopia and sit-ins were in full swing against widespread brutality. Just the cover image of three black men defiantly sitting at a lunch counter in front of an apprehensive-looking white waiter was confrontational, but it perfectly encapsulated the climate of the times.

Roach was one of jazz's fiercest, most outspoken civil rights campaigners. In 1952, he co-founded Debut records with fellow activist Charles Mingus, releasing his first album as a hard-bop band leader the following year. When Roach and Mingus organised a 'rebel festival' to protest against treatment of black performers by the annual Newport Jazz event, they signed to Candid Records, in the process forming the Jazz Artists Guild with other like-minds. Roach and Chicago writer-singer Oscar Brown started writing further tracks for their proposed *Freedom Now* suite – originally intended for the 1963 centenary of Abraham Lincoln's Emancipation Proclamation (Roach had played with Sonny Rollins on the 19-minute 'Freedom Suite' in 1958). The fraught social climate expanded the suite into a full album concept, Roach tracing slavery's trail of oppression from forced labour, brutal punishments and the sexual exploitation of female slaves to the celebratory 'Freedom Day' and 'All Africa' asserting an early form of Afro-centricity through the dramatic use of chants and percussion.

The album's stellar line-up included sax titan Coleman Hawkins and Roach's wife-to-be, Abbey Lincoln, as soul-searing vocal counterpoint to his blistering drum assaults. The terrifying 'Triptych: Prayer/Protest/Peace' still stands as the decade's most cataclysmic protest statement, described by *Downbeat* magazine's Don DeMichael as "the most devastating thing of its kind that I've heard… a vibrant social statement and an artistic triumph". The album got the couple blacklisted by the US recording industry for years. Roach died on August 16, 2007, and is now considered as important a civil rights figure as Robeson and Malcolm X.

In turn, Malcolm X cited free jazz as the music of liberation, declaring, "It's the only area on the American scene where the black man has been free to create." Ornette Coleman fused blues and jazz to African music to create alien new energy on albums such as *Something Else!!!* and *The Shape Of Jazz To Come*, funnelling rage, frustration, sadness and occasional joy through his flailing sax, much to the chagrin of the establishment and jazz's old guard. Coleman was one of the pivotal figures in breaking down barriers within black music, opening the floodgates for improvisation and expression through music, while debunking traditional structures and theories. Like tenor giant Albert Ayler's mutation of hymns and spirituals, Coleman was defining his own version of the field holler; the sound of survival delivered with his own personal slant. This new, unfettered musical freedom would be a crucial element in the evolution of the funk, as many jazz musicians subsidised their incomes by working the chitlin' circuit where the style gestated amid the sweat and inhibition-free environment.

Archie Shepp was another horn-tooting messenger channelling the hardship of his Philadelphia upbringing through his music. As he told Denise Sullivan in her superb book *Keep On Pushing: Black Power Music From Blues To Hip-hop*, "As a younger man, being exposed to modern music – black music – was really quite important to me, in the forming of my identity, in the forming of my goals. Even giving the blues all its due, people like Parker and Gillespie, Monk, actually provided younger black people with another image of themselves. They were really role models for me; they gave me somewhere to go."

Presaging what George would soon be doing to challenge and realign black music, the jazz trailblazers such as Shepp railed noisily against their music's orthodoxy, creating their own form of personal liberation which owed little to European heritage. As the jazz traditionalists scoffed, a new, young, mixed audience started to appreciate the rapidly evolving strain of urban blues which had soundtracked the beat movement before taking its own spiritually anarchic path to run amok amid the countercultural revolution. These visionary musicians included John Coltrane, Eric Dolphy, Cecil Taylor and Albert Ayler, who declared, "I must play music that is beyond this world" as he unleashed his soul-searing sax-skronk. Extraterrestrial band leader Sun Ra had landed

36

in New York by now, taking the metaphysical proto-Mothership to downtown clubs with his exotically costumed Arkestra, who we'll meet later.

Cultural polymath Everett LeRoi Jones (latterly known as Amiri Baraka) wrote in his renowned book *Blues People*, "This recent music is significant of more 'radical' changes and re-evaluations of social and emotional attitudes toward the general environment. But I cannot think that the music itself is a more radical, or any more illogical extension of the kinetic philosophy that has informed Negro music since its inception in America. Negro music is always radical in the context of formal American culture."

Coltrane became an icon to many and has since been hailed as jazz's answer to Hendrix – the biggest influence on Funkadelic. Both were blessed with natural virtuosity which, combined with countless hours of dedicated practice and devotion to realise their mind's most far-out musical visions. Both cut their musical teeth within conventional musical frameworks before busting loose to strive for a sonic Holy Grail that neither would ever admit to glimpsing. Coltrane's musical journey saw him join Miles Davis' first great quintet in 1955, explore hard bop and ballads on Prestige between 1956–58, kick the heroin habit which had dogged him for years in 1957, explore chordal and modal stretching on Atlantic between 1959–61, then ferociously forage into free jazz and spiritual fulfilment for Impulse! Records until he died shortly before his 41st birthday on July 17, 1967. Since his death, he has been endlessly feted in both jazz and rock'n'roll circles, but during the sixties his fearless experimentation incurred harsh criticism from disparaging critics and old-school jazzers. After bebop had been pilloried like punk 30 years later for replacing old traditions with unusual new ideas (which would gradually be assimilated into the mainstream), free jazz was largely dismissed as subhuman racket.

Rarely expressing overt political views, Coltrane preferred to channel his feelings through his music on charged statements such as 'Alabama', which lamented the deaths of four girls killed in the 1964 fire-bombing of a Birmingham, Alabama church. Amid rumours that, like many others, he was using LSD, he was welcomed at downtown New York venues like the Village Vanguard, pioneering barrier-trampling by appearing with rock names such as Chuck Berry and at happenings with Timothy Leary and Allen Ginsberg.

Continuing to shape the environment which spawned P-Funk's parallel universe, the civil rights movement found its figurehead when a young Baptist minister called Dr Martin Luther King emerged triumphant from 1955's Montgomery Bus Boycott where Rosa Parks refused to give up her seat for a white passenger. The resulting court case and boycotting of services organised by Dr King led to desegregation on the city's buses. Now a national figure, the eloquent, charismatic spokesman formed the Southern Christian Leadership Conference with other church leaders to provide direction for local organisations to fight racism and segregation non-violently. In 1961, Dr King and the SCLC took their desegregation lobbying to Albany, Georgia, singing songs of freedom and establishing music as a major element in what became known as the 'Freedom Now' movement. The laments descended from slaves provided the musical impetus for the freedom songs that bookended Dr Martin Luther King's appearances.

The March On Washington in August 1963 called for equality in employment, housing, education and voting, along with the passage of the Civil Rights Bill proposed by the Kennedy administration after Birmingham. Major civil rights organisations were led to the White House by veteran activist Philip Randolph and Dr King, with estimates of numbers attending reaching up to half a million. Music was provided by Bob Dylan, Joan Baez, Odetta, Harry Belafonte and Peter, Paul & Mary. Dr King gave his most famous speech after gospel queen Mahalia Jackson had set the scene with the stratospheric voice that had done more than anyone to take gospel's message around the world. She exhorted King to depart from his script and launch into the "I have a dream ... free at last" testimonial that changed history.

After John F. Kennedy was assassinated on November 22, 1963, his successor, Lyndon Johnson, used his influence to bring 1964's Civil Rights Act home. The bill banned discrimination based on "race, colour, religion or national origin" regarding jobs, accommodation or public facilities.

1963 also saw the civil rights anthem which caught the collective mindset of the country, as Sam Cooke reportedly wrote 'A Change Is Gonna Come' as his own protest song after watching Dylan sing 'Blowin' In The Wind' at the march on TV. His moving runaway slave opus provided a blueprint for black message songs, cracking the Top 40 when released shortly after the singer's death in late 1964. The song's inherent humanity elevated it above the insular, folk-derived staples of the gatherings and established soul music as a major force, both socially and in the charts. The march also inspired Chicago's Curtis Mayfield to write 'Keep On Pushing' for his Impressions, taking civil rights into the Top 10 after topping the R&B chart. In 2004, then Illinois State Senator Barack Obama used the song as the theme to his Democratic National Convention keynote address endorsing John Kerry's controversially unsuccessful Presidential campaign.

Despite the socio-cultural upheavals taking place, much of what went on during the sixties grabbed headlines but failed to crack the bedrock of conformist conservatism that lingered from times past, especially in those parts of America unaffected by progressive thinking in New York, Los Angeles and a handful of other cities. Before the army bleached him into Hawaiian racing car movie fodder, Elvis was the hip-thrusting symbol of rock'n'roll's newly awakened primal energy, translating for white audiences what had been electrifying the chitlin' circuit for decades. At the same time, four Liverpool teenagers were honing an act built on R&B and rock'n'roll in Hamburg's steamy clubs, while a bunch of more radical English blues fanatics were hatching their mission to spread their beloved music in the UK, never dreaming they'd be dubbed 'the world's greatest rock'n'roll band' by the end of the decade. Black music was dominated by those previously insular genres of R&B, gospel and jazz, which were ripe for cross-fertilisation. Rather than storm the barricades, George rode through the first part of this inflammatory decade trying to make it in America's institutionalised music business, initially using showtime traditions, pop song structures and gospel-spawned call-and-response vocals. Soon enough, however, he would react to his comparative failure by creating a wild new world in his own vision, taking the Parliaments to fame on pathways battered down by the new breed of radicalised African–American artists.

The Big Apple at the core of the music business was carrying on the way it had been since World War Two, with different movements and musical styles gestating and evolving in various enclaves of the five boroughs, often colliding to morph into new forms of music. The counterculture and nascent hippie movement gestated around New York pioneers in anything from Harlem jazz to Lower East Side agit-poetry, plus a new arrival in Greenwich Village called Bob Dylan, whose biting agit-folk gripped radicals of all races.

At the time, George was acutely aware of what was going on over the Washington Bridge in New York City's entertainment hub and desperately wanted to make his name there. Although increasingly ambitious, his success at this time was still on a more localised level as the Plainfield barbershop thrived as a successful independent black enterprise; this represented both a statement and achievement in those times.

After acquiring a 50 per cent share in the Silk Palace from owner George White in 1961, George continued to hustle in New York's Tin Pan Alley. The 10-storey Brill Building, which got its name from the tailors occupying the ground floor, dominated New York's entertainment industry in the fifties. By 1960, while it still housed hotshots Jerry Leiber and Mike Stoller, there was also the cheaper Music Building at 1650 Broadway. Both were a maze of cubicles furnished with a desk, phone and upright piano, which played host to the hordes of publishers, promoters and songwriters that continued to descend upon the city.

New York became the teen pop capital of the world, establishing a vital new musical form which spoke to girls undergoing hormonal lust pangs and boys craving to be cool – both sexes united by dreams and fantasies of love, romance and unrepressed sex. Thanks to some of the greatest pop songs ever concocted in a recording studio, the influence of New York's Tin Pan Alley was extended, its pop sensibility and hit stable culture a crucial influence on George.

With its sparklingly contemporary songs, spectacular dance routines and referencing of New York's virulent gang situation, 1957's blockbuster musical *West Side Story* became another influence on George's ideas about how music could be presented.

The original production had evolved from Jerome Robbins approaching composer Leonard Bernstein and scriptwriter Arthur Laurents with the idea 10 years earlier. Pressure of work caused the musical to be sidelined until 1955 when the trio reunited on another project and decided to revisit it in the light of recent publicity about gang warfare. *West Side Story* re-imagined Shakespeare's *Romeo And Juliet* with the Puerto Rican Sharks and Italian-American Jets taking the place of the star-crossed houses of Montague and Capulet. Romeo analogue Tony falls for his Juliet (Maria), sister of the Sharks' leader Bernardo. Their intense love affair accelerates as the violent rivalry between the two gangs builds to the fatal final rumble between the two gangs, soundtracked by classic songs including 'Maria', 'America', 'Somewhere', 'Tonight', 'Jet Song' and 'Cool'. This was many people's first exposure to US gang culture.

George's musical epiphany and inspirational catalyst came in the form of Smokey Robinson & the Miracles' 1960 single 'Shop Around', a breakthrough hit for Berry Gordy's revolutionary new Motown hit factory. Even in the nineties, George still proclaimed Smokey his idol, especially lyrically, explaining to John Corbett, "That's what made me put so many puns in songs, 'cause Smokey used to pun songs to death and I think that when I left Motown it was about, let's see how many different ways I can make the same concept come to light, some synonyms or antonyms. Smokey wrote the book on that shit. He's my favourite songwriter."

Starting as a songwriter for local acts such as Jackie Wilson & the Matadors, Berry Gordy heisted Detroit's Motor City nickname for one of the biggest black business operations in history. Although he had written hits such as 'Lonely Teardrops' for Wilson, he found out through bitter experience that the real money lay in producing songs and owning their publishing.

In January, 1959, Gordy started Tamla Records with his Wilson royalties and an $800 loan from his family, opening for business in the

Hitsville USA building on West Grand Boulevard. Tamla's first hit was Barrett Strong's 'Money (That's What I Want)', released nationally on his sisters' Anna label to make number two in the *Billboard* R&B chart. Gordy's first signing was the Matadors, who became the Miracles, whose fourth single, 1959's 'Bad Girl', was first released on the new Motown imprint on April 14, 1960 (locally – nationally it was released on Chess).

'Shop Around' also reached number two on *Billboard*'s Hot 100, becoming the label's first million seller. Smokey became Vice President of Motown, while Gordy family members took key positions in the company, whose roster expanded to encompass Mary Wells, Mable John and Eddie Holland, as the label rose from being 'The Sound Of Young Black America' to simply 'The Sound Of Young America'.

Developing talent from kids around the neighbourhood and nearby projects, Motown gave doo-wop vocal groups a soul respray with pop sensibility, turning songs into mini teenage symphonies led by the omnipresent, tambourine-enhanced stomping beat inspired by Detroit's automobile production lines. The back room of the house was converted into a studio, where the Funk Brothers added their super-tight magic to what would become one of music's most monumental catalogues. The squad included keyboardists Earl Van Dyke, Johnny Griffith and Joe Hunter, guitarists Joe Messina, Robert White and Eddie Willis, bassists James Jamerson and Bob Babbitt, drummers Benny Benjamin, Uriel Jones and Richard 'Pistol' Allen and percussionists Eddie 'Bongo' Brown and Jack Ashford.

For any ambitious young black songwriter, Motown was an aspirational beacon of hope. Rock'n'roll had successfully assimilated hillbilly and 'race' music but, facing opposition from conservative elements, became sanitised for white audiences. Squeaky clean pin-ups now fronted diluted black music to corner the hit market. Motown's vibrant new soul sound redressed the balance, at a time when Ray Charles, Jackie Wilson and Sam Cooke were also whipping up their individual brands of hysteria.

George later admitted that all he wanted to do was be heard and get on Motown. As he says in *An Oral History*, "To me, the fifties is still my music. But Motown was the first one of the family things ... I could tell when I heard the first drumbeat that it was a Motown record. And they were the first organisation where everybody in their groups had a set of nice suits, yellows and reds and greens. They was always clean. All the girls had new wigs."

In September 1962, the Parliaments, backed by guitarist Andy Birks, secured an audition with Motown in Detroit, but flunked for, as they were told, resembling the Temptations too much. Some would have seen this as a crushing blow, but the ambitious George took it in his stride. Keeping the barbershop running, he regularly commuted to New York where he now gained a new avenue of entry into the Gordy empire.

George became ensconced in the Brill Building throughout 1962 and 1963 after landing a gig as a Motown-related writer-producer as Gordy's disintegrating marriage resulted in his wife, Raynoma (Ray), establishing a New York office for Motown's Jobete publishing arm. The company's main aim was to come up with demos of their writing stable's newly delivered songs in the hope other artists would record them. Ray signed George to churn out the hits on the recommendation of songwriter-producers George Kerr (who had performed with the Imperials for two years as lead singer Little Anthony's replacement) and Sidney Barnes, fresh from working for labels including Chess, Blue Cat, Red Bird and Gemini. Both were Parliaments fans who'd already got their new group the Serenaders on the roster after hearing about Motown's new office. Sidney won the audition by bluffing his way into Ray's office on the first day while posing as a furniture shifter, and he and Kerr were also taken on as producer-songwriters. The latter was a regular at the barbershop, so took Sidney along to meet George and the Parliaments.

"He took me out to the barbershop where George Clinton did his hair," Sidney Barnes recalled in *An Oral History*. "I met George, I met the other guys. They were putting that lye in people's hair, laying it down. I might even have had 'em doing my hair that day. George Clinton was the leader of the thing. I could see that. And they were kids. When George Kerr and I got with Motown, he called George and had the Parliaments come over. We built up Ray Gordy about 'em…They passed the audition, they were good as hell, but they were so different."

George reckoned getting the Parliaments signed to a Jobete publishing deal would put Gordy's mothership in easier reach, although the songs he was coming up with were already idiosyncratic compared to mainstream fodder.

Sammy Campbell adds, "The Parliaments were nasty, they were funky, but they were doing doo-wop. George really, underneath, was what he is now. I mean, when you went to a dance, George was the funkiest dancer. He's just one of those cats. He glowed, man. Very creative guy. When I first heard his stuff on tape – way back to even his audition tape – it was harmony and melodies that nobody else was doing. Some strange shit. And I said, 'This guy's fantastic'. Everybody else went, 'I don't know, man'. So Berry signed George, and we worked with George on a lot of demos."

George's talent was obvious and, despite some finding his songs too weird, he was allowed to develop his own material, seemingly under little pressure from above. The Parliaments never got past demoing as the company's attention fixed on Detroit big boys such as the Temptations and Four Tops. Jobete even started an offshoot called Soul Records as an outlet for the Parliaments but, instead, went on to release the likes of Earl Van Dyke, Junior Walker & the All Stars, Jimmy Ruffin, the Originals and Gladys Knight & the Pips. Some copies of a song called 'I Misjudged You' (which Parliament revisited in 1975 on *Chocolate City*) are said to have been pressed up on another Motown subsidiary called VIP.

But George knew that in their current form the Parliaments would always be floundering in the long shadow of the Temptations, and at a disadvantage because they didn't hail from Detroit.

Jobete became such a success that Berry Gordy wanted it back, even if his main concern was what his ex-wife was getting up to and with who. "Berry had given Ray Jobete, but now it was doing so well he wanted it back," explained George. "So he stopped paying the bills! There we are in the Brill Building with Leiber & Stoller, Bobby Darin, all these, and the lights would go out just like in the ghetto because the bill hadn't been paid."

A woman scorned, Ray pressed up her own copies of Mary Wells' 'My Guy', a massive hit in 1964, getting the boys to sell them out of the trunk of a car so they could pay to keep the electricity flowing. Gordy retaliated by sending down right-hand man Barney Ales to close down the office and confiscate everything, although Ray was paid off with a few million and relocated to Washington. This left some of her old roster following Gordy to Detroit to see what they could pick up, including George, Sidney Barnes and George Kerr.

George continued cutting demos for Motown and producing outside projects. He put some of his money into a short-lived little label called Marton Records, in partnership with Joe Martin, Motown's distributor in Newark. George produced singles including Roy Handy's 'Accidental Love'/'What Did He Do?'

Still hanging on to the barbershop, George juggled his hairdressing commitments alongside a hectic schedule of writing and recording, sometimes having to hurry a 'do' because he had to run to the studio, leaving the goo-plastered noggin for someone else to finish. Some regulars made for Grady or Calvin to do their hair in case George suddenly vanished. After George White died in 1963 Ernie Harris bought the other 50% stake in the Plainfield barbershop which now became known as the Black Soap Palace.

"Silk Palace was really doing good by that time," recalls George in *An Oral History*. "Processing hair. We had two or three older barbers, who had their clientele, playing checkers and shit. Then we had the younger guys, who may be nodding, you know what I mean? I might have a girl in the back there. Somebody's head might be burning, talking 'bout 'Get this shit out my motherfuckin' head!' Congolese – fry that muthafucka! Just put it on your head with a comb or brush, grease your head to death, then wash your head out while you pat your feet and holler. Or you might get, 'I'm going to audition for my record thang. I'll tell my boy to comb you out. I put the waves in, so you gon' be cool.'"

George had been going to New York on the bus every day after working hours; making over a thousand dollars a week then spending it on cutting records and productions. "That was the only way to get to do my own thing, was to pay for it," he reasoned.

This experience can be seen as crucial in feeding what he would ejaculate into the world by the end of the decade, as P-Funk sprouted like a wild polar opposite to Motown's glorious but tightly regimented hit factory. Although he benefited from the songwriting training his Motown stint gave him, George's refusal to conform to the demands of the conveyor belt and display the requisite upwardly mobile demeanour resulted in nothing being released from that association under his or the Parliaments' name, although it did also plant the idea for his own stable of artists (even if the same personnel were signed to different labels using the same house band, rather than a roster on the same imprint).

In 1964, George was invited to team up with a millionaire hotel owner called 'Big' Ed Wingate, who ran the Golden World and Ric Tic labels and had installed a studio in his palatial home. Described by Sidney Barnes as "eight feet tall, black and ugly but sweet", Ed saw himself as a rival to Berry Gordy, having released successful singles by Edwin Starr ('Agent Double-O Soul', 'Stop Her On Sight'), the Debonaires and Shades Of Blue (cheekily inviting the Funk Brothers to moonlight for extra cash). After abandoning his Motown dreams, George accepted the invitation and Wingate paid for him to fly back to Plainfield every weekend to work at the barbershop, on top of a generous pay cheque. This Monday to Friday week in Detroit went on for two years.

Now boasting his first independent deal, George called up Sidney Barnes, the pair setting up a company called Geo-Si-Mik, bringing in Andrew 'Mike' Terry, who'd been playing baritone saxophone for Motown since the start, his hiccuping style adorning hits by the Four Tops and Supremes.

George was being paid well and, crucially for future projects, had a studio to explore for the first time, even if Big Ed locked him and Sidney in its basement confines until they came up with a hit song. George and Sidney were expected to respond if Ed got an idea, like when he heard the phrase 'I'm into something I can't shake loose' on the radio and woke the pair to demand an instant tune from it. The pair came up with the hip-swingingly catchy 'Can't Shake It Loose' for noted session singer Pat Lewis, which the Supremes covered on their *Love Child* album. George wrote the verses, while Sidney handled chords and hook. The pair also wrote 'I'll Bet You' at these gruelling sessions, originally for a singer called Theresa Lindsay, before it was covered by Jerry Butler's brother Billy and the Jacksons on 1970's *A.B.C.* (and given away courtesy of a Cornflakes offer). The young Michael Jackson also covered George's 'Touch The One You Love' in 1973, while Barbara Lewis made her chart debut with his 'Hello Stranger', reaching number three and topping the R&B listings.

George still found time to produce some tunes in the New Jersey-New York area, helming a girl group classic in the Pets' stomping, frugging mod favourite 'I Say Yeah' on Carnival (co-written with Fuzzy Haskins and Grady Thomas). In 1965, he arranged an underground soul classic, 'No More Ghettos In America', co-written by his barbershop comrade Ernie Harris. The track was sung by Stanley Winston and released on Louisiana's Jewel label (later to emerge as one of legendary UK DJ John Peel's favourite records, being in his famous black box of 100 indispensable seven-inch singles). All soaring vocals and melodic pianos with lyrics presaging the protest soul of later in the decade, it could be considered an overlooked pivotal milestone for George, giving a roaring gospel-tinged ballad a cutting-edge musical slant to fit the lyrics.

Elsewhere, America's white kids were witnessing pop music losing its virginity as the Beatles appeared on Ed Sullivan's TV show in 1964, followed by the more dangerous implications of exposing the nation's teenagers to the Rolling Stones. Motown-dominated black music was an influence on both these bands, but the climate it was produced in was a far cry from the suburban upbringing of many Beatles fans. Dr King's non-violent civil disobedience approach was starting to pall for some of his followers in the face of the brutal thuggery inflicted by his racist opponents. Since the thirties, Louis Farrakhan's Nation Of Islam had thrown down a harder line, taking a more confrontational stance than Dr King's peace-pushing gatherings. By the early sixties, they had become a galvanising force for the disenchanted and militant.

Malcolm Little from Omaha, Nebraska, was a former Harlem hustler who'd discovered the Nation's black separatist teachings while doing time for burglary. Soberly dressed and sporting spectacles, as Malcolm X he became a ferociously compulsive and intensely knowledgeable speaker on the streets of New York, berating civil rights leaders of the time for what he considered to be their attempts to infiltrate an already-corrupt white establishment. Having grown up with violence, he could unleash the kind of fiery rhetoric which struck a chord right down to the prison sub-culture which had brutalised him. He believed any successful revolution could only be bloody, as seen in Africa and Latin America, rather than the passive approach of waving banners and singing around camp fires. He would be proved ahead of his time but, in March 1964, Malcolm left the Nation of Islam, formed his own Muslim Mosque Inc and visited Africa and Mecca, the accompanying epiphany altering his views on black separatism, although he subsequently famously declared that America's 22 million African-Americans would have to achieve freedom "by any means necessary".

As the civil rights and anti-war movements grew, the government had increased its counter-intelligence missions, while politically motivated murders became increasingly frequent. Malcolm was killed with a shotgun while commencing a speech to the Organisation of Afro-American Unity at Detroit's Audubon Ballroom on February 21, 1965. Whether or not this was a plot by the Nation of Islam or the CIA remains unproved, but the outpouring of grief was tangible. Thousands descended on Harlem to view his body over a three-day period, Malcolm now elevated to a martyr, invoked by anyone with revolutionary inclinations, while younger black revolutionaries re-evaluated his messages. This caused schisms to develop within the civil rights movement as goals changed and the debate raged concerning the level violence played in its activities. Malcolm's supporters were further motivated by events such as the beatings of civil rights marchers in Selma, Alabama. The violence reached a crescendo in August 1965 as the Watts riots raged through South Central Los Angeles.

Meanwhile, the possibility of better employment, schooling and housing in northern cities continued to draw hordes of migrating southern African-Americans, increasing the numbers of disillusioned as the better life promised failed to materialise. Addressing years of ingrained racism was obviously impossible in some quarters, particularly the bigoted elements in the Deep South, whose neo-Nazi terror tactics further propelled the Civil Rights movement, spawning the Black Power movement looking for equality, dignity and political self-sufficiency. Waves of dissent continued to gather impetus in black communities, many favouring direct action instead of Dr King's peaceful approach. The more militant, radical Black Power movement thrived in its own right, initially declaring its intention to fight against racial oppression and establish separate social institutions with self-sufficient economy. Followers started dividing between the banners of Dr King's 'Freedom Now' and 'Black Power', a term first used as a slogan by Stokely Carmichael and Willie Ricks, organisers of the Student Nonviolent Coordinating Committee.

Carmichael was one of the foremost black radicals of the sixties, and also one of its most efficient organisers, helping transform neighbourhoods, forcing black studies at colleges and mobilising voters while instilling racial pride through solidarity. Like most conscious black radicals of the time, he acknowledged the importance of the music that accompanied the movement growing into maturity. In his book, *Ready For Revolution*, Carmichael describes the galvanising effect of soul and funk: "We are an African people, so it was natural from the beginning, from the spirituals right on up, music would be our weapon and our solace... This music reached people we couldn't otherwise reach. How effectively I can't say. But from it, one sensed an exuberant mood in the community."

After Malcolm X's death, James Brown rose as a suitably charismatic figure for the black community to look to for inspiration, his place in this story as important as Motown in paving the way for George, who opted to follow his own path when he came to the fork in the road on the cusp of achieving his own stardom. The Godfather of Soul boiled up black music into a brand new bag called The Funk, coinciding with his ascension from pop star to black hero figure, the intensity of his music increasing with the heat on the streets. It took the June 1966 shooting of James Meredith while walking a one-man March Against Fear from Memphis to Jackson, to turn the Godfather into a politicised cultural tornado. Working independently of organised civil rights activities, he wanted to draw attention to the vengeful white-on-black violence that was escalating in the wake of civil rights advances.

Brown visited Meredith in hospital, recalling in *Keep On Pushing*, "I was greatly affected by that visit and afterward, I intensified the pledge I had made to myself... It was no longer going to be enough to change the music of a generation; I had to try to change people's way of thinking as well." He resolved to use his celebrity status "for the good of my people".

The evolution of black music has been built upon social struggle, sometimes against all odds in restricted circumstances after desperately poor beginnings. James Brown will always embody this; crawling up from gutter hopelessness to achieve huge success and empowerment; a living, sweating role model coming from poverty to rule a musical empire built on sweat and soul – blazing a trail for the likes of Stevie Wonder and Marvin Gaye.

Brown was born in May 1933 in Barnwell, South Carolina, and was raised in an aunt's brothel in Augusta, Georgia, where he was dancing and singing by the age of six. As a teenager, he served a three-year jail stretch for breaking into a car to steal a coat. On release, he was taken in by singer Bobby Byrd's mother, joining his benefactor's gospel-doo-wop outfit the Flames. "He'd come out and sing," recalled Byrd. "He was in his teens. I thought he was very good, even then." Their first hit was 1956's 'Please Please Please', followed by 'Try Me' and a string of soul-soaked landmarks which, combined with Brown's supercharged stage act, swiftly gained a formidable following.

The turning point for the form soon to be called The Funk came in late 1964 when Brown recorded 'Papa's Got A Brand New Bag' for King Records. Sax titan Maceo Parker had recently joined his band, along with his drummer brother Melvin. Brown welcomed their youthful vitality as his music was becoming tighter and funkier. What came out of that session is widely regarded as the birth of funk.

The song defied all the established structural norms; being written on the one and three as opposed to the two and four, while bringing in gospel-style vocal refrains and downbeat thrust to activate the groin-level rhythmic surge accent which would soon become the essence of P-Funk. In *98% Funky Stuff: My Life In Music* Maceo explains how the song was actually "a simple blues with the emphasis on the drums and bass. The horn lines were punchy and infectious; you couldn't help but hum right along." When the time came for the saxophone solo, Brown "uttered a phrase that would forever change my life. 'I just want you to blow, Maceo, hey!'" He then played his first recorded solo on the track, cementing his position as one of the founding fathers of funk.

When 'Papa's Got A Brand New Bag' stormed the charts the following year, Brown knew he'd caused a cog in the universe to shift, and so continued to refine his new formula on outings such as 'Cold Sweat', 'Out Of Sight' and 'Licking Stick', which were built on jams with percussive guitar, bass and drums. Soon – in uncanny parallel with his rise as a black figurehead – Brown increasingly stripped his music down to a naked, pulsating groove. He had unleashed a new beat for the street which would go hand in hand with his increasing ability to inject his songs with the spirit of a time when the most defiant acts of integration could be found on America's dance floors at black music shows.

This was The Funk. Dating back to Shakespearian times and coming from the Flemish word 'fonck' for fear or dismay, funk by dictionary definition can mean a depressed mood, cowering fear or 'sombre, emotional state'. It was also a 17th century term for stench or 'funke' smell. Rickey Vincent's *Funk: The Music, The People And The Rhythm Of The One* is one of the most knowledgeable and enjoyable books I've ever encountered. His affinity with all things funky manifests through his style of writing and trenchant insights such as, "Most people do not realise that a significant musical movement occurred during the seventies, generated primarily by outcast musicians that were a black underclass in America. Funk spoke directly to those people, while others simply danced to it. Funk rests at the core of hard hitting dance music today. And the missing link for a lost generation of funky people to find their place in history."

Even if, at this point in time, George's music had yet to be infected by The Funk, he had a clear perspective of its dynamics, "Funk has a lot of meanings like dark, damp places like the womb or then you have the sweaty jazz dens that are funky … But it's been in the jazz music scene for a long time and it means hanging very loose and sweaty again. It always leads to that.

"Just playing loose and jamming, grooving, the simplest form of making music, which is probably the first. You know there's beating on a tree trunk with a stick, which is very funky."

By 1966, George was still composing and recording at a ferocious rate. The Parliaments released their third single in November 1966 on Golden World. Both composed by George and Sidney Barnes; the sweet and breezy 'That Was My Girl' is like a soppy dude answer record to Mary Wells' 'My Guy', while 'Heart Trouble' rides the patent Motown stomp with toupee-whisking strings, bassatronic undertow and tremulous lead vocal from Ron Banks of the Dramatics – all heralded by George's immortal opening line 'Worryation's got a hold on me, I can't think for myself'.

George's most startlingly assertive self-composed production from this time is also one of his most obscure, the Flaming Embers 'Hey Mama (What'cha Got Good For Daddy)' a mini-masterpiece of smouldering attitude, its twanging guitars (reportedly courtesy of Eddie Hazel) and classical lift presaging the moody Funkadelic blueprint.

The next key development in the Parliaments' increasingly complex story came after Big Ed sold his labels to Motown and his former partner, local DJ LeBaron Taylor, started Revilot and Solid Hit Records with Detroit businessman Don Davis. Geo-Si-Mik placed themselves on the maiden release by supplying a B-side to Darrell Banks' 'Open The Door To Your Heart' with the uptempo romp of 'Our Love (Is In The Pocket)'. George again displayed his original lyrical approach when producing his 'Look What I Almost Missed' for Pat Lewis, which would later appear as a Parliaments single. Co-writing with Holland and Dozier and co-producing with Gene Redd, he was behind Roy Handy's Northern classic 'Baby That's A Groove' on Stephanye in 1966 (and noticeable for the Parliaments' gusto in the male chorale). The song was later slowed down by Funkadelic to become 'Fish, Chips and Sweat', a non-album B-side.

Around the same time, George produced Debonaires duo Joyce

Vincent Wilson and Telma Hopkins, who'd had a string of flops on Golden World and now appeared on Solid Hit with Northern Soul groover 'Headache In My Heart' and 'Loving You Takes All My Time'. The last song is a breathtaking example of how George's writing and production skills had improved in the eight years he'd been working in studios; a master class of perfect touches such as killer key change, glistening bells and midway falsetto acrobatics driving a perfect upbeat soul groover. There hadn't been that many singles with only George's name below the artist's so this could be considered a milestone release. The girls would go on to become the Dawn singers for Tony Orlando.

The parallel career path of Sammy Campbell and the Del-Larks helped P-Funk acquire one of its key components: by 1966, Sammy had got into production, launching his Queen City label with 'SOS For Love', which he tried to place with Newark's larger Smoke Records, owned by one George Blackwell. Sammy was friends with a young local guitarist called Eddie Hazel, who worked as a staff writer for Blackwell and would soon go on to join the nascent Funkadelic with close friend and fellow barbershop kid Billy Nelson.

Born in Brooklyn on April 10, 1950, Eddie initially found himself relocated to Plainfield because his mother, Grace Cook, wanted him to grow up in an environment untainted by drugs and crime. While she commuted to her silk presser's job in Brooklyn, Eddie diligently taught himself the guitar that was given to him one childhood Christmas by his brother, while also honing his soulful voice in church. The 12-year-old Billy first met Eddie at one of the popular Plainfield backyard jam sessions, where he was playing the Surfaris' 'Wipeout' with a group of sparring guitar hopefuls. "When it came time for Eddie to take a lead solo, that motherfucker played some totally other shit," recalls Billy in *An Oral History*. "I knew then that he was good." The pair quickly became friends, jamming Motown hits in their backyards, joined by local drummer Harvey McGee. Billy taught Eddie singing, the latter reciprocated with guitar tips, the pair forming a locally gigging band despite both being under-age.

When Eddie moved to Newark to join Sammy at Smoke Records,

he worked as a staff composer out of a house on Newark's Chadwick Avenue for groups including the Exsaveyons and Herbs. "I wrote most of the songs at Smoke Records," recalled Sammy for *Classic Urban Harmony*. "Eddie did most of the music. I didn't know the other guys. They were from George Blackwell's little stable over there. [Blackwell] had so many groups coming in and out of there. They'd pay for the session. We had to provide the music and the songs.

"I didn't go there to be a writer for somebody else. I wanted George to put out 'SOS'. I ended up there almost a year and my record still never came out." Sammy fell afoul of Blackwell over the situation so, after a gun-toting showdown typical of the cut-throat nature of the business at the time, Queen City was reactivated with 'SOS For Love', which Blackwell also released on his own Vision label, unknown to Campbell.

Billy Nelson was another child barbershop veteran, several years younger than the Parliaments, who played a pivotal role in the early Funkadelic. Born in Plainfield on January 28, 1951, he risked beatings for years sneaking into the barbershop, earning some cash by sweeping up or singing and dancing for the customers by the age of 11. "I was like an employee," he remembers in *An Oral History*. "George processed hair and I assisted in part of that where I would wash people's hair and get them ready for George to style them. I always played guitar. I just kept on playing and listening to [the Parliaments] rehearse in the barbershop. So, I kept on bringing my guitar around, practising with them and with the jukebox. I got so good I could play whatever came on.

"A lot of people used to hang out in that barbershop 'cause it was definitely a popular place to be... the energy was intense and the only place to be. They had to decide whether they would go home or not. I was deep in the barbershop. To do that and survive was rough as hell in itself but then we all grew up in it like Garry Shider, Eddie Hazel, Tawl Ross, Cordell Mosson and his brothers. As we were kids growing up, they all had their own bands."

Billy and Eddie's band regularly played events organised by Sammy Campbell in Plainfield to celebrate public holidays like the Fourth of July and Thanksgiving. The bills were usually headlined by the Parliaments or Del-Larks, joined by other local bands including the Wonders, and Jo-Jo & the Administrators featuring the Boyce brothers.

While George and the Parliaments were now poised for their first success, the seeds of the psychedelic funk monster called Funkadelic were now being sewn by two backyard jamming buddies. Sparks would soon be flying in the creative cauldron of the barbershop as the ghettos erupted into riots while the outside world exploded in lysergic Technicolor.

Chapter Three

There's A Riot Going On With Laughing Sam's Dice

"We knew we wasn't gonna get on the radio back then that easy, so we wasn't losing nothing by just going crazy. I started looking at, you know, alternative realities."

George Clinton

"So, back then the food was cheap; the pot and peyote were cheap; the beer and tequila were cheap. Cheap but exquisite. The living was as the song says, 'easy'. Things were 'exploding' in performance and in combining various art forms: Civil Rights marches; the birth of folk/rock; Happenings, the rise in recording technology: two-track to four-track to eight-track and 16-track in just a couple of years. The invention of the glorious wah wah pedal in late 1966! Good sound systems so that you could star the vocals! The era was wonderful, but had its whiffs of tear gas and danger."

Ed Sanders, The Fugs, to author 2008

The flowers, freakouts and hallucinogenic drugs which rose out of the counterculture in 1967 to briefly bathe the world in an idyllic explosion of love, peace and epoch–making music became an unlikely catalyst to release George and his barbershop crew from the straitjacket of traditional soul and into the anarchic circus that was soon to take over the group.

Of course, there was also the acid and eye-opening effect George's old chitlin' circuit buddy Jimi Hendrix started having on the white rock fraternity as 1967 progressed. But, maybe strangely, another major event which untethered George's cerebral space hopper to send it bouncing into the cosmos was the hit single he'd been dreaming of for 10 years arriving in the form of '(I Wanna) Testify'. Or rather the similarly long-fantasised headlining show at Harlem's Apollo, which turned into a disastrous shambles but showed the Parliaments that smartly pressed uniforms, choreographed dance routines and perfect harmonies were not the way to go as conventional musical forms started disintegrating and recombining in new, undreamed of ways.

The hippie revolution had yet to hit nationally and it certainly wasn't a preoccupation for George when he went into a Detroit studio in late 1966 and recorded the celebratory but smouldering gospel-tinged lovers' anthem he'd co-written with Ron Taylor's brother Deron, with more than a hint of the Temptations in the ethereal vocal harmonies and dramatic staccato intro riff. Although billed as the Parliaments' first release on the new Revilot label, the single only featured George because the other members didn't have the financial means to get to Detroit and Calvin Simon had recently been drafted to Vietnam. Instead, George vociferously declared "I just wanna testify what your love has done to me" over harmonies from Motown session singers the Andantes and a jazz-loose but funky guitar and organ-driven tear-up from Golden World Records group the Holidays (who released 'Love's Creeping Up On Me' and 'I Know She Cares' that year). He co-credited the laconic flip side's 'I Can Feel The Ice Melting' to 'T. Lewis' – this was backing vocalist Tamala or Pat Lewis who was the mother of George's son Tracey. While it recalls the Motown sound to the point of pastiche, the song is slow enough to accentuate the crystal-clear harmonies (which, to these furry ears, presages the lustrous Parliament vocal tapestries to come), all helped along by George's production touches such as the inclusion of vibes.

When George returned to Plainfield with the master tape, the other Parliaments protested he'd sold out to sound white. "I didn't like the way George sang it," revealed Fuzzy Haskins in *An Oral History*. "It just sounded so light and commercial. It wasn't an R&B sound at all. Me and Grady and Calvin were like, 'Man you sound like you white!'" But when 'Testify' was finally released on February 9, 1967, it was picked up by the majority of radio playlists, especially on the east coast where it took up residence on New York's WABC, reaching number three on *Billboard*'s R&B chart and hitting the Top 20 on the main pop chart.

In addition to catapulting the Parliaments to chart success, the track was also covered by several singers, including Johnnie Taylor, who enjoyed a Top 40 hit with it in 1969. The single also became George's first record released in the UK, appearing on Track Records, home of Hendrix, John's Children, Arthur Brown and the Who, whose sophisticated psych classic 'I Can See For Miles' it followed on the release schedule that October.

The Parliaments were suddenly in demand, but still had no regular backing band at this point. George started by drafting in 17-year-old Billy Nelson on guitar, which was inevitable as his whole adolescence had been soundtracked by the Parliaments rehearsing in the back room of the barbershop every evening. Although a homecoming show at Plainfield High School saw the Parliaments greeted like local heroes, their first headline gig at Harlem's Apollo that June dissolved into a shambolic nightmare as their well-rehearsed moves collapsed, followed by the music provided by the house band now augmented by Billy. This further threw the singers, who forgot lyrics and routines to the point of colliding into one another.

The group was supposed to go to the venue and show the house band the songs the day before they were due to play. George, Billy and Grady went over, leaving the rest of the band at home rehearsing their steps. On the night it was a disaster, which Grady Thomas partly attributed to the group being thrown by the sudden star billing over the O'Jays and behaving like "a bunch of Laurel & Hardys and Three Stooges ... We put this routine together for a song called 'Six By Six' and, whoa we were bumping into each other." They also massacred Eddie Floyd's

'Knock On Wood' and the Four Tops' 'Seven Rooms Of Gloom' after Fuzzy forgot the words, later opining, "I don't think I've ever been so humiliated and embarrassed in all my life." Grady summed it up, cringing, "The place you wanted to go all your life … There was family out there. I remember the O'Jays, they was laughing at us. 'Oh man, we'll never sing anywhere else again. The Parliaments are through'."

The billing was swapped for the rest of the week, with the O'Jays moved to the top spot. The experience was a wake-up call for George, who told *Creem*: "When 'Testify' happened we still hadn't found ourselves," he reflected. "We were trying to get away from ourselves and be like other people. The first time we went into the Apollo Theatre we wanted to be there so bad, we practised like we never practised in our lives. Then we went out for the first show and froze. We didn't make it that day but the rest of the week we were the stars. The first day we were there they made us open up that motherfucking show. The O'Jays were the stars of the show, but we were bigger than them because we had a hit record. We were definitely the stars of the show but we blew so bad! We were trying to be really slick. We had no idea it was going to be that ragged. We only had half a routine. We would always get carried away somewhere in the song and forget about the routine. We were never a routine group."

This encounter with the harsh realities of showbusiness kick-started the transformation of the uniformed Parliaments into the senses-scrambling anarcho-orgy of Funkadelic. Previously, they would have tried to correct the looseness, but that started tapering off as wardrobe malfunctions became not only the norm but were assimilated into the band's act. "We always tried to correct it but we couldn't," recalled George. "Like, we would always lose our shirts so never had shirts alike. We just couldn't do it. After a while, we just started wearing anything.

"At first, it was funny, and then we started liking not wearing the same things… We didn't plan it, it just was. Then psychedelic came out and that gave it a legit name. We were already into it. By the time we hit the road with 'I Wanna Testify', we had cut our processes off. Just before 'Testify' everybody looked like us, so we cut our hair off, and still too many people looked like us. But we just couldn't keep the clothes alike."

The Apollo debacle and the subsequent shows left Billy feeling totally inadequate as the sole backing musician touring with the singers. He desperately needed instrumental backup so new members started clambering aboard the nascent Mothership during a break in the Parliaments' relentless touring schedule between May and August, 1967. Also unhappy playing guitar, Billy first suggested his buddy Eddie Hazel, while he switched to bass (getting tips from Motown four-string titan James Jamerson). Billy tracked Eddie down and found that he was still working for George Blackwell in Newark and, as with everything, the guitarist answered Billy's invitation with "Ask my mother". At first, she refused point blank as her son was only 17 and she was one of the many respectable citizens who considered the barbershop a scandalous den of sin and iniquity. But Billy was a frequent house guest at the Hazels, so he turned on the charm to bring Mrs Hazel around (she later recalled both Billy and George 'begging' Eddie to join their band). Never mind moving to Plainfield to keep her son away from drugs, her son had just got a free pass into the biggest pharmacy on the planet, but at least now the world would hear his unearthly talent.

It hadn't yet dawned on George that one of the greatest guitarists of the 20th century, with the potential to rival Hendrix, was among the kids sneaking into the Soap Palace, although later he recalled, "One of the older guys in the barbershop, Wolf, he was the one, in the beginning, that was telling me we should listen to this kid around the corner. Wolf had a room at Eddie's mother's house."

Billy has always been the proud standard bearer of Eddie's legacy, especially since his friend passed away, stating, "When it comes down to the bottom line, Funkadelic was me and Eddie, and everything else came round me and Eddie."

Drummer Harvey McGee played with the pair during incessant Motown covering sessions at the Nelson home. The nascent band would have recruited highly regarded guitarist Frankie Boyce and his bassist brother Richard Boyce from Jo-Jo and the Admirations, who had opened for the Parliaments many times, but the former had been drafted to Vietnam earlier that year, where he was killed. George brought in keyboardist Mickey Atkins from Harrisburg, Pennsylvania and, according to Billy, a drummer from Washington DC called Stacy, who struggled to hold his own under the bombastic alchemy afoot. That problem was solved when the Parliaments hit Philadelphia's Uptown Theatre for a short residency that September and Eddie befriended shit-hot house drummer Ramon 'Tiki' Fulwood, who played with all the visiting acts who didn't have a band. Billy and Eddie agreed that his thunderous metronome would be perfect for the new band and, when George and the rest of the group started procrastinating, told Tiki to just join in. His performance on set opener 'Knock On Wood' was enough for Stacy to quit on the spot and hand Tiki the Funkadelic drum stool.

Born in Philadelphia on May 23, 1944, Tiki had played with the Artistics and Tyrone Davis around the time of 'Can I Change My Mind' and brought his heavyweight funk tattoos as an essential anchor for the new band. "The epitome of that showtime shit, with power," according to Billy.

Around the same time, Lucius 'Tawl' Ross came in on guitar. Born in Wagram, North Carolina, on November 5, 1948, he grew up in Plainfield, playing bass in a rock band with future Funkadelic bassist Cordell Mosson's brother, Larry. Again, Billy was the connection as, after he switched to bass to make room for Eddie, he started visiting Tawl regularly for lessons. Like Eddie, Tawl favoured uncut emotional energy in his playing over innate chops. By all accounts, he was already further out there than George and slotted right in, with his chipped front tooth and derelict demeanour.

"Larry 'Cool Pop' Mosson and Tawl were, as far as style and lifestyle, attitude, on into the Mothership, showmanship – identical. And crazy? Whew! I mean, I didn't know what insane meant until I met Tawl and Larry Mosson," recalled Billy. "Them brothers was out to lunch. I knew what Tawl could do, just like I knew what Eddie could do, just like I knew what Tiki could do."

After the success of 'Testify', George was confident enough in the Parliaments' future to sell the barbershop. Meanwhile a follow-up single was needed, so the Parliaments recorded enough tracks for their next five Revilot 45s in one single session, including 'All Your Goodies Are Gone (The Losers Seat)' which was released as a single that October. The track, co-written with Fuzzy and Billy, shows the growing maturity throughout George's songwriting, lyrics and production. Displaying another unusual slant on romance, the song concerns a guy resignedly leaving the girlfriend who dumped on him and who is now on the skids; in the losing seat "without a love of your own, and all your goodies are gone". With a killer, much-sampled bassline, it's the kind of dark, gritty and hard-hitting love song for modern times which George excelled at in his Tin Pan Alley period and, although not obvious chart material, reached 21 on the R&B chart (and was righteously revisited on 1974's *Up For The Down Stroke*, slowed to a haunted, malevolent throb to bring out the emotional power of the lyrics). The old-school Motown harmony stomp of the flip's 'Don't Be Sore At Me' (co-written with Grady and Pat Lewis) is immaculately pulled off with superb harmonies, again almost to the point of pastiche.

'Little Man', another Clinton/Lewis composition released in early 1968 on Revilot, was more pop-rock in flavour (bearing a slight resemblance to Aretha Franklin's 'Chain Of Fools'). Its lyrics were directed at straights who didn't know what was going on. While the production was George's most ambitious yet, Mike Terry's arrangement stacked up fanfare trumpets, a complex swirling male-female backing chorale and the unmistakable tinge of psychedelic spangle. The flip's weighty funk-rocker 'The Goose (That Laid the Golden Egg)' injected the kind of foreboding drama not usually found in pop or soul, its complex brass and vocal arrangement adorning an early foray into George's use of nursery rhymes, fairy tales and folk sayings. Co-written with Eddie Hazel and Ernie Harris, this too would be revisited on *Up For The Down Stroke*.

'Look What I Almost Missed' was another brass-laden Smokey Robinson-style chugger (credited to George and Pat), while George and Ernie's 'What You Been Growing' was released around the same time. Effortlessly evoking the then-popular moody Motown style crystallised in such tunes as the Temptations' 'I'm Losing You', but with additional complex twists, the track also features another example of George's use of nursery rhymes with its 'Mary, Mary, quite contrary, how does your garden grow? Remember you reap what you sow'.

Also released in 1968, 'Time' was another smoothly harmonic upbeat pop-soul handclapper from the same session. It was paired with 'Good Old Music', which saw the Parliaments finally escape the Motown template and hoist the funk flag, foreshadowing things to come with its hamslapping funky beats, serrated guitars and roaring Hammond organ. With its "good old funky music" refrain marking George's first use of the term, the song opened the Pandora's Box wide enough to at least enable a glimpse of Funkadelic's gestating acid-funk behemoth.

That day also saw them record a cover of the Beatles' recently released 'Sgt Pepper's Lonely Hearts Club Band'. George had been a big Beatles fan since the mid-sixties, their songwriting, productions and experiments in embellishing the pop form that reached a peak when they embraced psychedelic having a profound effect on his music as his Motown fixation dimmed. George's view was that the Beatles played "everybody's folk music", incorporating anything from R&B to ethnic Indian, which opened up his world view to disparate forms of music.

The previous summer had seen the Geo-Si-Mik squad produce a successful version of 'Daytripper' for JJ Barnes, at George's suggestion. "They thought that was the brand newest shit in the world."

The Beatles are an under-recognised influence on George, whose style is more apparently related to James Brown, Sly Stone and Jimi Hendrix. A key element in the ethos which shaped him was that capacity to go outside of the ghetto and see what else was going on, then bring it back home and use it in his own thing. In the mid-sixties, this kind of racial barrier-trampling only happened in jazz, while pop (or rather, its marketing departments) liked to divide and segregate. The fact that the Beatles took a lot of their early influences from black music as well as rock'n'roll seemed to go unnoticed. "I think of them like I think of Motown, Sly, Jimi Hendrix," George told John Corbett. "All of them was creators of something special. The Beatles caught the wave too for a minute. Some of us are clever ... I supposed to be able to do it, too, 'cause I was around enough music enough different places ... I just call that clever. But some people just catch onto a thang, and to me the Beatles caught onto it. 'Cause you can't do that shit later. Circumstances ain't the same, it can't be done. When that thing come through, it just come through and everything you do is right."

In 1967, the world seemed to turn into one huge fun palace for a few short months. As a wide-eyed 12 year old, I was too young to go to UFO or any of the London happenings, but was excited and enthralled by the new names such as Love, the Seeds and Pink Floyd spangling up broadcasts from the Radio London pirate ship while reading about Hendrix burning his guitar at Monterey. Even Scott McKenzie sweetly suggesting wearing a flower in your hair got me trying it out at school, though it attracted hostile meatheads instead of blissed-out hippie chicks.

As the Vietnam War turned ever more abhorrent and the establishment tried to work out ways to bring down this loudly attired breed of exotic new hedonist, the older versions of those meatheads I'd encountered tried to beat up the hippies the authorities hadn't managed to squash yet – the movement relentlessly subjected to the usual, lowest common denominator media sensationalism. In the US, the idealism of flower power gave way to a harsh new reality of brutal cops and crackdowns brought on by the government panicking in the face of dissent and opposition. But, even if there was a global awakening of peace-loving consciousness going on, nothing had really changed in the ghettos, where it was still hard to see life beyond the corners ruled by daily drug rituals and racist police. There was time for peace and love where George came from, but also the harsh realities of pimps, whores and junkies. George would only use witches' castles in lyrics if they carried some element of social comment.

Apart from *Sgt Pepper* and Hendrix's *Are You Experienced* debut, George loved the high volume blues-rock which came with psychedelia, particularly the riff-based pyrotechnics of Cream, proclaiming, "I learned more about Robert Johnson from Eric Clapton."

The new breed of British blues musicians such as Clapton, Jeff Beck and, later, Jimmy Page paid homage to and amplified the form for the psychedelic era and beyond, their audiences now discovering trailblazers such as Muddy Waters, Howlin' Wolf and B.B. King. George wanted to splice to blues the legacy of black music rather than rock'n'roll, admitting that, while he'd been chasing the Motown mountain, the Brits had been honouring a strain of music that was so deeply ingrained in his psyche and upbringing he'd passed it by. "You couldn't deny that Eric Clapton was playing the hell out of it. But he gave up the respect."

Along with Billy and Eddie, he was also taken with vicious power trio Blue Cheer's shatteringly loud acid rock and the heaving drama of Vanilla Fudge, who were produced by Brill Building maverick George 'Shadow' Morton. George now took as much notice of white psychedelic bands as he did of his black contemporaries, envisioning a new area to operate in beyond the old laws of rock and soul.

At the start of the year, George was still aspiring to join Motown's elite black pop corps, rather than plug into the cutting-edge funk being developed by James Brown. But, after the Parliaments' usual ramshackle attempts to share bills with long-time heroes such as the O'Jays and Temptations, his ambitions to join the upper echelons of slick R&B were replaced by a desire to go with the freewheeling spirit of the times and form a group pushing personal liberation and fierce musical chops rather than synchronised crooning. He now dismissed the Temptations as sounding as old-fashioned as the Ink Spots in the face of the musical revolutions taking place.

The rock influence became amplified in the true sense when the Parliaments were supported by Vanilla Fudge at Connecticut's Sacred Heart College. When their equipment was delayed, they borrowed the Fudge's Marshall amps, triple-stack SVT mound and elephant-size fibre-glass drums. It could be said that Funkadelic was born that night when Eddie Hazel's brilliance was channelled through the same amps as his hero Jimi used. Within weeks, the Parliaments were sporting the same setup. "That's when we evolved into the real Funkadelic," declared Billy. Or, as George put it, "We just went totally loony."

George was already into wild crowd-stoking strategies which started with clowning, jumping into the audience and making them dance with the band. By the end of the set, they could have lost their suits but gained a girl's wig. Anything to get a reaction.

"The Del-Larks and the Parliaments were totally different," recalled

Sammy Campbell. "The Parliaments had two cats that were very spontaneous. That was Clarence 'Fuzzy' Haskins and George Clinton. These two cats were wild. That's what made these two groups so beautiful – the contrast. We were doing the ballads, the Moonglows and Temptations kind of stuff. We had our choreography down pat. The Parliaments had that wild, spontaneous thing."

George swallow-dived into the outrageous new persona he was creating, although he could turn on old-school stagecraft techniques if necessary. Right now, he would be acting the fool with licence to do anything that came into his head, regardless how wild that may be. He embraced 1967's most colourful psychedelic creations with a vengeance that knew no bounds of restraint.

This larval process started with the musicians not wanting to wear matching suits and Eddie and Billy (then a Black Muslim) eschewing processes in favour of Afros, as the band started sporting a ghetto version of cool street clobber crossed with psychedelic accessories. Individual band members developed their own images such as 'baby of the group' Billy sporting over-sized diaper, braids and combat boots. The singers also started developing their own looks, with Fuzzy, George's onstage foil, rocking tie-dyed longjohns, while Grady went for an 'Arabian Nights' look. George still felt he needed a gimmick, so he shaved his do into a Mohican and cut holes in sheets that he draped over his head like a Biblical robe, knowing the look could work after a test run through the streets of Newark. The band moved from wearing suits to the bags they came back from the cleaners in. George was also inspired by the wildly flamboyant example of Hendrix – to me, that's the ultimate – whom he had known as Jimmy James on the chitlin' circuit.

As a Hendrix nut since the moment I watched his first UK TV appearance in December, 1966, then a Funkadelic fan commencing five years later with a US import of the first album, my teenage brain decided back then that Jimi was their biggest musical influence, along with Sly Stone after he had his first UK hit in 1968 with 'Dance To The Music'. From scuffling pickup guitarist to toast of London's counterculture then the world, Hendrix was the first modern black rock star, whose act had also grown from an inability to maintain his stage uniform. This also became a key element in George's strategy as the Parliaments' superfreak transformation got under way, although the nascent Funkadelic took a far more theatrical approach. All of which surprised the hell out of Calvin Simon when he returned from Vietnam, full of hearing 'Testify' on the radio out there. The singer quit the group a couple of times as there was friction between the peace freaks and those that had been to 'Nam, eventually returning sporting a colourfully casual look.

As the group accelerated into their new "crazy" phase, promoters were shocked when the Parliaments rolled up to do the gig looking nothing like their smart-suited promo photos. The show inevitably careered into unbridled lunacy and outrageous behaviour, George reportedly pissing into crowds and jumping across tables to slap punters upside the head with his P-fella. Considering the furore and legal persecution which surrounded Jim Morrison's alleged onstage exposure in the late sixties, it's amazing he wasn't also dragged off to the courts, although this is maybe more indicative of the less rarefied level at which the Parliaments were then flying.

Although their cerebral mooring rope was cut loose, George continued utilising traditional elements from his previous 10 years leading a group. The ability to put on a show was an essential attribute for any black act traversing the country's clubs. There were already novelty acts such as Screamin' Jay Hawkins taking to the stage from a coffin, but the spectacular stage shows George was developing would become a new visual peak for live black music. In 1967, before George became ringmaster of one of the most spectacular stage shows any form of music has ever seen, his group had to make do with whatever they could find and amplify it with sheer craziness. If the Parliaments now horrified promoters and traditional soul fans, the pimps, hookers and street crazies couldn't wait to join the party, along with a growing hippie audience.

Lysergic acid diethylamide was the other defining element in the group's transformation into full-blown interstellar funk marauders, the major catalyst for the Parliaments' pupae to erupt into Funkadelic's butterfly. George recalls Billy being the first of the group to do acid.

"He looked younger than me, but he did it first. I said if it made him smile ... He never smiled. He was always talkin' shit. And I saw him, a Muslim, smiling like a pig. So I ordered some acid fast." The group volunteered for scientific acid tests at Boston's Harvard University, conducted by acid gurus Timothy Leary and Richard Alpert; offering themselves as willing guinea pigs to be observed for three hours then let loose to run wild afterwards. "I was belching lights and shit, I watched so many people do it and I saw they were happy and I *knew* it had to be all right," recalled George to Frank Broughton in *i-D*. "So when I took it I had pretty much already been high just from the electrodes of everybody else being high.

"We were older – 28, 29, we were from New York and New Jersey, We were from the gang-fighting days of the fifties. *Blackboard Jungle, West Side Story*, all of that was about our era. So when everyone started talking about love and peace, first of all we didn't believe that shit: 'You gotta watch your back'. But then we saw people really meant it. So we were older, we were going to take advantage of all this. There were all these nice girls and the guys were talking all that free love 'Oh I don't own her, she's her own person' and we were '*Oh my god!*' So before we knew it we were like that too. I never would let myself believe that drugs could make me write better or do anything, I refused to believe it. But I know they did now.

"We'd play this club in Boston called the Sugar Shack. We'd always be tripping. Everybody in the audience was tripping. People that didn't even take acid. We called them pimps, hoes and hippies. And the pimps were trying to get over to the hippie girls. They would take acid and they didn't know anything about acid so you'd see some pimp walking around tripping. That was the funniest shit in the world. He's supposed to be all cool and he's wandering about saying 'beeeeeautiful...'."

It's worth noting that the acid going around back then was far purer, and therefore more powerful, than it would be in subsequent years. My first time was orange California Sunshine in 1969 – the wallpaper came to life and my mates turned into giant tortoises. Heavy shit of the sort being guzzled by Funkadelic at the time but, in its own way, clean and much fun if you just went with the flow. Last time I did it was on a Primal Scream tour 25 years later and the difference was noticeable. Although it was still possible to float off on supreme giggling marathons, the stuff was noticeably weaker but spikier with speed additives. (The mind boggles at what might have happened if MDMA had turned up during Funkadelic's lysergic prime.)

While the tough inner cities seemed the polar opposite of the west coast's peace and love idealism, George and crew dived headlong into the unfettered gush of love-seeking hippie chicks and unlimited drugs. As a test student at the psychedelic school, George unsurprisingly pushed his lysergic research to extreme levels after that first trip, recalling in *An Oral History*, "I stayed loony for three years. I wore a sheet and nothing else in the wintertime. I never thought acid did anything for me musically, but a long time after I quit, I realised that it did make my tempo unlike most tempos out of Newark. The kids made you embarrassed to want to fight your wife, or be jealous, 'cause they were so 'peace and love'. For that moment, everybody really meant it."

George felt that love and acid were a necessary yin to the shocking yang of Vietnam. Even if the love, peace and flowers of the Summer of Love seemed corny and blissfully idealistic, he saw it as a necessary balance to the dark shadow of the atom bomb. Like many he believed the flower revolution and anti-war protests nonetheless went at least some way towards preventing further use of nukes after World War Two.

George's new attitude and his change in sound and image was typical of that crazy, seminal year but almost seemed to take place overnight. The Stones and Beatles had started widening their horizons through drugs and musical exploration two years earlier, before unleashing their takes on full-blown psych in 1967. George didn't have that long to consider his group's evolution, as events were moving too fast. His change *had* to be faster, balancing a desire to outdo everyone else's stage show with an emerging message to educate new recruits to the horrors being inflicted by society. If George and crew found their friends and families unavoidably affected by what was happening on the street, his interests and ambitions now also encompassed the global countercultural revolution.

Acid wired the P-Funk crew into the seismic developments taking place across the rest of the country. Any analysis of who were the most vocal exponents of the new drug culture in 1967 goes beyond the Beatles and Stones. The notorious Fugs extended New York City's lineage of cultural innovations from the Beats, bebop and experimental movements into the acid age, two years before the Parliaments abandoned their uniforms and routines. Their no-holds-barred aesthetic and extreme antics on and offstage laid the foundations for further wild behaviour. Fugs shows were shambolic, X-rated 'happenings', raising the bar for mayhem, nudity and profanity. Their music was based upon folk rather than funk, but it flew the same freak flag for personal liberation as George and crew would be doing by the end of that pivotal year.

Named after a sexual euphemism in Norman Mailer's *The Naked And The Dead*, this ragged, wild-eyed gaggle formed around counterculture poet and Peace Eye bookshop proprietor Ed Sanders (who published a poetry magazine called *Fuck You: A Magazine Of The Arts*), fellow poet Tuli Kupferberg, singer Ken Weaver plus crazed folk musicians the Holy Modal Rounders. The Fugs' debut album, *The Village Fugs Sing Ballads And Songs Of Contemporary Protest, Points Of View and General Dissatisfaction,* slapped down their manifesto over basic percussive backings laced with primitive Lower East Side folk-psych thrash. Tracks such as 'Slum Goddess', 'Supergirl' and the locker-room jollity of 'Boobs A Lot' were street-crude and stoned while 'CIA Man' and 'Kill For Peace' ripped into the government and Vietnam War. While George imagined black people in the Pentagon the following decade, the Fugs led a gathering aimed at exorcising the building in October, 1967. Ken Weaver's declaration that "A man who's laughing can't shoot a gun worth a damn" is pure P-Funk philosophy.

The Fugs' underbelly anthems propagated the two main messages which George started running with – opposition to the war and the promotion of freedom (in their case, mainly to get stoned and behave according to the spirit of the moment). Their 'I Couldn't Get High' contained the first lyrical mention of LSD. Swearing live and on record while being thrown off labels and banned from venues, the Fugs caused more deep-rooted moral panic than the Sex Pistols ever would and, if relaying graphic urban narratives over primitive beats constitutes rapping, then they can also be considered hip-hop pioneers. They also gave Hendrix his first fuzz box.

Ed Sanders described the magnitude of the Fugs' conceived threat to me in 2008: "Ever been picketed by right-wing nurses, as we were in California in 1967? We had to have a civil liberties attorney ready to be called when we toured. And while most fans were very friendly, now and then there was hostility, plus the FBI tried to get the Justice Department to indict us."

The Fugs' vital work in breaking down barriers of what could (or couldn't) be said helped pave the way for Funkadelic's 'Loose Booty' and other X-rated nursery rhymes. It seems incredible that controversy-stoking comedian Lenny Bruce endured relentless persecution from the establishment that same decade, his 1964 obscenity trial from a gig at the Café Au Go Go as socially significant in America as the Stones' drugs trial would be in the UK three years later.

While George would have become aware of the Fugs on his downtown clubbing missions, he always names Sly Stone as his biggest influence and the only other human to step out of the Mothership. Sly could be regarded as the second in the Holy Funk Trinity which started with James Brown and ended with George, who instantly recognised they were both peeing against the same tree. Sly came from Oakland, birthplace of the Black Panthers, taking hyper-active soul-revue excitement and giving it a psychedelic makeover in a mixed band. His sister Cynthia played the trumpet, Larry Graham thumbed his hugely amped-up bass and they hit with the force of a high-octane juggernaut.

Sly was born Sylvester Stewart in Denton, Texas during 1943, moving to Vallejo in the San Francisco Bay Area as a child, graduating from the town's high school in 1961. Something of a prodigy, he had mastered piano, guitar, bass and drums by the age of 11, forming a mixed-race high-school doo-wop band called the Viscaynes, who released a few local singles and later influenced the formation of the multi-cultural Family Stone. By 1964, he was working as a staff producer for the local Autumn Records, producing Bobby Freeman's Top Five 'C'Mon Let's Swim', in addition to performing production wizardry for bands including the Beau Brummels, Mojo Men and Grace Slick's pre-Jefferson Airplane Great Society. At this time, it was unusual for a young black man to be producing white rock bands in the studio.

In the mid-sixties, Sly became a popular local radio DJ at KSOL, singing his own commercials and sprinkling the Stones, Beatles and Dylan among the Motown and Stax records. Sly & the Family Stone was formed in 1967 after he combined his band, the Stoners, with his brother's Freddie & the Stone Souls in 1967, lining up as white drummer Greg Errico, trumpeter Cynthia Robinson, saxophonist Jerry Martini and bass Godzilla Larry Graham, later joined by Sly's sister Rose on keyboards.

In 1967, the group was signed to Epic Records by Columbia executive David Kapralik, who had been behind the Torchlight Productions project "to integrate negroes in the theatre, movies and the media" before joining legendary A&R man John Hammond at the company. October 1967's debut album, *A Whole New Thing,* was a critical success but a commercial failure with its screamingly energised soul, psychedelic take on old forms and animatedly personalised performances, led by Sly's stoned, snaky genius. After boss Clive Davis told them to come up with a hit, they produced the following year's chart-storming 'Dance To The Music', then repeated the trick with a string of Top 10 hits, including 'Everyday People', and four ground-breaking albums. Sly and his new psychedelic soul could be credited with making the classic Motown sound and styled-up black groups redundant after 'Dance To The Music', that same year seeing Norman Whitfield plant the Temptations on 'Cloud Nine' then embark on his own widescreen visions on tracks such as 'Ball Of Confusion' and 'Runaway Child'.

Unsurprisingly, a ground-breaking mixed-race band enjoying huge success revolutionising black music and attitudes by playing psychedelic soul with a rock'n'roll agenda scored a direct hit with George. In his preface to Jeff Kalis' Sly biography *I Want To Take You Higher*, George remembers how CBS executive David Kapralik was interested in signing Funkadelic after catching them at Boston's Sugar Shack in August, 1967, recalling, "He was blown away. He was ready to sign us as soon as possible. I was overwhelmed. This was the dude." Turning up at his office, Kapralik showed him photos of his new signings Sly & the Family Stone, revealing that he was leaving Columbia to manage them. Kapralik compared George to Sly, exhorting him to also become centre of attention while playing him the songs, pointing out that they were 'different'.

"I said, 'Damn right it's different!'" recalls George. "They were a mixed, beautiful group. Black, white and big afros. They looked like Funkadelic on Motown! We were very similar, but dark. They looked like a polished version of us." When he heard the music, "I didn't know what to think. Were they a white group? Their pop songs… were as pop as you could possibly get, but the black songs was as black and funky as Ray Charles and James Brown. They had the biggest afros in the world. I thought it was a Bay Area thing, like Huey Newton."

George's obsession grew, consolidated by 'Everyday People' and its B-side, 'Sing A Simple Song', "'Sing A Simple Motherfucking Song' was *the bomb*,' he enthused. "This was it. This song hit me just like 'What'd I Say' by Ray Charles. It was the funkiest thing I'd ever heard in my life, from Motown to James Brown to the Beatles. They were the complete package; they could play, sing, write and produce, and all superior to anybody I'd ever seen or heard before. I was so into Sly's records that I forgot I had gone up there to sign a deal for myself."

That same night, George took in a Sly gig at the Electric Circus on St Mark's Place, the happening downtown psychedelic club at that time. He made sure he got himself "some funky haberdashery for the night" because, "I knew I had to represent. So many people had compared us." On getting to the club, he took a tab of sunshine and proceeded to be blown away by Sly & the Family Stone. "They had the clarity of Motown but the volume of Hendrix or the Who. They literally turned this motherfucker out. That would be the impression that Sly left on me for the rest of my life."

After this epiphany, George became heavily influenced by Sly, especially the rock-charged attack and multi-faceted genre-grabbing which manifested along with his love of Hendrix on the early Funkadelic albums. Predictably, his competitive side came out and he sought to top the Family Stone as most exciting live funk onslaught around and had to outdo Sly's superfly space cowboy image. "We dug Sly before anyone else did," expounded George. "We had his album before he released a single, so nobody knew about Sly. We were already into the thing we're doing now, but we were still straddling the road for work's sake. We'd do our thing whenever we could."

Of course, George outgrew any notions of rivalry once he had established his own unique universe in which to cavort, his own success overtaking the increasingly troubled Sly the following decade. In 1969, George signed to Sly's short-lived Stone Flower label, but the venture folded after releasing just one single. It would be years before they saw each other again, and by then Sly would be opening for George.

While flower power swept the nation and hippie chicks were filmed putting flowers into soldiers' gun barrels, the ghettos reacted to the paucity of peace and love in their neighbourhoods by embarking on a summer of riots in 1967. Unrest had started in April in Nashville and Tampa, spreading to Cincinnati by June when a protester was shot dead by police. Newark's large African-American population had long been feeling disenfranchised as unemployment rose while manufacturing industries contracted, and the city's predominantly white police force stoked tensions by victimising blacks. The massive Newark riot started on the night of July 12 when a taxi driver called John Weerd Smith was arrested for overtaking a police car. Rumours spread he had been killed in police custody, which acted as the spark for six days of arson, looting and rioting which, after police retaliated and the National Guard were called in, left 26 dead and 725 injured by the time it subsided on July 17 (coincidentally the day that John Coltrane died of cancer).

The shockwaves from Newark spread to Plainfield, 18 miles away, starting on July 14 after a fight broke out at a local diner and around 40 young black men rampaged back to their West End housing project, hurling rocks at shop windows and police cars along the way. Trouble started again the following night, local residents claiming that it was stoked by militant outsiders preaching hate and violence among their vulnerable community. Rioting and looting again flared the next afternoon, exacerbated when a nearby arms factory was broken into and 46 carbine rifles liberated and passed around the streets of Plainfield. A state of emergency was declared. The New Jersey National Guard turned up in armoured cars to quell the situation, after which the police appealed for a truce and for the stolen carbines to be handed in. When that proved unsuccessful, police and National Guard cordoned off the area and conducted house searches looking for the weapons, recovering few. When the disturbances subsided on July 21 with tanks patrolling the streets, the death toll was just one police officer caught in a mob. The riot also left around 50 injured and caused thousands of dollars' worth of damage from arson or looting. Like everywhere else, the rioters looted their own local businesses such as the corner shops, many standing burned out for decades afterwards. The Black Soap Palace was the only building left unscathed. The Parliaments couldn't resist venturing into the action on the streets. "Like everybody else, you ran around and got whatever was lying in the street," said George. "The only thing I tried to take was big boxes of tissues and sanitary napkins. My stealing days or my riot wasn't that profitable."

The city would never be the same again as white flight took hold and poverty further kicked in, the riots and one final indignity precipitating George and crew's final move to Detroit, itself about to erupt into a riot of its own. During the Plainfield action, the Parliaments were returning from playing a show at Newark's Bradford Theatre with the Four Tops, unaware of the curfew being imposed. Police ripped apart their uniforms looking for guns and drugs, laughing all the way. When the Parliaments said they were singers, the police made them sing but still stomped over their uniforms, claiming they were looking for weapons.

"['Testify'] was a hit and the chance to get out of Newark," George explained to Paolo Hewitt in *Melody Maker*. "Newark was rioting all the time. We already had a riot scene so it was nothing big to Newark because people were getting frustrated in different parts of the town all the time. So when it happened, for us it was 'let's get out of town' because we got stopped by the police and National Guard and they took our brand new suits, stopping us to see if there were any drugs in the pockets. They knew we were in a group — 'Hey, we got the

Temptations here. Ha ha ha'. So we said 'fuck this' and hit the road. By the time we hit Detroit we were playing with Martha & the Vandellas, David Ruffin, a whole bunch of us, and [the riots] started there ... Us having got out of town and having a hit record, we were just saying, 'Let's see what we can do to keep surviving until this thing blows over'. The group stuck together real tight then."

But the Parliaments had left one riot only to land right in the middle of another one.

Chapter Four

Motor City Madness

"The whole point of Funkadelic was not to tell people what to think, just tell them they could think."

George Clinton

There was indeed another riot going on when George and crew arrived in Detroit in 1967 to accelerate the process which would lead to the birth of P-Funk; one of the largest in US history in terms of destruction and body count.

Detroit at that time was America's fourth largest city, world famous for Motown and the automobile industry, which had grown from Henry Ford founding his company there in 1903, spurring massive growth during the first half of the 20th century. The Motor City was regarded as taking a progressive lead in race relations with a large black middle class which had worked its way up over the decades in different professions. Detroit boasted black congressmen, judges and city representatives in the Michigan legislature. Lower down the totem pole, unemployment was rising and black workers were often treated badly if they managed to land a job at the auto plants so there was widespread disaffection with social conditions, underfunded schools, the non-realisation of promises and – particularly – the predominantly white, often racist police force.

After the riot a *Detroit Free Press* survey showed that the main problem locals felt before the riot was rampant brutality from corrupt police officers.

It all finally went off in the early hours of July 23, when police raided an unlicensed after-hours drinking club (of the speakeasy type then known as a 'blind pig') in the office of the United Community League for Civic Action, on the corner of Twelfth and Clairmount streets on the city's Near West Side. Such clubs were an important part of Detroit's black social life as discrimination excluded African-Americans from many of the city's bars and clubs.

After the latest in a long series of heavy-handed raids on black clubs, the police were met with some mild opposition, to which they duly over-reacted. In turn, this caused the situation to escalate into a mass looting spree, which then erupted into an orgy of fire fights and arson, eclipsing Detroit's 1943 race riot (caused by discontent about distribution of labour in the auto industry). After an estimated 10,000 rioters had smashed, ransacked and fought for four days, the carnage ended when Governor George W. Romney sent in the Michigan National Guard, and President Johnson deployed the US Army. The aftermath saw 43 dead (33 black, 10 white), 1,189 injured, over 7,000 arrests and 2,000 buildings destroyed. Again, many black businesses were burned out, the affected areas staying ruined for decades, while white flight to the suburbs intensified, the feverish mass evacuation eventually also sweeping Motown and the auto industry out of the city.

The riots divided communities and widened the racial divide, raising both black militancy and the fears of whites. The *London Free Press* later described Detroit as "a sick city where fear, rumour, race prejudice and gun buying have stretched black and white nerves to the verge of snapping". While the riot succeeded in creating awareness of the situation that caused it, with the black community receiving more government attention afterwards, it blitzed any hope the city had of thriving economically.

While the riots inspired several songs, including John Lee Hooker's 'The Motor City Is Burning' (later covered by the MC5), which proclaimed, 'My home town is burning down, worse than Vietnam',

Berry Gordy was looking for a house in Hollywood – the first step of Motown's eventual move away from Detroit. It's ironic that George moved onto the home turf of the former employer whose hit factory he'd failed to penetrate, just as Gordy was planning to relocate. George now set out on the untamed new direction which his Motown experience had helped motivate, Detroit's incendiary rock'n'roll becoming another key element in the evolution of P-Funk, the city providing the epicentre as its empire expanded.

Motown's flight typified the city's decline after the 1967 riot, precipitated by the gradual withdrawal of the automobile industry. Detroit today is almost unbelievable, the population diminished by almost half since then, leaving whole neighbourhoods like ghost towns, abandoned houses standing like rotten teeth in vacant lots. Colossal, previously bustling commercial and public buildings such as the railway station have been shut down and left to fall into ruins, along with the huge old factories. Detroit is actually becoming unique as farms spring up on vacant ground in the city centre and underground artists stream in attracted by the cheap rents (and some by the ruins to turn into mammoth installations).

In some ways, it's like a return to the mid-sixties when Detroit was a haven for outlaws, outsiders and counterculture activists. George saw how every radical group in America had found they could operate below the radar there, unlike higher-profile big cities such as New York or LA. "Motherfuckers could get crazy without nobody paying them too much mind." The Motor City also boasted a large hippie community into which draft dodgers could easily blend.

With Canada just over the river, subversives and dissidents had gathered in and around Detroit for centuries. The city had been the last major pit stop for the underground railway which transported runaway slaves from Dixie through a network of sympathisers and co-conspirators until the end of the Civil War in 1865. Many ex-slaves found work in the textile factories before the following century's vast automobile plants developed. Assembly-line drudgery ruled the lives of many, to the exclusion of artistic endeavours. By the sixties, the city had become a haven for draft dodgers who could sneakily commute between Detroit and Toronto. With the social and cultural revolutions rocking Detroit more than other US cities, it provided a perfect fertile environment for the crazy new world of Funkadelic to develop among like minds, lunatics and hard-line rock'n'rollers.

When George arrived, Detroit's high-octane rock'n'roll bands were laying waste with their punk-presaging portents of things to come, while the city had been a vibrant breeding ground for trailblazing jazz, blues and proto rock'n'roll for decades. Innovation seems to be in the water supply as, since the eighties, the Motor City has continued to lead in the field of techno, sculpted in bunkers by electronic dance guerrillas such as Underground Resistance, continuing the electronic revolution started by Juan Atkins and Derrick May in the mid-eighties. All revere George as the pioneer who once lived in the same 'hood.

Before that, Hastings Street nurtured the blues in its teaming bars and clubs during the forties and fifties, John Lee Hooker settling in the city after migrating from the south. The Black Bottom section stood alongside New Orleans, Chicago and St Louis in the fifties Jazz Age, its illustrious sons including Elvin Jones, Kenny Burrell, Ron Carter, Thad Jones, Paul Chambers, Yusef Lateef, Milt Jackson, Donald Byrd, Sonny Stitt and Alice Coltrane. Gospel-wise, Oliver Green's the Detroiters were first to introduce instrumental backing to the traditional unaccompanied vocals. The sixties saw the Reverend C. L. Franklin find success with his recorded sermons on Chess Records' gospel offshoot, particularly the album of spirituals recorded at his New Bethel Baptist Church which marked the debut of his daughter Aretha.

The fifties also saw the rise of Detroit natives Little Willie John, Hank Ballard and the Midnighters, kiss-curled teddy bear Bill Haley (who scored an early rock'n'roll success with 'Rock Around The Clock'), and Jack Scott, who pioneered rockabilly's conjoining of that music's primal energy with country music. 1959 saw Wilson Pickett and Eddie Floyd emerge in the Falcons, their 'You're So Fine' sometimes considered the first soul record. It was released on Fortune Records, the city's biggest blues, soul and gospel operation – a family-run concern, overseen by Jack and Devora Brown, which paved the way for Gordy the following decade. R&B giants who came up in the fifties on Fortune included Nolan Strong, the Diablos frontman who was Smokey Robinson's major influence and inspired the first Parliaments recording, and sleazy proto-rapper Andre Williams.

While Strong was an obvious influence on George and the early Parliaments, the lascivious Williams showed it was possible to make a living out of talking about life as it really was in the inner cities, being one of the first to carry ghetto ribaldry into the mainstream. Born in Alabama in 1936 and hitting Detroit as a 16-year-old orphan, the profane Williams ploughed similar street-soiled turf to that which George would tread as he defined the juke-joint tradition of dealing with risqué subject matter and the joys of eating 'Pig Snoots' over rough, jumping rhythms. He couldn't hope to compete with his friend Nolan in the vocal department, so he delivered his vivid ghetto narratives as proto-rap spoken word, laying a dishevelled blueprint for filth and uproar on outings such as 'Bacon Fat' and 'Jail Bait'. Williams went on to write hits including 'Shake A Tail Feather' and 'Twine Time', manage Edwin Starr and produce the Contours. Between 1965 and 1966, he popped up on Wingate with 'Loose Juice' and 'Do It' and Ric Tic with 'You Got It And I Want It', placing him in George's Motor City orbit around this time before signing to Chess for a string of hits. Inevitably, their paths would collide, Williams writing for P-Funk the following decade, before falling into years of drug abuse and homelessness.

When George and the Plainfield squad touched down in Detroit, the city was in the throes of another musical revolution, spearheaded by the high-energy rock'n'roll of the MC5 and Stooges, who had a major impact on both his music and his stage shows. Earlier in the decade as the Beatles and Stones made their mark, the city had experienced a healthy garage rock scene with bands such as Unrelated Segments, Terry Knight & the Pack, Underdogs, Fugitives, Lords (featuring redneck axe warrior Ted Nugent), Suzi Quatro's Pleasure Seekers and energised white soul boosters the Rationals. In 1965, Mitch Ryder & the Detroit Wheels gave the UK charts a dose of Motor City mayhem with 'Jenny Takes A Ride' and 'Devil With A Blue Dress On'.

By 1968, at a time when east and west coasts were still exploring rock ragas and indulging in proto-prog whimsy, Detroit rock'n'roll kept its pedal to the metal, reflecting the city's large radical population and blue collar no-bullshit attitude. 1969 saw the establishment of *Creem*, Detroit's own underground rock magazine, which mirrored the city's myriad musical developments, partly through features and reviews sent in by readers. Lester Bangs, one of the most influential music writers of all time, started here, before going on to have his wild gonzo rantings appear in *Phonograph Record*, where he recounted the coalescing of the Motor City scene: "There was a new generation of young whites around Detroit and Ann Arbor who had finally decided that, much as they dig reproducing, they did not want to *produce* one more hubcap! No! And all their lives they had been hearing metallic, mechanical rhythms in the din from the factories that destroys the hearing of everyone in this city just as the pollution of the water in the Detroit River forces them all, much as they might resist, into drinking alcoholic beverages every day and night.

"So the young white kids picked up this sheet-metal din, hearing how close it was to the rattly clankings of rock'n'roll, and turned it into a new brand of rock'n'roll which was more metallic, heavy, crazed and mechanical than anything heard on the face of the earth in 6,000 years of Western history."

Leading the charge with their blistering turbo-charged rock'n'roll, the MC5 pre-empted the energy and urge for change which would fire UK punk a few years later. The group formed in 1964, their line-up solidifying at singer Rob Tyner, bassist Michael Davis, drummer Dennis 'Machinegun' Thompson and guitarists Wayne Kramer and Fred 'Sonic' Smith. They began playing Stones, Who and Yardbirds covers before hooking up with jazz critic John Sinclair, who became their manager and spiritual guru. The MC5 was a reaction to what Kramer described to *MOJO* as being "very frustrated with the slow pace of change, and what we viewed as an intolerable situation, between racism, police oppression, the war in Vietnam, outmoded drug laws. We took the lead from the Black Panther Party in that they were the vanguard and voice for their community. We felt we could be the vanguard and voice for our community."

The MC5's *Kick Out The Jams* debut album, recorded live at Detroit's Grande Ballroom in October 1968, arrived with the impact of a Molotov cocktail through a plate-glass window, unleashing a crazed gaggle of rock'n'roll assassins preaching revolution and channelling free-jazz fury through hot-wired guitars, tracks such as 'Rocket Reducer Number Nine' and 'Starship' setting new templates for stampeding high-energy rock'n'roll and just how incendiary that music could get. One of the free-form jams which unfortunately didn't make the record was called 'I'm Mad Like Eldridge Cleaver'.

In his book *Miami And The Siege Of Chicago*, Norman Mailer likened the Five to "an interplanetary, then galactic, flight of song, halfway between the space music of Sun Ra and 'The Flight Of the Bumblebee' … the roar of the beast in all nihilism, electric bass and drum driving behind out of their own nonstop to the end of mind."

One afternoon in July 1977, I spent a few hours with Rob Tyner, who described the environment into which George had planted himself in 1967: "Now we would be looked on as middle-of-the-road but in those days we were the maniac fringe. We were faced with the situation where we were, stylistically speaking... I hate to say this it sounds so dumb... ahead of our time. We tried to change people's musical and social beliefs too quickly and too radically. Then there's this vast social backlash that happens. The cops don't wanna know about it because they have to change their attitudes about everything. They like everything pretty much as they've got it, pretty much because they've got control over it, and the government don't want you to do it because it changes everything. You're talking about a new social order, and I know new order sounds a little ominous. There's always been this resistance to change, especially when it comes to rock'n'roll for some reason.

"I wanted us to be totally original. I thought what we were doing was totally unprecedented, at least in rock'n'roll. There was plenty of jazz music, like Sun Ra, where people improvised and played for free. When we started doing it with electric instruments, the energy levels that we achieved were so profound that audiences either absolutely hated it or went crazy. I thought that it would be a long-term effect."

Just as George wanted to smear his new take on funk with rock'n'roll, Wayne Kramer craved to make the music of the spheres, as propagated by the free-jazz players who he says, "opened the door for me and showed me how to start breaking the boundaries in the world of rock. If I took my best Chuck Berry solo, you know the highest velocity I could play it, and moved it to the next level, I would be going into the kinds of things that Albert [Ayler] was trying to do with his saxophone or that Pharoah Sanders was trying to do – to move into a more pure, sonic dimension… start to incorporate polyrhythms and subdivisions and move out of the western concepts of rhythm and outside the concepts of western harmony. Those were the things we were trying to do in the MC5."

These ideals also fed into the Stooges, the Five's little brother band and Detroit's other most notorious live phenomenon. Fronted by the charismatic, confrontational Iggy Pop, guitarist Ron Asheton, his drummer brother Scott and bassist Dave Alexander, they churned out a racket of stunning brutality, with nihilist anthems such as 'No Fun' alongside their demonic free-form pile-ups.

Detroit's free-jazz-influenced high energy rock'n'roll tipped the nascent Funkadelic further into their unholy hybrid of psychedelic rock'n'roll and nasty, humping funk. Sharing the same agent as the Five, Stooges and Bob Seger, George and the band were cast into a world crawling with drug-toting crazies, voracious women, cultural visionaries and intense musicians bent on channelling the mood of the times into a revolution. It fitted his current world view like a rubber glove while, for the first time, placing George alongside the most cutting edge musicians in the country, including the Detroit rockers and New York's free-jazz figureheads. As future P-Funk producer Bill Laswell, who grew up in the Detroit area and recalls seeing Funkadelic sharing bills with the MC5, says in *An Oral History,* "It was very common to see Funkadelic on a bill with a rock band like the MC5. It was an interesting time, because a fan of the MC5 had already been educated… about the roots, the source of energy music. These are people that are already being exposed to John Coltrane, Albert Ayler and Cecil Taylor. To them, Funkadelic was just an extension of that energy that they were experiencing at the time."

And we mustn't forget Sun Ra. If he hadn't stumbled across himself in New York, George would have had a tough job not noticing the man from Saturn when he was invited to the Motor City by John Sinclair to share bills with the MC5. This was confirmed by noted Detroit correspondent Ben Edmonds in *Sun Ra: Interviews & Essays*, edited by Sinclair in 2010. He writes, "Detroit funk-rock fusioneer George Clinton, himself an alien from a weird planet called New Jersey, has never attempted to deny the mark of the Arkestra on his Parliament-Funkadelic 'Mothership' extravaganzas of the seventies."

These parallels obviously went beyond any mutual flying saucer fixation. Both led and conducted large ensembles built around faithful core musicians which would often act as stepping stones to other projects, while their albums would often be culled from a large pool of already recorded material as the tapes rarely stopped rolling when the band was fired up.

The connection between George Clinton and Sun Ra is also based on their similar personal mythologies; the key elements of that being outer space and craziness, while both also became the subject of some mythologising. They mutually used space imagery to refer to their African heritage and as a metaphor for overcoming the social marginalisation experienced by African-Americans during the last century, Ra referencing slavery and the racism he'd seen at close quarters down south. Ra and Clinton took black culture where it had never been before, while remaining aware of their roots and the street, and were branded 'far out' or 'crazy' as they assumed alter egos and personas anywhere between visionary starship captain to circus ringmaster, wielding tangible shamanic holds over their congregations. The pair also developed their own slogans, key phrases and song titles which doubled as rallying calls – the conceptual chasm between Ra's 'Space is the place' and Clinton's 'The Mothership connection is here' is not that vast. George and Ra set their music apart from the mainstream, subverting, then massively influencing, what came later.

Just as Blaxploitation movies cast black actors and actresses in leading hero roles for the first time, so their panoramic sci-fi visions and story lines placed George and Ra beyond earthly rules and prejudices, the boundaries between science fiction and social reality an optical illusion. In George's case, this became a licence for 'anything goes'.

I've lost count of the number of times writers and fans have misrepresented Sun Ra as some kind of delusional eccentric, or dismissed George as a drug-crazed space case. Black music has often referenced insanity as a term or excuse for getting out there. Ra embraced this practice on titles such as 1963's *Cosmic Tones For Mental Therapy* and George celebrated it by exhorting his throng to "free your mind and your ass will follow" at every opportunity. Both saw the infinite possibilities of space as a way to heighten their idiosyncratic paths; sanity the ground from where to take off on their flights into the unknown, entering that uncharted zone where traditions and inhibitions go out the window as unfettered inspiration beams in. Live tapes of Ra's Arkestra and Funkadelic in full flight during the early seventies show two groups of musicians achieving often spectacular liftoff, though both could be controlled by their respective leaders by hand signals and had the virtuosity to return to ground level at a gesture.

While George enjoyed astronomical success, proper recognition took years to materialise for Sun Ra. Born early in the 20th century in racism-clenched Birmingham, Alabama, Sun Ra was first to create his own universe and appoint himself a messenger from the stars, claiming to hail from Saturn as he led his exotically clad ensembles through their space chants while declaring 'Space is the place' with the same fervour James Brown would later give 'Say It Loud I'm Black And I'm Proud'. He had come from playing piano and arranging for big bands before settling in Chicago in the early fifties, steadily assembling the Arkestra and introducing his space-age consciousness and attire by the middle of the decade.

Ra often talked of the out-of-body dream experience which laid out his life's mission. In *Space Is The Place* he says, "My whole body changed into something else. I could see through myself. And I went up... I wasn't in human form... I landed on a planet that I identified as Saturn... they teleported me and I was down on stage with them. They wanted to talk with me... They told me to stop [attending college] because there was going to be great trouble in schools... the world was going into complete chaos... I would speak [through music], and the world would listen."

After recording futuristic albums such as *Sun Ra Visits Planet Earth*, he relocated to New York City with his faithful Arkestra members in 1961, influencing the east coast free-jazz movement as his quest to play the music of other worlds intensified. Ra released much of his music on his pioneering independent Saturn label, where he could run wild presenting the latest instalment in his ongoing cosmic philosophy in limited runs to be sold at shows with sleeves hand-decorated by band members – something a major label never would have allowed.

Although self-releasing albums such as *Secrets Of The Sun*, Ra's first widely available records coincided with the escalating mid-sixties cultural revolution. Two volumes of *The Heliocentric Worlds Of Sun Ra* appeared on the mysterious ESP-Disk label, whose roster included the Fugs, Albert Ayler, Pharoah Sanders, Timothy Leary and the Godz. The album deconstructed traditional jazz forms to a prehistoric level, from desolate soundscapes to squalling blasts.

While the band played New York's downtown clubs through the rest of the decade (including the Electric Circus), Ra also took his Arkestra to Detroit in June 1967 at the invitation of John Sinclair, sharing bills with the MC5, returning in May, 1969. The MC5 were major fans, using Ra's 'There' poem for 'Starship' on *Kick Out The Jams*. As writer Ben Edmonds observed, "MC5 and Sun Ra were visionary brothers-in-musical-arms, fearless explorers charting unknown territory the rest of us might one day occupy."

In the same way that George rejected the uniformity of starched suits, Sun Ra had binned stage uniforms during the fifties, first adapting a discarded theatrical wardrobe from a production of Robin Hood, before overseeing his musicians making their own combinations of shiny, star-daubed robes and Egyptian-influenced headgear. "Costumes are music," he declared. "Colours throw out musical sounds." George's mob were continuing along the same lines, dry-cleaning bills now a thing of the past as he simply took the sheet off the hotel bed, cut a hole for his head and put it on, usually with a pair of boots and nothing underneath. Like Ra, he would refine this image over the years at the same time as rewriting his status in African-American history.

George, with typical adaptability, really got into the wild Detroit scene, as the Parliaments played alongside Ted Nugent, Iggy Pop, MC5 and Bob Seger on the same bills at rock'n'roll clubs. One story that went out had George and Iggy getting betrothed, but *Creem* didn't pick up on it, as hoped, because the magazine knew it was a spoof.

Being embraced and promoted by Detroit's high-energy bands further liberated George while alerting him to the possibility of a whole new audience, his new positivity heightened by hanging out, dropping acid and listening to the incendiary music being produced. Soon, George's attire for a night out clubbing could consist of pink hot pants, fishnet stockings, a fur coat and a load of proto-bling jewellery, topped off with pink shades. Only a year earlier he would have been sporting a neat suit.

For some time, George had felt that the old-school black music industry from which he'd come had been spiritually left behind by the new post-Panther audience and that the old order was a dead end for the untamed beast which now pulled his creative chariot. Funkadelic had no corporate record company grooming them for the mainstream, so could go wherever their newly unleashed inventive demons took them. In keeping with Detroit's musical tradition, they played politcally charged blues for the working class, for radical blacks looking for the sound of the street and white crowds who loved the unfettered wildness and drug-crazed racket. "We had that cult following in the beginning," recounts George. "We toured at a time when being a hippie was the hip way of life. We could eat out of people's plates in restaurants and it was cool. We could survive then."

Inevitably, outside of Detroit they could find themselves caught between their two target markets – young blacks open to funk conversion and white rock fans who worshipped Hendrix. As George explained, "We was too white for the blacks, and we was too black for the whites. Whites could go for one black guy up there, but not 10. We was young enough to be as horny as hell, so all that shit that everybody was afraid of was there."

Since freeing his ass from show routines, George didn't change or tone down his onstage antics for anyone. Even his fellow band members could get hacked off by his increasingly wild onstage behaviour, Billy recalling a show at New York's Cheetah Club attended by representatives from the William Morris and Premier booking agents, the largest at the time, who were wining and dining them. George was told, in no uncertain terms, not to strip off his sheet. "Of course, with the band riding high on acid, George stripped off then ran across the bigwigs' table, which stymied any future business relationship." Billy also claims that George did the same one Christmas at Detroit's prestigious Twenty Grand club, where Berry Gordy and family, including his mum and dad, were sitting in the front row.

George denies telling Berry to kiss the ass he was alleged to have waved in Gordy's face, or chain-whipping him round the chops with his P-torpedo, but matter-of-factly owns up to the stripping. In *An Oral History* he recounts, "I was naked, probably. And I probably poured some wine over my head, then it dripped all down my dick, and as I run across *all* the tables in there – I don't know if Berry was there, but I know the family was there – I would run up and down the table, up the bar, and wine would drip down so everybody say it looked like I peed in everybody's drink. But I was too out of it to even know if I did or not."

Future manager Ron Scribner told Rob Bowman, "George was thinking loud is good, outrageous is good, controversial is good, whatever would shock. I had never been exposed to anything as outrageous. There was no black act like them. Sly was comparatively homogenised...these guys were the punk of funk."

In March 1968 the Impressions released Curtis Mayfield's gently affirming black pride anthem 'We're A Winner' while, from the UK, the Rolling Stones' 'Jumpin' Jack Flash' signalled their return with a new strain of incendiary rebel rock. It became another volatile year of riots, protests and political unrest with Martin Luther King and Bobby Kennedy assassinated. That October, at the Olympic Games in Mexico City, Tommie Smith and John Carlos gave the clenched-fist salute after being presented with their medals for winning gold and silver medals in the 200 metres.

Although colour boundaries were disintegrating in neighbourhoods, relationships and music (although not always smoothly), funk's politically charged sex machine reflected lives and locales which would never be fully integrated. The ghettos still needed to find hope in figures they could identify with. James Brown had already risen to the status of black celebrity leader after the death of Malcolm X. Even if he would soon become the royalty-approved Beatles to George's forecourt-spraying Stones, in 1968 Brown was a strict, consummate entertainer with enough clout and charisma to quieten riots and instil devotion befitting a ghetto Messiah (with a little prodding from the Panthers).

Dr King was assassinated by hapless ex-con James Earl Ray at the Lorraine Motel in Memphis on April 4, prompting endless conspiracy theories later on but, at the time, sending the US into a panic that the previous year's riots were going to look like campfire singalongs by comparison.

James Brown was booked to play Boston's Garden the night following Dr King's assassination, persuading the mayor to let him go ahead and televise it to keep the heat off the streets. He went on to play the show of his life and Boston remained peaceful that night. Elsewhere it was a different story as riots broke out in more than a hundred cities. Then Brown lost some credibility with a misfire of a single called 'America Is My Home' and an ill-judged tour of Vietnam army bases that was roundly condemned by anti-war protesters, not least because it was becoming apparent that black soldiers were being sent on the most dangerous combat missions, resulting in a disproportionate number of fatalities. According to sideman singer Hank Ballard, Brown was advised by gun-toting Panthers to show he was down with more militant elements. So he released a milestone called 'Say It Loud, I'm Black And I'm Proud', a turning point for black music which became everything from political slogan to declaration of defiance and empowerment as the word 'Black' was reclaimed from being a derogatory term used by whites. As funky as a rhino's foreskin, the song topped the R&B listings and cracked the *Billboard* Top 10. It also became unofficial anthem of the Black Power movement, followed by similar empowerment outings such as his 1969 cut, 'I Don't Want Nobody To Give Me Nothing (Open Up The Door, I'll Get It Myself).

Although it proved inestimably influential, Brown was downplaying his new anthem within a year. In his autobiography, *James Brown: The Godfather Of Soul,* he says,"The song is obsolete now," he insisted. "But it was necessary to teach pride then... People called 'Black And Proud' militant and angry – maybe because of the line about dying on your feet rather than living on your knees. But really, if you listen to it, it sounds like a children's song. That's why I had children in it, so children who heard it could grow feeling pride... The song cost me a lot of my crossover audience. The racial make-up at my concerts was mainly black after that. I don't regret it, though, even if it was misunderstood."

Two months after Dr King was killed, presidential favourite, Senator Robert Kennedy, who supported civil rights and was turning against the Vietnam War, was also gunned down following his victory in the California primary election.

Detroit, which burned for two weeks after Dr King's death, was particularly volatile during this period of severe discontent, not least because of the escalating zeal of an angry police force. After an arson attempt on John Sinclair's home, the MC5 operation moved out to the college town of Ann Arbor, but the band still had regular brushes with the law as the police repeatedly tried to haul members in at their own gigs. Sinclair responded by answering Black Panthers honcho Huey Newton's declaration that white people who want to help the struggle should form their own party by setting up the White Panthers towards the end of the year. Sinclair's manifesto was based on the creation of "a cultural revolution through a total assault on the culture by any means necessary, including rock'n'roll, dope and fucking in the streets".

The police stepped up their persecution of the MC5, putting them under surveillance, under pressure and under arrest if one of them even broke wind in the wrong direction, or so it seemed. The group's reputation as drug-crazed harbingers of free love and Black Power-sympathising revolution boiled down every element of the establishment's paranoid hatred of the counterculture into one loathsome entity, which had to be exterminated, also by any means necessary.

Along with the rock and jazz influences they were being exposed to in Detroit, George and the band were still feeling the British influence as they embraced post-psych blues outfits such as Ten Years After and the first incarnation of Jethro Tull. George was also struck by his beloved Cream planting Pete Brown's mythology-influenced lyrics over their thunderous blues rock.

Next arrived the musician who would enable George to spectacularly establish his method of entering another musical world, such as classical, by soaking it up then belching it out in his own distorted image. In late 1968, the Funkadelics were joined in Detroit by Plainfield keyboard prodigy Bernie Worrell, another former barbershop kid who would soon be playing a major part in shaping the P-Funk sound with his dazzling keyboard and arranging skills derived from European classical music.

Born in Long Branch, New Jersey on April 19, 1944, Bernie moved to Plainfield when he was eight, having already learned piano by the age of three and given his first concert the following year. His parents wanted him to be a classical pianist but his relentless practicing was punctuated by sneaky listens to R&B radio stations. No piano teacher would touch him because of his young age, until Fay Barnaby Kent – who taught him from eight to college (she went to see Funkadelic in her eighties, telling George she could hear every lesson she'd given Bernie in his playing).

When Bernie went on to study at the New England Conservatory of Music, he played clubs at night, becoming singer Maxine Brown's bandleader for a few years. Much to his mother's displeasure, he had also been sneaking into the barbershop. He reunited with George after finishing his conservatory training, becoming the magic ingredient in the band after first writing lead sheets, then holding out until the money met his requirements. Bernie's musical heroes included Beethoven, Chopin, Mozart and Schubert, along with Hendrix and Duke Ellington, his European classical training providing the symphonic touches, complex arrangements and classical lyricism that worked so well juxtaposed against the dirty P-Funk grooves. George actually tried to deter the band's efforts to give Bernie a funk makeover and swing his style towards their nasty groove, as he was now nurturing ambitions to break into the progressive market and reasoning that "what he can bring from the conservatory can help us compete with the Jethro Tulls and King Crimsons".

"We made a groove that was religious," crowed George in *An Oral History*. "We could vamp forever. The only thing that made that intellectually appealing – 'cause the jazz musicians would say, 'Oh yeah, they're funky'. And I'm like, 'You're not going to look down your nose – you ain't gonna do this like you did blues'. 'Cause Bernie Worrell could take any groove and make it Beethoven, Bach or any jazz thing you want it to be, right within the groove. He taught us all to make it what some people might want to call 'legitimate'. Bernie's classical, he includes jazz and everything else. Bernie can make music out of anything that makes a noise. So the contradiction was done on purpose – the classical things against the real simple-minded, silly, basic."

For the next two years, George had his own Magic Band which, as with Captain Beefheart's recruits, incorporated a disparate array of personalities and talents whose joint effect when combusting together could be apocalyptic, spiritual or just one colossal funk bomb. The difference between George and Beefheart was that Funkadelic musicians weren't dictated their every move on pain of punishment and could take the music any way they felt it within or without the perimeters of the song.

Unhappy with Revilot's distribution and lack of payment, George fell out with LeBaron Taylor and refused to record any more Parliaments tracks for the label, despite being under contract. The group now worked all its business through a single holding company called The Parliafunkadelicment Thang, jointly owned by himself (as sole manager) and fellow Parliaments Thomas, Simon, Haskins and Davis. In military terms, George was now the General, the Parliaments were Captains and the Funkadelics would be his soldiers who could work their way up through the ranks.

This left Revilot to release one final Parliaments single, 'A New Day Begins'/'I'll Stay' that year, then licensing it to Atlantic subsidiary Atco in May, 1969, making the R&B Top 50. After Revilot folded, the Parliaments name and catalogue was cast into legal limbo while they waited for their contract to run out. For now, the Parliaments were in frozen recess.

The days of competing with Motown and the name of his original doo-wop group coming to an end propelled George to use the often brilliant resourcefulness that became one of his trademarks. He simply got around the problem by suggesting that the backing band of Nelson, Hazel, Ross, Atkins and Fulwood make the records, with the singers "guesting". The group was initially called the Funkedelics, then Funkadelic. The name arose out of stoned banter while the group was driving home from a gig. Laughing at old doo-wop band names such as the Del Vikings, the crew gigglingly pondered such a moniker for the psychedelic era. Funk spiked with acid. According to Billy in Rob Bowman's liner notes to *Music For Your Mother*, Eddie said "the Del Funkloroids or some shit like that. We all laughed and I said 'no, like Funkadelic.' It came out of my mouth, that's the truth. As soon as that name came out, man, there was a little silence and then George started talking about 'well yeah, y'all ought to call yourself Funkadelic and we'll have Parliafunkadelicment Thang.' He came with that exactly right after I said it. Not even 10 minutes later he started talking about the whole concept – a label called Funkadelic, the group Funkadelic and the whole conglomeration/production situation, Parliafunkadelicment Thang. It all came out in that car the same day."

Their first vinyl appearance under the name, then still in transition, was a one-off that year on the (very) short-lived Funkedelic [sic] label set up by George and Ed Wingate (who reportedly sold Golden World to Berry Gordy for a million dollars). Produced by Mike Terry, the A-side is the supercharged 'Whatever Makes My Baby Feel Good', credited to singer Rose Williams, George Clinton and the Funkedelics, funky southern-fried soul buzzing with a hallucinogenic undercurrent. The flip side's instrumental shows a band champing at the bit; funky and dynamic with a blistering Eddie Hazel guitar groove detonating near the end.*

Detroit record distributor Armen Boladian knew the Parliaments through handling their Revilot releases and dealing with George on his frequent visits. He started Westbound Records to release the new project. "Psychedelic music was kind of starting at the time," explained Boladian. "George loved that music, but thought there should be good old funk connected to it. That's where Funkadelic came in."

"Armen Boladian is the cause of Funkadelic," states Fuzzy. "He's the one that gave Funkadelic a shot at it."

"And I didn't worry," added George "'cause I looked at B.B. King in '69 or somewhere around in there, he was getting his first award. I had listened to him all my life with my mother, and he was just now getting recognised as great. So I said, 'At 28, man, we may as well relax and just make a track record.'"

Given this lifeline, the switch from Parliaments to Funkadelic suited the transition already taking place within the group. "Funkadelic came about because of the individuals involved," said Billy. "Here you had five different individuals playing five different grooves, and [they] made it work. George never told us what to play. We played what we wanted to play and what we felt to play. You couldn't beat that configuration."

Funkadelic would release an immaculate string of albums on Westbound between 1970–76, but the first time the 'A Parliafunkadelicment Thang' credit appeared on a record was first Westbound single 'Music For My Mother' – an early template for Funkadelic's gutbucket dirt-throb, alchemical field hollers and fried guitar scratchings glazed in eerie luminescence, topped with new sax player Herbert J. Sparkman's hipster space-ghetto-drawl.

Composed by George, Eddie and Billy, the song invokes Jim Crow paranoia combatted by the strains of raw funk wailing in the distance,

---

* When I was being bodily evicted out of my Newark slum apartment on Saybroke Place in 1989, with scary-looking officers standing there, there was only time to grab a few essential possessions. This was one of them, along with my other Funkadelic 45s, and I've still got 'em!

the band a ghostly chorus of siren spirits as Sparky intones, 'I recall when I left a little town in North Carolina/I tried to escape this music/I said it was for old country folks/I went to New York, got slick, Got my hair made, heheheh, No groove, no groove, no groove, no groove, I had no groove, But here it comes! But now, fly on baby...'

Radio stations refused to play the single, fearing it might spark more rioting. Boladian later admitted the song "was just totally against the grain of what was happening in those days ... but you were having fun, and maybe just looking to see how far you can go with something. But, believe it or not, the record got played and the record sold. It was not a huge record, but it was certainly the kick-off of what was to come."

After the first single Sparky, Eddie and Billy quit in the first of many conflicts with George about finances. They moved to Newark and started gigging as Sparky & the Pimpadelics, who became the house band at pimps and dealers' hangout the Cadillac Club. When various Parliaments descended to repossess a guitar and bass amp, they were greeted by a crickets' chorus of safety catches being unfastened as numerous weapons suddenly appeared.

The Parliaments got their guitar back... and also their guitarist, as Eddie Hazel returned to the fold.

The journey begins. One of the earliest Parliaments photos, George on left. P-FUNK ARCHIVES

The Parliaments testify at Palisades Park Amusement Park, New Jersey, 1967. L-R George Clinton, Grady Thomas, Ray Davis, Fuzzy Haskins.
P-FUNK ARCHIVES

sychedelic dandies on shot used on promo postcard for 1968 Parliaments 45 'A New Day Begins'. P-FUNK ARCHIVES

he classic early Funkadelic promo pic, Eddie Hazel in hat. P-FUNK ARCHIVES

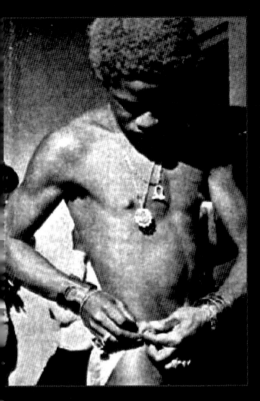

Diaper man Tawl Ross fixes his pin. P-FUNK ARCHIVES

Chief George takes Detroit, 1969. P-FUNK ARCHIVES

...iki in the studio. P-FUNK ARCHIVES

P-Funk support the Free John Sinclair campaign started in 1969 after he was jailed for marijuana possession (with MC5 neighbours The Up). P-FUNK ARCHIVES

Funkedelic Records' first and only 45. KRIS NEEDS ARCHIVES

Trailering the debut LP; 'I'll Bet You' 45. KRIS NEEDS ARCHIVES

First Funkadelic 45 (and 'A Parliafunkadelicment Thang' billing) 1969. KRIS NEEDS ARCHIVES

'I Wanna Testify': 1967 hit in the US and Vietnam. KRIS NEEDS ARCHIVES

Funkadelic as defaced by George. KRIS NEEDS ARCHIVES

Free Your Mind...And Your Ass Will Follow. KRIS NEEDS ARCHIVES

MAGGOT BRAIN

FUNKADELIC

Side One

Maggot Brain 10:10
(E. Hazel, G. Clinton)

Can You Get To That 2:45
(G. Clinton, E. Harris)

Hit It And Quit It 3:44
(G. Clinton, B. Nelson, G. Shifa)

You And Your Folks, Me And My Folks 3:29
(G. Clinton, B. Worrell, J. Jones)

Side Two

Super Stupid 3:53
(E. Hazel, B. Nelson, L. Ross, G. Clinton)

Back In Our Minds 2:35
(C. Haskins)

Wars Of Armageddon 9:28
(B. Worrell, G. Clinton, L. Ross, R. Fulwood)

All Songs Published by Bridgeport Music, Inc. BMI

Produced by George Clinton
A Parliafunkadelicment Thang

Executive Producer: Armen Boladian
Bernie Mendelson: In Charge of The Eegangas
Cover Photography: Joel Brodsky
Inside Cover Photography: Ron Scribner
Album Design: The Graffiteria/Paula Bisacca
Art Direction: David Krieger
Album Supervision: Bob Scurbo
Album Co-ordination: Dorothy Schwartz

For information or Promotion:
Big Band Music Industry Public Relations
15 Brookbanks Dr., PH 4
Don Mills, Ontario, Canada
(416) 449-0984

Fear is at the root of man's destruction of himself. Without Fear there is no blame. Without blame there is no conflict. Without conflict there is no destruction

But there IS Fear: deep within the core of every human being it lurks like a monster; dark and intangible. Its outward effects

fear of intensity, fear of inadequacy, fear of emotion, fear of GOD, fear of knowledge, fear of death, fear of responsibility, fear of sin, fear of virtue, fear of guilt, fear of punishment, fear of damnation, fear of the consequences of our actions, and fear of our own fear? How many of us recognize the presence in ourselves of these?

And if some of us recognize some of them, are we prepared to see the full extent of them? Do we know just how afraid we are? And do we know the effect that our fear has on our lives? Do we know how completely we are governed by our fear?

And do we know that the world is governed by the sum total of every human being's fear, and that no one is not excluded?

Nothing before me but thong: George at 1971 Lincoln Festival. COURTESY OF COLIN MOSS OF SUPPORT BAND SCAPA FLOW, UKROCKFESTIVALS.COM

Parliaments hit New York: Ungano's February 16, 1970. P-FUNK ARCHIVES

CREEM

HAIL ERIS
ALL HAIL DISCORDIA
VOL. 2 NO. 16

Dr. Tim
Welcome Here

tographs by Ric Siegel

Parliafunkadelicment Thang

When the Parliament-Funkadelic trample on stage, everything is suddenly transformed. It's just like hearing rock and roll or John Coltrane for the first time; you really don't know what's happening, but whatever it it is, it won't hurt you. It sounds and feels too good.

They come on dressed as clowns or magicians or maybe this time it's African kings or Zulu warriors. The array of bizarre costumes is seemingly never ending. Their show is a combination of dance, singing and all types of weird sounds coming from the amps. Whatever it is, it's not like *anything* we're used to hearing.

Continued on page 26.

Chapter Five

Mommy, What's A Funkadelic?

"When Woodstock happened, to me rock'n'roll was over. 'Cause everything was for sale then. Before it was, 'Do you want to share a joint? Do you want to share a tab? ... At Woodstock it was 'Acid five dollars a hit', 'Weed ten dollars a lid' ... Now people was making acid to make money. It seemed like they had turned the electric off. No more pretty trips."

George Clinton

The 13-minute clip from a show called *Say Brother* broadcast some time in 1969 on Boston's WGBH has to be one of the most priceless pieces of archive gold preserved for digital posterity, capturing the moment the Parliaments toppled into Funkadelic. Literally.

The sequence starts with the band in silhouette already pumping a low-slung funk groove, lining up across the stage as Tiki, Billy, Eddie, Tawl and Mickey. Fuzzy, Calvin, Grady and Ray make their entrance from the front, led by a visibly energised George, clapping and swaying around each other in a loose approximation of Motown dance steps. Fuzzy starts giving it the full throttle on a song called 'Into My Own Thang' as, gesticulating next to him, George, looking young and crazy in his Mohawk and clad in tight dungarees, intones, "We will not harm you" before his "Soul is a hamhock in your cornflakes" and "Soul is

97

the ring around your bathtub". The catchphrases collide with more chanting, including a snatch of 'What Is Soul', wailed and moaned with gospel fervour.

It seems as if they're making it up as they go along as, suddenly, George frantically gestures that the song is ending, and launches throatily into 'Testify'. This is the most electrifying part of the clip, the band on fire, George ripping the lead vocal out of his now sweating chest and the whole ensemble a gyrating blur of hats, smiles and hippie gear. After that it all goes off, referencing Sly and Stevie Wonder's 'I Was Born To Love You' with the crowd now dancing around the band as they build to a climactic freakout around 'Friday Night, August 14', which would appear on the second Funkadelic album. The spot doesn't so much end as dissolve into mock gear-trashing chaos. The last shot is Eddie facing his amp, extracting Hendrix-style feedback squalls while the others play-fight and roll away.

Now, it's hard to imagine that this was the kind of stunning ritual that the band's crowds were getting blasted with at the time, usually in more explicit and extended forms. The Parliaments were kissing the decade they'd come up in goodbye as Funkadelic, visibly leaving their past behind and flying into the new decade by the seat of their bell-bottoms with tangible joy.

1969 had been a cataclysmic finish to a tumultuous decade; the Charles Manson killings, Woodstock festival and Rolling Stones' Altamont bloodbath dominating its final few months. The Americans dropped some men on the moon on July 20, suddenly making space a much closer place. While the war in Vietnam continued to claim America's young, the counterculture went overground into the front rooms of the country's white masses. In August, the appalling Manson Family murders shocked the world with their psychotic brutality, carrying enough deranged hippie commune resonance (and claiming to draw inspiration for some of the atrocities committed from the Beatles' 'Helter Skelter') for the media to go into knee-jerk overdrive – blaming the underground *en masse*, rather than the two-bit thief with failed musical ambitions responsible.

Just a week after the murders, the three-day Woodstock Music & Art Fair took place on a farm in upstate New York. It was the biggest musical gathering the world had ever seen and one occasion where the sixties dream of peace, love and unity became reality, leaving it as the ultimate symbol of the Cultural Revolution, even a mythical embodiment of the decade itself.

The sight of Country Joe encouraging the huge gathering to take up his 'F-U-C-K' chant, and singing the loudly anti-Vietnam 'I Feel Like I'm Fixin' To Die Rag' were highlights of the *Woodstock* movie that played a part in marking 1969 as the year music started to become corporate, with the festival itself defining a new kind of super-gig with lucrative spin-offs that precipitated the early seventies music business boom. George saw the festival as the death of rock'n'roll's original spirit, explaining in *An Oral History*, "When Woodstock happened, to me rock'n'roll was over. 'Cause everything was for sale then. Before it was, 'Do you want to *share* a joint? Do you want to *share* a tab? ... At Woodstock it was 'Acid five dollars a hit', 'Weed ten dollars a lid' ... Now people was making acid to make money. It seemed like they had turned the electric off. No more pretty trips."

Having said that, Woodstock could also be considered a milestone for the profiles of black artists outside the confines of blues and soul – Greenwich Village protest soul giant Richie Havens, Bay Area Latin-rockers Santana, Sly & the Family Stone and Hendrix providing some of the most memorable performances.

Havens and his two sidemen opened the festival by default when the band booked were delayed in traffic, playing a magnificent set of his spiritual protest songs, many drawn from his recent fifth album, *Richard P. Havens 1983*. Pouring sweat in his floor-length orange robe, he wasn't allowed to leave the stage as there was still no band to follow him. Despite exhausting his repertoire, Richie was repeatedly redirected back onstage by stage manager and MC Chip Monck, eventually forced to come up with 'Freedom' on the spot using elements of the spiritual 'Motherless Child', bringing the crowd to its feet as he swayed and stomped into the history books and provided the festival's first magic moment and a modern freedom anthem. Chip once told me that

'Freedom' was just something that he made up at the time. "Every time he decided to walk off I'd say, 'Excuse me Richie, nobody else is here yet.' He'd go, 'Oh, fuck'."

"It was crazy and overwhelming but it was great," said Richie, who would now be known for life as the man who opened and conquered Woodstock. It was also Havens who in 1966 had suggested to Hendrix he might try his luck in the Greenwich Village clubs and later gave him the words to Dylan's 'All Along The Watchtower'.

Despite going on at 3.30am in pouring rain and experiencing shocks from their crackling equipment, Sly & the Family Stone got one of the most vociferous receptions of the whole festival with their supercharged superfly soul revue tear-up through their stoned soul picnic basket. Never could a killer version of 'I Want To Take You Higher' have been better timed and placed, Cynthia Stone later commenting, "Sly was like a preacher. He had half a million people in the palm of the hand."

Hendrix closed the festival, taking the stage at around seven on the Monday morning with his new six-piece multi-racial band Gypsy, Sun and Rainbows, which saw original Experience drummer Mitch Mitchell joined by Jimi's old Army buddies, bassist Billy Cox and rhythm guitarist Larry Lee, plus Afro-Latino percussionists Jerry Velez and Juma Sultan. Criminally, their fluid, African-flavoured percussion percolations were mixed right down, so – while Jimi's incandescent reinterpretation of 'The Star Spangled Banner' as a searing roar of pain and napalm was held as the defining rock performance of the sixties – his first major attempt at escaping the barriers imposed on the Experience went unnoticed and unacknowledged.

The popular line is that, if Woodstock was a celebration and show of strength for the counterculture that had mushroomed during the decade, the Stones' Altamont nightmare the following December was when the sixties dream died – setting an altogether darker tone for the seventies. Altamont was a free concert which went horrifically out of control, held at the last moment by the Stones, who hired the Hells Angels as security for $500 worth of beer. They proceeded to get psychotically blasted, lashing the crushed crowd with pool cues and stabbing Meredith Hunter, a young black man in a lime-green suit, who pulled a gun in front of the stage and hoisted it towards Mick Jagger. Writer Robert Christgau wrote in 1972 that, "Writers focus on Altamont not because it brought on the end of an era but because it provided such a complex metaphor for the way an era ended."

Combined, these events realigned the socio-cultural landscape that greeted the new decade. Musically, 1969 had roared ahead rather than milking the more transient traits of the last few years: epoch-making debut albums emerged from George's fellow Motor City marauders the MC5 and Stooges, as black music evolved rapidly across the board, from the social conscience and Sly Stone production traits infiltrating Motown to the self-funkacising Hendrix influencing Miles Davis' new electric direction on *Bitches Brew*.

Somehow, George managed to straddle all this and more when Funkadelic went into Detroit's Terra Firma studio to record a first album which would comfortably stand alongside the most vitally innovative black albums of the era (and, thankfully also in the Kensington Market record bin where I stumbled on a copy the following year and spent many minutes studying the mirror-image cover and track titles such as 'I Got A Thing, You've Got A Thing, Everybody's Got A Thing' and 'Music For My Mother'. I'd never heard, or indeed heard of, this band Funkadelic but had soon rectified that situation).

'Mommy, What's A Funkadelic' – the first song of the first album to bear George's name as leader and producer – planted the seeds of the P-Funk mythology and opened the gate into his deep-fried cosmic soul consciousness as he declared, "If you will suck my soul, I will lick your funky emotions", announced he is "not of this world" but assured that he "will do you no harm, other than pee in your Afro", concluding "It's called Funkadelic music and it will blow your funky mind". These messages loom out of a druggy, hallucino-drift processional containing effects that presage dub and rewrite the psychedelic soul rulebook with Bob Babbitt's stalking bass joined by renowned guitarists Dennis Coffey and Rare Earth's Ray Monette, plus keyboardist Ivy Hunter, along with Billy, Tiki, Mickey Atkins and eerie falsetto females.

Two versions of the single were issued, featuring different B-sides:

first the bluesy vamp of 'Qualify And Satisfy', which would appear on the album, then 'Open Our Eyes', a soaring, Hazel-sung cover of Leon Lumpkins' 1958 gospel classic made famous by his Gospel Clefs. It could even be pretty much a straight piano gospel workout until Eddie weighs in with his flickering firefly wah-wah over some roaring sound effects near the end. With lyrics including, 'Grant us thy lovin' peace, and let all dissension cease, let our faith each day increase, and Master – lord please – open our eyes, open our eyes', such an impassioned spiritual outing was possibly the last thing anyone expected for the flip of a Funkadelic record at that time. It can only be a tribute to Professor Leon Lumpkins, the great Newark religious song composer (despite his name being spelt wrong on the label – ironically with the 'p' missing).

The single reached number 22 in the R&B charts and a creditable 60 in the pop listings. At one point, Funkadelic's old-school Motor City soul take on George's Jobete era 'Can't Shake It Loose' had been scheduled between 'Music For My Mother' and 'I'll Bet You' as Westbound 149, but never saw the light of day. Already covered by Pat Lewis on Golden World and the Supremes on 1968's *Love Child* album, it can safely be assumed that the move was seen as a step back in the face of Funkadelic's rapid evolution. The projected B-side was the early stage instrumental 'As Good As I Can Feel'. The tracks remained in the vaults until seeing the light of day in 1992 on Ace Records' *Music For Your Mother* singles compilation.

Somehow, George managed to straddle all this and more when Funkadelic went into Detroit's Terra Firma studio to record a first album which stands alongside the most innovative black albums of the era. Released in March 1970, Funkadelic is no-holds-barred and nasty, psychedelic and gutter-grimy, draped in scorching guitars, stoned soul vocals, eerie field holler gospel chorales and liquid Hendrix-homaging, spiked with dub-presaging mixing desk trickery such as cross-panning and phasing. George was recasting The Funk for modern times, coating it in cosmic philosophies, ghetto ribaldry and black consciousness. He described the record as, "the beginning of our psychedelic era", its darkly dangerous social comment living up to his declaration that "We gonna be the blackest, we gonna be the funkiest, we gonna be the dirtiest".

The cavernous, radioactive sound added to the deep, druggy aura, created by George exploring the studio, as he recalls, "We were playing stuff in the studio that the engineer didn't even want his name on. You turned on a Funkadelic record with earphones on, drums running across your head, panning the foot, we panned everything. Matter of fact, you didn't even have to be high to get off into that."

During the sessions, the rhythm section quit in drug-stoked mutiny, so George recruited some of Motown's finest Funk Brothers. Eddie was first to return, joining a new band including Mickey Atkins on keyboards, drummer Zachary Frazer and Tawl Ross on bass. When Billy was persuaded back, he grabbed the bass and got Tawl to play rhythm guitar, replacing Atkins with Bernie Worrell.

'Mommy, What's A Funkadelic' – first song on the first album to bear George's name as leader and producer – planted the seeds of P-Funk mythology and opened the gate into his deep-fried cosmic consciousness as he declared, "If you will suck my soul, I will lick your funky emotions", announced he is "not of this world" assured that he "will do you no harm, other than pee in your Afro", concluding "It's called Funkadelic music and it will blow your funky mind". Bob Babbitt's stalking bass is joined by renowned guitarists Dennis Coffey and Rare Earth's Ray Monette, plus keyboardist Ivy Hunter.

The spaced-out 'I'll Bet You' amps up Tiki's drums, underpinning a firestorm of guitars and moaning, chanting reverie around Eddie's vocal. The incantatory nature of this new kind of murky voodoo funk recalled Dr John's recently released Gris-Gris album, born from its creator's years of hustling in New Orleans' sleazy underbelly.

An edited version was released as Funkadelic's second single, coming in two versions featuring different B-sides: first the bluesy vamp of album track 'Qualify And Satisfy', then 'Open Our Eyes', a soaring, Hazel-sung cover of Newark religious composer Leon Lumpkins' 1958 gospel classic made famous by his Gospel Clefs. It's an unexpected straight piano gospel workout until Eddie weighs in with his firefly wah-wah, but the song made a fine tribute to Professor Lumpkins (despite his name being misspelt with the 'p' missing).

The single reached 22 in the R&B charts and creditable 60 in pop. At one point, Funkadelic's old school take on George's Jobete era 'Can't Shake It Loose' was scheduled as a 45 after 'Music For My Mother'. Already covered by the Supremes on 1968's Love Child album, it would have been a step back after Funkadelic's rapid evolution. Along with projected B-side instrumental 'As Good As I Can Feel', the track remained in the vaults until Ace's 1992 Music For Your Mother compilation.

After 'Music For My Mother', Fuzzy's 'I Got A Thing, You Got A Thing, Everybody's Got A Thing' marks Bernie's P-Funk debut on swirling proto-prog organ recalling UK Hammond maestro Vincent Crane's searing work with Arthur Brown. An unholy, glorious roar, it would be the third single in April 1970, making the R&B Top 30.

'Good Old Music', 1968's ground breaking single which introduced the Funkadelic name and sound to the world (and which George produced a version of by the Magic Tones for Westbound in 1969) is remade and stretched into eight minutes of dense, howling blues, Calvin wailing over its claustrophobic grind introduced by Tiki's turbo-thwacking breakbeat, blessed with one of the best funk drumming sounds of all time. All the promise of the single version had been delivered and elevated into a funk skyscraper.

'Qualify And Satisfy' mutates the riff from Muddy Waters' 'I'm Your Man' with gravel-blues lead vocals by Calvin, before the stoned immaculate grand finale of 'What Is Soul' and its swirling haze of snaking guitar riffs – George fires off catchphrases such as 'Ain't nothing good unless you play with it, and all that is good is nasty' and insisting that Soul can also be 'a joint rolled in toilet paper', alongside 'chitlins foo yung', all punctuated by much cackling and post-bong coughing.

One of the great debut albums winds down in a cloud of smoke and baked studio banter. The time had come for Funkadelic to start licking the country's funky emotions. From now on, George would be ready with sound-bites which, though often similar, often seemed like he was working out new definitions of The Funk. "Funk is something that one feels and everybody has the ability to feel it," he explains. "The irony is, the more one thinks about it, the harder it is to get the feel of The Funk.

It's just done… Stripped to its bare roots, all of [black music] is funk. It is that product we produce, and no one can do it like we do it… Funk is whatever it needs to be, at what time that is."

George also promotes the idea that The Funk is something that hits the first time someone plays an instrument, then, "You lose it through thinking you're cool as you learn how to play technically. When you first start playin' that groove, you're so glad that you got it, you play it for*ever*. And then as you start getting technical ability, it gets boring to you. So you have to be able to go back to that no matter what you learn, remember to always keep that in your repertoire. What you first started out doing? That's valuable."

Funkadelic received their first positive review from Geoffrey Jacques in *Creem*, who said, "In light of most of the present shit that passes for music these days, *Funkadelic* is a welcome ray of sunlight. Everything flies around here, through your ears, off the walls and everywhere else sound can travel… If Sun Ra were playing rock'n'roll, what would he sound like? Listen to Funkadelic. This record is a cross between *Their Satanic Majesties Request*, *The Best Of Sly & The Family Stone*, with a little Sun Ra spirit/influence thrown in for good measure…This first Funkadelic record is amazing. It just may go down as one of the year's best."

Funkadelic spent 30 weeks in the R&B lists, reaching number eight and also making number 126 in the pop charts, which was enough to green light an immediate follow-up.

While Sly & the Family Stone's effect on Funkadelic has been established, George always cited Hendrix as a massive influence on *Funkadelic*, this highly noticeable element growing as the band got tighter. Jimi's pyrotechnic arrival in 1967 swiftly influenced the group's image and stage act while his three albums, *Are You Experienced*, *Axis: Bold As Love* and *Electric Ladyland,* showed up as sonic and lyrical inspiration on the music (as they were on black music as a whole, it would emerge later).

"Funkadelic was the beginning of our psychedelic era. Jimi Hendrix was the king of it at that time. I knew him as Jimmy James, and he wasn't playing like that, he was with King Curtis, went over to England

and did that album that he did, *Are You Experienced*. I was like, 'Hey shit! He's doin' it',," enthused George. "As far as that style, we was already doing it slightly ourselves anyway – and then Sly came along. And we did *Funkadelic*, and *Free Your Mind … And Your Ass Will Follow* was the next one, that was *blatantly* psychedelic. We just said, 'Let's go all the way crazy'. That was a whole crazy album."

Soon-to-be P-Funk bassist Bootsy Collins adds, "Jimi Hendrix was the cat that said not only can you play guitar, I want you to come up front and do the wild thing. Back in that day, brothers weren't cool with being freaky and being out there like that."

Of course, Jimi also remained a mighty influence on Eddie, whose stratosphere-scraping soul flights and flame-snorting blues-rock riffage were all over the Funkadelic albums he appeared on, particularly the first three. Eddie embraced Jimi's post-Woodstock Band Of Gypsys trio with Billy Cox and drummer Buddy Miles, which made its debut over New Year's Eve at New York's Fillmore East as a return to his black roots. Crucially, the Gypsys displayed a solid power-funk bedrock on tracks such as 'Power Of Soul' and 'Who Knows' that connected to the musical world Jimi had started out in and could appeal to the black audience who had previously avoided psychedelic rock. (Jimi probably would have been tickled at the west coast P-Funk homaging hip-hop crew Digital Underground sampling 'Who Knows' on their *Sex Packets* album.)

"[Jimi] wanted a black band and a black drummer," said Buddy Miles. "He wanted to get together with the roots, going back to what he really loved, which was basically soul, R&B and blues." Although reviews were mixed, Jimi lived up to his statement in the *New York Post* that, "I want to bring it down to Earth. I want to get back to the blues, because that's what I am."

At the shows (recorded for a contract-fulfilling live album), Jimi also unleashed what is considered by many to be his greatest guitar solo of all time as he ripped into the dark heart of his powerful new Vietnam statement 'Machine Gun' – drawing Coltrane comparisons from Miles Davis and being described by Fillmore promoter Bill Graham as "the most brilliant, emotional display of virtuoso electric guitar playing I have ever heard… He just stood there, did nothing, just played and played and played… Aside from Otis Redding, there will never be anything like that show."

"When Jimi started playing with Buddy and Billy in the Band Of Gypsys, I think he brought what he was doing all the way out," Davis asserted. "But the record companies and white people liked him better when he had the white guys in his band… But Jimi Hendrix came from the blues. Like me. We understood each other right away because of that. He was a great blues guitarist. Both him and Sly were great natural musicians, they played what they heard."

'Happy new year, Goodbye '69, What you can do for me, is kiss my behind,' warbled Jimi as he played his first notes of 1970 on the Fillmore stage. Sadly, his management stifled the Band Of Gypsys by the following month in order to revive the money-spinning Experience. The following September, Jimi would be found dead in a West London hotel, surrounded by circumstances that have attracted conspiracy theories ever since.

The Band Of Gypsys came at the end of a year which had seen Jimi trying to reconnect with the black crowds who'd felt alienated by his huge success in the British and American white rock markets. It's interesting that George was busy placing bludgeoning, Jimi-style sex riffs and his acid-stoked ethos over weighty funk groove foundations, throwing in an over-the-top stage act, and could be accepted by both Detroit's white audiences and black crowds at the city's Twenty Grand club. In her autobiography, *Rage To Survive,* R&B goddess Etta James wrote about Jimi and Sly Stone as black men who were also hippie figureheads, presaging what George was starting to get off the ground: "By asking 'Are You Experienced?' in his song, Jimi got a lot of people to start looking for an answer. I dug the hippies. I related. I saw them as rebels the way I'd been a rebel, except they were mixing rebellion with love. I liked their attitude. It was a whole generation of young white kids who were sweetness and compassion. They treated black men and women like sisters and brothers and seemed determined to put the racism of their parents behind them. It was naïve and idealistic, but hey, who not?"

Apart from his pioneering black power trio, Jimi had been making an effort to reach out to black crowds alienated by his mainstream success, including agreeing to play a Harlem street fair held at 139th Street and Lenox in aid of the United Block Association in September 1969. He was concerned that, although the world's biggest rock star, he was hardly known – much less appreciated – in the place where he had lived and played earlier in the decade. Hendrix records were never played on black R&B radio stations, so playing a concert in the heart of Harlem would be a good move. "Sometimes when I come up here, people say, 'He plays white rock for white people, what's he doing here?' Well, I want to show them that music is universal, that there is no white rock or black rock," Hendrix explained. "Some of these kids haven't got six dollars to go to Madison Square Garden – besides, I used to play up here myself at Small's."*

Topping a bill that also included Maxine Brown and blues singer Big Maybelle, by the time the Hendrix band got on stage after midnight the crowd had dwindled from five thousand to a few hundred, some throwing eggs and catcalling. Jimi announced 'Voodoo Chile (Slight Return)' as "the Harlem national anthem". During the Band Of Gypsys' Fillmore stint three months later he introduced it as "the Black Panthers' National Anthem". Jimi was asked to play benefits for the Panthers and, although agreeable, was always vetoed by his manager Mike Jeffery, who was terrified of any association emerging that might alienate white audiences and damage his marketability.

Jimi invited the Panthers to provide security for his 1970 Seattle stadium appearance. "There was so much great music at that time, so much great music from the white community, from the black community, and Jimi Hendrix just brought the two together," recalls Panther Party Captain, Aaron Dixon, in Rickey Vincent's *Party Music*. "Jimi really represented this whole rebellious nature of young America."

Hendrix also showed respect and support for the Last Poets, the group of Harlem black nationals who spiked jail toasts and politically charged missives with urban commentary over bare percussion to provide a

---

* Small's Paradise on 138th Street, the site of several Jimi gigs during Harlem days.

blueprint for hip-hop. The two major long-playing ghetto statements of 1970 were *Funkadelic* and the Last Poets' hard-hitting eponymous debut album. But whereas George was flying over the tenements on lysergic wings or plunging to gutter level in search of female company, the Last Poets were the righteous sound of militant Harlem, berating their own people for complacency and drug abuse as much as the white man for obvious crimes against humanity.

Jimi recorded with founding poet Alafia Pudim, later known as Jalaluddin Mansur Nuriddin but here trading under his Lightnin' Rod alter-ego, the same name he used on 1973's street poetry concept classic *Hustler's Convention*, which can be viewed as the first modern rap album. In one continuous, 12-chapter track he tells his player's tale over smooth funk backdrops from studio luminaries such as Kool & the Gang, Eric Gale, Cornell Dupree and Bernard Purdie.

In November 1969, Jalal and the Poets' label boss Alan Douglas made an early visit to the New York studio Hendrix was using for the Band Of Gypsys, intending to record the Poets' 'Doriella Du Fontaine' with Buddy Miles. The track was based on a street story that concerned a pimp and his doomed hooker. When Jimi turned up, he joined in with some understated liquid guitar, the trio cutting the 13-minute original on the first take and then overdubbing bass and organ. The track was finally released on Celluloid Records in 1984. Jimi also recorded commercials for the first two Last Poets albums.

In 1985, I had the pleasure of spending an afternoon with Jalal and fellow Poet Suliaman El-Hadi in a central London hotel. It was with some trepidation that I went to meet them. I was a weird-looking apparition then, with black spiky dreadlocks. What sort of reception would I get? Maybe it helped that, as when I first interviewed George, I was clutching original pressings of some choice albums, here the Poets' debut, *This Is Madness*, *Chastisement*, *At Last* and *Delights Of The Garden*. Jalal turned out to be warm and articulate, explaining the group's history, the reasons they had to form and their lyrics, while also commenting on the current state of the hip-hop monster he had been so crucial in kick-starting. Even by 1985, hip-hop had become a multi-million dollar business, which rankled with Jalal, who said he'd never made a cent out of any of his albums, even when his 'Wake Up Niggers' appeared on the soundtrack of cult movie *Performance*. "They're into show business," he stated, coldly. "I'm not into show business. We show; that's our business. We're not in the business to entertain, but enlighten. There's a difference."

He continued, "Basically the first album was the sum total of my lifetime experience, because oppression brings about mental imbalances, which translates into negative emotions, which resides in the pit of my stomach. That's why you get that expression, 'I can feel it in my gut'. Our combined ages were over 100 years, so you were listening to 100 years of oppression, which was being spat out like a snake spits out venom. I started writing in order to have an explosion, to channel off the frustration. The implosion, the oppression. The situation was serious, like a disease.

"They insult your intelligence. That's what we try bringing to the forefront of people's minds: don't allow your intelligence to be insulted. Nothing will change unless you physically change it with your own hand. First you gotta change yourself, then you can change that which is around you."

Jalal believed that Jimi Hendrix was trying to change at the time he was seeing him. "He was trying. He could see he had to. The roots was severed. And he was out of contact with his people. He had alienated them – not on purpose, but he got swept along by his popularity with white people. He was really happy just jamming. When I met him he appreciated what the Poets did because it reinforced his black roots, but he was not interested to step out of that being a black pop star appreciated by whites. My impression was that he identified his status; he communicated this to me with his eyes.

"We had a handshake at that time called the Black Power handshake which went [he grabbed my hand to demonstrate]. I taught him this handshake because he didn't know how to do it. All the brothers knew how to do it but Jimi didn't."

Even if Hendrix didn't manage to successfully engage the black market while he was alive, his superfreak cool and proto-superfly image fed into the Blaxploitation heroes of the seventies. After Jimi's death he was duly acknowledged as one of the greatest black musicians of all time and among the most important figures in shaping music to emerge during the sixties. When Hendrix died, Funkadelic were just getting started. "George Clinton's Parliafunkadelicment Thang captured perhaps the most authentic replication of the Hendrix legacy, recording as Funkadelic," attested Rickey Vincent. And, as I'll keep saying, Eddie Hazel was the nearest living embodiment of his supernatural magic, even claiming to carry some of Jimi's spirit in him.

Along with James Brown, Jimi Hendrix and Sly Stone, Miles Davis was the other key figure during this transitional time for the cutting-edge black music that George was now reshaping in his own unique vision. 1969's *In A Silent Way* laid out Miles' new electric style, swathed in psychedelic rock influences. It received a rave *Rolling Stone* review from Lester Bangs, who proclaimed it to be "the kind of album that gives you faith in the future of music... All at once it owes as much to the techniques developed by rock improvisers over the last four years as to Davis' jazz background. It is part of a transcendental new music which flushes categories away and, while using musical devices from all styles and cultures, is defined mainly by its deep emotion and unaffected originality."

Recorded the same weekend as Woodstock took place, Davis' next album, *Bitches Brew,* is up with *Funkadelic* and *The Last Poets* as one of the pivotal works of the new decade's first year. The double album's alien-sounding new form of electric space-funk improvisation reflected the trumpeter's love of James Brown's guitar-driven street grooves, while extending Hendrix's expanded sonic horizons. Predictably, Davis' introduction of electric instruments and appearances at rock festivals incurred the blinkered wrath of jazz's old guard who, once again feeling threatened by something new and fearless, gorged from the same well of reactionary bile hurled at Dylan in 1965 for strapping on a Stratocaster.

As would soon happen when the new electric jazz caught on, Miles didn't just hijack funky rhythms and blow over them. The increasingly stark music he made through to the mid-seventies was all pulses, moods and textures, spaced to infinity. Miles had been a lifelong hero and inspiration for Hendrix. The respect became mutual after Miles' wife, Betty, took him to Alan Douglas' spouse, Stella's, boutique for an image makeover and bombarded him with the sounds of Hendrix and Sly, influencing *In A Silent Way* and, particularly, *Bitches Brew.*

The pair met through Douglas, immediately hitting it off and talking for hours about music. It was inevitable they would jam and hatch plans to record together. Douglas booked a session at the Hit Factory to record three tracks from each musician for a projected album (one rumour has Hendrix sending Paul McCartney a telegram asking if he would play bass). As the session was due to start, Davis famously asked for $50,000 before he would set foot in the studio, resulting in Douglas cancelling the session. Hendrix still remained enthusiastic about working with Davis until his death, telling *NME*'s Roy Carr, "Like Miles, I want to invent a new kind of music, a new kind of jazz... It was supposed to happen several months ago, but money got in the way, money always gets in the way, but that's just Miles."

If anything, Hendrix influenced Miles more after he died, the latter saying in 1973, "I tell the guitar player that if he likes Hendrix or Sly to play something like that, just to open it up. Hendrix had no knowledge of modal music; he was just a natural musician, you know, he wasn't studied, he wasn't into no market, and neither am I."

Miles often battled against his audience, the critics and his record company to let his creativity take his music beyond the mainstream jazz market. He picked up many young, white fans, who ignored generic boundaries to rank him alongside Jimi, Sly, Sun Ra and (before long) George as fearless innovators who were changing the times. Speaking as one of those young, white kids, I can vouch for the excitement and danger buzzing through that amazingly innovative time and how it felt perfectly natural to take a short hop from James Brown and Jimi to the new outer limits being charted by Miles and Sun Ra.

George careered even further into the realms of acid rock on Funkadelic's second album, released in July, 1970. *Free Your Mind ... And Your Ass Will Follow* was one of the records which George picked out of my P-pile in 1989, proudly recalling, as a massive beam lit up his face, "I made this one up on the spot, acided out of my mind. 'Let's see if we can record a whole album while we're tripping on acid!' This one I recorded and mixed in one day. I did most of those records in one day."

Amid the weird sonic booms, howling rock and dismembered funk, George was celebrating liberation of the brain, behaviour and sexuality, continuing to explain as he defaced the gatefold sleeve's naked girl who can be found spread-eagled within: "If you think about it… if you free your mind, if your mind is working it knows what to do about anything. If you feed your mind with information it will lift you out of the shit."

Bernie Worrell was chucked in at the deep end for his first album as a fully-fledged P-Funker, but rose to the occasion to give an idea of the vital role he would be playing in the sound and arrangements. "I could take everything I had been doing, now here's a vehicle, a way to – totally free – create something," he recalled. "Writing, composing, performing, recording. Back then it was like, 'Hit it!' You know, *Free Your Mind … And Your Ass Will Follow* is one day. All that stuff is raw, it's feeling. We didn't mess it up with no overdubbing crap. That was the shit, that's the P-Funk! That throb, that thang."

Working for the first time at Detroit's United Sound studio, birthplace of many future P-Funk classics, George also saw the album as his answer to the Beatles' *Sgt Pepper's Lonely Hearts Club Band,* but the abrasive gonzo belches sometimes sound like he's having a bad trip as violence and desolation hover around the latent funk. The album sandblasted away anything that was left of sixties hippie bliss to reveal torn psyches letting off steam in the hedonistic sandbox of personal liberation.

The gonzoid title track, which subverts Christian themes into a mystical funk, predates space rock with headfuck cross-panning, screaming feedback and coruscating Booker T organ adorned with call-and-response vocals as the girls chant 'the kingdom of heaven is within' under George and Ray's exhortations – all sounding like it was mixed in a wind tunnel. 'Friday Night, August 14' is a heaving proto-rock/funk blend of socially conscious lyrics sung by Billy Nelson, suffused with wah-wah action wrapped around twisting, shrieking guitars and the kind of crashing, reverbed drum adventurism being explored by Sun Ra in the sixties.

Also rocking out of its gourd on one of the classic Funkadelic riffs, 'Funky Dollar Bill' features bass vocalist 'Sting Ray' Davis' lyrics inspired by seeing his band colleagues in drug-addled catatonia and thinking it wouldn't have happened without money, which can buy land, wars and life, but also "the kind of life where the soul is lost". The song is sung quite histrionically by Billy (him being among those who were most wasted), pointing towards the explosive Funkadelic sound to come with Bernie's splintering avant barrelhouse piano solo recalling Mike Garson on David Bowie's 'Aladdin Sane' over Eddie's dizbusting squeals and priapic wah-wah.

Glazed in whirring acid, the churning sex-grind of 'I Wanna Know If It's Good To You' humps like Sly on a loudly romantic mission from gutter to boudoir, gouged by Bernie's screaming organ alongside Eddie and Billy resuscitating old lyrics such as 'Your honey tastes sweeter than the honey that replaced the rain since I met you'. Bernie's prowling keyboards over the lengthy home-stretch vamp could have sat comfortably on beefier British prog outings of the time. This was the track selected for release as a single.

When not being cross-panned into oblivion on the mixing desk, Funkadelic's sound on these tracks is an unbridled rock surge tempered with inner funk momentum while the slowies heave in the lower reaches, the blood in the group's collective groin bubbling with the chemicals in their heads. Funkadelic were now a seriously good acid rock band, although 'Some More' weirdly tops its swinging, Hammond organ boogie remake of the Debonaires' 'Headache In My Heart' with gurgling fish-like vocals from Eddie and more dubbed-out drum effects.

Lasting barely over 30 minutes, the album closed with the bizarre 'Eulogy And Light', an ironic, pimp's-eye rewrite of the Lord's Prayer written by Ernie Harris, which is testified by George over the formerly pure gospel tones of 'Open Your Eyes' run backwards through the tape deck. Starting with "Our father who art in Wall Street, hallowed be thy butt", he asks forgiveness for robbing and selling drugs to kids, expressing gratitude for his Cadillac and smug satisfaction at attracting envy from the poor as he walks "through the valley in the shadow of poverty", all thanks to "the Good God Big Buck". George's monologue

114

gets more demented as the surreal reversed gloop unravels, spluttering to a halt in more mixing desk vocal lunacy.

Free Your Mind... (as the strait-laced voiceover announced it on the radio ads, minus the ass) peaked at number 11 on *Billboard*'s Black Albums Chart and 92 on the Pop listings.

That same month, another album appeared featuring the same cast under a different name. Having regained the Parliaments name, George changed it to 'A Parliafunkadelicment Thang' before settling on 'Parliament'. At the invitation of former Motown producer Jeffrey Bowen, a regular at Funkadelic's Twenty Grand gigs, George signed them to Invictus, the label set up by Edward and Brian Holland and Lamont Dozier after they left Motown. For eight years, Invictus was a hotbed of scintillating soul, releasing material by Freda Payne, Chairmen Of The Board and 8th Day, while sister label Hot Wax played host to the likes of 100 Proof Aged In Soul, Honey Cone and Laura Lee. George essentially presented the label with the same band under a different name, initiating the web of projects built around core personnel that would escalate throughout the rest of the decade. He signed the deal after finishing *Funkadelic*, which meant recording of Parliament's album overlapping with the next Funkadelic and resulted in both albums being released in the same month. "Sure, neither company liked it much, but we had been caught before in this business so we felt it safer if we had an escape clause," reasoned George as he tried to explain what amounted to contractual bigamy. "So, Funkadelic stays with Westbound and Parliament stays with Invictus. They don't really like it but it keeps both companies working hard trying to do better than the other!"

George contended that Funkadelic was "purely emotional with very little intellectual content", while Parliament was "very subtle and professional". However, with the latter's first album, *Osmium*, Invictus got something unlike anything anyone else was doing, including the band itself – especially when the bagpipes came in.

My several years spent in New York City in the eighties were dominated by trying to plug the gaps in my P-Funk record collection. I regularly traversed the independent downtown record stores and scanned the wares of the old guys on the sidewalks spreading out their record collections for sale on a Sunday evening. This could turn up trumps, but never a copy of *Osmium*. Now it's been reissued with bonus tracks it's possible to experience one of the strangest items in the P-Funk catalogue. Although the band are heard for the first time without a full blown acid fry-up across a brace of tight, steaming funk-rockers, the music also veers into country, classical and bagpipe anthems. With George rapidly finding his studio feet, the album is co-produced by Jeffrey Bowen, under his wife, Ruth Copeland's, name (to avoid contractual issues with Motown). As a singer-songwriter in her own right, Ruth collaborates on some of the album's key tracks, heavily affecting its overall atmosphere.

One of Invictus' first white artists, Ruth hailed from the cathedral city of Durham in northeast England and reportedly sang in local folk clubs in the mid-sixties, releasing two singles on Mercury in 1965. It's not known how she hitched up with Bowen but he had got to know Holland-Dozier-Holland while writing and producing at Motown around 1967, working with Marvin Gaye and Martha & the Vandellas. Whether her involvement was a business move aimed at pleasing Jeffrey and the label, or if George simply fancied Ruth's statuesque frame isn't known, but the Funk Mob ended up recording *Osmium* at the same time as playing on Ruth's own Invictus debut album. Inevitably both projects ended up feeding and spilling into each other.

Much of *Osmium*'s diversity is down to Ruth, including her prayer on spine-chilling gospel hymn 'Oh Lord, Why Lord', an extraordinarily impassioned plea against racism. Calvin Simon's emotion-charged vocal quakes on lines like, 'Why is that I must suffer without even a cause?' countered by Ruth's operatic tones while the choir swells over the poignant melody from Pachelbel's 'Canon In D'. The idea comes from a 1968 single of the same name by soulful Spanish baroque-pop outfit Los Pop Tops, led by Trinidad-born singer Phil Trim, who receives a co-writing credit with Ruth.

Being a down-home country romp, Ruth's 'Little Ole Country Boy' sounds truly odd for a P-Funk album, Fuzzy's animated rasp surrounded by quicksilver steel guitar which could have graced a Flying Burrito

116

Brothers album, its jew's-harp and yodelling heisted by De La Soul for 'Potholes In My Lawn'. "I loved that album," giggled George. "We even had a country and western number on there!" The song provided the B-side to all four of Parliament's Invictus singles (possibly because no R&B radio DJ would ever play it, compelling them to concentrate on the A-side).

Ruth's finest moment has to be the epic closer, 'The Silent Boatman', one of the oddest outings in the P-Funk songbook. After beginning gently with some acoustic guitar, bagpipes breeze in playing 'The Skye Boat Song', before George kicks into Cecil B de Mille mode with Bernie's church organ and massed choir joining the riverside clapping and wailing. All this for what's basically a soul-racked ode to the Ferryman of Death. Even stranger, it was released as a single, unfortunately not selling a fraction of Paul McCartney's bagpipe smash 'Mull Of Kintyre' in 1978.

Elsewhere on the album is the more customary Funkadelic-style funk rock, although 'My Automobile' starts with a discursive preamble and doo-wop singing that harks back to the barbershop, before Fuzzy rides a mutant Sun Records rockabilly scuttle into a down-home car song reminiscent of the Stones' similarly wasted drawlers of the time. The slow-burning, organ-lashed dirt-funk of 'Moonshine Heather (Takin' Care Of Business)' predates 'Cosmic Slop' in singing about a mum forced to sell moonshine to support her 14 kids. 'Put Love In Your Life' starts with an impassioned semi-spoken introduction before easing into a Doorsy organ vamp, unusually featuring lead vocals from Sting Ray before a quick change leads into a convoluted stop-start arrangement recalling Frank Zappa's complex rush-hour mini-opera outings.

On the rockers, the Funkadelics have never sounded so tight, energised and on the button. *Osmium* kicks off with 'I Call My Baby Pussycat', written by George, Billy Nelson and Eddie Hazel, released as a single under the name A Parliament Thang. Hot, hard-rocking and squealing with dog whistles set over a heavyweight Sly-style turbo-soul drive, it's nothing like the back-alley sleaze epic which would appear on *America Eats Its Young* two years later. Eddie leads the frenetic primal surge of 'Nothing Before Me But Thang', co-written with George,

Bernie and Ernie Harris. As with several of the funk-rockers, it comes on like a hyperactive Chairmen Of The Board on heat. The stanky, wailing 'Funky Woman' was Bernie's first co-write, his big organ riffs evoking UK proto-progsters Atomic Rooster.

'Livin' The Life' is a classic of its time, boasting much meaty blues-rock riffage, and a pulsing midway jazz piano solo, with Eddie on fire and a soaring chorus straight out of *Hair* featuring Ruth Copeland. The home stretch fadeout is the kind of hoodoo shuffle Jimmy Miller was producing for the Stones at the time with Bernie outdoing Nicky Hopkins in the gospel piano pummelling stakes.

One of the most unique outings in the sprawling P-Funk catalogue, *Osmium* ventured into musical areas George never returned to and further confused a public still getting to grips with *Free Your Mind....* Unsurprisingly it stiffed, hence the high going rate for original copies before it was reissued.

The album has also been re-released under the names *First Thangs* and *Rhenium*, adding the three subsequent singles and out-takes such as the prototype 'Loose Booty' and George-sung 'Fantasy Is Reality', which would later pop up on the P-Funk Earth Tour and coined the tautological line 'I'm free because I'm free of the need to be free'.

Even if *Osmium* bombed, Invictus continued releasing the aforementioned singles, starting with the scorching blues-rock riff onslaught of 'Red Hot Mama' the following year. Written by George, Bernie and his unaccredited wife, Judie, Eddie and Tawl's wall of guitars and the hammering piano provide more fiery hard rock, which cried out to be revisited by Funkadelic and soon was. This was followed by 'Breakdown', written by George, Ruth and guest singer Clyde Wilson of 100 Proof Aged In Soul, who'd recorded in the sixties as Steve Mancha for Don Davis' Groovesville label.

Ruth Copeland's album, *Self Portrait,* followed in October, boasting a stellar P-Funk cast including Eddie, Bernie, Tawl, Billy and Tiki, plus Dennis Coffey, Bob Babbitt, Ray Monette, the Detroit Symphony Orchestra and the Choraliers Gospel Singers. While this was another oddity in the P-catalogue with orchestral ballads such as 'The Music Box' (her first single), 'Thanks For The Birthday Card' and the yearning 'No

Commitment' (B-side of her second single's take on 'Hare Krishna'!), the album's close proximity to the creation of *Osmium* becomes particularly evident when George, Tawl and Eddie have a hand in the songwriting, as in the fuzzy acid grind of 'Your Love Been So Good To Me' and Hazel-laced blues-wailer 'I Got A Thing For You, Daddy'. Ruth's own version of 'The Silent Boatman' is dreamier, as her voice rings plaintively over a bed of blissful organs, while 'Un Bel Di' bizarrely heists Puccini's 'Madam Butterfly' with a majestic Eddie joined by the Detroit Symphony Orchestra under Ruth's operatic trilling.

With Berry Gordy acknowledging that something revolutionary was going on in his backyard, the P-Funk influence spilled into Motown during the late sixties and opened the door for the seventies. One of the biggest changes took place in the Temptations. Their transformation from 'My Girl' harmonies to conscious outings such as 'Cloud Nine', 'Ball Of Confusion' and 'Message From A Black Man' were initially credited to producer Norman Whitfield's reluctant concession to Sly's highly successful rock'n'soul, but it took Funkadelic to infect the label with cutting-edge black rock. George has claimed that the music to these and the Temps' 'Psychedelic Shack', released that March, was derived from Funkadelic songs after Whitfield attended their shows with a tape recorder. He also reckoned their intro theme provided the hook to the Temptations' 'I Can't Get Next To You'. Although the call-and-response expertise is obviously all Temptations, the hefty guitar shenanigans are pure Funkadelic, but George was happy his efforts were being listened to and acknowledged by his old heroes, so he didn't slip into legal mode (although he might have done 40 years later).

It wasn't just their music. Funkadelic's unique sartorial style showed up in the wardrobes of Motown acts after the store on Plum Street where they bought their fringed Indian vests and other exotic apparel started being patronised by the Temptations and the Jacksons. "That's why I knew we changed the way people were approaching music in Detroit," says Billy.

With new manager Ron Scribner now handling their bookings, Funkadelic started building a live following by traversing the country's clubs and halls, making anything from $2,000 to $10,000 a night, depending on the city. When they played Bermuda they were greeted like the Beatles in 1964. Comedian James Wesley Jackson did a warm-up routine for the band at many of the shows.

By now, Detroit regarded Parliament/Funkadelic as its own. In the definitive Motor City music history he wrote for *MOJO* magazine in 1996, Ben Edmonds, who was there, states: "The P-Funk gang fits comfortably into any discussions of Detroit rock'n'roll. It was the audiences in the rock venues that encouraged George and even egged him on. He could never get too far out for these Detroit kids, as he'd seen when he did shows with the Stooges and MC5. This made him entirely too far out for the rest of the country, but they caught up eventually. And it was certainly nice to see little pieces of Detroit rock consciousness being fed back into the black music spring that had so nourished it."

Parliament/Funkadelic scored a major feature in the October 1970 issue of *Creem*. Writer Geoffrey Jacques, whose name could normally be found after the magazine's jazz reviews, based his feature around the gig he'd seen at the local Edganster Park Fairground: "When the Parliament/Funkadelic trample on stage, everything is suddenly transformed. It's just like hearing rock'n'roll or John Coltrane for the first time; you really don't know what's happening, but whatever it is, it won't hurt you. It sounds and feels good." He describes the group being dressed as clowns, magicians, African kings and Zulu warriors, while George looks like "the last of the Mohicans in bell bottoms… a totally outrageous person, with his head shaved, save for a distinct five o'clock shadow on the top".

He continues, "Whatever it is, it's not like anything we're used to hearing," comparing them to Sun Ra's Arkestra or the kind of store-front church service that will "hypnotise and seduce their audiences with their mad rituals". George is on form, explaining how the band can pack out clubs in Boston and Detroit and colleges, while 'Testify' earned them a spot on Robin Seymour's local TV show *Swingin' Time* with the MC5. "We had died down in the white clubs because everything was psychedelic then," continues George. "We were still straddling the road. After they had forgotten about us, we went into our own thing completely. When we went into Funkadelic, we started getting into the black thing. We're popular with blacks in Detroit. We're popular in Boston but it's half and half. Here in Michigan, we're gaining a large, white crowd, but Detroit is still predominantly black. We get even more exposure between blacks and whites. But we like it across the board. We hate to be restricted."

George posits his radio-play theory that Funkadelic couldn't be classified, so were deemed too weird. "It's not strictly rock and roll, it's not strictly rhythm and blues. It's everything. Like radio stations don't know; they try to make us R&B because we're black. The black stations don't want us to change. The white stations don't play us because we didn't come up the R&B ladder. This bothers us because we didn't want to be categorised as anything. All of us have things we want to get into. If you're put into any kind of category, they won't let you out of it. We want to be able to do whatever we want to do. As long as we're making a little money we'll do it. That's one reason we have two labels and the double name. The Parliament album is completely different from the Funkadelic album."

The *Creem* feature also mentioned a forthcoming Invictus project which, to my fevered P-infested knowledge, never materialised, although a joint album with Iron Butterfly of 'In-A-Gadda-De-Vida' fame called *Heavy Funk* would have been intriguing. George explained that the plan was to feature a 400lb white woman on the front cover and a 380lb black man on the back.

Even if that never happened, George and crew had created a ghetto funk master-work, an acid-fried nuclear experiment and an intriguing oddity that also marked their maturing as a fearsome recording band, plus they had catalysed a bizarre but unique period piece. Now heroin showed its allure to some of the younger musicians, the trip would be strange but not very long, as Funkadelic greeted 1971 on the supernova hayride that would burn itself out during the creation of its greatest work.

Chapter Six

Looney Tunes And Scary Melodies

"The drug experience in P-Funk is as integral to the P-Funk experience as perspiration is because everything had to do with the higher consciousness in some way, shape or form."
Rickey Vincent, *One Nation Under A Groove* documentary.

The first time this writer can remember Funkadelic appearing in the British music press was a story about their outrageous stage act running into controversy, illustrated with a photo of George in a leopard-skin jockstrap; printed *after* their May, 1971 UK tour.

In retrospect, thank the Lord for the jockstrap. This was a risky time to get the old chap out on a stage, as Jim Morrison had found in Miami in March 1969 when he was hauled in and charged with the felony of lewd and lascivious behaviour and five misdemeanours; two counts of indecent exposure, two of public profanity and one of public drunkenness. In September 1970, the Lizard King was found guilty of the flashing and swearing that his bandmates insisted never happened. Morrison was subsequently sentenced to six months' jail and given a $500 fine. Jim was appealing the conviction when he was found dead in his bathtub in July 1971 but, until he died, this most high profile of busts had hung over his head and caught the public imagination, further feeding the establishment belief that rock musicians were a moral threat to society. Jim and many others believed he had been made a scapegoat for the counterculture.

Even the Beatles weren't immune as the naked cover of John Lennon and Yoko Ono's *Two Virgins* sparked all sorts of moral panics and prosecutions, while the MC5 had to replace a 'motherfucker' hollered on their *Kick Out The Jams* album with "brothers and sisters". In 1970, Janis Joplin was fined $200 for violating local obscenity laws in Tampa, Florida while Jefferson Airplane copped a $1,000 fine in Oklahoma for onstage profanity. The following year, President Nixon was saying rock albums should be screened for content and any records containing drug references be banned, while the Federal Communications Commission was threatening the licences of stations that played songs glorifying drug use or failed to exercise responsibility in selecting music. (This last action would be vetoed two years later for violating the First Amendment).

The Fugs had long boasted an FBI file and now Alice Cooper had started to make his presence felt as what *Creem* magazine called "the wildest, most unusual rock group to ever make the scene". Alice had returned to his native Detroit in mid-1970 after being shunned by the west coast for cross-dressing and the notorious "chicken incident", which saw a crowd rip a bird to shreds after Alice tossed it into their midst, mistakenly assuming that poultry could fly. He regularly faked his own execution in an electric chair amid a blizzard of pillow feathers and, with 1971's breakthrough *Love It To Death* album, containing the generational anthem 'I'm Eighteen', Cooper was about to enjoy his stint as a chart-topping public enemy number one.

In the case of Funkadelic, stories had filtered through the underground and stoked a degree of notoriety before their visit. Geoffrey Jacques described a Detroit P-Funk show in his October, 1970 *Creem* story, writing: "The bizarre act is attacked with an almost religious fervour, as if you were witnessing a service at a store-front sanctified church. The Parliament-Funkadelic seem to hypnotise and seduce their audience with their mad rituals. Well before the act is half over, the P&F have

123

the audience joining in, and here, when an audience rush the stage, it is not just to tear the clothes off their favourite rock star, but to join him in his dance. It is as if they are caught up in the ritual of praise, the Holy Spirit caught hold of their bodies and won't let go."

Jacques comments on the band's "reputation of being obscene", admitting "they are a very raunchy, coarse band, in the same way as, say, Iggy Stooge or Mick Jagger. At the least, they're excellently raunchy and even though they shrug off the accusations of being obscene ('It's only in your mind') they are among the best at it.

"If the group ever assumes the status of a major attraction (one which, in certain areas of the country, they are nearing) you can expect that very coarseness which seems so charming now to be labelled 'obscene', the same way that Jim Morrison's was, the same way that a lot of Janis Joplin's has been, the way Iggy Stooge's may be or Mick Jagger always was. And that intensity is, of necessity, to be closely linked with sexuality – in all of the above cases, to be sure, and the Parliament/ Funkadelic are no exception here, either. Coupled with that, their appeal is multi-racial, a problem which few black performers have ever had to deal with... primarily because they were castrated before they could make the attempt. Only Sly Stone and Jimi Hendrix, among black performers, have been able to pull off what the Parliament/Funkadelic are attempting and Sly had never emphasised the sexual. Hendrix has and he's been roundly blasted in many circles for it.

"George Clinton has been known to bound into the crowd, Red Indian headdress streaming after him, and emerge wearing nothing more than a scarlet jockstrap. One wonders if a black man can get away with that, without being accused of pretension (under the guise of fear), even in the supposedly liberated, theoretically leftist world of rock. They might have to give up what might ordinarily be their greatest asset (their sexuality) in order to 'Make It'."

Obviously, George had already ticked most of the government's naughty boxes, from onstage profanity to indecent exposure, but he was so far under the establishment radar in terms of success and profile that he wasn't yet considered a threat to the white middle-class kids America so wanted to protect. Like the MC5, he was based in Detroit and even playing to the same crowds as they were, but in the rest of the US he was still playing venues such as Boston's Sugar Shack and the chitlin' circuit gigs which had been unbothered hotbeds of carnal celebration and unbridled hedonism for decades.

In 1971, post-psychedelic Britain enjoyed a healthy club and university level blues, rock and proto-progressive rock scene, with bands such as Genesis, Van Der Graaf Generator and the Groundhogs playing to crowds sporting long, stringy hair, greatcoats and denim. The MC5 toured early in the year but, otherwise, onstage flash and high-energy guitars were only to be found in the likes of Mott The Hoople – the first band in the UK to sport platform boots and lay the foundations for glam rock and punk.

Meanwhile, black music fans had their own world of Northern Soul all-nighters, connoisseur discos and tacky niteries for the indiscriminate cavorter. There was very little outlet for the music on the radio or TV, which meant specialist publications such as *Blues & Soul* and the odd mention in the rock and pop weeklies were the only way their music was known about outside of the clubs. The Parliaments had acquired something of a reputation in the soul clubs after 'Testify' but Funkadelic, which was hardly Wigan Casino material, were practically an unknown entity in the music papers they should have been dominating – although Pye International had recently released the first two albums in the UK. Speaking as someone who came up in the white rock'n'roll world but loved black music and didn't live in London, there were few ways this most revolutionary of bands could filter through. It was all about the grapevine, intrepid detective work following a rumour something was outrageously great, or just a happy accident, like turning up the first album while rummaging in the Kensington Market record bins.

In the UK, where Mick Jagger had been called "obscene" when he still had his pants on, it wasn't unusual for 'Fire' singer Arthur Brown to drop his Hellfire strides and I still remember the evening in 1971 I sat at the side of the Watford Town Hall stage next to Hawkwind's statuesque dancer Stacia, who was just about to take the stage totally naked.

Funkadelic made their first sortie to the UK in May 1971, playing venues including Leeds Locarno, Liverpool Polytechnic, Kirklivington

Country Club, Chester Quaintways, Crawley's Fox, the tiny London Country Club, Southend Kursaal Ballroom, Cardiff University, London Roundhouse and Croydon Greyhound. A prestigious spot at the Royal Albert Hall was said to have been pulled when a copy of *Free Your Mind ... And Your Ass Will Follow* found its way to a certain Marian Herrod, the venue's lettings manager, who was mortified by the naked lady on the cover. She had likewise banned Frank Zappa's *200 Motels* from the venue in January for profanity, and Mott would be blacklisted from the venue indefinitely in July for inviting their audience to join them on stage, a regular occurrence at Mott gigs.

When Funkadelic arrived they made a point of visiting the Royal Albert Hall in Kensington, complete with hired donkey, which laid a loaf on its venerable steps. Up the road from the hall the P-Funk crew explored the delights of Kensington Market. "I got my first pair of high platform boots from Kensington Market," George told Jasper the Vinyl Junkie in *Soul Underground*, "and some leather stuff made there, and of course, the Kings Road too. It was great. We really did have a ball."

George had already predicted the band would have a blast in the UK when he spoke to *Melody Maker*'s Chris Charlesworth on the phone before the visit, declaring, "I think we're gonna have one really good time when we come. We don't know a lot about English audiences but I don't expect they will have seen anything like us before; not visually anyway."

Pleasantly surprised to encounter "a level headed and sensible young man" rather than the expected "freaky acid head", Charlesworth caught George at his most charming, outlining the Funkadelic manifesto and trying to diffuse the notoriety filtering over to the UK by that time, particularly about their stage act. "I think people misunderstand the appearance of the group. People misinterpret things we do and say on stage, like wearing jockstraps and using phrases like 'suck my soul'. The act is pretty wild but it's not designed to hurt anyone. We do a number about people praying to the dollar bill... People thought we were pulling the Lord's Prayer down but we weren't.

"Offstage, we're very different people. The stage show is just something we do to make people sit up and listen when we play. We had a hard time getting the new style over during the first year. It's only really been in the past year that things have come on. Originally, we were with a small company in Detroit and we had to do just about everything ourselves."

The big London show was the Roundhouse, the old engine shed in Camden Town which hosted Middle Earth and popular Sunday afternoon hippie rock extravaganzas. Funkadelic also made an appearance on the tiny stage of the hip Speakeasy club, which is where the photo of George in his leopard-skin jockstrap came from. When I saw this in one of the music papers, it was the first time I'd seen Funkadelic featured in any of them. The visit disappointed soul boys coming to hear 'Testify' and shocked but often delighted rock fans who, back then, attended their local club or university shows on a regular basis to see their mates. Both camps wondered what the hell was going on up there as this ragged bunch of black freaks in surreal fancy dress cranked up the guitars to deafening levels, previewing songs from the newly finished but unreleased *Maggot Brain*.

Melody Maker's rock scribe Chris Welch wrote glowingly about the "all action soul band" which "blew minds" and provided "sheer entertainment" at the Speakeasy and Roundhouse, describing how, "The Speak was aroused from its frequently blasé semi-hostility to music to shout, yell and jump on chairs.... Funkadelic, in their brightly coloured gear, by their sterling efforts, and rhythmic expertise, are obviously destined to become even more popular, especially among fans of wild, polyrhythmic rhythms."

Even if the London show met with fingers stuck in ears and scratched heads, some of the out of town gigs still went swimmingly as white crowds picked up on the P-Funk spirit. George told *Blues & Soul*'s John Abbey that these receptions reminded him of the positive way that Funkadelic were now being accepted in the southern US. "It's just that we appeal to the people down there," he explained. "Our outlook to music is their outlook to music. And some of us are from the south so we understand the people down there, too. But, you know, the same situation in the south is here in England; the people accept us in just the same manner. We did a date in Cleethorpes the other night…"

127

George then recounts the near-nightmare of that particular gig, supporting Afro-rockers Osibisa, then hot in the UK with their "crisscross rhythms that explode with happiness" and an eponymous debut album. I had seen them three months earlier and can think of worse bands for Funkadelic to share a bill with, but manager Ron Scribner described how it could have turned into a disaster after it took an hour to get Osibisa's gear off the stage and Funkadelic set up, leaving them just 45 minutes before curfew. "The group really needs an hour and a half to really get into something. So we couldn't really get it together yet the ovation was incredible; they clapped and stomped their feet and demanded the group come on for encore after encore. It's funny because most people are really startled and frightened when they see the group for the first time. The whole thing depends on how the group performs; the audience gets excited and sometimes loses control of itself... the girls in the audience are often frightened and they start to disappear from the front of the stage. And then others get caught up in some kind of spell."

With the band playing to mainly white crowds of hippies and soul boys, album sales didn't rocket after the trip to a country which, on the whole, wasn't ready for Funkadelic's onslaught. It would be November 1978 before P-Funk landed in the UK again. By then, punk had swept the country and given its moral guardians something closer to home to sweat about. In terms of shocking press, music fans and authorities, Funkadelic were up there with the first confrontational proto-punk outfits, testing the boundaries of what could be got away with on stage. In the ultra-conservative early seventies, they represented an affront to prudes, bigots and the narrow-minded.

As Geoffrey Jacques had said as he concluded his *Creem* feature on Funkadelic the previous October, "Those in control of the rock industry, especially those in control of black music, obviously aren't prepared to unleash a Black Jim Morrison (in the person of George Clinton or otherwise) on their minions. Certainly, the white kids *can* accept that, if they're given as Hendrix has already shown, because of the very mystique associated with miscegenation in this country. It's another taboo, and like any other taboo, white youth is ready to bust it open.

"Somehow it seems that a white band with this much potential would have achieved much more at this point. It may be that the innate racism of the rock scene is *exactly* what's holding them down; they've paid enough dues by now, they've got their show together, there's not much more that they can do. Still, 10 years ago, who'd have thought rhythm and blues would suddenly emerge with this many-headed Hydra? That soul has been able to spawn such a bizarre hybrid, while the Supremes, Temptations and so many others have become the white supper club hits, is testament to its immense virility. All that remains to be seen, in the case of the Parliament/Funkadelic, is whether or not the insidious white racism of the record industry and the rock'n'roll scene will allow that virility to emerge undiluted."

Released in July 1971, there are many who consider *Maggot Brain* to be the best Funkadelic album of all, managing to distil the band's pounding hard rock, soaring gospel balladry, cranium-fried proto-metal and wigged-out cosmic psych into one devilish beast. Sadly, it marked the last time the original Funkadelic band would creatively combust in the studio together as rebellion brewed in the ranks, mainly over financial issues like back pay. But *Maggot Brain* is an awesome final shot, the high peak of Funkadelic's early phase.

Their third album in 18 months, it fared less well than its predecessors and stalled outside the *Billboard* Hot 100 by eight places. However, the album was popular within the black community, reaching number 14 on the R&B chart.

Maggot Brain was George's first serious comment on the crisis enveloping the Vietnam War, which was spiralling out of America's control. "We had to realise that our brains and minds – which we thought would bring the solution to all the problems – were fucked up themselves," he asserted. The title is derived from Eddie's nickname, but there's also been a story about George finding his overdosed dead brother, Robert's, decomposed body in a Chicago apartment, the cracked skull inspiring the song, title and scary African woman's zombie head on the cover. George later rebuked that one, declaring, "It's not that gory!"

The time-stopping 10-minute title track is one of Funkadelic's most renowned statements, featuring Eddie Hazel's searing guitar traversing a stairway to hell as the closest he got to generating the spiritual catharsis achieved by his idol Hendrix. His performance was described by writer Greg Tate as providing Funkadelic's 'A Love Supreme'. Once, when I was listening to 'Maggot Brain', it occurred to me that Eddie would have recorded this shortly after Jimi's death and maybe this was his own personal requiem to him. "Eddie claimed that he had some Jimi Hendrix spirit in him," said Sidney Barnes. "He really did. That's why he's not with us any more, because the truly genius like that, they're tormented. He had too many demons, and he couldn't get away from 'em."

"I listened to Jimi a lot," Eddie told *Guitar Player* magazine. "It was very uncanny that our styles were alike, but that is what I was hearing inside. I wanted to make the guitar an extension of my singing. My style is really like solo vocalist guitar."

The often repeated tale about Hazel's stellar performance has George telling him to imagine he had just been told his mother had died then finding out it wasn't true – all on super-strength Yellow Sunshine acid. Before the guitars gently ease in upon the haunted riff, George intones his litany: 'Mother Earth is pregnant for the third time/For y'all have knocked her up/I have tasted the maggots in the minds of the universe and I was not offended/For I knew I had to rise above it all, or drown in my own *shit*...'

"It really is a cosmic song," said George. "When we first did it, the whole band played on it but I just didn't use anything but him and the other guitars. All I had to do was tell him to think of something sad. He said, 'Oh man, motherfuck this, why don't you think of something sad?' So I was suggesting any stupid thing that was totally horrible. Well, he was feelin' it now."

When mixing, Clinton left the first take's tour-de-force guitar reverie unencumbered by the rhythm section, who can be heard trying to sketch a loose groove in that version, which was included on the Ace reissue. "I had four baby junkies; they decided to go to sleep right there on the session," he recalled. "So I had to make a record out of whatever I got … But the rest of the band sounded like shit! So I faded they ass right the fuck out and just let Eddie play by hisself the whole fuckin' track."

Eddie played his solo in a pentatonic minor scale in the key of E, putting it through a fuzz box and Cry Baby wah-wah pedal, glazed with dub-style delay. The late Garry Shider wells up with tears on the *One Nation Under A Groove* documentary as he declared 'Maggot Brain' to be "the sound of a brother crying his soul out. Maggot Brain is a state of mind … to get you out of a heroin mood, OK? The way I understand it, George put Eddie in the middle of a whole bunch of amps; just surrounded him with amps and said 'Play'.

"Billy and Tawl came out with the chords that night. Those chords are minors against majors. They said you couldn't do that but they proved it all wrong. So I just sat there and got hypnotised into this. Eddie just had to sing to hisself on guitar."

"I was listening to Funkadelic for as long as I can remember," recalled future P-Funk guitarist Dewayne 'Blackbyrd' McKnight, in *An Oral History*. "'Maggot Brain' fucked me up. It was emotion – the sounds that Eddie was making, and the way he was playing the notes that he played. I don't know where he was at the time he was doing it, but damn! That's what I think got me – just emotion-wise. I don't think I had heard a song like that with, like no drums, no bass, and playing like that. When I figured out the song as far as notes, I discovered then that some of the phrases Eddie was playing were really quite uncommon. He was playing some different stuff."

After his early death in 1992, Eddie Hazel was made for posthumous icon status, his super-cool image and stratospheric guitar flights placing him only a few steps to the side of his hero, and above any other guitar warriors since. Like Hendrix, Eddie operated in his own sphere of playing, the lightning bolts of liquid virtuosity pouring from his fingers glistening with inner pain and turmoil, like a luminous cry from his soul. I'm lucky to be old enough to have seen Hendrix (at the Royal Albert Hall in February 1969). For this 14-year-old fan, his presence and charisma were overpowering and his playing still unlike anybody I've seen since, inspiring previously unencountered inner tingles and soaring sensations as every note hit home. As has been subsequently revealed, Eddie was capable of invoking similar spiritual shock, awe and beauty.

"Eddie was a really funny guy, always laughing," future bandmate Jerome 'Bigfoot' Brailey told me. "He was real sensitive. He would just break down and start crying for no reason. He was just a cool guy. He could just play the guitar. He wasn't ego'd out about playing. He was really soulful. They didn't even use him a lot on the singing but he had a killer voice." George couldn't get Eddie to sing anyway "'cause he start crying all the time. He was one of those real serious emotional dudes." Asked about Eddie in 1994, George simply said, "Mr Maggot Brain. His music will be here forever. His was a ball of sensitivity. He just felt everything. He'll be here for a long time."

The rest of the album raised the bar for Funkadelic's lysergic black rock onslaughts but also introduced new subtleties along with key new band members. Also released as a single, 'Can You Get To That' marks the P-Funk debut of Garry Shider, singing on this rework of the Parliaments' 'What You Been Growing'. Born in Plainfield on July 24, 1953, Garry was the barbershop kid who first met George at the age of seven, having sneaked out of church to have his hair waved. Now he was old enough to join the band, having nearly ended up with a career in gospel, singing behind the likes of Shirley Caesar and the Mighty Clouds Of Joy by the age of 10. "We had the family band at the church, and we went around to other churches to perform. In fact, we were going to make gospel records before I got into rock'n'roll, got into this funk stuff. My father was finished with me. I blew the whole shot!" In truth, Garry had never been the same after hearing the Parliaments practising in the barbershop. He simply grew up and into Funkadelic, after first playing in US Soul with best buddy Cordell 'Boogie' Mosson, later becoming George's high-profile right-hand man and band leader. Garry also had no problem later taking up the oversized diaper mantle (originally sported by Tawl Ross), earning his 'Diaper Man' title.

'Can You Get To That' was the gentlest that Funkadelic have sounded so far; gorgeous gospel-flavoured doo-wop soul with lyrics which change the original version's break-up song to a realisation that love, co-operation and karma are the way to rise above negative elements.

Amid the album's bombast, it glistens with Tawl's featherlight acoustic guitar, deep piano resonance and a tour de force vocal arrangement that sees the boys joined by Pat and Diane Lewis and Rose Williams on the verses and interplaying harmonies on the choruses. All this is rounded off with Sting Ray's doo-wop bass exclamations and his solo verse, 'When you base your life on credit and your loving days are done/ Checks you sign with love and kisses come back signed 'Insufficient funds'.' It was an early outing for the kind of gospel-flavoured unison vocals which would characterise many P-Funk songs and, notably, the spin-off girl-group, Parlet.

By now, Bernie was co-producing and arranging, injecting Funkadelic's often sprawling bombast with light, shade and melody, while never detracting from the funk any more than turning the overheating amps down. In the volatile atmosphere of the studio before the split, Bernie became a target for dissent from the younger members when they weren't fighting among themselves, often stepping in between the vociferously complaining Billy and older Parliaments. "I had to be the moderator, 'cause the Parliaments were older," explained Bernie. "I'm in the middle. That shit was funny."

Gary also guests on 'Hit it Or Quit It', a raging, organ-charged blues-burner sung by Bernie with a scintillating jazz organ solo and Eddie spontaneously combusting near the end. The song had already been released as a single by Bobby Freeman on Westbound's Eastbound subsidiary. The track would also become a Funkadelic seven-inch, flipped with a churning instrumental called 'Whole Lot Of BS'. 'You And Your Folks, Me And My Folks' has been described as a sequel to 'Hit It Or Quit It', appealing to the poor to hang together, otherwise they'll never find equality. The chorus resembles an old folk rhyme first published in Thomas W. Talley's *Negro Folk Rhymes (Wise Or Otherwise)* (1922), the first substantive collection of African-American secular song. From the start, George appropriated old songs and rhymes for his own patchwork constructions, which could effortlessly straddle field hollers, nursery rhymes and spirituals in the same track. Even at his furthest out, he hung on to the original roots of black music.

Eddie also rears up on the ferocious proto-metal grind of 'Super

133

Stupid'. The song's lyrics (which he sings) concern an addict who buys the wrong drug to feed his habit. The lyrics are based on one of the exploits which earned him the nickname 'Maggot Brain', 'Super Stupid bought a nickel bag, thought it was coke but it was skag' referred to a show in Boston where Eddie, who was striking out blind with no contacts, went out to score bugle and obliviously returned with a bag of smack, which he chopped out and snorted.

Fuzzy's 'Back In Our Minds', sung by George and Tawl, boasted stand-up comedian and P-Funk warm-up man James W Jackson on jew's-harp, McKinley Jackson on trombone, and the rhythms of Eddie 'Bongo' Brown, whipping up a sleazy New Orleans shuffle (which the Stones were absorbing into their own 'Lovin' Cup' around this time). The 10-minute 'Wars Of Armageddon' closes the album with George's intoned comments on the psychic investment in war, including such declarations as, "The cathetic mum ruffians of madness continue to hasten total biological Armageddon for the benefit of consumerism' and 'more power to the people' (along with 'more power to the pussy, more power to the Peter'). The listener is plunged into a sound effects-milking collage of voodoo drums, sirens, mooing cows, hippo flatulence, screams, orgasms, electronic wobbling and Eddie's demented guitar. This most extreme example of Funkadelic's experimental side has been called their 'Revolution Number 9' after the Beatles' surreal *White Album* collage.

Maggot Brain sported apocalyptic sleeve notes from the Process Church Of The Final Judgement religious sect, whose preachings would grace the next few P-Funk albums. George was an avid reader of books on UFOs and mysteries like the Bermuda Triangle. Many of these were passed on to him by Ron Scribner (who George remembers attending Funkadelic gigs), who liked to wear a long white robe and introduced him to the cult. "They wore robes and big crosses and stuff. Being white, they looked really strange in all the places we went." At first, the more spaced out in attendance thought that Jesus had arrived and started apologising profusely for their sins.

Started by Robert and Mary Anne DeGrimston in the mid-sixties as a Scientology splinter group, the Process Church was controversial at the time, but grew into a global concern. Its first headquarters were in an abandoned salt mine in Yucatan, Mexico, before they settled in New Orleans. By the early seventies, they had centres in Detroit and Toronto. Homing in on people's emotional triggers and insecurities using Scientology's E-Meter, they believed in ironing out mental traumas to bring out the individual's subconscious goals and assimilate them into the group with a sense of calm and extended family camaraderie. (Later the E-Meter was replaced with the P-Scope, I kid you not.)

If that sounds quite harmless, the cult was accused of being a 'black-caped, black-garbed, death worshipping church' made up of the 'mindless snuffed', who believed they were visionaries warning of the coming apocalypse. It was a cult of contradictions, black-clad members sporting bling consisting of conflicting silver crosses and the Goat of Mendes as they worshipped both Christ and Satan (which prompted misunderstandings that they were a Satanic cult). They believed Satan would reconcile with Christ and the pair would come together to judge humanity at the end of the world, the former to execute Christ's judgement. In their initial manifesto, the Process Church recognised Jehovah, Lucifer and Satan as the three great gods of the universe. Jehovah was the only recognised God, bringing retribution, demanding discipline, dedication and ruthlessness in duty, purity and self-denial (!). Lucifer urged followers to enjoy life, value success, be kind and loving and live in peace with one another. The Church believed that man's self-centred qualities had brought Lucifer into disrepute, wrongly identified with Satan, who dealt with both the highest spiritual peaks and lowest levels of human behaviour, such as violence and gross over-indulgence. In between man and the three great Gods swarmed an entire hierarchy of lesser gods, super beings, angels, demons, watchers and guides. The Process believed that all these patterns existed within everyone, but their main doctrine was the unity between God and Satan, opposites who, when united, would bring together Jehovah and Lucifer.

"In the conversations I had with George regarding the Process, there was never any grand plan that I can recall," reveals Ron Scribner. "He saw those as things that related to him. They were in the same space in his mind as taking sayings and taking principles and putting them into music."

In other words, these mysterious writings were just another element for George to play with, while also elevating the group further above normal black outfits. Believe it or not, some seriously believed for years that the Church was an invention because of the Process in the name – just George referencing his day job at the barbershop? – until closer study revealed it to be something that might have been considered a bit risky if he had taken it more seriously.

George admits that the huge quantities of acid being ingested at the time meant that they were goofing a lot of the time, diffusing any hint at being pretentious with surreal mirth. But what George and the gang found hysterically funny drove devout P-Funkers across the globe into research, speculation and even conspiracy theories.

"I guess we really did get loony and didn't know it," admits George. "I wasn't no guru 'cause I'm still trying to get some pussy. I don't want nobody taking me seriously like I ain't... But I ain't no fool either. I knew we made a big step. We came out of the ghetto, where you got to watch your back about everything. Now here I'm gonna take something that ain't got no reality to hold onto whatsoever, but it felt good. It was a permanent smile on my face. I don't regret that. I don't regret nothing I did, if I did it. I try to find out what's the best lesson I can learn from it. I look at anything like that; what is it trying to tell me? And if it's something that's hurtin', I usually find out about it before it has a chance to hurt bad."

Shortly after *Maggot Brain* was released, the heroin George protested about during its recording overtook acid and cocaine as drug of choice for the younger band members, as paranoia and semi-comatose inertia replaced their initial exuberance.

Tawl Ross departed in horrific circumstances in 1971 after participating over-zealously in a group drug-guzzling game involving Yellow Sunshine acid and pure methedrine. Billy recounted to Rob Bowman how the band used to play these dare games with drugs. That night in London, Ontario, he recalls George, Grady and Fuzzy taking about three tabs of acid each, while Tawl took at least six. While Fuzzy and Grady spat theirs out Tawl snorted line after line of methedrine. "When the acid set in, he just started going wild with it. He was hallucinating so bad that I could see the hallucinations. I could see him sitting in the hotel room talking to his mother who had been dead for at least seven or eight years. I had a little acid in myself so I could actually see what he was seeing. I could actually see him leaning over a coffin talking to his mother and his mother leaning out of the coffin talking back to him... When we got to that gig Tawl was totally out of it and he stayed that way." An extreme casualty of the P-Funk lifestyle, Tawl was not to be heard of again until 1995.

Tawl was initially replaced by Memphis guitarist Harold Beane, who'd been playing with Isaac Hayes. By this time, the live show had turned into a two-hour funk orgy, many of the group still spinning on acid, whipping both themselves and the rabid crowds into sweat-steaming trances of continuous groove momentum as the set built to its screaming climax. Funkadelic's reputation was quickly spreading on a word-of-mouth level, faithful crowds in clubs such as Boston's Sugar Shack now looking and behaving like the band. "Everybody in there was dressed like Funkadelic," recalled Sidney Barnes. "Oh, they rocked that joint. They had people getting naked in the Sugar Shack. When an act like George, which was so different, got to a place that was full of people that just accepted their differentness, they went all out. And when they went all out, it was like a good fuck. They made the club grunt."

"The Parliafunkadelic methane has brought you... you," says George at the conclusion of the outrageous gig captured on Ace Records' 1996 CD *Funkadelic – Live – Meadowbrook, Rochester, Michigan – 12th September 1971*. It's just after *Maggot Brain*, and the band have bust the leash, heading off into the stratosphere as a thundering rock-funk juggernaut. Armen Boladian decided to record the show for a possible live album, without telling the band, then shelved the project, leaving the tape with engineer Ed Wolfram until 1996, when it ended up on the mighty Ace label.

The recording shows the structure of the sets at that time (and is a pretty fair representation of what they'd hit the UK with a few months earlier). That night marked the debut of Tyrone Lampkin, the former Apollo house band drummer who impressed George and Bernie when his band Gutbucket supported Funkadelic at a gig in Connecticut. He had only joined the week before with no rehearsal.

"Tyrone Lampkin and I were like two peas in a pod, because he had schooling," said Bernie. "He'd do rudiments, big band style, all his rudiments. Jazz. He was a trained musician – classical training in the drum corps, which is very demanding and precise. Plus he has the God-given natural thing, plus he had the ability to be able to mix his beats into the funk thing. Him and Billy Cobham was the only two doing that, the way they were playing those drums."

"Tyrone was like a lead drummer," asserted Garry. Tyrone stayed for years, assuming a major role, but was still finding his feet this night, going out of sync occasionally and prodding the short-fused Billy to walk off.

After the mega-riff bombast of the opening 'Alice In My Fantasies' (then a new, untitled instrumental), they're into 'Maggot Brain', Eddie shattering vertebrae as he sets off on his solo, taking his time until liftoff occurs around five minutes into this version, the band rising to the occasion as he rips emotional torrents out of his guitar, like his own answer to Hendrix's 'Machine Gun'. He is astonishing here; his control of deep feedback near the end is simply beyond these realms. Bernie sculpts a sublime keyboard solo under Eddie's sobbing wah-wah, both joined at the song's soul, their instruments colliding like lovers before ripping their own hearts out.

'I Call My Baby Pussy' starts as a fast version, which has to be aborted by George when Tyrone spirals out of control, before levelling into the elongated slow-burn sex groove which would appear on the next Funkadelic album.

Calvin handles the slow-burning new version of the old Parliaments single 'All Your Goodies Are Gone', which goes on for 15 minutes, simmering gospel harmonies adding to the old-time ghostly atmosphere with organ and flash-flood breakdowns. It's the Parliaments' old doo-wop teleported to the church at the end of the universe and supremely effective (especially given that the song's original message was to a fallen woman who done him wrong).

"If [the musicians] are feeling a certain way on a certain day then that's the way it's gonna come out," explained Calvin Simon. "Basically, that's what Funkadelic is to me: what you feel and that. That's the way it comes out on record. Sometimes it was really good. Sometimes it was real bad but at least you had an opportunity to do it."

'I'll Bet You' and 'You And Your Folks...' don't break for applause, just flow in a druggy funk-trance with chants and exhortations from George ('I'm as high as a motherfucker', he gleefully confesses). By the closing jam around 'Free Your Mind ... And Your Ass Will Follow' they're like a runaway train, Fuzzy screaming and preaching next to Calvin's gospel tones while Eddie and Billy spark off each other like there's no one else in the room.

By early 1971, George, Eddie, Billy, Tiki and Bernie had returned to play on Ruth Copeland's second album, *I Am What I Am*. Jeffrey Bowen still believed in his wife's talent and, after the *Self Portrait/Osmium* interaction, Ruth was still well within the P-Funk gravity.

The album displayed a harder, gospel-blues feel than her debut, as the savage Funkadelic acid-rock sound charges anti-war tear-up 'The Medal' and the stoned soul hump of George co-write 'Don't You Wish You Had (What You Had When You Had It)', complete with stellar skydiving Hazel solo. Co-written with Eddie, 'Suburban Family Lament' is a sublime slice of molten funk, driven by Tiki's deft beats and Eddie's languid guitar hump, over which Ruth screams and wails her heart out. Bravely, she deconstructs and amps up two Stones songs: 'Play With Fire' turned into a sinister, spaced-out incantation for eight minutes before they plug into the ominous malevolence of 'Gimme Shelter', boosted by Ruth's apocalyptic performance and Eddie turning in another blinder. It's a treat to experience the original Funkadelic let loose on the Stones. 'Crying Has Made Me Stronger' is possibly Ruth's finest moment of all as she lets rip on a soaring gospel blues that was also co-written with George. The album's first single was yet another George co-write called 'Hare Krishna'.

Funkadelic also backed Ruth at her live shows. There was some rivalry between Bowen and George, which would have made this

139

something of a power play with the Funkadelics as pawns. During a big convention-centre date supporting Sly & the Family Stone in Chicago, Ruth got three encores, introducing Funkadelic on the third before they came out and rocked the house down before Sly's set. Sly then told Ruth she would have to find another band or another gig.

In 1972, she contributed to the self-titled debut album by McKinley Jackson's the Politicians, co-writing opening track, 'Psycha-Soula-Funkadelic'. She split with Bowen in 1972, disappearing before resurfacing on RCA in 1976 with third album, *Take Me To Baltimore*, but it didn't sell. Ruth Copeland then vanished, never to be seen again, but can be safe in the knowledge she made a brief, but memorable, contribution to the evolution of the P-Funk.

Ruth's album would have been one of the last times the original Funkadelic line-up recorded together in the studio. Now that hard drugs were top of several members' shopping lists, tempers were highly combustible. This was particularly true of the outspoken Billy, who argued that since the younger Funkadelic were attracting many of the fans, the rhythm section should make at least equal wages as the Parliaments singers. He also demanded the back pay owed to the band, but gave up when George gave him his marching orders in the form of awarding Bernie his position of the band's musical director. "When I got to the point where they considered me a troublemaker, George's way of letting me know it was time for me to go was by making Bernie the bandleader," recalled Billy. He was supported by Eddie, who was also sinking into addiction.

George was torn because Billy, Eddie and Tiki were like his own kids; to the point where Billy's mother had given him legal guardianship as a proviso if they took him on the road. George's admonishments to the unruly element must have sometimes resembled parent-style discipline, but the kids still sidestepped from acid to smack. Famously trying to avoid confrontation, George once responded by refusing to pay them their money because, "They would only use it for dope".

"The Parliaments were getting paid more than us," reasoned Billy. "But they didn't care, especially Bernie. And Tiki, as long as he got enough money to get high. Pretty much the same with Eddie. It's a motherfuckin' shame. The main reason why shit turned out the way it did – messin' with drugs. It was a top fucking priority, man."

After walking out, Billy and Eddie ended up in Los Angeles working with Invictus acts such as Chairmen Of The Board. After the guitarist returned to George, Billy ended up working for 10 years with his band the Love Machine.

The Funkadelic bassist's position was now vacant but Cordell Mosson was waiting in the wings and ructions in James Brown's band were about to send over a larger-than-life bass-wielding Funkateer who would play an invaluable part in booting the P-Funk into its predestined orbit.

Chapter Seven

America Eats Its Young

"I didn't know what the fuck I was doing but I had a feeling that it would work. All I did was incorporate all the different places that I worked at. I threw everything together from Motown, the fifties and the doo-wop thing, the sixties with 'The Lion Sleeps Tonight', the Tokens, the Chiffons, Phil Spector and his vibe of compounding voices onto a wall of sound. I took all the different things and threw the shit all together."

George Clinton

One June afternoon in 1989, George Clinton is sitting on a couch in a little office somewhere in the concrete labyrinth of the Warner Brothers building in New York's Rockefeller Center.

A mass of rainbow hair extensions and giggling, he is in buoyant mood after the previous night's three-hour funk-affirming P-Funk All Stars marathon at the Palladium on 14th Street. In fact, George could have walked straight off the stage as he attacks the refreshments he's brought along with gusto and expounds on The Funk, prodded by the priceless pile of P-Funk albums I've thrust in front of him. Like any seasoned professional I've interviewed, from Keith Richards to Captain Beefheart, George is in his element when expounding before an obviously obsessed fan who happens to be writing a story about him. Today it's a walk down memory lane for a special P-Funk edition of Tommy Boy mogul Tom Silverman's monthly tip-sheet *Dance Music Report*, George getting increasingly animated as the snorting and smoking goes on.

The only time the ebullient mood he has been displaying all afternoon visibly darkens is when he picks *America Eats Its Young* out of my pile. If an album such as *Free Your Mind...* has elicited fond acid-related reminiscences, 1972's epic double album casts him back to a particularly dark period in America's history, when the increasingly grotesque Vietnam War was making its presence felt on the streets in the form of irrevocably damaged returning veterans. They might have survived the war but now had to face life back in the real world, often addicted to heroin and minus a limb or two. The government didn't seem to give a shit, especially for its black servicemen.

"Yes, this is what that's about," exhaled George. "No-one wanted to talk about it back then. Even the vets didn't want anything to do with it. People don't understand what to survive is.

"The Vietnam War was happening when I made that album. It was about the heroin in Vietnam. That whole war was about heroin. The Golden Triangle... But this album also reminds me of what's happening *now!*" George bangs the table so hard the Columbian mountain he's scaling nearly flies off the coffee table.

The Golden Triangle straddling the mountains of Myanmar, Laos and Thailand has been one of the world's main opium-producing regions since the twenties. It was supplying most of the world's heroin at the time of the Vietnam War, including to the US via CIA agents, it has since been revealed. As the fighting in Vietnam continued and the situation became increasingly desperate, many US soldiers switched from the marijuana prevalent at the time to easily available heroin; anything to anaesthetise the unimaginable daily horror.

By 1972, with barely a third of Americans believing the US had not made a mistake sending troops to Vietnam, peace protests were sweeping the US while the troops themselves were getting increasingly disillusioned or out of control. By the seventies, although the military was being withdrawn due to overwhelming public outcry and the obvious pointlessness of the whole exercise, the conflict had spiralled into a mess of war crimes and horrific slaughter; a whole generation seemingly drafted to surefire death, madness, mutilation or addiction. Direct US involvement would end in August 1973 with the passing of the Case-Church Amendment by US Congress, while the capture of Saigon by the North Vietnamese Army in 1975 marked the end of the war as North and South Vietnam prepared to unify after all, at a cost of 58,200 US service members' lives.

In addition to dividing the original Funkadelic, heroin had increased its hold in the inner-city black neighbourhoods. It's now known that black troops were routinely sent on the most hazardous missions in Vietnam. Those who managed to come out alive often bore deep mental scars which manifested in various ways as they found it hard, often impossible, to settle back into normal life. Abandoned by the country they'd served, they'd come home addicted to face another kind of dangerous jungle as they were tossed aside and forgotten. The cities were teaming with dispossessed vets who had lost jobs, homes and marriages, now addicted and hustling on the streets or begging to survive. Some could only show their stumps for change. Talking to vets on my downtown New York travels in the eighties – often inevitable if you sat in a dive bar for longer than 10 minutes – these guys felt harshly treated by the government. When sneering cops carried out their nightly sweeps, addicted veterans were thrown in the holding cell next to the street junkies and small-time dealers.

That day I met George I had just come out of three years immersed in that same epidemic while living in New York's Alphabet City. Every day consisted of traversing the blocks around Avenue B, waiting for the proverbial man and, if triumphant, negotiating the wire fence and piles of rubble before reaching the shooting gallery in an abandoned building on Second Street and Avenue B.

There, I met a cross section of local junkies, from Puerto Rican hookers and ancient bag ladies to young black guys, some of whom had returned from Southeast Asia nursing their habits. At the time I was writing for a Canadian magazine and did a Christmas With The Homeless piece based on the day-to-day scoring and survival rituals

144

and hours spent hanging out with this cross section of forgotten city life. Many of the junkies were quick-witted and intelligent, but had just been dealt bad breaks.

I particularly remember a quiet, articulate black man in his thirties called Al, who made his dope money selling clean syringes in the shooting gallery 'foyer'. He would tell me how he believed the ghettos had been flooded with smack since Vietnam's heyday as a way of keeping the people down, dazed and controllable. Earlier that decade, crack had barged in like a crazy man at a slumber party but pre-gentrification New York in the eighties was still awash with homeless people looking for a fix. Quiet, hollow-eyed and haunted-looking, the vets weren't hard to spot. One called himself 'Miami' because he hailed from the city of that name. He was one of the few who scared me and one of the only ones who eventually ripped me off. Al told me Miami had been to Vietnam as the latter never mentioned it. He was clearly disturbed and I'd be surprised if he was still around now.

The mood always lightened whenever the corner missions had been a success and those assembled started talking about music. Hip-hop hadn't really infiltrated here but they perked up when someone spotted the latest George-related album I'd unearthed on the street and my P-Funk obsession came up, talking about how they'd grown up with this music. A lovely Spanish hooker called Lucy had seen the Mothership land when she was a teenager. It was in their blood. The way Al and the regulars bantered and howled about their P-Funk experiences was like a more animated version of white guys sitting in the pub talking about the Stones, except here they were cooking up spoons rather than downing points of beer. I thought about them when I was sitting with George that afternoon, having managed to escape that life when I started the Tommy Boy job. Most of them wouldn't be so lucky.

"I missed the war just 'cause I was a little older than everybody else," George recalled. "I knew a lot of people that went to Vietnam, that died as soon as they got there. But they convinced us black people that it was the best alternative that you had. All my friends had the choice of going to war or going to jail. Every time you'd do something wrong, 'Why don't you go join the army?' the teacher would suggest to you. And they thought they was doing you a favour. All the kids we were playing to they was all running away from home to avoid the war, or little girls were running away because their boyfriend was getting ready to get drafted. I didn't really pay attention before that. And then we began to realise that the CIA was actually starting these wars. They were the ones getting us in trouble."

Although *Maggot Brain* was George's first overtly anti-Vietnam War broadside, the often misunderstood and even under-appreciated *America Eats Its Young* was his grand statement on how the conflict and other elements were afflicting his country. George commented on this appalling situation in his own way, starting with the title and gatefold sleeve, which he designed with Ron Scribner to replicate a one dollar bill (emphasis on the One). Instead of laurel branches and arrows, the eagle in the Great Seal is gripping a hypodermic syringe and emaciated child while, in the middle, the Statue of Liberty is standing with evil bloodshot eyes and vampire fangs sinking into one of the babies she's cradling, one missing half its skull and the brain. This was another George trait that was starting to emerge; a liking for adapting and respraying immortal American symbols and traditions to fit the concept he was brewing at the time. In this case, he was holding up America's invincible dollar and defacing it to convey his message of money, war, heroin and death. The title is easy, Vietnam having swallowed up a whole generation of Americans.

Although the sleeve proclaimed, "This album is dedicated to all the young of THE WORLD!", the Process Church blurb offered another oblique slab of the kind of manifesto that would be abandoned by the next Funkadelic album. This particular rant, about 'the agony and conflict of America' explains the album's title with a pessimistic tint as it declares 'America eats its young – maybe. But America is also our child, as now how we all have made it... America reflects to us what we have come to. The state of America is our state.' It concludes 'The only way is to love our enemies!' Seventeen years after the album first appeared, George can't resist drawing atomic dogs on the cover. Kathy Abel's lyric book insert unveiled the Funkadelic logo they still use today.

Couched in George's most ambitiously epic production to befit the socially conscious themes bristling among the love ditties and reworks, Funkadelic's most sprawling and densely populated album could only be a double in the grand tradition of the Stones' *Exile On Main Street*, released in May the same year. I've always placed it among the great double albums, such as that murky basement masterpiece, Dylan's *Blonde On Blonde* and Jimi's *Electric Ladyland,* which all simply needed the extra vinyl to accommodate the gush of songs recorded. Of course, many used the format to indulge whims they felt their audience couldn't live without, such as Pink Floyd's *Ummagumma,* but George steered the steaming hydra of *America Eats Its Young* into a brilliantly complete entity which now stands as one of his mightiest achievements and most potent statements.

The album was also an attempt to hit the mainstream, replacing the acid-fried landscapes of previous records with structured songs embracing the sense of concept inspired by the Who's 1969 rock opera *Tommy*, even nodding to the labyrinthine arrangements of progressive rock. With his old-school soul background, George knew Funkadelic had the chops to bust out of the lysergic undergrowth and clean up with more direct material, rather than the acid lunacy of the first three albums, which were constructed out of jams which had been gestating on stage.

To pull off such a massive work George decided to lay off the acid, still looking quite pleased with himself when he told me, "That album was really a test to see if I could do it straight after all that acid. All the ones before that I did on acid. I wanted to see if I could make any kind of sense! The songs have got horrible names but they're pretty straight. I did that album straight. I mean, as much as I *could* do it and prove to myself that I could control myself. The sixties was over, so I tried to regroup and see if I could write an album of songs that was chronological."

Four years on from its release, George was still full of admiration for the Beatles' *Sgt Pepper's Lonely Hearts Club Band*, which had now been joined by *Tommy* at the top of his works to aspire to. Pete Townshend's double set telling the story of the deaf, dumb and blind boy even influenced George's Mothership visions. With both these albums, it wasn't so much the individual songs but the scope opened up in threading them around each other. The acid period was now officially done with and from now on George's albums would carry some kind of loose concept.

It's interesting that George has regularly cited bands as unlikely as Jethro Tull as influences at a time when black music was going through a major purple patch of landmark albums and anthemic singles. During the time he was working on *America...*, 1971 saw such milestones as Marvin Gaye's era-reflecting *What's Going On* (inspired by his brother Frankie coming back from Vietnam and Malcolm X's autobiography), answered by the cracked genius of Sly Stone's chart-busting masterpiece *There's A Riot Goin' On*, the southern soul seduction of Al Green's *Let's Stay Together*, the Staple Singers' 'Respect Yourself', Undisputed Truth's 'Smiling Faces Sometimes' and the O'Jays' 'Backstabbers'. In 1972, Stevie Wonder continued his coming of age metamorphosis with *Music Of My Mind* and *Talking Book*, while George's old boss Berry Gordy started the short-lived Black Forum offshoot to release speeches made by the likes of Dr King, Stokely Carmichael and Amiri Baraka's fierce black nationalism poetry. But George was now firmly on his own path in his own laboratory, believing that, rather than try to outdo Motown's new socially conscious music, he could strike into the heart of the massive white market.

"We felt that the early shit was over, the cool 'dos, and the hippie thing was done, with sheets and things," he explained. "So we went right on to *America Eats Its Young*. That's when we started saying, 'OK, let's see if we got any brain cells left.' Black was still popular but if you're gonna do something you got to do it better than the black groups *and* better than the white groups. And *Tommy* and *Sgt Pepper's*, to me, was the classiest two pieces of music that I had ever seen where everything related to each other. So I wanted to do one of those kind of things."

The album's multi-hued complexity still polarises opinions, some finding it indulgent or impenetrable, while others call it the transitional step from the acid storms of the original band and the golden run of

Funkadelic albums ahead. *America Eats its Young* was almost two years in the making at studios including Manta Studios in Toronto, Artie Fields in Detroit, Master Kraft in Memphis and London's Olympic. The now studio-savvy George took full production duties, using endless reels of tape until he got the desired result as tracks were built up – often using whatever the musicians were throwing in – then arranged by Bernie and George. There's said to be a warehouse stacked with reels of out-takes, jams and sketches from the sessions which spawned *America Eats Its Young*, some of which later went through myriad changes and stylistic alterations before their perfectionist creator deemed them fit for release. Despite sometimes being wrought into strange and wonderful shapes, classic song forms harking back to doo-wop, Motown and soul proliferate, while the blazing funk-rock is, if anything, tempered with the British rock influence that George had embraced. With Bernie, he had someone who could take that element and work it into the ongoing Funkadelic creative process.

As the first album recorded without recently departed original core members Eddie, Billy, Tiki and Tawl, *America...* is another example of George snatching victory from a potentially desperate situation as Funkadelic didn't exist as a physical band when recording commenced. With George, Bernie, the sole surviving Funkadelic, and Calvin Simon relocated to Toronto, recording started in earnest at the city's Manta studios, where George had done a deal while it was still being fitted out and not yet open to the public.

As befitting an epic, the album not only featured the proverbial cast of thousands but it also saw the gestation of a new Funkadelic nucleus including Bernie, Garry Shider, Cordell Mosson and Tyrone Lampkin, who were joined by the likes of drummer Zachary Frazier, guitarist Harold Beane, steel guitarist Ollie Strong, James Jackson (on 'juice harp') and a full-blown string orchestra. The Toronto sessions also featured session titan Prakash John, who'd go on to become an essential part of Lou Reed's albums and touring bands.

America Eats Its Young was barbershop kids Garry Shider and Cordell Mosson's rite of passage into Funkadelic or, as the former put it, "I don't know what happened, but when that album was finished, I was in the group." Somehow George had gained his devoted lifelong lieutenant along with his killer bassist bandmate Cordell 'Boogie' Mosson, along the way creating a great lost chapter in P-Funk history.

Although he had sung 'Can You Get To That' on *Maggot Brain* by overdubbing his vocals in New York, the 18-year-old Garry had yet to commit to full-time P-duties. He had already joined United Soul, a Plainfield-based outfit formed in 1968 which included Tawl Ross, brothers Cordell and Larry Mosson, Peggie Turner, 'Slim' Edwards and drummer Harvey McGee, which became the first signing to George's new talent stable – Parliafunkadelicment Thang Inc – marking the start of the P-Funk empire.

While envisioning them in his band, George also wanted to remove Garry and Cordell from the heroin epidemic crippling or killing so many local teenagers, and which had already gripped some of the band. In an act of funk intervention, he sent them to Canada, away from temptation.

"Everybody in the town damn near shot dope," recalls George. "It was deeper than New York. Thirteen and 14 years old… It was a scholastic town; it wasn't Newark. But somehow, prior to '59, somebody had come through there with real dope. I didn't really know nothing but about reefer, and I had just got that myself. *The Man With The Golden Arm* cured me of ever thinking about heroin being recreation. Even with all the acid and stuff we were taking, heroin or angel dust never appealed to me at all. I did my share of coke. But with all of it, I never got to the point – other than acid. I would've taken acid forever if I could've but it stopped working after a while. You just be up all night."

United Soul recorded tracks for what should have been their Westbound debut album with Bernie, Fuzzy and Sting Ray handling production, plus other musicians who were around pitching in. First they planned to release a single of 'Baby I Owe You Something Good' – originally written for singer Frankie Boyce and recorded by the Parliaments in 1967, coupled with Fuzzy's 'I Miss My Baby'. The single was credited to 'U.S. Music with Funkadelic', already suggesting some assimilation into that band, rather than them being presented as a stand-alone act. This was borne out when the 45 never made it past promo status and no album followed despite it reaching the track-listing and mastering stage, although no test pressings have ever turned up.

Ace's miraculous 2009 reissue reveals it as one of the hidden gems in the vast P-Funk archive. Garry sings throughout the five tracks, his voice bearing the rich hallmarks of his gospel background as he reaches the highest peaks before swooping down through his soulful range. 'This Broken Heart' is a yearning cover of a 1959 doo-wop single by New Jersey vocal group the Sonics, complete with a romantic spoken interlude and drenched in strings, celestial backing girls and crashing proto-prog dynamics. The track wasn't wasted, as an edited version popped up on 1973's *Cosmic Slop*. Then it's their energised gospel-rockabilly rework of 'Baby I Owe You Something Good', Funkadelic's new drummer Tyrone Lampkin laying down hi-octane rhythms, while Toronto vocal duo Doctor Music supply church-wailing backing vocals. The song would finally find a home when it was reworked again for 1975's *Let's Take It To The Stage*. Side One was set to end with the metallic funk hiss of deeply resonant individuality anthem 'Be What You Is'.

Side Two kicks off with Fuzzy's 'I Miss My Baby', his gorgeous soul ballad about a situation going on with the mother of his child. The backing track was recorded in Toronto while Garry's impassioned vocal and the Debonaires' Telma Hopkins and Joyce Vincent's lush chorale were overdubbed in Detroit. Somewhat short, the projected album would have closed with a booming sleaze-monster called 'Rat Kiss The Cat On The Navel', which fizzes with jagged acid-funk and sinister nursery rhyme-flavoured vocals that could have sat comfortably on the previous three Funkadelic albums. I'd bet my luminous P-Funk cod-piece that's Eddie scything and screaming through its smashed, blocked funk vamp.

United Soul split after recording the album, leaving Cordell and Garry to join Funkadelic. Garry eventually became musical director, guitarist and the Star Child, earning the nickname 'Diaper Man' after taking to the stage in an over-sized nappy. Despite cutting his musical teeth backing gospel stars, he seemed destined for the P-Funk life, his strong, soulful voice propelling many P-songs heavenwards over the next 40 years. Cordell, or 'Boogie' as he was popularly known, joined with less fanfare than the approaching Bootsy but appeared on as many tracks, taking over live after the latter went solo, anchoring countless classic tracks with his naturally fluid feel. Sadly, Boogie passed away while I was writing this book in April 2013.

With two invaluable new recruits in the Funkadelic engine room, George was able to concentrate on the job in hand. Without the acid, his brain hovered like a sharp-eyed hawk over his beleaguered country, swooping on suitable subjects to turn into songs, while a couple of old ones were remade and remodelled to fit into the new concept. *America...* shows him acknowledging what he'd done and experimenting with what he would do next. George's lyrics took on a more social, environmental and political edge, toughening up his version of the hippie ideology that drove the 'free your mind' ethos using ghetto nursery rhymes to comment on the virulent heroin situation.

1972 saw James Brown release 'King Heroin', his serious and well-intended smack sermon over the backing track of 'It's A Man's World'. Next to that, George manages to sound both silly-fried and super hip over the relentless metronome guitar chug that powered one of Funkadelic's most merciless grooves. 'Loose Booty' was slang for a smackhead, referring to the bowel-relaxing properties of withdrawal or easy nature of fix-obsessed females. George and Harold Beane wrote the song, which was recorded in different styles, including a 10-minute tryout version that includes George referencing Dave and Ansell Collins' 'Double Barrel' by declaring "I am the magnificent".

George now hits like a ghetto Bob Dylan in the way he can use oblique surrealism to cloak biting socio-political barbs and reach across racial and gender lines. Black Panthers Bobby Seale and Huey Newton held up Dylan's 'Ballad Of A Thin Man' as the song which most got to the heart of black oppression. Newton identified Dylan's "geeks" as poor blacks and his "freak" as the white guy who passes by, watching the hell of ghetto life as if it was entertainment but now called to confront the conditions he created.

On this album, George was carrying a message and what he described as 'logic' in his funk, as evident on beautifully constructed outings such as his and Garry's 'If You Don't Like The Effects, Don't Produce The Cause' – an environmental whammy laying into hypocrites who blather about change but don't take any action, or 'Biological Speculation', whose ecology-with-a-twist lyrics concern man's relationship to nature and the manner in which it will eventually resolve oppression. Co-credited to Ernie Harris, co-owner of the barbershop, the track started life at Olympic, ending up veering between choral soul and a form of country, thanks to Garry's rustic guitar picking and David Van de Pitte's pedal steel flourishes. These echoed the cosmic country then imbuing the Stones at the time through Gram Parsons.

Van de Pitte was also responsible for the silken strings and steel guitar arrangements that seem beamed in from another age on the title track, 'Everybody Is Going To Make It This Time', as well as across 'If You Don't Like The Effects...' and the gooey ballad, 'We Hurt Too'. During the late sixties and early seventies David was behind the arrangements on Motown sparklers by the likes of the Temptations (including 'Ball Of Confusion' and 'Psychedelic Shack'), Marvin Gaye (*What's Going On*), the Four Tops, Jackson 5 and Stevie Wonder.

Meanwhile, Bernie contributes sublime string arrangements to 'A Joyful Process', 'Wake Up' and 'Miss Lucifer's Love', Fuzzy's histrionic vocal showcase where he professes his love for the woman in the title (not necessarily Satan as some have suggested). "She just wants to satisfy" goes the chant and that can only be Eddie's guitar keening over everything like an incandescent ghost.

It's been said that the album acted as a kind of testing ground for George to experiment with different styles to see what worked. 'You Hit The Nail On The Head' coins a genre best described as prog-funk, opening with a torrent of convoluted rhythm and Bernie's raging, Keith Emerson-style organ dropping into sitcom-theme breeziness, as the lyrics work on both personal and political levels before another complex future-funk mutant enters the fray. 'Balance' also piles on thick organ riffing and abrupt time changes recalling nobody so much as Brit-prog outfit Van Der Graaf Generator's epic melodrama *Pawn Hearts*, shot with Motor City madness on the mid-song blow-out and topped with busy Bootsy vocal. It's another ecological 'logic track', asking nature to explain how she intends to get the balance right between oppressed and oppressor. Started in London, the song now stands as a seminal black rock prototype.

Steering back to the essence, there's also a bona fide P-Funk classic with Bernie's 'A Joyful Process', which takes Sunday-school favourite 'Jesus Loves Me' into a diamond-hard groove propelled by his snarling clavinet topped with starburst horns and the kind of melodic strings favoured by Chic a few years later. Subsequently issued as a single, the track made the R&B Top 40.

The album featured two reworks: the lovelorn but jaunty Motown throwback 'That Was My Girl' – the 1965 Parliaments song co-written with Sidney Barnes that still spills into a sliding, skidding organ jam at the end. Then there's the new bedroom version of 'I Call My Baby Pussycat', my unashamed, even guilty favourite on the album. Its stealth-groove dynamics are a masterclass in pin-drop precision as it detonates into screaming climaxes that, again, can only be another holdover from Eddie. A live favourite, the song dates back to *Osmium* as 'I Call My Baby Pussycat', co-written by Billy and Eddie. After its scrabbling intro, the track settles into the slinkiest of groin-friendly undertows for Fuzzy's priapic, hog-breathed vocal, the sultry chorale cooing 'I call my baby pussy, P-U-S-S-Y' as he professes his barely containable lust. Beneath the dubbed-out sex fog, the sound references barbershop doo-wop, while lines like 'I'm the tomcat and you're my lil ol' pussy' and 'Wild and warm is my pussy' hark back to R&B's tradition of innuendo. The twist is that he's butt-clenchingly powerless against the unwanted power of this particular pussy.

The heaving stealth groove then abruptly whips off its jockeys and piles into the album's title track. On the original vinyl, this gave the impression Fuzzy and his pussycat had fallen into a mass orgy – going by the writhing carpet of ecstatic moans and shivers accentuated by Eddie's translucent guitar flickers and Van De Pitte's sweet strings. Then comes George's barely decipherable basso monologue declaring that America is 'a bitch' that 'sucks the brains' of her 'great grandsons and daughters', like he's translating the album's sleeve. The moans of pleasure seem to turn into racked sobs. Coming after the lascivious

'Pussy' it makes for one of the most underappreciated sequences of genius in all P-Funkdom.

With their languid salacious swoon and slow-crawling bedroom tempo, tracks like these or the Van de Pitte string outings could be seen as George's answer to Isaac Hayes' symphonic epics which had introduced a sexy new sophistication into black music with 1969's *Hot Buttered Soul*. The former Stax Records backroom dynamo's silky stretched-out treatments of modern popular classics might be considered the polar opposite of George's non-stop nasty funk orgy, but both men were tapping into different strains of inner-city blues remedies: Ike the seductive bedroom Goliath with a vulnerable soul and heavy charisma, whereas George let out the craziness and corner talk while making commenting on the world fun and funky.

The story behind 'Everybody Is Going To Make It This Time' is a tad confusing. Sources including the usually reliable *Motherpage* state that the track was recorded in London in 1968 with Cream drummer Ginger Baker, who George always cited as a favourite. This is unlikely, as George's first trip to London and its Olympic studios was during the 1971 UK tour. The song is uproariously widescreen, anthemic and drenched in torrential positivism offset with an undercurrent of desperate realism, bolstered by Van De Pitte's strings and Bernie's sepulchral organ. Calvin Simon turns in a blinder, declaring that mankind has the potential to grow and change for the better but at the moment it is heading full-tilt into empty-souled consumerism, referencing the album sleeve on the line 'Our country and our cities, they have been betrayed for money'. The soul revue-style vamp of 'Philmore' is the first major P-Funk showing from William 'Bootsy' Collins and his older brother Phelps (aka 'Catfish'), who'd come straight from the James Brown band. Bootsy brought his own brand of spaced-out street cool to the crew. Whereas Eddie seemed to possess a direct line to Hendrix's soul-generated emotional flow, Bootsy flamboyantly mated Jimi's sensual looseness with Funkadelic craziness, soon absorbing both into his star-shaded persona as funkiest bassist on the planet.

Bootsy was born on October 26, 1951 in Cincinnati, Ohio, while Catfish was born in 1944 (so named because Bootsy thought he looked like a fish). As his family moved around the city, Bootsy always managed to hang with the coolest street gangs, reasoning, "I always managed to get in the street gang that was considered the baddest. I told lots of jokes, and for some reason, the females found me pretty attractive, so the fellas thought it was a good investment to keep me around."

With Catfish established as one of the most fearsome guitarists in Cincinnati, Bootsy taught himself bass so he could play in his band the Pacemakers, who also included drummer Frank 'Frankie Kash' Waddy. Playing nights and weekends, the band would meet after school at the King Records studios, mainly working with producer Henry Glover. By late 1968, the Pacemakers were backing the likes of Bill Doggett, Marva Whitney, Bobby Byrd and Hank Ballard, whose touring band they joined on the road in the James Brown Revue. Bootsy first met Brown while doing a Doggett session the Godfather was producing on a track called 'Honky Tonk Popcorn'. This led to Bootsy, Catfish and Kash doing more King sessions, adding trumpeter Clayton 'Chicken' Gunnells and tenor saxophonist Robert McCullough.

In March 1970, after firing his existing band a few hours before show time, the Pacemakers provided Brown with a quick replacement – Bobby Byrd flying the wide-eyed group to the gig in Augusta, Georgia that same night. Stepping out on to the biggest stage they'd ever been on in front of the largest crowd they'd ever seen, all the gigs playing J.B. songs behind imitators paid off and they acquitted themselves in startling fashion, careering through the hits in a frightened mid-stage huddle. Brown was delighted enough to pay them $450 each, hire them on the spot and provide new equipment and the requisite uniforms. After a few weeks deliberation, which saw him reject names including Blackenizers, New Dapps and New Breed, Brown decided to call his new band the J.B.'s.

The new J.B.'s stripped down and honed Brown's sound into taut, pulsing funk, rarely doing more than two takes as they were soon working seven days a week either in the studio or on the road. The first song they recorded (under the impression they were rehearsing) was a single called 'The Grunt', followed by another instrumental called 'These Are The J.B.'s' then the monumental 'Get Up (I Feel Like Being

A Sex Machine' that July. The pumping bomb which turned loose early seventies funk was the most graphic embodiment of sexual heat the world had seen, reaching number two in the R&B chart and 15 nationally.

"Me and Catfish came up with that groove on 'Sex Machine'," says Bootsy. People ask me how come I didn't get paid for things like that back in the day, but we wasn't thinking about our names being on the record as writers because we didn't even know nothing about that. We were just so excited that we were actually playing with James Brown... I couldn't wait to get home to tell my friends I just cut a record with James Brown." Other hits they appeared on included 'Brother Rapp', 'Talkin' Loud And Sayin' Nothing', 'Soul Power', 'Get Up, Get Into It, Get Involved', 'Super Bad' (going to number one on the R&B chart and 13 on the pop listings), 'In The Jungle Groove' and 'Give It Up Or Turn It Loose'.

"What James Brown meant to me was total bliss," states Bootsy. "I had never ever seen a black man take care of that much business and have fun at the same time. This cat was so bad at the time; he produced his own records, had his own picture on them, had his own promotion men. These were things I didn't understand, but I realised later how on-it this man was."

Fred Wesley was installed by Brown that December to control the new bloods, who had rapidly got on the good foot with nightly lysergic assistance. Bootsy was now stepping out to play "lead on bass to make things a little more entertaining" – which worked two ways for Brown by driving crowds wild but taking the spotlight off Mr Dynamite. "It was really difficult [for me] to take over as leader because Bootsy was clearly leader of the majority of the band," explains Fred. "Also, the young guys in the Bootsy band didn't give Mr Brown the respect the old guys did. They were, for the most part, footloose and fancy free and had nothing to lose if they lost favour with the man. These wild and crazy guys were not the job-dependent, family-orientated people J.B. was used to having under his control. There was nothing he could threaten them with. They didn't care. Mr Brown exercised his control as well as he could by manipulating the money and the individual egos.

These guys were not going for the mental bullshit. They were very close for the main part and saw through Mr Brown's efforts to divide and conquer.

"In fact, they had become bored with the gig and were looking for something else to do. Bootsy and his brother Catfish were on the verge of leaving when I arrived, and I really do believe curiosity about me kept them staying as long as they ended up staying."

Frankie Kash likened playing with Brown to "partying with your father. We loved him, we respected him, we cherished what we got from dealing with James Brown, but we was a little bit too wild for him. He used to incorporate a fining system into his show, in his dance. And he did that to us one time, he fined Catfish, something Catfish did. And when James looked back, we were all laughing so hard until he never did that again… And he used to ask us, 'Man, you cats, all the time you're grinnin'… What you takin'?' We were takin' acid and all that shit!"

Bootsy, Phelps and Kash left after the March 1972 European tour, feeling restricted by the discipline and demands (also after a particularly strong acid trip convinced Bootsy that his bass had turned into a snake after he broke all the strings, which didn't go down a storm with the Godfather). On returning to Cincinnati, Bootsy formed the House Guests with Phelps, Waddy, 'Chicken', Rufus Allen, Ronnie Greenaway and Robert McCullough, plus Spinners singer Philippe Wynne. They released two singles on their self-titled label – 'What So Never The Dance' (a minor hit) and 'My Mind Set Me Free Parts 1 & 2'.

The House Guests moved to Detroit in 1972, turning down joining the Spinners when Philippe became their second lead vocalist. The group stayed with singer and band promoter Mallia Franklin, whose sister was shacked up with George. Something of a key figure in George's Detroit days, Mallia became known as the Queen of Funk, George referring to her as a 'Funk scout' when she included him in her local networking. Mallia sang on P-Funk albums of the time, including Parlet. Married to Nathaniel Neblett of New Birth, she introduced George to Bootsy, and also to Junie Morrison in 1978.

Living up to their name the House Guests spent a few months staying at Mallia's place. She booked them into Detroit's Soul Expression club, where they played from nine in the evening until six in the morning, although George first encountered Bootsy while sharing a bill on a show promoted by her manager, Dick Scott, in Toledo, Ohio. "Bootsy was backing up a singer called Gloria Taylor, who had a large R&B hit ['You Got To Pay The Price']," recalls Mallia. "I saw this bass player with some hot pants on and some lace body-stockings. And he had a tambourine taped on his foot and he was keeping the beat, and never lost it. I said, 'Damn! George needs to see him'. Because they were dressed so funky and Sly Stone-ish."

George was impressed, remembering, "[Mallia] brought everyone around. I saw Bootsy and I said, 'Wow, I didn't know we had an extra man in the band'. He already looked like one of P-Funk. When it was time for us to grow a little more he was one of the first people I called. First Bootsy played with us, then his brother Catfish, then the whole House Guests … They had just left James and they came with us. I already knew the Ohio Players, who I knew Bootsy was real close with. Mallia brought him around and it didn't take long to figure out who he was."

Fred Wesley maintains that "George connected with Bootsy because he had been affiliated with James. Even though it was a short affiliation, that's why George wanted some of that. It all comes from wanting to have a piece of James Brown."

"Bootsy had a perfect personality," said George. "He had magnetism no matter what he was doing, whether it was serious funk or silly love songs."

Brown had taught Bootsy the principles of the One, the foundation on which the funk is built, which puts the emphasis on the first downbeat. "The One started at the James Brown school of funk," explained Bootsy. "He used to tell me, 'You're playing a lot of things all around the One but you're not playing the One… Play the One then play that other stuff' … So James made us more aware of the One and dynamics, which Funkadelic had never experienced before. We didn't have to be totally wasted to make you feel us."

★

The first time I met Bootsy and encountered his engaging mix of unearthly funk charisma and silly mischief up close was in June 1990, amid the old school New York ambience of the Gramercy Park Hotel's piano bar, which had been a haven for artists for decades. He was everything a long-time P-Funker could have hoped for, draped over a chair in his star shades, face lit up by that ever-present grin, also rising accommodatingly to being confronted by a weird-looking British devotee hurling trivial questions. As with George, to be sitting in a bar chatting and laughing with someone I'd worshipped from afar for years was pretty surreal. That he turned out to be so articulate, friendly and sparklingly intelligent didn't take away from the Bootzilla mystique but did establish him as one of the most genuine figures I have interviewed in over 40 years of doing this.

Maybe Bootsy sensed I wasn't about to stitch him up but, after the warm-up phase of the interview, started opening up about the darker times and when he left P-Funk's chaotic orbit, almost like he was telling someone this for the first time, or even just trying to get it clear in his head. As he willingly submitted to the same gruelling album-signing process I'd put George through the previous year, he talked about his time before P-Funk with the Godfather, and leaping from Brown's tight regime to Funkadelic's cosmic crazy gang. "Oh man… some of the craziest stuff happened with George, as opposed to James. James' thing was the way of living straight up and be on time thing while George's thing went against all odds. I was just in the middle of it. Here's James; one extreme. Here's George, the other extreme. It was like, 'OK, here you are, right in the middle. To me, that was a good place to be."

From sharp suits to space costumes. Bootsy grins. "It was good because I always wanted to do those [wild] things. Do what you wanna do and be yourself. You're not tied down or anything, but when I was with James, I wanted to do that too, because I wanted to be in both sides of it. I wanted to be in uniform. I wanted to do the routine; 'Look like we all together'. I wanted that at that time. And then as time moved on I was growing into another thing because the acid came out, the trips and peace and love start happening. It was like, 'Oh man', and bands started moving from the back to the front of the stage. And we got caught in that. We stopped wanting to play behind people. We wanted to be on the front of the stage, and, when I hooked up with George, that's what happened. It was like, 'Oh man, this is the place to be!' It was like when they say there's a thin man in a fat man's body waiting to get out; just waiting to get out, man! George didn't have no restrictions. It was like, 'Whatever funky, you bring it, just come on with it. There it is, give it up.' When I seen what happened, I couldn't believe it. Oh God, there's no morals behind this guy with this, you know what I'm saying? So we just took it on.

"Funkadelic was crazy, meaning it was looser. You had room to do stuff. James' thing was, 'OK, if we had a certain line we stayed on that line'. If we had a move, we stayed on that move. Funkadelic you could take that line and stretch it. You could take that line and add fuzz. You could have aeroplanes on your record. James' thing was strictly the groove. One groove and one groove only. That's what I did; I took the groove that I got with James and I took that to P-Funk. George already had the craziness going. It was all about. All we needed was that serious groove. I feel that was my contribution, bringing over that groove with Fred Wesley and Maceo. They added that horns thang. That's what radio started taking note of, when they could tap their feet a little bit to it because, aside from me, they didn't know what the heck was going on. It was just being born then because George and me was collaborating on this stuff, mixing our chemistries together and it just started to work it.

"George would give me the freedom in the studio I never could have got with James. With James, it was like, 'You don't play this, you play bass'. I was already understanding all of that then. I already knew that I wasn't gonna be there for too long. I knew that I was there for a reason and I knew I was picking up, and I was learning. Just the idea of being with James was so incredible and I knew I had to go through that phase, but I wasn't looking at it like themselves with it. It was perfect timing, but I didn't have anything to do with it. I was just in the right place at the right time, I guess. And the same thing happened with George and myself. I just happened to be in the right pace at the right time. Even if I hadn't worked with James or George there was so much going on back

161

then. I was going to be someone with somebody doing something, but I guess it just happened that these were the guys I was relating to in the back of my head when I didn't know."

Although he sang on 'Balance' and played bass on 'Loose Booty', the self-composed 'Philmore' was Bootsy's only major contribution to *America Eats Its Young,* but that was enough to open the door. Bootsy and Catfish joined the Funkadelic touring band for a while before returning to Cincinnati, still with the ambition to lead their own group. Bootsy describes taking part in *America Eats Its Yo*ung as "an awakening for me. That whole first trip, it was like, 'Wow, this is so cool. This is what we've been waiting to do'. They were crazy times."

Chapter Eight

Standing On The Verge Of Getting It On

"Verily, those soulfulifically jaded swashbucklers of agitproptic burnbabydom – FUNKADELIC – have descended from the original Galaxy Ghetto to cleanse they wayward souls THROUGH MUSIC worthy of the immortals themselves."

Pedro Bell, *Cosmic Slop*

We found ourselves getting off on people getting scared.

Bootsy Collins

Never mind the rock operas which influenced *America Eats Its Young*, maybe Funkadelic could have made a major impact sooner if they'd found the right Blaxploitation movie to feature in. By 1973, these films had become the biggest phenomena to hit the cinemas that decade and the Funk Mob seemed to be living in a drama of their own making on account of all the comings and goings within the camp.

1973 also saw the start of the surreal graphic P-Funk mythos when Funkadelic hit on its famous in-house visual side through the revelatory work of artist Pedro Bell, who almost single-handedly carved a whole legend in felt-tip pen across the mutant ghetto-scapes of those renowned album covers.

Raging all the way through the feet-finding years of Funkadelic and then Parliament in the first part of the seventies, Blaxploitation films were now a major element in ghetto life, a new manifestation of the black power which had arisen out of civil rights militancy to inspire roots research and acknowledgement of African-American history and culture. This new form of pride was loudly declared through ongoing musical innovations in jazz and soul, as commentators such as Gil Scott-Heron (initially inspired by the stark Harlem poetry of the Last Poets), was firing out eloquently scathing indictments such as 'The Revolution Will Not Be Televised', 'The Get Out Of The Ghetto Blues' and 'Whitey On The Moon'.

Although the idealism of the previous decade had been trussed and muted by law, the transitional sixties had paved the way for integration and set wheels in motion which would change US politics forever. Meanwhile, Black Power's attitude and imagery morphed into a new style, in many ways similar to the one being pursued by George. Black was now beautiful, unity between "brothers" and "sisters" mushroomed on the streets, while fashion statements such as Afros, flamboyant threads and hefty bling adorned the new loud, proud audience.

Now the revolution *would* be televised, as the latest dos, outfits and dance crazes were flaunted every week on the all-powerful *Soul Train*, while *The Flip Wilson Show* heralded a new era in TV entertainment with its skits on ghetto life. *The Mod Squad*'s street-wise undercover cops presented white America with the sort of characters that would dominate Blaxploitation movies as black actors and actresses were cast as heroes in places they might not usually be seen. This was not lost on George.

Ghetto life was now being shown to the world in the movies and music, its residents noisily identifying with the cool, powerful heroes who could be good or (often preferably) baaad, as in pimps, hustlers and dealers. Many aspired to the glamorous lifestyles, whooping at the pink Cadillacs with leopard-skin trimmings roaring through the tenements in this self-contained world where the white guys inevitably came out as bumbling, racist honkies. Predictably, characters with stereotypical Blaxploitation traits started showing up everywhere from Bond films (1973's *Live And Let Die*) to New York cop dramas like *Kojak*, but the biggest evidence of their influence came later when characters and screenplays were reincarnated in gangsta rap and infiltrated music videos. The rise of Blaxploitation films also coincided with funk becoming a universal language.

It has been harrumphed that the term Blaxploitation was derogatory; the films dismissed as exploitative cartoons pushing superfly stereotypes. Predictably, cash-ins came fast and sometimes dreadful as Hollywood tried to reclaim audiences from TV and attract black crowds to downtown theatres abandoned in escalating white flight. The crucial point was that, after decades of secondary cliché parts, these films marked the first time black actors had taken romanticised lead roles. Having sat in an uproarious eighties New York Blaxploitation crowd amid the similar kind of unbridled enthusiasm to that which I saw greet George at Harlem Apollo, it was obvious that black audiences hadn't tired of this elevation in cinematic status, cheering on their heroes in the way white audiences had more sedately fawned over James Bond since the early sixties. Many characters were exaggerated and saddled with traditional Hollywood blueprints for detective, horror, kung fu and western movies. Despite this, black characters led the plot and the 'hoods were the setting rather than a token trip into the danger zone. Years of oppression and suppression were being symbolically overcome on the big screen.

Rarely has a cinematic genre translated so comfortably and distinctively into its musical counterpart. Black music went widescreen, soundtracks becoming classics in their own right. The way that the worst film could have the coolest soundtrack opened another avenue in the entertainment industry, exposing millions to black sounds as its musicians found well-paid work scoring the action. Blaxploitation gave invaluable breaks to Earth, Wind & Fire, Roy Ayers and Willie Hutch, and spawned landmark albums for Isaac Hayes, Curtis Mayfield, James Brown, Marvin Gaye and many more. Gushing out until disco took over, these soundtracks were crowding the second-hand bins by the following decade, but subsequently inspired much fevered crate–digging after the sampling revolution found them as fertile a source for hip-hop's breaks and beats as the P-Funk.

Apart from Booker T & The MGs' cool music for 1968's *Uptight*, the Blaxploitation soundtrack breakthrough came via Melvin Van Peebles' score played by an unknown Kool And The Gang for his 1971 independent venture *Sweet Sweetback's Baadasssss Song*. Dedicated to all the 'Brothers and Sisters who've had enough of The Man,' this is the one credited with starting it all, independently written, produced, scored, directed and starring its financier, Melvin Van Peebles. The story concerns a black male prostitute on the run after saving a Black Panther from racist cops, helped by the ghetto community. Required Panther viewing, it struck a chord and became a phenomenon in grossing 15 million dollars.

Van Peebles attacked the score with similar flair, bringing in the fledgling Earth, Wind & Fire through the recommendation of his secretary, who was dating one of the band. The soundtrack was released before the movie to generate publicity because Peebles had no money for advertising. Awash with vibrant funk instrumentals, the collage-like set mixes field hollers, dialogue and abstract dissonance, complementing a film made through one man's will and stubborn determination.

The film paved the way for *Shaft* and *Super Fly* to start the black gold rush. Produced by Gordon Parks with a $500,000 budget, *Shaft* saw the charismatic Richard Roundtree swagger, shag and shoot through his title role as a private detective rescuing the daughter of a Harlem gangster from the Italian mob. The film was critically well-received and grossed 13 million dollars. From Charles Pitts' immortal wah–wah intro, Isaac Hayes' title track is an architectural soul genius realised by the Bar-Keys, and made him the first African-American to win an Oscar for a non–acting role. The rest of the score traverses the essential mood pieces and 25 funk mantra 'Do Your Thing'. It became Stax's biggest-selling album, opening the floodgates for soundtracks like the film did for movies.

Although Hayes' career had been going beautifully up until then, the film cemented his status as defiantly chrome-domed figurehead.

He had originally agreed to take on scoring *Shaft* if he could audition for the lead role. This never happened, but he got to make his movie debut three years later in action-packed bank-heist blaster *Three Tough Guys*, swiftly followed by playing a besieged bounty hunter in *Truck Turner*, supplying dynamic soundtracks for both, notably the latter's epic 'Pursuit Of The Pimpmobile'.

1972's *Super Fly* was created on a shoestring by (son of *Shaft* director) Gordon Parks Junior, producer Sig Shore, and screenwriter Phillip Fenty. Played by Ron O'Neal, Youngblood Priest was the first of the genre's flamboyant hero villains. His character was based on a real coke dealer's stories that included the customary last big score before retiring from 'the life'. With a $300,000 budget (some raised from real pimps and pushers, with location power drawn from hotwired streetlights), a key factor was Buddah president Neil Bogart enlisting Curtis Mayfield for the soundtrack. Buddah distributed his Curtom imprint, which was one of the first labels owned by an African-American recording artist.

While in the process of leaving the Impressions, Curtis had released his eponymous first solo album in September 1970, displaying funk and psychedelic flavours as he tackled political and social issues on tracks such as the ominous race relations warning '(Don't Worry) If There's A Hell Below, We're All Going To Go' and 'We The People Who Are Darker Than Blue', while creating a new soul anthem in 'Move On Up'. He followed it with 1971's *Curtis/Live* and *Roots* sets before arriving at *Super Fly* the following year. Although he had been a star by his teens with the Impressions, Curtis knew life on the other side of town, hailing from Chicago's notorious Cabrini-Green projects. Already a beacon of black pride since capturing the civil rights mood with 'People Get Ready' and 'We're A Winner', he agreed to record the soundtrack for no upfront fee – going through the script scene by scene to catch each track's essence, drawing inspiration from his old 'hood. Recording at RCA's Chicago studio with his well-drilled band, he produced more music than asked for, resulting in the finished movie being cut to the soundtrack (predating music videos). Topped by that angel-breathed force of nature of a voice, the soundtrack is staggering in its breadth and had an era-defining influence, staying at number one for five weeks and selling over two million copies.

The album's sublime exercise in liquid funk storytelling has been called 'the black *Sgt Pepper*' on account of its era-capturing breadth, including the sublimely insidious title track, junkie laments, romantic instrumentals and hectic car chase. Unusually, Bogart released 'Freddie's Dead' as a single six weeks before the movie opened to packed houses in the autumn of 1972. The following year's *Superfly TNT*, directed by O'Neal with screenwriter Alex Haley, was less successful, soundtracked by Funkadelic's old touring friends Osibisa.

Curtis recorded more soundtracks: 1974's *Three The Hard Way* (starring screen giants Jim Brown, Fred Williamson and Jim Kelly joining forces as an unstoppable sleaze-fighting trio). The film's all-vocal backing featured his old group the Impressions on Temptations-esque outings such as 'Something's Mighty, Mighty Wrong'. Others included *Let's Do it Again* (the combination of Mayfield's songs and mighty Staple Singers predictably marvellous), *Claudine* with Gladys Knight & the Pips (a moving urban tale starring Diahann Carroll as an under pressure welfare mom in a Harlem slum) and *Sparkle* for Aretha Franklin. In 1977, he would team up with Mavis Staples for *A Piece of The Action*, which featured instrumentals that strayed onto P-Funk turf.

Before these films, black crime novels by the likes of Iceberg Slim, Donald Goines and Chester Himes were the outside world's only glimpse into the lives and locations portrayed in Blaxploitation movies. The authors wrote from experience, Slim being a reformed hustler who started by publishing his autobiography, *Pimp,* in 1967. Detroit's Donald Goines was another former pimp, trying to escape jail by feverishly churning out brutal street novels such as *Dopefiend* in the early seventies to support the heroin habit he picked up during the Korean War after lying about his age to join the Air Force. His Kenyatta character led a Panthers-style organisation dedicated to cleaning up the ghetto.

Chester Himes had been writing short stories and novels since getting out of jail in the thirties, and was considered by many to be the equal of crime specialist Raymond Chandler. He was a major influence on George's favoured novelist Ishmael Reed, who said that Himes "taught me the difference between a black detective and Sherlock Holmes". Based on one of Himes' Harlem novels centred around hard-boiled black detectives Coffin Ed Johnson and Gravedigger Jones (which he wrote between 1957–69), *Cotton Comes To Harlem* was directed by Ossie Davis a year before *Sweet Sweetback's*. The story concerned a dodgy preacher and dollar-stuffed cotton bale going missing uptown. Galt MacDermot's sprightly funk soundtrack forged a blueprint that countless others would subsequently follow.

1974's *Willie Dynamite* is considered a genre classic, largely on account of its intelligently conceived morality tale concerning the rise and fall of super-pimp Willie 'Dynamite' Short, as he rebels against a union proposed by the camp and sinister pimp-in-chief, Bell. The understated urban funk score was written by jazz veteran J.J. Johnson, with Martha Reeves singing director Gilbert Moses' words on the theme song, while 'Gospel Family' sees Mothers Of Invention keyboardist Ian Underwood dueting with jazz veteran Pete Jolly. Roscoe Orman, who went on to front *Sesame Street*, takes the prize for the most outrageously attired pimp in all of Blaxploitation, and could well have helped provide a visual plan for Dr Funkenstein's upcoming splendour.

1973's *Gordon's War* reflected the post-Vietnam fallout that also inspired George around this time. Paul Winfield plays a soldier back from the battlefront to find his Harlem neighbourhood blighted by smack and his wife dead from an overdose, so he rounds up his ex-army homeboys to clean it up in a far-fetched but rip-roaring rampage. For reflecting the despair of the streets, it ranks with the best. Even the poster, with the hero stomping a giant heroin needle, is a killer. The thrillingly nasty soundtrack was supplied by a cooking band called Badder Than Evil, while Barbara Mason sings the film's central ballad, 'Child Of Tomorrow'.

Along less serious, more P-friendly lines, came oddball novelty outings such as 1972's *Blacula*, a low-tech horror foray concerning an African prince bitten by the Count at a Transylvanian house party two centuries earlier who awakes to run amok in modern LA as Drac's soul brother. It became one of the biggest-grossing movies of 1972, spawning further horrors such as *Blackenstein* and *Dr Black and Mr Hyde*.

A new breed of strong, foxy black women appeared after *Coffy* ("They call her Coffy and she'll cream you"), which stars Pam Grier as a nurse whose dope-addicted sister gets stricken by contaminated smack, prompting a vigilante revenge rampage which leaves a trail of dead dealers, pimps and mobsters. Roy Ayers turns in a smooth jazz-funk score with members of Ubiquity. The film established Pam Grier as the archetypal queen of Blaxploitation, consolidated by 1975's *Foxy Brown*, which sees her avenging her boyfriend's death at the hands of a drug syndicate, leaving a trail of bodies and castrating one particularly hapless villain. Singer/songwriter Willie Hutch created a taut and funky score stoked by the pioneering use of drum machines, later repeating his triumph with the soundtrack to *The Mack*. Vying for Pam's crown, *Cleopatra Jones* starred Tamara Dobson as a flamboyantly Afro'd undercover agent bringing down evil lesbian drug baroness Shelley Winters.

Although George had his hands full during this period reshaping Parliament and Funkadelic, his funk inspiration James Brown leapt aboard the Blaxploitation bandwagon. Starring Fred Williamson, 1973's *Black Caesar* remade the 1931 gangster movie *Little Caesar*, following Tommy Gibbs' violent life from Harlem childhood to facing the mob and racist cops. The same year's *Slaughter's Big Rip-Off* saw Jim Brown reprising his role as a Vietnam veteran up against the mob. James Brown was between *Get On The Good Foot* and *The Payback* so on top of his game. Working closely with Fred Wesley and Charles Bobbitt, his two soundtracks didn't have to depart from his signature sound, boasting outings such as 'Down And Out In New York City', 'Brother Rap' and Lynn Collins' 'Mama Feelgood'. He was going to score its sequel, *Hell Up In Harlem,* but instead the tracks ultimately became *The Payback*, leaving Edwin Starr to lend his raw tones to a crack session band including guitarist Dennis Coffey, bassist Chuck Rainey and Crusaders keyboardist Joe Sample, with the resulting album released on Motown.

Marvin Gaye's soundtrack venture came with 1972's *Trouble Man* in which Robert Hooks stars as supercool South Central private dick/ pool hustler, Mr T. His conflict with local kingpin Big is enhanced by Gaye's lustrous soundtrack recorded in LA with various Funk Brothers and members of Hamilton Bohannon's band.

Films with immaculate scores came thick and fast in the first half of the seventies, the most notable (if only for their music) including *Across 110th Street* with Bobby Womack on the evocative theme song and score by veteran jazz trombonist J.J. Johnson; recently emerged walrus lurve king Barry White's tight score for 1974 inner-city gang drama *Together Brothers*; Donald Byrd and the Blackbyrds on blazing jazz-funk form for basketball murder drama *Cornbread, Earl And Me*; Herbie Hancock's cool backdrops for civil rights satire *The Spook That Sat By The Door;* Charles Earland orchestrating street funk with Sun Ra-recalling synth on 1974's *The Dynamite Brothers;* Lloyd 'Stagger Lee' Price singing the theme to *The Legend Of Nigger Charley*, a western that was followed by *The Soul of Nigger Charley* (soundtrack by Lou Rawls). Even George's hero Smokey Robinson clambered on the wagon with the lightweight *Big Time*.

The blackest Blaxploitation got was *Dolemite*, which featured comedian Rudy Ray Moore avoiding white-run directives by baffling them with the fast-talking doublespeak of 'The Toast'. The soundtrack mixed the Soul Rebellion Orchestra's dirty funk with Moore's proto-rap rhyming.

Unsurprisingly, Sun Ra put black people in space a few years before the Mothership: while in Oakland in 1971, he was approached by producer John Coney to make a documentary for PBS. This resulted in *Space Is The Place* – the best encapsulation of his philosophies, humour and music on film. Featuring the Arkestra alongside a cast of actors, it combines elements of Blaxploitation with biblical epic tropes to create one of the era's classic period pieces. Traversing the universe in a spaceship fuelled by music, Ra finds a planet suitable to revive the black race, returning to Earth while battling with mega-pimp the Overseer who, along with the FBI and NASA, sends him back to space after he offers black people an 'alter-destiny'. Production was tortuous and the film heavily edited, sneaking out and disappearing fast but destined to be a cult classic (with two soundtracks).

Apart from illustrating how times were changing regarding what black-related projects could get away with in the outside world and maintaining many musicians' careers, Blaxploitation changed fashions and attitudes on the street, while the soundtracks provided black music with new impetus. All this action fed into the twin-headed monster George was helming now that he'd got the double album out of his system. The Funkadelic and Parliament albums of the seventies were like psychedelic Blaxploitation movies with killer soundtracks covering all the bases of modern urban blues, thrusting sex grinds, full-blown freakouts and mental car chases. George was still taking the ghetto to the stage, led by black heroes and with a fresh new plot.

Released in June, 1973, *Cosmic Slop* ushered in Funkadelic's middle phase golden run after the epic excess of *America Eats Its Young*. Mainly recorded at United Sound, it was George's first stab at being radio-friendly with shorter, tighter songs. For the first time, none exceeded six minutes. The newly streamlined band featured Detroit lead guitarist Ron Bykowski, Funkadelic's first high-profile white member. Bernie knew him from playing in 8th Day, introducing him as a musician renowned for his smouldering, sustained tones. Ron emerged as the perfect foil to Eddie's flights and became the master of the long lunar note, coaxed out of a sizzling guitar no one else could touch. Although not credited, all the Parliaments also sang on the album. "The *Cosmic Slop* album was me, Boogie, Ron Bykowski, Bernie and Tyrone," recalled Garry. "United Sound had this little mike in the control room and we'd be out there cutting a track and George would be in there hollering through the mike like he's onstage, which would give us the hype."

George was seriously on the case, later admitting he now had success on his mind: "When we saw that that sixties thing was over I did *America Eats Its Young* just to show that I could get chronological. I got that out of my system, then it was about: let me do some real neat Funkadelic records. *Cosmic Slop* was the first one we got actual serious airplay on. And it was workin'. Blacks was seriously into it. Black colleges was seriously into the experience now. All that had just passed with the white groups, the blacks had their own version of it by now... We was getting much neater at being psychedelic. And the musicianship... they were able to play it when they wanted to play it, and not play it when they didn't want to play it. Tyrone Lampkin was a real good jazz drummer, and he kept it funky but really tasty."

In the 1989 *P-Funk History* I described *Cosmic Slop* as the taming of the Funkadelic beast, but it was more akin to George attempting to channel the band's ethos into a more digestible form for radio and the masses; realigning the sound with renewed funk quotient, memorable melodies and delicious vocal harmonies while still carrying lyrical or sonic twists in its tackle-bag. Although you couldn't say that to Garry, who was initially unhappy at the new direction: "That's when George and them decided we got to take this crazy stuff and get it played on the radio. I was into the rock stuff, all the nasty stuff. That's what the older Funkadelics, the early heads were really into. By the time it got to *Cosmic Slop* it was like, 'Do you want to make some money at this?' George was ready to make money."

Ironically, Garry rips one of the all-time greatest P-Funk vocal performances from his young soul on the astonishing title track. The bassline which drives the number's coiled-spring stealth-groove is the first thing an unaccredited Bootsy came up with when he joined Funkadelic, originally bolstering another song he was working on, which was opening the live shows. The weird snare tattoo and heat-seeking beat was an early contribution from Tyrone. Garry puts himself in the place of a kid whose impoverished mother is driven to prostitution to feed her five kids. She's trying to keep it a secret along with her dignity but every night they can hear her begging God for forgiveness and understanding of what she's being forced to do to survive in an immoral world. The chorus goes, 'Then the Devil said, "Would you like to dance with me? We're doing the cosmic slop".'

"I don't know where [George] got the lyrics from, or how he came about 'em, but it was almost like he was telling my story," revealed Garry. "There was seven of us, we were in foster homes, and all kinda shit. My mother, I can remember her out hustling to get the cash to feed us. So I could relate to it. Through that song, I learned how to identify with characters – take a lyric and become the character... that was one of the hardest things too, 'cause I remember George saying, 'Think of Curtis Mayfield while singing it. Put yourself in the position, put yourself in his state of mind'. Took me about a week, but I got it."

"The melody is like a spiritual hymn," said co-writer Bernie Worrell. "If you take away the words and just hum it, it sounds like down on the plantation." But 'Cosmic Slop' did nothing when released as a single and was only the second Funkadelic 45 not to chart.

'March To The Witch's Castle' was the anti-war track George had told me about and the album's other major social comment. It remains one of the era's most potent comments on the plight of the returning Vietnam veterans. George references a pointless meeting between them and President Nixon at the White House, while relating the tale of an addicted, mentally ravaged soldier who comes home to find his wife has married someone else, believing that he'd perished in the jungle. America really was like the Witch's Castle for soldiers returning home. The only track recalling Funkadelic's earlier experiments, the band brew up an atmosphere reminiscent of Fleetwood Mac's 1968 UK chart-topping instrumental, 'Albatross', with a mountain-hauling chorale under George's ghostly slowed-down intonations concerning the 'nightmare of readjustment' the veterans were facing on coming home to find they had lost more than just limbs or sanity. It's at odds with the usual P-lunacy, but the track whips up a chilling form of timeless contemporary blues. This wasn't the first time blacks had felt used. Returning from their considerable presence in World War One, black soldiers living in the south could still find themselves facing a lynching. After Vietnam, they were simply swept under the carpet.

The rest of George's concerted stab at a radio-friendly record contains more concise works adorned with freewheeling studio mischief. The lazy, one-dropping lope of 'Nappy Dugout' eases in with a syncopated groove that New Orleans' Meters would have been proud of, stripping the first album's sparse funk template of lysergic flatulence. Perhaps it was inevitable that, sooner or later, someone would bring a duck call to the studio. Speaking as one who knows, the amount of fun to be had with a quack pipe is immeasurable, so it can be said that Funkadelic used theirs as tastefully as possible.

Funkadelic's fearless black rock trailblazing continues on George's proto-metal 'Trash-A-Go-Go' (concerning a guy given a jail stretch for pimping his girlfriend to feed his drug habit despite his pleas of undying love) and 'Let's Make It Last', predating Joan Jett's 'I Love Rock'n'Roll' chord structure, as Garry passionately extols the virtues of long-standing relationships over one-night stands. The song was co-written by Eddie, who sails through the ether with some Jimi-style talking wah-wah.

'No Compute' can still have Clash fans spluttering into their boxsets with its jazzy shuffle blueprint for 'Jimmy Jazz', which would appear on *London Calling* six years later. George's tale of gutter realism finds him waking up horny from a dream, looking for a partner and finding an agreeable lady. Looking at his conquest later ('breath smelling like a 1946 Buick') he feels guilty before realising that he might have pulled a transvestite.

No Funkadelic album would be complete without its remakes and the bouncy reworking of the Parliaments' 'Heart Trouble' into 'You Can't Miss What You Can't Measure' is huge fun as Garry, Sting Ray and George trade lines like they're back in the barbershop with decent microphones. 'This Broken Heart' is the same United Soul cover of the 1959 ballad by the Sonics that provided the group's first single, while 'Can't Stand The Strain' revisits 1968 single 'Whatever Makes My Baby Feel Good' with lead vocals by Garry.

Cosmic Slop planted the nascent P-Funk game plan on the launch pad along with the first taste of its mythology and new look. This was enough to set the album apart from anything else going on in black music at the time and give it 20 weeks on the R&B chart. After the previous LP's gruesome images and Process Church blather, Boladian put pressure on George for a different cover strategy. "People are starting to get the wrong idea about us," agreed George, who brought in young Chicago artist Pedro Bell. Instantly converted after hearing the first album on the radio, he became a 'maggot' (a P-Funk devotee). Garry recalled meeting him at a funk festival for the first time dressed as Darth Vader. Pedro changed the public face and defined the mythology of Funkadelic with his intricate designs. He also constructed P-Funk's literary legend with his wildly surreal notes on urban black life. As George's website attests, his 'stream-of-contagion text rewrote the whole game. He single-handedly defined the P-Funk collective as sci-fi superheroes fighting the ills of the heart, society and the cosmos... As well as Clinton's lyrics, Pedro Bell's crazoid words created the mythos of the band and bonded the audience together.' Creating another parallel Afro-centric mythology along with the Blaxploitation movies, his words and images were vital in creating alternative ways in which black people saw and spoke about themselves in seventies America. The new language he was coining provided George with concepts and phrases he used in the music.

As a child, Pedro learned to draw from his brothers, managing to find a link between Genesis in the Bible, dinosaurs and Godzilla, which led him to science fiction and inventing his first fantasy creature – the Rumpasaurus. He was another that became sucked into Funkadelic's orbit after hearing the first album on the radio, becoming a regular at gigs following a 1971 Chicago appearance. Before long, he was designing their gig flyers and posters while helping George with his make-up on the chitlin' circuit. Pedro had graduated to press kits before George asked him to do the sleeve for *Cosmic Slop*, which he accomplished in three weeks using the title track and pimping as his theme. Using magic markers (!), he came up with the grotesquely disfigured naked lady as his first mutation of black life scenarios, introducing himself as Sir Lleb (Bell backwards) and setting P-Funk's mythos into motion with the kind of words derived from signifying and street slang he would call 'zeep-speak': *For virtual decades of alembic time parsecs, I have gazed upon the so-called highest life form on this planet with unbridled disgust! For the very source of life energies of Earth have become the castrated target of anile bamoozlery from homosapiens' rabid attempts to manipulate the omnipotent Forces of Nature! Their directionless efforts to achieve the metaphysical state of godliness, eons premature to evolutionary destiny have, indeed, become an invitation to species extinction.*

George left Pedro to illustrate each album in any manner that grabbed him after he'd described the idea and played a few tracks. "I'm a writer who happens to be an artist," he insisted. Pedro's distinctive graffiti-predating comic-book style would now illustrate each album's concept, songs and characters, his testimonies becoming much more than simply being something to pore over while the album was playing. Vinyl pressings became works of art as he illustrated more than two dozen albums, from Funkadelic and its spin-offs into George's solo career. He's also been called the forefather of 'The Black Age of Comics'.

"Funkadelia on a two-dimensional surface is about chaos," declared Pedro. "There's either all yin or all yang. And no balance between the two. I figured if the audience could get past some of these comics, maybe some of this stuff will start makin' sense, maybe it won't. I'll at least make it interestin.

"People thought Clinton and I worked in close co-operation in terms of putting the package together. That wasn't the case at all. He rarely saw any projects that were in progress and very few that were finished before they were already out. And none of my liner notes... I was in a hell of a position. I was an artist and art director for an organisation that was ultimately responsible to a record company. I didn't have to take orders, got paid and talked as much smack as I wanted. I had a degree in Funkology day one. I was just a cruise missile lookin' for a place to land. In the late sixties, I was goin' through the black power thing, the drugs, the tart actions. On the music tip, I was seriously into Frank Zappa, Jimi Hendrix and Sun Ra [none of whom, by the way, were particularly popular with blacks at that time]. Blue Cheer was another group I was geared towards. I really had access to both sides of the radio channel... I said, 'Dag! There's something that can be done with the Hendrix thing. Blacks ain't up on that yet but there's goin' to be something to it.'"

While presenting his ghetto retort to peace and love with 'provocative, scan'lous, completely out-the-box' creations, Pedro highlighted and distorted another world based on the philosophy, 'Hey, we're out here in the *ghet-to*, and things ain't like that.' He wanted to create a black version of his hero Frank Zappa's self-packaging and presentation, influenced by the hot rod monster concepts of artist Robert Williams, explaining, "With all those elements happenin' on the music tip and all those other elements on the external tip, the Funkadelic evolutionary thing was just something that was going to happen."

Incredibly, Pedro often had to work as a security guard or postal worker to survive. He was understandably miffed when a message from Kiss about a potentially lucrative album-cover job, which would have helped boost Funkadelic's profile in the white market-place, mysteriously didn't reach him. Even more amazingly, having helped shape the seventies, Pedro was broke and living in poverty when tracked down fighting eviction from a Chicago slum by the city's *Sun-Times* five years ago. Then 59, he was practically blind and receiving dialysis three times a week after severe hypertension damaged his kidneys. He revealed he fell out with George around 1994. "George Clinton gets a lot of credit for the conceptual dimension of P-Funk, but actually Pedro Bell was a big part of that with his texts and imagery," said Pan Wendt, co-curator of a 2009 Toronto gallery exhibition called *Funkaesthetics*, which featured some of the original artwork Pedro kept stored at a friend's house and was then considering selling to private collectors. When news of Pedro's plight got out, those who'd admired him as one of music's most innovative artists of all time got together to play benefits. These included the Black Rock Coalition Orchestra's January 2010 Miracle For A Maggot Funkraiser event in New York, which saw the likes of Bernie Worrell, Vernon Reid, Ronny Drayton, Andre Lassalle, Kelsey Warren, Melvin Gibbs, Luqman Brown and J.T. Lewis jamming on 'Cosmic Slop' and Hendrix's 'Who Knows'.

While 1974 also saw George reconvening Parliament to commence its flight path to the Mothership by scoring a hit with the title track of its comeback album *Up For The Down Stroke*, George and the Funkadelics were practically living at United Sound studios as the groove factory cranked into the conveyor-belt-style action that would be forged into albums over the next few years. Funkadelic was still firing like a blow-torch after breaking into the rich funk strata which birthed *Cosmic Slop*, but their black rock essence was never better encapsulated than on *Standing On The Verge Of Getting It On*, released in early 1974 as possibly the most cohesive album of all under the Funkadelic name. "There is nothing harder to stop than an idea whose time has come to pass. Funkadelic is wot time it is!" wrote Pedro Bell on the cover, providing a future catchphrase for Public Enemy mainstay Flavor Flav.

Despite being produced quickly during a transitional period, the album became a milestone, exploding with monolithic riffs and crowd-boosting chants that remain part of the band's set to this day. Part of its success was down to Eddie Hazel's blistering form, co-writing every track with George (including some under his mother's name, Grace Cook, for publishing rights purposes).

Once again, Pedro demonstrates why he's one of the main reasons I despise downloads and even CDs – his cover based on George's idea for 'some tripped out landscape... some kind of freaked out chariot with folks scrambling around' looking like a cartoon sci-fi Hieronymus Bosch version of the Beatles' *Yellow Submarine* cast into the space ghetto. Band credits are planted under their mini-portraits. George is credited as 'Supreme Maggot Minister of Funkadelia, Vocals, Maniac Froth And Spit; Behaviour Illegal In Several States'. The Parliaments are tagged for the first time with their vocal ranges: tenor Calvin Simon, Ray 'Sting Ray' Davis on 'subterranean bass vocals', 'licensed genie' 'Shady' Grady Thomas and 'A Prototype Werewolf Berserker Octave Vocals' credited to Fuzzy. The singers are joined by Garry's 'doo-wop vocals' and 'sinister grin', 'Space Viking' Bernie, 'World's Only Black Leprechaun' Boogie and the returning Tiki Fulwood, plus Tyrone Lampkin on percussion and 'polyester soul-powered token white devil'. Ron Bykowski is credited with 'stun guitar', while Eddie is 'Smedley Smorganoff'.

Under the heading 'Wet Epic Debauchery', Pedro declares George to be the last man standing out of the big four who also include Hendrix, Sun Ra and Sly: *AS IT IS WRITTEN HENCEFORTH... that on the Eighth Day, the Cosmic Strumpet of MOTHER NATURE was spawned to enclose this Third planet in FUNKACIDAL VIBRATIONS. And she birthed apostles Ra, Hendrix, Stone, and CLINTON to preserve all funkiness of man unto eternity... But! Fraudulent forces of obnoxious JIVATION grew. Sun Ra strobed back to Saturn to await his next Reincarnation, Jimi was forced back into basic atoms; Sly was co-opted into a jester monolith and... only seedling GEORGE remained! As it came to pass, he did indeed begat FUNKADELIC to restore Order Within the Universe. And nourished from the pamgrierian mammaristic melon paps of Mother Nature, the followers of FUNKADELIC multiplied incessantly!*

The title track unleashes the full-bore hippo-on-heat hoedown often

179

credited as the first decisive statement in P-Funk die-casting and a major R&B chart hit when released as a single. It was born out of a chant that went up before the group took the stage, whereupon Fuzzy would ask 'People what you doing?' to be greeted with a rousing 'Standing on the verge of getting it on!' On the album's unedited version, the track starts with George intoning one of his favourite lines, 'Hey lady, won't you be my dog and I'll be your tree … and you can pee on me' before booting into the mass chorale, Garry's rhythm guitar churning beneath Eddie and Ron's twin leads. The lyrics stretch beyond normal party incitement to become the first of several calls for punters to get off their arses and into positive action, as propagated by the likes of Gil Scott-Heron and the Last Poets.

On the single version, it was flipped by George and Eddie's 'Jimmy's Got A Little Bit Of Bitch In Him', George adopting the ironic Zappa narrative style as he talks about the way Jimmy's inner bitch demon is ready to bust out. He based the character on a friend he knew from a local record store in Detroit. "The dude was just finding out *himself*," he recounted to John Corbett. "And so far he was asexual, he hadn't done nothing'. I said, 'Shit, the worst motherfucker is the one who don't do nothing'… We used to joke with him about that. That's funny, he thought we were the lightest ones on him. We said the harshest shit, but he said we were easier on him than his family was." The song was a favourite of Garry's, who explained, "Every Funkadelic album had one outsider song, while with everything else we would try to get on the radio. That was us telling the industry 'Fuck you, we still stuck one in on you'. That's the stuff that kept us going."

'Red Hot Momma' reaffirms the album's status as Funkadelic's rockiest, with a supercharged update of *Osmium*'s remake of the Parliaments track which had originally been the second Invictus single*. It begins with the gang discovering the giggle potential of helium or varispeeding their voices, cackling like a gang of rowdy mice as George revisits the 'It's not nice to fool Mother Nature' and 'who is this bitch?' monologues first heard on *America Eats Its Young*, before the group crash

---

* This is the latest spelling of 'Momma', following 'Mama' and 'Mamma'.

in and uncork the brown champagne. With Eddie diligently following his orders to play like Hendrix (nimbly pursued by Bykowski), the band continued jamming ferociously. This also resulted in the B-side 'Vital Juices', when the track was released as a single the following year. 'Red Hot Momma' was sometimes mated with Hendrix's 'Who Knows' when played live. The snarling, crashing 'Alice In My Fantasies' sees Eddie further uncaging his Hendrix beast to maul the 'Izabella' riff into an incandescent solo befitting the bombast raging around him. Funkadelic used to start their shows with this then-untitled instrumental version, as heard on *Live: Meadowbrook, Rochester, Michigan 12th September 1971*. The new words appear to have George being seduced by Alice, but demurring in the face of her demands, 'The freak said I would even owe her my devotion' causing him to fantasise about how it might be with no strings attached.

George and Eddie's 'I'll Stay' is a deliriously smooth, seven-minute revamp of the late sixties Parliaments ballad 'Please Stay', with flickering dual guitars and heart-gurglingly glorious vocals pledging to hang in until the lady relocates that loving feeling. The compact but lustrous 'Sexy Ways' harks back to JB's funk with an airy boner-battling vocal from Garry. 'Good Thoughts Bad Thoughts' takes the album out on an ethereal 12-minute guitar meditation, like 'Maggot Brain' after the trauma and catharsis have subsided and reflective calm set in. Eddie's luminescent cloud flashes recall the Grateful Dead's Jerry Garcia or Jimi at his most spiritual. Being the George monologue track, he weighs in near the end with a final message of 'Good thoughts bring forth good fruit/Bullshit thoughts rot your meat.'

Assisted by the success of the single, the album reached number 14 in a 12-week chart run, their best showing yet.

Outside of the newly minted P-world, late 1974 saw the release of another Great Lost P-Funk album when the Parliaments' former label Invictus released *Skin I'm In* by their old labelmates Chairmen Of The Board. By this time the group were off the label and Invictus was on its way out, the tracks dating back to late 1972 when Eddie, Billy, Bernie and Tiki did the sessions after temporarily leaving George.

Chairmen Of The Board was formed as a flagship act by Holland,

Dozier & Holland when they set up Invictus in 1967, led by hiccuping lead vocalist General Johnson along with singers Eddie Custis, Danny Woods and Harrison Kennedy. Their first big hit was 1969's 'Give Me Just A Little More Time', followed by '(You've Got Me) Dangling On A String', 'Everything's Tuesday', 'Pay To The Piper' and 'Finders Keepers'. One of their greatest steel-sharp urban vocal group soul outings, 'Working On A Building Of Love', was a big UK hit in 1972. They also recorded the original version of 'Patches', a hit for Clarence Carter.

The General had just lost his songwriting partner Greg Perry when *Osmium* producer Jeffrey Bowen appeared to take his place, now working for Invictus in an official capacity rather than moonlighting from Motown. The first Chairmen single he worked on was early 1973's 'Finders Keepers', which made the UK Top 30 with its Stevie Wonder 'Superstition' vamp and urgent chorus.

Jeffrey unearthed the 1972 tapes, delighted to find them harbouring nuggets of early Funkadelic gold such as the chomping 'Everybody Party All Night', laid-back wallop of the title track and a remarkably orchestrated funk suite based around Sly's 'Life And Death In G & A'. The retro-purist General disowned the album on its release, describing working with Funkadelic as 'horrible', although *Black Music* magazine named *Skin I'm In* among its albums of the year and it's become something of a cult funk classic.

Meanwhile, the Funk Mob's Detroit stamping ground had changed since the close-knit vibrancy of the scene which embraced them in the late sixties. Debilitated by heroin, the MC5 were dissolving and Stooges practically self-combusting, leaving newer groups such as Grand Funk hitting big with safer, basic fare. Having moved to LA after the 1967 riots, Berry Gordy had closed up the last bastion of Motown's golden age by shutting the Hitsville UK studio by 1973.

However, there were still groups to be found at subterranean levels, some of which wouldn't be heard by the outside world until years later. Black Merda have been called the first all-black rock band, active in Detroit between the mid-sixties and early seventies (reforming in

2005). Lining up as school friends guitarist Anthony Hawkins, bassist VC L. Veasey and drummer Tyrone Hite, they first worked as session musicians for labels such as Golden World and Fortune in early sixties Detroit (which would have brought them into George's orbit). They then changed their name to the Impact and played sessions with the likes of Wilson Pickett, Gene Chandler, the Chi-Lites and Spinners, along with some Motown acts. They also became Edwin Starr's backing group after playing on his 1965 hit 'Agent Double-O Soul', renamed the Soul Agents.

By 1967, the trio had started indulging their love of Cream and Hendrix, releasing their version of 'Foxy Lady' as a single that could be the first Jimi cover on record. With Anthony's younger brother Charles coming in on second guitar they started noticing the hard rock elements infiltrating Detroit's soul courtesy of the Funkadelics, trying it on an approving Starr while striking out in their own right in 1968. Rejecting Murder Incorporated, they settled on Black Murder as a name in response to the number of African-Americans being killed by police and the Ku Klux Klan at the time. Veasey wanted the public to know how bad the situation was. The spelling of 'Murder' was then duly slanged up.

After backing Starr on his incendiary classic 'War', along with a stint with the Temptations, Black Merda went under their own name and signed to Chess Records, which released their self-titled debut album in 1970 but failed to promote the disc due to management changes at the label. A second album suffered the same fate when released in 1972 and the disillusioned band broke up, returning to session work. The Hawkins brothers reformed Black Merda in 2005 after being rediscovered by black-rock devotees, reissuing the original albums and recording two new ones; *Renaissance* and *Force Of Nature*. Mining a tougher rock seam than the Funkadelics, Black Merda display a conscious fire and merciless chops when dealing out grit-logged tracks such as 'Prophet' and 'Cynthy-Ruth', which the *Detroit MetroTimes* named as one of 100 Greatest Detroit Songs Ever.

Whereas Black Merda came from the epicentre of the Detroit sessions scene, punk-presaging power trio Death were one of the few black bands to form in the city after witnessing gigs back in the day by the MC5, Stooges and Funkadelic. Comprising the Hackney brothers David, Dannis and Bobby, it was assumed black Detroit kids only gravitated towards Motown but Death favoured high-velocity guitar carnage and socially aware messages on tear-ups such as 'Politicians In My Eyes' and 'Freakin' Out'. By 1974 they were building a formidable local legend, which prompted MC5 guitarist Wayne Kramer to declare that "Death are the true progenitors of punk."

"We were three black brothers playing straight-up white rock," said Dannis. "It was loud. It was hard-driven. After we had finished a song, instead of clapping and cheering, people would just stand there and look at us like we were weird." The band recorded demos at Groovesville studio because George had worked there, and also used P-Funk haven United Sound. Columbia Records president Clive Davis was impressed enough to offer a deal, on condition they change their name. Many bands would change their sex to get a deal but David refused, saying death was the one thing in life you could be sure of and stuck to his guns. This scenario repeated itself with subsequent interested companies, the trio only managing one independently released single ('Politicians In My Eyes'/'Keep On Knocking' on Tryangle in 1976) before changing their name to Fourth Movement and going into gospel.

David Hackney, the band's motivating force, died of lung cancer in 2000 aged 48, leaving Death to become one of the more fascinating mysteries of Detroit's early seventies music scene. This state of affairs endured until Chicago label Drag City released the original single and other tracks on an album called *For The Whole World To See,* followed by *Spiritual/Mental/Physical*'s collection of demos. Recently, the surviving brothers have revived the name and recorded a new set entitled *III*.

With Parliament well and truly under way, Funkadelic appeared again with *Let's Take It To The Stage* in April, 1975, continuing the weighty funk-rock sound littered with experimental urges and surreal comedic touches. It was the first of two albums the group had to deliver to discharge their Westbound contract, but it's anything but the ragbag creation that might suggest.

Eddie spent the best part of a year incarcerated in a California prison after smoking angel dust on a flight and a confrontation with an air stewardess. His replacement was 17-year-old Michael Hampton from Cleveland, Ohio – nicknamed 'Kidd Funkadelic' because of his age. Michael tells the story that, in summer 1974, having just graduated high school, he went with his cousin Lige to see Funkadelic at Cleveland Public Auditorium as his first concert. He remembered George squirting the front rows with his funk hose and attended the after-show party thrown by local manager Ed Sparks at his home where, fancying getting involved with a band, he had set up equipment in his front room. When Funkadelic arrived, he prodded Michael to play 'Maggot Brain' on guitar, which he proceeded to do with note-perfect precision. "He was sitting on this little Fender amp," recalled Garry. "I knew Mike was going to be with the group then, 'cause he played it note for note. Eddie couldn't even play it note for note." Two weeks later, he got a call from Tiki, the next week he was playing his first Funkadelic gig – the 'Maggot Brain' showcase which he still performs to this day as the live set's tour de force.*

Declaring that "we grow guitar players", George describes Hampton as "one of the finest guitar players there is. The majority of rock'n'roll players just take a solo and get on down. A few of them play the melody of the main part of the song. Michael actually played rock'n'roll but he played the melody of the songs like a horn player would do."

Another (slightly disturbing) triumph of a sleeve by Pedro Bell ("A little too much mutant science on that one") listed a slimmed-down line-up including the Parliaments singers and Garry 'Doo-wop' Shider, Bernie, Boogie, Tiki and Hampton with George as 'Maggot Overlord'. 'Alumni Funkadelic' are Bootsy, Billy Bass, Eddie and Bykowski, and a singer called Gary 'Mudbone' Cooper from a group called Madhouse.

'Good To Your Earhole' starts proceedings in hell-raising axe fashion, riffs a-chomping and searing, swooping guitar work, which can only be that of pre-incarceration Eddie (whose mother again receives a composing credit). Glistening, percussive rocker 'Better By The Pound'

---

* Included on the free 45 given away with 1978's *One Nation Under A Groove*.

was released as a single, Garry and Eddie singing about society in a positive fashion hinting at later one nation groove unity while a guesting Billy Bass takes off on his own private flight.

'Be My Beach' marks the returning Bootsy's sole appearance on the album. After the madness of touring in 1972 and early 1973, he had retreated back to Cincinnati, saying "Constant touring with such a manic, consciously lunatic, drug-consuming crew led to complete mental and physical breakdown." This track is enough to stamp his stoned-cool new Bootzilla persona into the P-Funk consciousness, its initial Hendrix inspiration evident. It was the first time that those now-familiar tones first slinked out of the tin as Bootsy has the hots for a girl but is told there's more beaches by the sea. 'No Head No Backstage Pass' is a roughshod groupie-whoopee churn dealing with a favourite subject of rock'n'rollers. George was first to put a funk slant on it.

The fabulous title track takes sly digs at the competition over a languorous JB guitar vamp, playing the dozens with James Brown ("the godmother"), Dufus and Earth Wind And Fire ("Earth, Hot Air and No Fire"). Its slow-burning dynamism presages oncoming Mothership raps as another illustration of the thin fence between George's two bands. Released as a single, George's rewriting of nursery rhymes continued while the humour was getting more warped. "All of us used to just sit around and blow a joint and just start talking and acting crazy, and out of these conversations is how all this happened," recalled Sting Ray. "George would take these thoughts that were thrown out in the conversation and start putting [them] to tracks."

'Get Off Your Ass And Jam' is a short, sharp party chant with surging guitars that showed the influence of the Motor City's high-energy rockers. 'Baby I Owe You Something Good' is the United Soul tune amped into a gospel workout, showing that a basically religious song can be thrown into any setting. Calvin Simon's stratospheric vocal ups the atmosphere of church fervour. Gary sings several leads on the album, but 'Stuffs And Things' is his strongest, riding a pumping cack-cannon funk groove featuring Michael Hampton's first appearance on record while Bernie invents the G-Funk synth snake. LA vocal group Brandye's Telma Hopkins and Joyce Vincent add to the vocals. 'The Song Is Familiar' is a love song with soaring chorus and old soul throwback qualities on this album's seemingly requisite straight song, riding the kind of beat which would underpin hip-hop ballads 20 years hence. This album's experimental finale, 'Atmosphere', sees Bernie embarking on another organ and synth excursion that references Sun Ra and is sprinkled with subliminal XXX-rated cheekiness from George and Bootsy.

The album went R&B Top 20, continuing the essential groundwork in establishing Funkadelic as a separate entity to Parliament. As George reflected, "So you got *Cosmic Slop* and *Standing On The Verge Of Getting It On* and *Let's Take It To The Stage*. You could feel it was coming. It was being more and more accepted. We knew just about how funky to be to get on black radio. And we was getting on a lot of white radio at that time, too. Before that, it didn't matter 'cause we weren't gonna get on *nobody*'s radio, so it was better to be crazier and do it extreme. Those three albums, we was bringing to the norm."

Of course, George's 'norm' is another man's 'warped', but having retained the qualities which gave Funkadelic its unique spaced superfly aura, he had strived to mash funky soul and black rock together into sharper songs peppered with crowd-detonating slogans and radio-friendly reference points packing underlying social comment.

Soon it would be time to watch the skies.

Chapter Nine

Space Is The Place

"His style was simultaneously insane and right on."
  Scott Hacker *(Can You Get To That? The Cosmology Of P-Funk)*

"It had always been spiritual. Now it was really spiritual"
  Garry Shider

After Parliament returned, they seemed to go from blacker-than-black to bigger-than-big in the space of a year, enrapturing their core audience with two successful feet-finding albums before George finally landed on the world stage touting a spaceship, a mega-selling record and their expansive P-Funk mythology.

After stirring on the previous albums, P-Funk had become its own living Blaxploitation movie and crowd-unifying entity, a code of life, and even a religion that would spawn hardcore followers calling themselves 'maggots', 'clones' or 'funkateers'. The 'P' has been explained as standing for Plainfield Funk, Pure Funk or just an abbreviation of Parliament-Funkadelic. In a decade of cults, the only rituals were at gigs, with George the preacher spurring on his congregations to heights of euphoric craziness and frenzied joy. Believing in a form of cosmic oneness rather than any established religious ideology, he eschewed imposing any direct Biblical views on his audience and approached P-Funk with his usual larger-than-life humour but, in the decades since the Mothership first descended, its philosophies have taken on a deeper significance.

In terms of sheer numbers and devotion, P-Funk injected its seventies continuation of the Black Power ethos that had manifested in Blaxploitation with enough fun, rock'n'roll and killer tunes to beguile white audiences. With George's songs and concepts becoming more defined and complex, it wasn't long before serious dissections and theories started emerging on the meaning of the P. George cleverly inverted and made cool words that had previously been used in a negative fashion, such as 'funky', 'stupid', 'nasty' and 'bad'. As he used to boom from the stage, "All that is good, is nasty." There were a lot of ingrained barriers to trample as, even in children's stories, the white knight was traditionally the good guy while his grunting opponent was invariably black clad. One of George's first moves was to tear off the conceptual armour and replace it with a cosmic codpiece.

Looked at now, George was creating a modern form of black folklore, doused in science fiction and sporting a creation tale as he built the parallel universe that was then brought to life every time Parliament-Funkadelic took The Funk to the stage. The over-the-top alien pantomime that had grown out of the mutilated bed-sheet era presented a new form of black liberation achieved by being a freak and plugging into the new groove. Rickey Vincent writes in *Funk* that it was "rooted in ancient African spiritual systems in which sexuality and spirituality are united in harmony with the essential *life force*. The Funk returns to that same singular orientation in which intellect, ambition, desire and sexuality all exist as part of a greater whole." In effect, George was blowing apart ingrained western constraints by ditching mundane reality, language restrictions and sometimes even his clothes to take his audience to a sexed-up spiritual plane filled with funk and freedom.

The time was right for such wild expansions, as black artists enjoyed the sea change in opportunities and popularity that was permeating TV, the movies and bringing entertainers out of the underground. In 1974 Illinois comedian Richard Pryor opened the floodgates for the kind of

X-rated humour that had been the lifeblood of black clubs for decades by releasing *That Nigger's Crazy*, his brilliant procession of ghetto vignettes and characters drawn from drunks, junkies, cops and hookers. "Black is what's happening," said George at the time. "Richard Pryor is selling a million records without being played on the radio. To me, Richard Pryor sounds typical of everybody I grew up with. Civil rights, the whole freedom thing has opened it up."

While Funkadelic traversed and translated ghetto street action and its characters into the P-Funk worldview, for Parliament George created minor gods as black comic-book archetypes. He was building a space chariot to bring the Funk home to the beleaguered inner cities and leave the Earth's atmosphere to pull off his vision of creating the ultimate black soundtrack for the times. In the hands of certain progressive rock artists, this would have seemed monstrously self-indulgent, but George added the crucial ingredients which set his band apart; silliness, humility and bonkers drug mayhem, along with the most awesome butt-shaking music on the planet. In many ways, the P-Funk mythology could be seen as a natural progression from the Parliaments at the Apollo in the mid-sixties.

Writing for Pagan Kennedy's book *Platforms: A Microwaved Cultural Chronicle Of The 70s*, commentator Scott Hacker said, "P-Funk seemed to believe that music wasn't so much something that you made with your instruments as it was something that you caught with them, as if funk was out there in the form of an ancient residual energy left over from the big bang. It was as if their basses and horns were finely tuned, specialised antennae dialling into cosmic leftovers. Funk became a unifying presence – the godhead as manifest to anyone willing to laugh and boogie at the same time... The crowd could be as badass as the band."

It was time to take the band and P-Funk to the next level. George knew he had to up the concepts, expand the sound and tap into the mainstream in order to knock the masses being enthralled by David Bowie for six. To this end, he recalled Parliament, last heard three years earlier against the bagpipes of *Osmium* and now required to give the original singers and Garry Shider a bigger platform, a vehicle which would take him to the radio then the stadiums. With the counterculture winding down or being assimilated into a mainstream now obsessed with Bowie and getting over glam-rock, it was time to take the P-Funk to the people.

With Funkadelic in the middle of working off the two remaining albums in their Westbound contract, George had needed a new record company to realise his dreams for Parliament. This materialised in the shape of his old friend Neil Bogart's Casablanca Records in late 1973. Born in New York City and raised in the Brooklyn projects, Bogart was a key figure in the bubblegum pop explosion of the late sixties after joining Buddah Records from Cameo-Parkway. Although he had enjoyed huge success with the likes of Ohio Express and 1910 Fruitgum Company, Bogart had grown tired of the corporate restrictions at Buddah, leaving to start Casablanca in 1973 and taking fellow execs Larry Harris, Cecil Holmes and Buck Reingold with him.

Based in Los Angeles and initially financed by Warner Brothers, he named the label after his favourite film and because he shared his surname with its star Humphrey. The first signing had been low-rent New York glam hopefuls Kiss, who'd emerged from the city's post-New York Dolls/pre-CBGB limbo period and changed their fortunes by adopting cartoon characters and obscuring their faces in black and white slap. Their limp first three albums tanked, but their stage show was gaining popularity and notoriety with its pyrotechnics, fake blood and levitating drum kit. Bogart's fraught relationship with Warner Brothers resulted in chairman Mo Austin giving him Casablanca to run as an independent, but by 1975 he was facing bankruptcy. He decided to take a shot capturing Kiss' popular live pantomime on the *Alive!* double album released that September. It went gold, catapulting band and label into the big league.

When Bogart signed Parliament, the label was still in its infancy, but he knew George from their Buddah days, and so he didn't need filling in on Funkadelic. He was more concerned with what the future held for Parliament. As far as George was concerned, that was a simple matter, as he felt Casablanca would be a good home for the expansive concepts trapezing around his brain at that time. It would also fit Bogart's raging ambition to make his signings hit the mass-market bullseye. As he liked to say, "Why head for the mountaintop when you're reaching for the sky?"

Bogart's faith was immediately justified when first single 'Up For The Down Stroke' jumped to number 10 on the R&B chart and 63 on the Hot 100 in June 1974, providing George's first major chart placing since 'Testify' and Casablanca's first hit. Written by George, Bootsy, Fuzzy and Bernie, this quintessential P-Funk anthem marked Parliament's rebirth with a call-to-arms: 'When you're hot you're hot, look at what you got'. Boasting a steely new sheen, the track showed how Parliament was now firmly on the One, shifting the musical emphasis away from Funkadelic rock with a heavy (unaccredited) brass presence. This brought a soul-revue edge to the stripped-down unit that included Bernie, the returning Bootsy and Cordell Mosson on basses, drummers Tiki Fulwood and Gary Bronson plus guitar power from Ron Bykowski, Garry Shider and Eddie Hazel.

From the cracking opening salvo with George swiping at Tricky Dicky Nixon and laying down his funk manifesto, Parliament were back to ignite the party and the people. Bootsy was also back, and this time he meant business, fiercely nudging his liquid hump under the urgent brass and defiant choral chant (which, for reasons best known to me then, I wrote that "you can wear as a pair of underpants" at the time). UK dance duo Coldcut cite the song as their favourite 45 of all time.

Released on July 3, 1974, *Up For The Down Stroke*'s blurred sleeve photo depicts intergalactic super stud George clad in big red cape, silver chains and a voluminous codpiece towering over a group of distressed space damsels who seem possessed by some unseen force which is probably the power of the funk. It all seems to be going off to speaking-in-tongues levels of possessed rapture, which could be early evidence of George's recent reading of African-American author Ishmael Reed's 1972 experimental novel *Mumbo Jumbo*, another major influence on George's P-Funk philosophy. Rickey Vincent recalls asking him where he got his intergalactic funk concepts from in 1985. "Have you read *Mumbo Jumbo*?" he replied.

sh garbage; Robert Matheu's original photo for *Creem's* Stars' Cars spread. ROBERT MATHEU

Up For The Down Stroke decorated by George and Bootsy.
KRIS NEEDS ARCHIVES

The Clones Of Dr Funkenstein signed by George. KRIS NEEDS ARCHIVES

Pedro Bell makes his debut with *Cosmic Slop*. KRIS NEEDS ARCHIVES

Away from the stage: Dr Funkenstein working in the Detroit funk lab
with assistant Jim Callon. P-FUNK ARCHIVES

h, the name is Bootsy, baby. P-FUNK ARCHIVES

The Brides Of Funkenstein. P-FUNK ARCHIVES

Queen Of Funk Mallia Franklin & the Brides' Dawn Silva. P-FUNK ARCHIVES

Long-serving guitar messenger Duwayne 'Blackbyrd' McKnight. ALDO MAURO

Ra levitates New York's Squat Theatre, early eighties. TAV FALCO/THE PANTHER BURNS

Air traffic controller Glenn Goins & keyboard navigator Bernie Worrell 1977. STEVE LABELLE/© SERGE DODWELL

Garry 'Starchild' Shider prepares for takeoff, Philadelphia 1977. DIEM JONES

On the road; Cordell 'Boogie' Mosson. JEROME BRAILEY

For the ladies: Uncle Jam. P-FUNK ARCHIVES

wesome: the landing of the Mothership. P-FUNK ARCHIVES

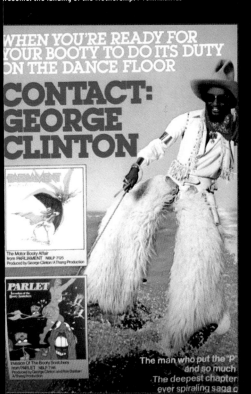

The Boogie Man warms up, 1977. STEVE LABELLE/© SERGE DODWELL

Sir Nose D'Voidoffunk at Flash Light launch 1977. ROBERT MATHEU

Mutiny On The Mamaship. KRIS NEEDS ARCHIVES

The funky drummer; Jerome 'Bigfoot' Brailey. P-FUNK ARCHIVES

Set in twenties New York City, the novel concerns a Haitian voodoo priest called PaPa LaBas (who practises from his Mumbo Jumbo Cathedral) who finds himself in opposition to the Wallflower Order, an international organisation trying to end the 'Jes Grew' virus unleashed by Voo Doo Generals, which infects Chicago's twenties Jazz Age and the post-war bebop revolution. It's "electric as life and is characterised by ebullience and ecstasy", influencing people to listen to music, dance and be happy. Spread by black artists, 'Jes Grew' grips its victims in frenzies of euphoric jazz dancing, representing the freedom and identity they're reclaiming after years of being squashed and trampled. The Wallflower Order is defeated because there is no vaccine against the black dance crazes they want so desperately to crush.

Mumbo Jumbo is laced with voodoo traditions, conspiracy theories, Harlem renaissance writers, the Afrocentric theories of Marcus Garvey and occult author Henri Gamache (who maintained that the prophet Moses was black). Disorientingly presented in a non-linear style, the book plays on the relationship between race, black magic and technology, alongside many other elements. Writing in his own street slang and taking many creative diversions with the text, Reed's portrayal of jazz hitting recipients at gut level and making them dance also plugs in at groin level for the funk which, at this time, also 'jes grew'.

Up For The Down Stroke was a perfectly timed taster of the new Parliament sound. The group was well and truly back in session. Bootsy felt it too, telling me, "When *Up For The Down Stroke* came out, I think that was the first. It's like the chemistry just started working."

The Spanish guitar-inflected 'Presence Of A Brain' was written by George and Garry (about a deep thinker) and was sung by Eddie whose softly heartfelt vocals were often dwarfed by his guitar playing. With its shadowy rhythm and web of billowing interacting harmonies the song is the album's only real funk departure, but shows how George was prepared to venture outside the funk box to explore new sonic strata.

'I Can Move You (If You Let Me)' is a swirling Garry-sung One-plopping funker written by George, Boogie, Bernie and Bootsy (on deadly form test-driving the rectoplasmic bass drops he'd deploy on his first solo album). 'I Just Got Back (From The Fantasy, Ahead Of Our

Time In The Four Lands Of Ellet)' is a lightly psych-glazed ballad by composer Peter Chase (who also wrote 'For Everyone Under the Sun' on jazz organist Jimmy Smith's *Root Down* live album in 1972). His bird whistling solo is unexpected but graced with its own spangled charm as the blissful utopia of this other world kicks in, fitting Parliament's take on the kind of wistful hippie wafters still common at that time. You can almost picture the trees clapping along here.

Maintaining the tradition already established by Funkadelic, the vibrant new songs were joined by rewired versions of previous singles 'Testify', 'The Goose That Laid The Golden Egg', 'Whatever Makes My Baby Feel Good' and 'All Your Goodies Are Gone'. As Fuzzy explained, "We would be playing these things on stage and when we needed a song in the studio we would record it as we were then doing it."

The storming take on 'Testify' was boosted by Bernie's synchronised clavinet chomp (similar to the one he used on the Chairmen Of The Board's 'Skin I'm In'), while George's vocal is in a different universe to the original. 'The Goose' introduces 'the man in the box', a primitive rhythm machine providing an unusual bedfellow for the simple guitar riff (like early Funkadelic stripped of the effects) while stellar Parliaments harmonies curl around George like an echo beaming in from the old barbershop. 'All Your Goodies Are Gone' now becomes a spooked sleaze-groove topped with a subtly malicious vocal. Led by Bernie's undulating piano, the understated band are perfectly in touch with the song's simmering internal dynamic.

'Whatever Makes My Baby Feel Good' returns again to that first Funkadelic single, which nearly provided the album's title. Here it is refashioned into a gorgeously languid stoned piano blues with sobbing vocals and stinging guitar from Eddie, while the harmonies are pure Parliaments magic.

Bootsy was back after his two-year hiatus, stepping forward to claim his destiny as the most well-known P-member after George. "Funkiest motherfucker in the world on a bass!" declared the latter in 1993. "Bootsy's got some other kind of rhythm, him and his brother Catfish too. There ain't too much more rhythm outside of Bootsy."

Although he'd dipped his platform star boots into Funkadelic's albums since *America...*, Bootsy had yet to fully establish his presence in the burgeoning P-Funk empire. Maybe George was waiting for the right time or album concept. 1975 was the year Bootsy burst out in a big way, his electrified bass globules and superfly space dude persona appearing on all the Parliament albums released on Casablanca. Bootsy was now becoming George's telepathic songwriting partner. "George adds on to me when I'm in the studio and I add on to him," he told me in 1990. "There's a certain thing you don't get from nowhere else. It's just there. I know that when I was in the studio it felt like that. It was different."

Bootsy remembered his time getting settled into George's groove in the early seventies being initially difficult before the funk just started growing, declaring, "The Funk was a bad word when George and myself came out with the first stuff. At one time it was illegal to say on the air. Plus, it was kind of rowdy.

"Any time something is that new, people tend to back off from it for a minute, and if it starts working they'll start coming in. We had fans in New York but our records never got played. I think New York was an area where they just had their own format that didn't have nothing to do with the rest of the world. And they still like that. I think they never wanted to be affiliated with the funk. That kind of left us out on the air but the live shows were working. We sold out Madison Square Garden two nights in a row."

With Casablanca covering his increasingly happy ass, George was ready to take Parliament all the way, especially now the main songwriting team had solidified at Bootsy, Bernie and himself. Released in March 1975, *Chocolate City* can be seen as the stepping stone between re-entry and the heights soon to be achieved with the *Mothership Connection*. "We knew we was getting popular," explained George. "And then we got right to *Chocolate City*. That was straight-out commercial. When we had brought Parliament back out with *Up For The Down Stroke*, it was still a semi-rock band. *Chocolate City* was straight-out sophisticated J.B.'s or Sly funked up."

Released in April 1975, *Chocolate City* was George's love letter to

Washington DC, selling around 150,000 albums in that area alone. The city had earned its 'Chocolate City' nickname due to its large black population. The phrase had been in use since the early seventies on Washington's black radio stations WOOK-AM and WOL-AM, whose Bobby 'The Mighty Burner' Bennett said it expressed DC's "classy funk and confident blackness". It was the first major city to pick up on the Parliaments and Funkadelic, whose first singles were caned on those radio stations and where they were hailed as gods after the legendary show at Howard University in October 1972. Funkadelic routinely sold 20,000 albums in the DC area.

Rather than dwell on white flight 'vanilla suburbs', George celebrates a safe stronghold ("my piece of the rock") to honour P-Funk's passionate DC following. He was also inspired by the irony of one of America's worst ghettos being situated just blocks away from the President's palatial abode. The album's cover shows the Lincoln Memorial, Washington Monument and Capitol Rotunda rendered in melting chocolate.

I first heard the renowned title track in no lesser place than Noel Edmonds' Chelsea record shop and had to steady myself on his beard as George boomed in over Bootsy's lava-popping bass throb, which slurped around Bernie's drastic piano grunts. It's an exercise in controlled atmosphere-stoking, as brief female interjections of 'gamin' on ya' periodically erupt under minimal percussive pulses for one of George's most effective political statements. He's assumed the (then vanishing) persona of a hip radio jock to intone with impossible cool, 'Hey CC, this here's the White House but that's only a temporary condition', before naming other chocolate cities such as Newark, Gary, LA, Atlanta and New York. He makes the point that DC had an 80 per cent black population (*'You don't need the bullet when you got the ballot'*) and runs through a roll-call of his fantasy administration – Muhammad Ali as President; Secretary of the Treasury Isaac Hayes; Minister of Education Richard Pryor; Secretary of Fine Arts Stevie Wonder; and First Lady, Miss Aretha Franklin. Although George's Funkadelic narratives had previously echoed radio disc jockeys, this track saw him fully adopt the persona he would retain for the next Parliament album. Black radio DJs were a major aspect of George's youth, firing up the music with larger-than-life hyperbole. As Alan Freed was among the first to play black music to white teenagers in the early fifties, George would be responsible for turning a new generation on to The Funk from this album onwards. The track was released as a two-part single that May, making number 24 on the R&B chart and 94 nationally.

Chocolate City got P-Funkers dancing rather than splashing about in the band's boggle-eyed experimentation. Its piledriving supersoul bristled with pride and unpredictable danger on tracks such as the inflammatory 'Ride On', an electrifying rump-shaker that positively crackles with up-for-it energy and audacious diamond-cutter bass. 'What Comes Funky' is unashamedly dripping with the One, along with other elements that react to and recombine with its clipped turbo-rumble. 'Bigfootin'' and 'If It Don't Fit (Don't Force It)' flagrantly stomp, while 'Together' (originally recorded by Bootsy and Catfish in their Complete Strangers group with Gary 'Mudbone' Cooper) is a masterclass in light and shade, lashing its taut butt-bubble bass funk to stretches of soothing chorale draped with Brecker Brothers brass. The track boasts a standout early appearance from Mudbone on backing vocals, which hint at what would follow from the gestating Bootsy's Rubber Band.

Bone grew up on the perilous streets of East Baltimore. As a youth he became obsessed with James Brown to the point of being billed as the "Baby James Brown" in his first group, Ricky & the Chips, who got as far as opening for the Temptations and Stevie Wonder. By the time he hooked up with his next band, Madhouse, he was feeling the influence of Hendrix and Zappa, bringing his brand of 'sweet-voiced melodies and wild ass attitude' to *Chocolate City* at George's invitation, then staying on for the upcoming run of classic Parliament albums.

Also in the line-up are Garry, Boogie, Prakash John, Eddie and Tyrone Lampkin, as the Parliaments upped the voltage on their harmonies. 'Let Me Be' draws from seventies DC gospel with Eddie's vocal cracked and pleading with convincing desperation. Amid the funk-soul bombast it's the album's moment of naked strangeness, with only subtle strings and electronic keyboards set alongside Bernie's enthusiastic jazz-scattered piano pounding. Sumptuous soul ballad 'I Misjudged You' beautifully pays homage to DC R&B group the Unifics (best known

197

for 1968's 'Court Of Love' single featuring future P-Funk drummer Jerome 'Bigfoot' Brailey) with Isaac Hayes-style wah-wah and strings. (A frenetic sixties-style funky soul out-take called 'Common Law Wife' showed up in the *George Clinton Family Series*.)

Mothership Connection was released that December to inaugurate Parliament's rise toward becoming one of the biggest groups in the US. It presented the P-Funk mythology as a concept album that would be accompanied by a spectacular stadium show the following year. This album revolutionised the Funk, bust black music out of its remaining shackles and displayed the singers and players at the top of their game; pointing at an intergalactic future but still embracing Motown soul, gospel and even nagging pop choruses. Its original title was *Landing In The Ghetto*.

"We had put black people in situations nobody ever thought they would be in, like the White House," states George. "I figured another place you wouldn't think black people would be was in outer space. I was a big fan of *Star Trek* so we did a thing with a pimp sitting in a spaceship shaped like a Cadillac and these James Brown-type grooves, but with street talk and ghetto slang."

The James Brown-type grooves now ran deeper as Bootsy and Catfish had been joined by J.B.'s titanic trombonist Fred Wesley, sax maniac Maceo Parker and trumpet legend Richard 'Kush' Griffith, who'd been driven away by James Brown's financial and behavioural restrictions to hook up with funk's most happening thing. Now dubbed the Horny Horns, they were ready to play a key part in the oncoming string of classic P-Funk albums.

Fred was born the son of a big-band leader in Columbus, Georgia on July 4, 1943. He took piano and trumpet lessons, switching to trombone at the age of 12, when he was presented with one by his father. After playing with the Ike & Tina Turner Revue in 1962, Fred joined Hank Ballard & the Midnighters before hitching up with Brown. The first session he played on was 'Say It Loud I'm Black And I'm Proud', his slide an unmistakable ingredient when J.B.'s Funk stew was at its hottest on albums such as *Say It Loud, I'm Black And I'm Proud, Sex Machine,*

Hot Pants, There It Is, Get on The Good Foot, Black Caesar, Slaughter's Big Ripoff, The Payback, Hell, and *Reality.* He also released albums as 'Fred Wesley and the J.B.'s', including *Food For Thought* and *'Damn Right I Am Somebody'.* Fred became J.B.'s bandleader but by 1975, was feeling exploited, underappreciated and abused.

When Bootsy left the J.B.'s he and Fred promised each other they would work together again, and duly kept in touch. Holed up in New York's Americana Hotel one night, Fred heard a knock on his door. Opening it he was greeted by what looked to him 'like creatures from outer space'. The gaggle of hats, leather and shades was actually Bootsy, along with George, Bernie, Garry and Boogie, here to invite Fred to join P-Funk. They played him a cassette of raw grooves they were looking to get smeared with his trombone magic. "What I heard scared me again," he relates. "All rhythm tracks. Funk. Bass, guitar, drums. Musically simple, but with an attitude. A Sound. Aggressive like I'd never heard before. Bold, overwhelming, compelling ... This music was brand new. It was what I was doing with James but with an attitude that was fresh. It was the next step for funk, R&B, and all popular music."

When Fred asked what they needed from him, George replied "Gimme something baaad". He had just played him the basic tracks from *Mothership Connection* and the first Bootsy's Rubber Band album. After prevaricating, Fred finally walked away from Brown after being spiked with acid before an ill-judged show at New York's Madison Square Garden, fed up with walking on eggshells. He would now take his belief that "funk and jazz are basically the same thing with emphasis on different elements and playing with different attitudes" to P-Funk and, having been given an open field to run in, would try to prove that theory with seismic results, soon pulling an equally cheesed off Maceo Parker out of the J.B.'s to join him.

Born on February 14, 1943 in North Carolina, Maceo handled alto, tenor and baritone saxophones, becoming part of the deal in 1964 when Brown sought out his drummer brother Melvin. Maceo went on to become MC, band leader and dynamic tenor player, and the cry of 'Maceo!' became a regular feature of the group's live sets. In 1970 Maceo and Melvin left Brown to start Maceo & All The King's Men, touring for two years. Maceo returned to the Godfather in 1974, seeing his own single 'Party' make the pop charts. Subsequent albums *Us* and *Doin' It To Death* cut a mean path as Maceo & the Macks – the discs issued as part of Brown's deal with Polydor for his new People label. He also appeared on the same landmark James Brown albums as Fred Wesley.

Maceo was told that George, Bootsy and Fred were talking about starting a record label and wanted him in at its inception. He promptly quit Brown's group and met Fred in Detroit. First, George had a wealth of rhythm tracks that needed Fred's horns, so Maceo duly joined the funky sweatshop at United Sound where crew members worked around the clock churning out grooves. The next few months saw Maceo and Fred along with trumpeters Maurice Davis and Marcus Belgrave lay down tracks which would appear on *Mothership Connection*, *Let's Take It To The Stage* and *Stretchin' Out*, luxuriating in the state-of-the-art multi-track recording equipment.

"I knew what I was getting myself into," Maceo admitted in his autobiography. "I'd seen George at the Apollo several years before, and the only thing I really remember about the show was thinking to myself that he was absolutely *crazy*. During the chorus of 'Loose Booty', he'd turn his butt around to the audience and a spotlight would shine on it. When my friends and I saw that, we fell out laughing. This guy was too silly. I never thought in a million years I'd actually be part of his band one day. But once I found myself on stage with him, I discovered that his theatrics had gotten worse (or better, depending on your perspective)."

"See, Fred had schooling and everything too. We clicked," recalled Bernie. "The 'Gamin' On Ya' and 'Handcuffs' sessions in New York with Fred Wesley, Maceo Parker and the Brecker Brothers was an event, one of the highlights in my life as a horn arranger. Because I never believed that the Breckers would be playing my charts, or Fred Wesley and Maceo, let alone having them all together on one session."

"Work, and life in general, with the Funkadelic people was, literally, 'nothing but a party'," recalled Fred. "George was not only the boss but the party master as well. He was always laughing and joking, trying to keep everybody relaxed. It was clear that he was in charge but he ruled with a soft, friendly respectful approach that made everyone feel comfortable. Creativity was the order of the day. All day. Every day. Nothing that popped into anybody's mind was dismissed. Everything, no matter how crazy and unconventional, was considered... On the other hand, George, Bootsy and [engineer] Jim [Vitti] paid strict attention to details when it came to putting innovative ideas on tape. The groove was ultimately important, but using the multi-track recording techniques allowed us to stretch it to and beyond its current limits."

Fred goes on to describe George as the boss, Bootsy second in command with "faithful and dutiful lieutenants" Bernie, Garry and Glenn Goins always present with suggestions. The latter is another of P-Funk's under-recognised talents who really could have risen to major stardom out of the P-chaos had he not been cruelly struck down at an early age. For the next three years his soaring gospel vocals were one of P-Funk's most lethal weapons. Born on January 2, 1954, Glenn grew up in Plainfield, playing with local groups including the Ambassadors and Richard Boyce & the Presidents before becoming a member of the Bags, who released a single in 1972 called 'It's Heavy'. One day he got called to the Mothership.

Jerome 'Bigfoot' Brailey was another new recruit who ended up occupying the drum stool during P-Funk's most successful period. If anyone has travelled the Funk Road, it's Bigfoot. He told me, "I started playing drums after seeing the Beatles on the *Ed Sullivan Show* in 1964. That's what I wanted to do now – be in a band. I actually started on trombone but it started leaving a ridge on my lips. I was trying to attract girls and stuff but my lips were all red and swollen. I knew I wanted to be a drummer but had to wait until that teacher had left the school before I could change my instrument. I actually started playing drums around 14.

"It was wild because my mom got me my first kit, a little three piece Ludwig and I just listened to records at first. Motown and Stax was happening at the time. Every Sunday one of my mom's sisters would come by and put on a Motown record and want me to play behind it. 'Play with this record!' I got the R&B thing down at a young age and started listening to John Bonham from Led Zeppelin. I listened to all kinds of groups. After playing with records, I wanted to add my stuff in.

I just incorporated it into my style the way I would have done if I had played it. That just developed over the years, I guess.

"I started with a local high-school band called the Montclairs, with Wah Wah Ragin (later Motown session giant Wah Wah Watson). He's playing on the Unifics record and became a big session guitarist. We started together playing with Donny Hathaway, who I met when we were actually rehearsing. By that time, I was at Howard University in Washington."

After leaving Howard in 1967 Hathaway found work as a songwriter, session musician and producer, arranging 1968's 'The Court Of Love' for DC doo-woppers the Unifics, who Jerome had joined. "We were actually recording the Unifics material when I was at Howard University," recounts Jerome. "I was in Virginia but DC's only a hundred miles away so we'd get the bus. We recorded 'The Court Of Love' in the old Ed Sullivan building in New York, where they had a studio in the basement. I met Donny Hathaway then. I was actually still in high school when I started doing the sessions with them and everything. During the summer months when I was out they took me to New York to play the Apollo Theatre.

"While I was on tour with the Unifics, the 'Steps were checking me out. I liked the brothers because they were around my age. The Unifics were older guys. The 'Steps let their drummer go and we were on the same tour together so I was playing with both the Unifics and the 'Steps on the same tour. Finally, it was like, 'I'd rather play with that group because we're all about the same age. I liked the Stairsteps. They had a killer live show. They were stepping around on stage and catching the licks that I was playing."

Jerome appeared on *Soul Train* with the Stairsteps after they hit with the sublime 'Ooh Child'. "*Soul Train* was just starting, a lot of stuff was just starting to come out. That's me in the corner with the floppy hat playing the drum kit!" The song was recorded with Curtis Mayfield for his Windy City label. "We did a lot of shows with Curtis, both solo and when he had the Impressions. We were all kids so it was like... We knew these guys was cool but we didn't realise at the time how large they actually were, you know what I mean?"

Next, Jerome hooked up with the Chambers Brothers, the Mississippi-born outfit which foreshadowed Funkadelic's down-home psychedelic black rock with their church-roots-gospel vocal style. After relocating to Los Angeles in 1954, the brothers started performing folk and gospel in Southern California as a foursome, with Joe and Willie on guitars, Lester on harmonica and George on washtub bass. In the early sixties, they ventured outside the gospel circuit, playing folk coffeehouses and the renowned Ash Grove club, where they hung with the likes of Reverend Gary Davies, Hoyt Axton, Ramblin' Jack Elliott and Barbara Dane. The latter introduced them to Pete Seeger, resulting in an appearance at the 1965 Newport Folk Festival. By that time, the Brothers had become the first black band to electrify their sound, sparking uproar but drawing attention from white audiences, not least Dylan. Shortly after, they released their debut album, *People Get Ready*.

The Brothers' only hit was 1968's 'Time Has Come Today' written by Joe and Willie and leading their third album, *The Time Has Come*. After a run of less successful singles and bad breaks led to their split in the seventies, they reformed in 1974 to record *Unbonded* and the following year's *Right Move* for the Avco label – which is where Bigfoot came in.

"I met the Chambers Brothers while performing on *Soul Train* with the Five Stairsteps," he recalls. "They were actually on that show. They were interested in me because I was wearing the big, floppy hat. I was six foot two and they were all tall guys. They were like 'This guy looks like he should be with us!' We exchanged numbers and it was like maybe about six months later; I was in Virginia and I got a telegram from Hawaii asking if I would like come up to Stamford, Connecticut where they were living. They wanted to meet me as they were interested in me working with them. So I went up to Connecticut and it was like *boom*!

"It was crazy because each one of my career moves was like a step going up – the Stairsteps higher than the Unifics, then the Brothers was higher than the Stairsteps. I came in and they did an album that CBS never released – *Oh My Lord, Oh My God*. Then we did *Right Move*, produced out in San Francisco in 1975 with David Rubinson (producer of 'Time Has Come Today').

"I had met the Funkadelics on the chitlin' circuit but they were a real underground group because they didn't have a hit. By the time I was with the Chambers Brothers I had all the Funkadelic records. On the road I was always playing Funkadelic music and they used to ask 'Why you always playing that when you're with us? And I'm like, 'Well I'm with you guys and I know your stuff but this is the kind of music I like'. This is the early Funkadelic I'm talking about; *Free Your Mind...* . I knew Eddie, Tiki, Billy and Bernie so I was tight with the band. I was also tight with Grady Thomas. During that time they were more of a group and it wasn't George in charge of everything.

"I wanted to try and get Eddie in the Brothers with me. We did a show together and did 'Time Has Come Today' and Eddie got up. I remember he was playing and rolled his head back and kept on playing and I kept playing and the Brothers walked off the stage! They got mad because me and Eddie just tore it up. They said, 'Well, I guess you guys won't make it in this group' and I was like 'Well, we had fun'. They thought he was a little too far out for them.

"I was back on the west coast, doing on and off gigs with the Chambers Brothers and also playing with Fuzzy Samuels, who used to be the bass player in Stephen Stills' Manassas and had a band with PP Arnold. I was getting ready to move back to the west coast then Grady Thomas left a message that 'George wants to see you'. I had everything in the back of a semi-truck and said 'You'll have to call me later'. About three weeks later I got a call from one of George's managers saying that he was coming to town looking for some outfits. He wanted to come to LA and check out a bunch of clothing stores. We cruised around and I remember one of the managers called and let Tiki know that they weren't gonna use him any more. George said, 'What did Tiki say?' and the manager said, 'Well, he start crying'. So they asked me if I would do the gig. I said, 'Yeah, let me think about it', because I still had some gigs with the Chambers Brothers.

"On the day my youngest daughter was born, I was at the hospital in Southern California. I remember my daughter was born on August 20, 1975 and I was supposed to witness the birth. I was at the hospital with the robe on and everything and the nurse came and said, 'Mr

Brailey, you have an important call'. So I went to get the phone and it was George, calling to see if I wanted to do the gig. He told me what he would pay me and I was like, 'That's not actually as much as I make with the Chambers Brothers but I want to get in this group. So I said, 'OK, that's cool, I'll do it'. And I went back and my daughter was born. I'd missed her birth!

"So he was in LA and about two weeks later I met him at the airport. He was standing there and he had my equipment and all these freaks with him. My wife was pissed off. She said 'Look at all these girls. Now you're just going to leave with all these women and go on tour.' I said, 'I'm just getting the gig, all those women are with George.' So we flew from LAX to Akron, Ohio. I just went straight on the stage and did the show and that was it. I never rehearsed with them a day in my life.

"Maybe about a month later, we went to Detroit and started working on *Mothership Connection*. The first day I went in we did 'Unfunky UFO' and then Bootsy came up with this little tune and we did 'Give Up The Funk (Tear The Roof Off The Sucker)'. So that's how I hooked up with P-Funk."

'Give Up The Funk (Tear The Roof Off The Sucker)' would become the first P-release to go gold. "I mean, I was *in* after that," says the drummer. "I also co-wrote 'Do That Stuff' and me and Mike Hampton wrote 'If You Got Funk You Got Style'. Me and Mike also wrote 'Field Manoeuvres'. It went on *Uncle Jam Wants You* after I'd left. And they tried to tell people Tiki played on that! Tiki had passed away so he was not on that record. George always had a problem with his writers. He'd always give it to Bootsy and Bernie every time. We'd go in the studio and it was never like 'OK here's the sheet, here's the tune we're gonna go over. I want you guys to play this'. It was like we'd just go in and start a groove. I'd just start locking into something.

"When I was playing a track instead of playing the beat all the way through, I always liked to see if there was a change I could work around. I'd always try and play a lick that was different from what I started with, then somewhere along the way I would go back to that lick or part of that lick that I started with and it would end up different. I'd try to lock on and vibe with the tune; compose on the tune instead of just playing straight through. That came from my coming from doo-wop. I knew what the changes would be when they were singing, when to put in a lick or bunch of fills.

"The stuff that I did I couldn't have been high. Everything I played on a record I always concentrated on. 'Right, this is a record, this is not a live show'. I got hip to all that at a young age. When you play on a record it's totally different to what you play live.

"Years before I went through Cincinnati with the Chambers Brothers and can remember Bootsy hanging out backstage looking like Sly Stone tripping on acid. He told me would never work with George again in his life. He'd played on *America Eats Its Young* so I guess he got ripped off or something. Soon as I went to Detroit, he's there with George. I'm like 'Oh, OK'."

Most of the recording was done across around-the-clock sessions at United Sound in September 1975. The group crashed at the University Motel over the road if they hadn't already curled up comatose on the studio floor. "That was home right there, boy; a little dump hotel," recalled Gary. "You could record all night long, long as you wanted to. Then, when you got tired, just walk on across the street, flop over there in the bed."

As one of the band members with a family home Jerome was not so impressed with the Spartan arrangements. "I hated Detroit. Not the city as a whole but George had us in this sleazy hotel with like four or five of us in a room. We had mattresses on the floor. LA was cool because we recorded in Hollywood Sound. Going back to LA for me was almost like being at home, but when we went to Detroit we were all squeezed into this sleazeball motel right across the street from the studio. We could walk over there but the hotel was like the pits, one of those drive-in type joints. But it brought The Funk out of us.

"We were like young kids, just out there having fun and trying to survive. I had never got into the drugs scene. I was married at the time. I had my kid and my little house plus I had worked with other people. Over the years, I had seen older groups and how they kept falling by the wayside, doing drugs. My mom raised four boys so we were pretty cool, you know?"

The musicians showed stanky solidarity when George declared he wouldn't bathe until an album was completed, but some inevitably buckled under his assembly line regime of keeping the tapes rolling while musicians played until they dropped and were replaced by the next substitute. The only other artist I've encountered who took their studio marathons to such extremes is Keith Richards, but he was allowed to spend nine days on a guitar riff. Obviously both had a mutual friend called bugle helping them along. George was now producing albums by Parliament, Funkadelic and Bootsy and had to keep being fed grooves and new music. Boogie described George as 'the referee', recalling "With *Mothership Connection* it was like they was pressing us. We had to have at least two albums out every year... Sometimes it took more than we could give. It was just phenomenal to go in the studio and work from 12 in the afternoon and you look around and it's two days later."

"We just went in and tracked and tracked," recalls Bigfoot. "It was like just playing in the studio and stuff got on different albums. I remember when we did 'If You Got Funk You Got Style' and we were just in the studio jamming on something and I could see George up in the control room, laughing and tooting. I could see him putting something up his nose. I thought 'He's up there getting high' but he'd hit the record button while we were doing it then go 'That's enough, that's enough'. Then a month later you'd hear the track on an album with their names as writers and everything. We just went in and recorded and recorded tracks and they'd end up a Parliament album, or a Funkadelic album or a Bootsy album, or a Horny Horns album, all from us just tracking and tracking."

Fred bears out this picture of a funk assembly line: "The recording was getting to be a little confusing... We were doing horns to many tracks in different stages of development. It was hard to tell which tracks were Parliament, which were Bootsy and which were just material to be named and used later. Some tracks had titles, some didn't. Some had vocals, some didn't ... I approached it all as a challenge and really took liberties on the tracks that didn't have a clear direction. Our policy was to completely cover the tracks with horns and deal with how they were used during the mixing process. I didn't know it at the time, but with the horn arrangements I was inspiring the theme for many of the songs.

"And I was having the time of my life. Doing some hellafied horn tracks to some hellafied rhythm tracks. We didn't have to worry about how long it took. We didn't have to worry how much it cost… I got to continue to work although in a much more relaxed atmosphere. When George showed up at the studio, the only worry was, 'Did he bring the goodies?' He almost never disappointed us."

Mothership Connection was P-Funk's equivalent of the kind of breakthrough album or all-round peak which happens once in a band's career; crafted in an ongoing creative surge by a band getting on beautifully without notable casualties. George and songwriting partner Bootsy were on a roll of deceptively complex arrangements and robust crowd-pleasers with superclear sound quality and panoramic vision realised by singers and a band rising to the occasion. The album was the commercial package George had been striving to create for years without compromising his original mission, striking the humungous chord that would cause Parliament's popularity to soar over the next three years.

George's initial reference points for the album's inspiration were the *Outer Limits* sci-fi TV show and radio commercials for home remedies scattered with street slang which then stretched way beyond anything known to man as he started building a parallel black universe. According to George, the concept was solidified after an incident where George and Bootsy experienced a UFO 'visit' while driving back to Detroit from Toronto. "We saw this light bouncing from one side of the street to the other," he recounted. "It happened a few times and I made a comment that 'The Mothership was angry with us for giving up the funk without permission.' Just when the light hit the car, all the street lights went out, and there weren't any cars around… I said, 'Bootsy, you think you can step on it?'"

George has re-told this story several times: "I told Bootsy to step on it so we could get away from there but ever since then things have really begun to happen. It was like somebody out there saying they were hip to the Mothership and they approve. We were very nervous about the project. We had a concept that was the bomb but black audiences have never really bought a concept album. We decided to save most of the concept for the second album (*The Clones Of Dr Funkenstein*) and put the hits on the first release to grab attention."

P-defining gems such as 'Make My Funk The P-Funk' illustrated George's story about the Mothership landing on Earth to bring back pure funk to replace the nasty grooves the planet had lost. The Funk was now something to be nurtured and worshipped, both as an irresistible sensual motion on the groin-walloping One and essence celebrating the word Funk's original aromatic meaning: dirty, sexy, sweaty and visceral.

George's masterstroke was applying it to popular sci-fi stereotypes and making the Mothership land in the ghetto before it invaded the stadiums. Parliament in 1975 took recent trends such as glam rock to their largest and loudest extremes, George's silver platform boots boasting nine-inch heels. When Bowie broke through as extraterrestrial future rock star Ziggy Stardust three years earlier he used just a strobe and a sparkly top. By 1974 he was fronting the ultimate cocaine-fuelled extravagance of the Diamond Dogs Tour's enormous onstage city. Huge productions were now the way to go, so George came up with hits that carried the visual potential to carry that kind of extravagance to black audiences and cross over into the exploding white rock market.

While preaching absolute freedom, George steered Parliament's Mothership clear of any repatriation to Africa. On the album it's a symbol of P-Funk's universal message, symbolising a spiritual return to roots and music invoking its original function as a sweaty sex ritual soundtrack. After *Mothership Connection*, George found himself placed at the forefront of what became known as 'Afrofuturism' (predicted in *Mumbo Jumbo* over 20 years earlier). This re-examined and reassessed historical events with a black sci-fi edge. Sun Ra is credited as the first Afrofuturist through his linking of ancient Egypt with outer space.

The P-Funk manifesto and the Mothership can also be seen as parodies of several things, including the Nation Of Islam's Wallace Fard and his protégé Elijah Muhammad with their "wheel in the sky" UFO of God's chosen people, who were non-whites (the original man). According to the Nation, a mad scientist called Yakub created the white race as an experiment, the end result being that the weaker race would rule the stronger one, before the Wheel In The Sky returned to destroy the enemy of God's People. Wallace disappeared in the thirties, said to have gone into this metaphorical forerunner of the Mothership. George declared that the funk "was placed among the secrets of the pyramids until a more positive attitude towards *this* most sacred phenomenon, 'Cloned funk', could be acquired. Here in these terrestrial projects it would wait for the Kiss that would release them to multiply into the image of the chosen one, Doctor Funkenstein." One interpretation is that Dr Funkenstein is Wallace Fard, George poking fun at the theories and myths common to black communities before and during this time. The DJ-related monologues were his way of voicing his messages, grand schemes and world view. In the process, he was setting a template for rapping, complemented by Bigfoot laying the foundations with his block-rocking beats.

"When I first started doing this stuff it was, 'Oh man, he's not singing, he's just rapping all through the songs – and the kids are loving it! Why, why, why?! He should be singing'," remembers Bootsy. "People would criticise. There was so much criticism going on. We were just, 'Why don't they just leave us alone and let us do the things we want to do?' If we hadda listened to them there would have been no P-Funk. *If* we'd have listened… George was nuts and was rebelling. I wasn't listening to no-one, I was rebelling. That's what I think it takes. I ain't saying go out and practise it all the time. I'm just saying that sometimes it takes a certain amount of rebellion to come up with something new, 'cause when it's fresh people go, 'Nah, nah, I can't stand that crap'.

"That's what was happening with George and myself when we first started really. We were delivering to the radio stations and it was like 'Nah, nah!' [he makes a Dracula-movie cross gesture]. Then the kids got into it by seeing us. They would come to the concerts and freak out. Then we started selling out concerts; that's what caught the records on and that's when the records started selling. Next thing you know, the radio had to start playing it because when we was doing it funk was like illegal, you know what I mean? It was like, 'You can't say that on the radio', but we said it so much it was like if you didn't say it you better get hip. 'This is *the thang*! The kids are into this.'

"That's what was happening with that and man, I'm seeing the same thing happening today. It's the same thing. 'Wow! It's like you never know you're going to go through that kind of thing when you're growing up and you're a kid. You never think you're going to be looking back seeing that same kind of thing."

And, of course, George had found someone with equal ambition and vision in Neil Bogart who, most crucially, would foot the bill for a Mothership when the time came. The album was created with the extravagant stage show in mind, as George explained: "What really gave me the idea to do it is I got with Neil Bogart, 'cause I knew that he would promote it at that end. He was a good promotion man. And once we did *Chocolate City* – putting black people in situations they have never been in, and it worked, I knew I had to find another place for black people to be. And space was that place... Put niggers in places that you don't usually see 'em. And *nobody* had seen 'em on no spaceships! Once you seen 'em sittin' on spaceship like it was a Cadillac then it was funny, cool."

The *Mothership Connection*'s funky space odyssey begins 'Chocolate City' style with George as space DJ Sir Lollipop ('chocolate coated, freaky and habit forming'), hijacking the airwaves with radio station WEFUNK ('home of uncut funk... The Bomb') before easing into the 'Make my funk the P-Funk/I want my Funk uncut' chant over the band's simmering dynamism on 'P-Funk (Wants To Get Funked Up)'. This new strain of time-release space-funk dynamite was deftly prodded by the Breckers' horns, Bootsy's hump, Bernie's keyboards and an urgent chorale, underpinned by Bigfoot's superbly subtle groove accentuations. 'Mothership Connection' introduces Star Child who conducts a tour of the Chocolate Milky Way galaxy, referencing 'Swing Low, Sweet Chariot' to add to the spiritual undercurrent continued on comments such as 'You have overcome, for I am here'. George's black utopia was now concentrated on the entire universe rather than one chocolate city.

The upbeat 'Unfunky UFO' sees Garry, George and Glenn trading lead vocals about aliens who want to steal The Funk. 'Supergroovalisticprosifunkstication' comes daubed in Bernie's weird synth-tweaking lunacy, embroidering a relentless chant over Bootsy's unstoppable throb. 'Handcuffs' harks back to vocal group origins, giving the Parliament singers a classy Stax-like funk field to cavort in amid gorgeous muted brass and Beatles-y backing vocals.

'Give Up The Funk (Tear The Roof Off The Sucker)' was the album's biggest hit, making number 15 as a single. Coming straight in with Sting Ray's baritone it's a pure groove vehicle with a massed choir extolling the Funk in the nasty fashion that would soon become the norm. Girl rappers the Sequence provided one of the first P-Funk covers on their 1981 Sugarhill single 'Funky Sound (Tear The Roof Off)'. Unusually but commendably, they credit Bigfoot, George and Bootsy as composers.

Mothership Connection goes out on 'Night Of The Thumpasorus Peoples', Bootsy and Bernie's *tour de force*, with the former bubbling to the fore in one of his finest bass stretches and the latter coaxing dirty noises out of his synth. The 'Da da da' scat hook and growling baritone sax belches provide the ideal coda. The album became the most successful P-Funk outing so far, reaching number 13 in the *Billboard* chart and going gold (it was later ranked 274 in *Rolling Stone*'s 500 greatest albums list).

As the intense sessions wound down, Don Davis (who co-owned the studio with George) asked if Funkadelic would play on a new song for singer Johnny Taylor, who he managed. Garry, Glenn, Bootsy, Bernie and Tiki duly laid down the backing for 'Disco Lady', which went on to hold the number one spot on the *Billboard* Hot 100 for four weeks, going platinum.

As he was prone to do after happening on fresh new talent, Frank Zappa offered the band $500 a week to come to his house for some sessions, particularly headhunting Glenn Goins. "But I could smell that; that's the first step," said Garry. "It never fazed me. Funk is home."

They turned the Mother down and wouldn't regret it as the next step was taking it to the stage. And not just any stage.

Chapter Ten

The Awesome Power Of A Fully Operational Mothership

"After I saw how things worked (at Casablanca), I bought the spaceship and he paid for it with our royalties. I don't mind, because he wouldn't have paid us if I hadn't bought the spaceship."

George Clinton

1976 was the year the funk bomb went off as George followed the recently released *Mothership Connection* with four major P-Funk albums drawn from the creative cooking pot that was bubbling fiercely at United Sound Studios.

April saw Parliament's first US top 20 gold single with 'Give Up The Funk (Tear The Roof Off The Sucker)' reach number 15. The Mothership saga then continued with their stellar next instalment, followed by the debut of Bootsy's Rubber Band in August and two Funkadelic albums released in September and October on different record labels – all followed by one of the most breathtakingly audacious live shows the world has ever seen.

When Parliament toured through 1975 they were already selling out auditoriums from Kentucky to Cleveland, playing their most prestigious gig so far at New York's Madison Square Garden on August 16. The early months of 1976 saw the group headlining similarly sized venues like Nassau Coliseum and Philadelphia's Spectrum. They were soon to be joined by Bootsy's Rubber Band for shows that would mark Fred Wesley and Maceo Parker's entry on to the P-Funk stage before they double-dated with Parliament on the Mothership towards the end of year. Up until now, the pair had just been toiling in studios in Hollywood and New York, as well as at United Sound. Fred described the sessions as being "like a musical laboratory staffed by many on-call funk scientists, each skilled in his particular field of endeavour". He was also quite shocked at the crotch-grabbing and simulated orgies that accompanied George's X-rated live moves, pronouncements and rhymes, deeming them the kind of things "I thought would get you arrested and put in jail if done in public".

The first P-Funk show that Fred and Maceo witnessed first-hand was at Washington's Capital Center in front of 20,000 screaming, mainly black P-punters in early 1976. The pair were there to watch the show and work out the best places for them to be called forward once their horn parts had been devised.

Fred observed that the dressing room was "more like an army preparing for battle than band getting ready to do a show". Each night, the band piled into the 'Funk Trunk' to grab their stage gear – Bigfoot's silver suit and boots topped with pith helmet; Fuzzy's tie-dyed long johns and alien monster mask, new boy Michael Hampton's long black cape and fencing mask; Calvin's understated American Indian look; Grady's all-purple Arab garb; Garry's Holiday Inn towel diaper; George's sheet-and-boots combination and everyone slapping on wild make-up. For his first night Fred dressed with caution in his wide-lapelled brown suit and a green shirt, daringly worn without a tie.

Coming from James Brown's frugal setup, Fred was taken aback at the mountain of keyboards, guitars, drums, amps, speakers, lights and a monitor system bigger than the Godfather's entire sound system. Unbelievably, each member of the band had their own white hippie technician. With the stage in darkness, Bigfoot started a groove before every musician blasted the low E which brought the lights up to reveal the band staring menacingly at the crowd before launching into 'Cosmic Slop'. This erupted into a lengthy guitar solo from Michael Hampton, before Garry and Fuzzy started delivering those pain-driven lyrics.

"When the other singers came in, the sound was so full and so musically perfect that you could have been listening to the Mormon Tabernacle Choir," recalled Fred. "But what you were looking at could have been aliens from the moon." After marvelling at the panorama of musical styles on show ("all played with serious funk attitudes") he describes George's entrance as when "things really got going. He was like the party master. He didn't sing, didn't play an instrument, but he did direct the whole show, telling who to play where and what, guiding the audience through all the singalongs and dances... He was everywhere, wearing only a sheet, so you know he flashed everybody at one time or another. At one point, he brought the guitar players together, and they all went to the edge of the stage and challenged the audience by making phallic gestures with the necks of their guitars. Only thing was, George didn't have a guitar."

Plans were afoot for a tour which would open with Bootsy's Rubber Band and close with Parliament/Funkadelic. Fred enlisted trumpeter Rick Gardner for the Rubber Band brass section he was putting together with Maceo. Rick came from a group called Chase, who had been fronted by four trumpeters before they were all killed in a plane crash. The trio joined the rest of the Rubber Band at Bootsy's mother's house in Cincinnati to rehearse their live show in her little basement. With Ms Nettie and Bootsy's family cooking and looking after the boys, they whipped up the live set from songs which would appear on *Stretchin' Out In Bootsy's Rubber Band* when it was released in August.

The group then moved to a large rehearsal studio to fine-tune the production. Bootsy didn't have his star bass or specs yet but all his shiny new equipment was in white and red. It was also adorned with stars. Bootsy now had Warner Brothers and management financing a concerted plan to promote him as a solo act while he worked out an identity for himself.

Finally the time had come. Bootsy's ascent to highest profile P-Funk spin-off, George's second-in-command and songwriting partner had been far from overnight. In fact, it was five years since J.B.'s escapees the House Guests had bailed out Funkadelic after the departure of the original line-up before Bootsy buckled under the on-the-road madness and went back to Detroit to form his own band. He had loomed on a couple of Funkadelic tracks since then, unveiling his Bootsy persona on 'Be My Beach' and writing the immortal bassline for 'Cosmic Slop' without a credit. George had wanted a Bootsy project as his first P-Funk spin-off but first had to grab the bassist back from Los Angeles where he was being groomed by George's rival Jeffrey Bowen, who we met before with Invictus. Bootsy duly returned, in time for *Up For The Down Stroke* and the start of Parliament's golden run. He was also clutching demos of sumptuous new songs he'd been writing such as 'I'd Rather Be With You' and 'Vanish In Our Sleep' that would perfectly complement the songs he started writing with George. The pair briefly became a kind of funk Lennon & McCartney, catalysed by their chemistry and mutual sense of humour.

"I think me and George fed off each other so much it was like a right and a left arm," Bootsy told me. "We had never talked too much. It was always a natural thing. He knew what I needed and what I wanted and I knew what he needed and what he wanted. It was one of them kind of things. It didn't take too much explaining. Just like your old lady, when you find yourself having to explain so much and then she still don't understand. It's like 'Why am I doing this? Why am I explaining when it keeps getting worse?' Over and over. But we never had to do that. It was like 'Da da dee, yeah yeah'. We didn't know what we was doin', we was just doin'. When I came to find out that people were *studying* what we were doing."

"Bootsy and I were walking down the street when it was time for him to do an album," recalled George. "I said, 'I'm gonna have to do a record with your band Bootsy'. At that time he was a Funkadelic but he was so dynamic it didn't make sense for him just to be a Funkadelic. He had to do his own thing, because we were a psychedelic band mainly. He was like a horn band from the James Brown school of music, so I said, 'We gotta get a band for you.' He said, 'Well what would be a nice name?' Off the top of my head, I said, 'I'm gonna call it the Rubber

Band... stretchin' out with the Rubber Band. When I get a pun I can just go crazy and do it from every possible angle, with his alias Casper the friendly ghost. That one was done in a matter of 10 minutes walking up 43rd Street in New York. All of that was done between the hotel and the store."

The Rubber Band began in the studio when Bootsy, Garry, and Michael Hampton were hammering the 'Stretchin' Out' groove and it started catching fire, prompting the bassist to exclaim "Man, we're stretchin' out on that one!" Hearing this, George leapt up yelling "That's it, stretchin' out *in a Rubber Band*!"

George has also explained that being such a distinct character meant that Bootsy had to have his own thing and this required a certain amount of persuasion: "Bootsy didn't want to use his nickname. I said, 'Man, you look like a Bootsy, you got to play on it. You ain't got to be egotistical about it, but you got to play on what's natural.' So we did the song 'We Want Bootsy'. He was so embarrassed, he didn't want to do that. I had to do Dr Funkenstein just so he could do Bootsy."

"I've always looked at it like Bootsy was one of George's alter egos," observes Frankie Kash. "Bootsy was the cat that George maybe would have been if it wasn't so much work. You understand what I'm saying? Didn't nobody even know who George was. We'd get through doing a show, George and I would walk through the crowd, and people would be like, 'Which one is George Clinton?' He got off on that one for years."

George also cited Bootsy's Rubber Band as widening P-Funk's appeal to different ages, stating, "Bootsy and his group came in and that was a whole different concept within itself. So what I did was record Bootsy by himself with another group, recorded Parliament which sounded like that but was a little more grown up. Bootsy was aimed more at kids – we called it silly serious. Parliament was a little older and Funkadelic was for a little older than that."*

---

* *Funk* author Rickey Vincent memorably described Bootsy's Rubber Band as "the *exposed genitals* of the P-Funk vibe".

Bootsy's House Guests bandmates were all for the new band, which was sometimes called Bootsy's Early Sun in its early stages. "We'd always wanted to do a solo project, so we broke away to set up Bootsy's Rubber Band," recalled Frankie. "George was totally all for that. He nurtured it... our rhythm section teamed up with their horn section. Maceo and Fred were our idols. Plus, they really dug it."

"Eighty per cent of the P-Funk songs I worked on was tracks I put together," reasoned Bootsy. "That's what I was used to doing and that's what George wanted at the time. George knew how to use what he had. He was a music chef."

"Where I figure that I might have done at least one thing that had a little intelligence in it was the fact that we tied all the groups together," asserted George. "One could support the other when necessary, it made us less vulnerable. Also I know how the system likes to play one artist off against another, so we were able to get round that. Like when Bootsy came along, it was obvious that they would eventually shoot for him as the star... And sure enough, as he got more popular, people started telling me, 'You're the one that made him and now he's using you', while at the same time they were telling him exactly the same thing about me. But before he'd even started doing his first album, we spent a month on a boat in Miami, just fishing and tripping and talking about what was bound to happen and what we could do to plan our way around the system. So when it came time for them to pit him against me I said, 'I ain't gonna rap now 'cause everything I say is incriminating now we're both big. Just remember what we talked about two years ago.' And he went away, it took him about a month, and he came back and said, 'Yeah, just like we planned it.' And that in itself kept us past the point where we're supposed to bust up."

If George created the solo opportunity, Bootsy's look was all his – the star glasses, star bass, sparkle and miracles of platform boot design were all of his devising, along with that languid cartoon Hendrix vocal delivery. "The whole stage thing for Bootsy was my idea," he affirmed. "George and I never talked about my image. George left that up to me. That's why we got it on so good." Now, it's a fabulous enduring visual for him to have fun with forever. Nothing Bootsy wears can be too outrageous, no platforms too tall or cape too dazzling. But it must also be remembered that he revolutionised bass playing in black music, creating the primal throb of 'Sex Machine' and exploring new effects in his quest for the perfect Bootsy groove.

"When he came back, he had just started getting into gadgets," recalled Garry. "That put a whole 'nother side on it. He became the Jimi Hendrix of the bass."

Bootsy also invented other characters to spring out of his ultra-cool rhinestone rock star from another planet, including his monstrous evil twin Bootzilla and Casper the Friendly Ghost (based on the TV cartoon). George was on lyrical overdrive, dubbing the fans 'Funkateers' because he heard that Bootsy was raised on the Mouseketeers. "All George needed was a spark, and that's what I did for him," said Bootsy. "What he did for me, I probably haven't realised it all yet."

Along with Bootsy, Catfish and Kash, the Rubber Band consisted of Fred, Maceo and white classically trained keyboard player Frederick 'Flintstone' Allen. Vocals were handled by Bootsy in his Casper persona ('kind of friendly when I want to be, and funky otherwise'), Leslyn Bailey (who would soon flee the group, freaked out by the untamed behaviour raging around her), while singers Gary 'Mudbone' Cooper and Robert 'Peanut' Johnson handled the slowies.

After a Spartan "pre-tour tour" tightened the Rubber Band into suitable shape and they added yet another J.B.'s refugee to the brass section in Richard 'Kush' Griffith, the group undertook a run of dates with Parliament/Funkadelic leading up to the album's August release. These often featured bands of the day doing an opening slot, including Rufus and Natalie Cole, but usually the Brothers Johnson. Fred Wesley recalls Bootsy taking a while to settle into his new frontman role and display the kind of confidence which would ignite the band's onstage combustion. He recalls the show in Orlando, Florida where Bootzilla emerged in all his glory during his cataclysmic bass solo in 'I've Got The Munchies For Your Love': "He worked it like he was making love to the entire audience, slowly and methodically bringing himself, the bass, the band, and everybody in the audience to an explosive orgasm. After that everything caught fire... From then on, Bootsy's Rubber Band had arrived. It was and always will be the funkiest and most dynamic band that ever was. The vocals, the horns, the rhythm and, of course, Bootsy have never been topped or even equalled before or since. I just knew that we were soon to be the hottest band around."

Fred was less happy with the business arrangements – he saw himself as a founder member of the group, but was still on regular fees for arranging, playing gigs and recording (where at first George was paying him double the union scale). Worried that no matter how big the band became that would be it, he confronted George and Bootsy at various times but the issue kept being put off. This meant he had no royalties or publishing contracts. Instead he raised his fee for arrangements and George got a deal with Atlantic for him and Maceo to record under the name of the 'Horny Horns'. The name came from George's wife Liz who remarked during a blowing session "That sure is horny". Fred maintains she was referring to the preponderance of brass. The advance kept them happy for a while.

Meanwhile, the elevation of Bootsy to P-Funk's next solo star rankled with some of the musicians. "I remember every night we'd have Hugh Masekela or the Brothers Johnson or the Bar-Kays opening up for us then Bootsy would go on and go nuts," says Bigfoot. "At the end of each show George would call Bootsy back up. I'd be going to Glenn, 'Why's he calling up Bootsy? This is P-Funk'. We spanked Bootsy's band every night. But he always put Bootsy back on, putting Bootsy in everybody's head and it used to piss us off. 'What's happening with him and Bootsy? What about P-Funk? What about us?'"

The discontent brewing with the Horny Horns, Bigfoot, Glenn (and also the Parliaments singers who would quit after the Earth tour) took a backseat for the rest of 1976 as many elements which defined P-Funk took shape. George was on too much of a roll in the biggest year of his life to sit down and work out balanced career plans for his musicians. Also there were a lot of drugs about. As he told Lloyd Bradley when he asked if there were jealousies or hierarchies in P-Funk: "Oh sure, but you can't avoid that. It never got to the point where I was like having to play the schoolmaster keeping the kids in order. Mostly it was people coming to me saying they weren't being utilised enough, and I'd have to say, well you can't be doing everything, besides, I'd tell 'em, just listen to the results."

Unusually for P-Funk, the *Stretchin' Out...* sleeve features a photo of the artist, as Bootsy rides a motorcycle in through the mist. He was now toting his original 'space bass' made in Warren, Michigan by Larry Pless of the Gus Zoppi music store. It can be seen leaning against a chair on the back sleeve, white and dripping with The Funk. The 'space bass' is certainly the most dominant sound on the album; popping, swooping and gnashing through side one's turbo-funking 'Stretchin' Out (In A Rubber Band)'. That riff remains one of the most incendiary in all of Funk; a seismic bedrock being ram-raided by Garry and Mike Hampton's guitars before Casper floats in to introduce himself against cheeky backing vocals, nagging horns and Bernie's sci-fi theatre keyboards. Already a new sound and funk dynamic had been introduced into the P-Funk canon, as continued on the merciless 'Psychoticbumpschool' maintaining the pressure 'with some bump music'. 'Another Point Of View' harks back to the House Guests era, as a mean Funkadelic-style riff emerges from the bubbling sonic cauldron. It's immensely tight and complex as the riffs surge and swallow-dive with that J.B.'s schooling firmly in evidence.

Side two sees Bootsy drop the tempo and unveil the Rubber Band's sensual side which would fly on epic pantaloony hump ballads such as 'I'd Rather Be With You'. Boasting Mudbone's first major performance and a blaster of a Bootsy solo, this sublime slice of major soul surgery was the album's first single, reaching number 25 on the R&B charts. Laying out the future Bootsy pattern of booming funk-ups on one side and ballads on the flip, it's followed by Leslyn's *tour de force* 'Love Vibes'. The track's R&B flavour is untypical of the album but perfect foreplay for the slinky 'Physical Love', which boasts Eddie Hazel materialising as a blazing asteroid counterpart to Bootsy's liquid whomp. The album closes with the impossibly dreamy 'Vanish In Our Sleep', which reflects upon society's rules for romance.

In what turned out to be a truly ground-breaking album, Bootsy had started the ball rolling for his new persona while establishing a surreally humorous wordplay blueprint for the future and a scorching brand of funk, countered by P-Funk's new take on the ultimate sweet soul ballad. And who else can do the wobbling Bootsy war yelp, one of the silliest noises of all time?

Meanwhile, Parliament's follow-up to *Mothership Connection* had to be a stone killer. George had deliberately put the upfront hits from the United Sound sessions on *Mothership Connection*, leaving the deeper conceptual outings for the follow-up. Released in July 1976, *The Clones Of Dr Funkenstein* was lighter and more melodic, with multi-tiered vocals and Fred Wesley's lush horn arrangements to the fore. Although misread at the time as being a bit of an anti-climax after its uproarious predecessor, the album could be seen as the most accessibly commercial P-Funk release of this period.

This time, George's cosmological concept revolves around intergalactic leader of the descendants of the Thumpasaurus Peoples, Dr Funkenstein. The Doctor is the master technician of Clone Funk who can cure all man's ills because 'the bigger the headache the bigger the pill' – the pill being his omnipotent baaad self. If archangel Star Child's arrival was the 'Mothership Connection', then this is his secret boss – whose forerunners were super-intelligent aliens who hid the secrets of The Funk in the pyramids for five thousand years. Only now was the time right for Earth to receive them via the Clones – Children of Productions responsible for keeping everyone on The One and capable of funkacising whole galaxies.

Most tracks are Clinton/Collins/Worrell compositions with Glenn and Garry pitching in. As most of the tracks were drawn from the United Sound sessions, the personnel is pretty much the same. After a dramatic organ intro and George's scene-setting 'Listen while I tell you of the Clones' is played backwards, 'Gamin' On Ya' steams in with prime J.B.'s-style horn-driven funk. The vocal revisits a line from the earlier Parliaments anti-Vietnam single 'Come In Out Of The Rain' – 'People keep waitin' on a change, but they ain't got enough sense to come in out of the rain.' Dr. Funkenstein announces himself on the track of the same name, laying out his narcissistic 'kiss me on my ego' spiel, which is fed by the girls' saucy 'We love to funk you Funkenstein, your funk is the best'. The provocative 'Children Of Production' is the deepest track. It concerns the 'biological time bomb' created to 'blow the cobwebs out your mind'. This refers to powers–that–be creating divisions in society to keep friction brewing.

'Gettin' To Know You' is this album's gorgeous Garry vocal outing, providing further evidence that this album marked a peak of Fred's horn arrangements. With a hook inspired by a favourite crowd chant among the girls in St Louis, 'Do That Stuff' was the obvious single (reaching number 22), achieving bass–drum–guitar nirvana with cool vocal interplay between George, Glenn, Garry and Taka Khan. Bernie's sprightly synth theme was later hijacked to great success by dance producers Röyksopp. The music also revisits the instrumental part of 'You Can't Miss What You Can't Measure', which was itself a reworking of 1965 Parliaments single 'Heart Trouble'.

'Everything Is On The One' is another subtle funk masterwork, garnished with audaciously trumping bass gurgles, seriously dynamic brass and a naggingly catchy chorus. The Goins–sung and composed 'I've Been Watching You (Move Your Sexy Body)' uncurls into one of the great P-Funk ballads drifting slinkily through twinkling baroque–psych bridges into an erogenous smooch-fest. Glenn also sings 'Funkin' For Fun', his wall-shaking intro heralding a gospel-hotwired knees–up harking back to *Chocolate City*. Rather than outer space, *The Clones...* sounds more the coolest city album thanks to those multi-tiered horns, Bigfoot's deftly understated pulses and the Newark church fervour of an increasingly assertive Glenn Goins.

The Clones Of Dr Funkenstein became Parliament's second gold album, reaching number 20 on the *Billboard* album chart while its second single 'Dr. Funkenstein' reached number 43. Now George had deftly pulled off the potentially hazardous next album he was in an even stronger position with Casablanca. Happily, the label was similarly strong, after its fortunes were swivelled the previous year when Kiss finally took off with their live album, the success of *Mothership Connection* and Neil Bogart getting in early on the rising disco movement by signing Munich-based diva Donna Summer to cause a sensation with soft-core moanathon 'Love To Love You Baby'. This started a run of success for Donna that continued until the end of the decade as she became the Queen of Disco and racked up a string of ground-breaking electronically driven dance hits produced by the visionary Giorgio Moroder.

This success put Bogart in a position to finance George's idea for a spectacular stage show to go with the *Mothership Connection* concept – the P-Funk Earth Tour. Through 1976 and 77, the show would become America's main musical arena attraction, overshadowing similar spectacles such as the Hunger City of David Bowie's 1974 *Diamond Dogs* tour and the Stones' lotus stage of 1975. The Bowie shows set a new precedent for presentation, with theatricality eclipsing spontaneity to a degree hitherto unseen in rock, but Bowie, perhaps distracted by his own excess, declined to connect with his audience, a deliberate ploy but one which not only seemed at odds with rock's traditions but also confounded his audience. The Stones' tour was much the same as ever, only on a far bigger stage which seemed to dwarf the group. Ribald as ever, a huge inflatable cock rose up during 'Star Star', but their concert at Earls Court in 1975 is probably the worst time I've seen them in 46 years of avid Stones gig-going due to the appalling sound and Keef's practically inert state.

The Mothership show was just as spectacular but, with the cavalcade of costumed P-Funkers churning out uncut funk with deadly crowd-detonating dynamics among the barrage of cartoon-like props, crucially managed to reach out to and include every one of the vast crowds who flocked to see it.

The Mothership was P-Funk's biggest, most successful project, as George took his crew into the kind of 20,000 capacity arenas normally used by big rock bands with the kind of show he'd dreamed of since *West Side Story* opened up the road from his old Broadway office. "We'd been planning that since the Who's *Tommy* and *Jesus Christ Superstar*," said George. "We'd been planning to do a funk opera for a long time, so when *Mothership Connection* was a hit record, we put it all together."

In 1975 Maurice White's Earth, Wind & Fire show demonstrated how they'd come a long way from the *Sweet Sweetback's Baadasssss Song* soundtrack by scoring massive success with their chart-friendly pop-funk draped in African imagery. Combining J.B. funk essence with contagious chorus action, 'Shining Star' was a number one pop hit that year. Their *That's The Way Of The World* album also cleaned up, quickly followed by live double album *Gratitude,* capturing the mega-tour which raised the bar for black bands' live shows with its glam-informed costumes, flying musicians, rotating drum kits and a new variation on the human cannonball routine.

It was all about the budget, and George shrewdly managed to obtain the necessary financial backing for his own grand plan out of Neil Bogart. "It was our money to start off with. We did the big Mothership show because we paid for it ourselves," explained George. "After I saw how things worked (at Casablanca), I bought the spaceship and he paid for it with our royalties. I don't mind, because he wouldn't have paid us if I hadn't bought the spaceship. This way I was able to use that spaceship on the road to promote Parliament, Funkadelic *and* Bootsy... So although we only got paid one album's worth of royalties from Casablanca, we ended up with a budget for promotion the same size or bigger than the white groups were getting. Which was much more to us than money, which we probably wouldn't have got anyway."

"George called me and he said, 'Sidney, guess what? I got a spaceship," recounted Sidney Barnes. "'You got a what?' 'I got a spaceship, man. It comes onstage.' George was one of the first black arena acts – George and Maurice White – and that's only because their shows were so extravagant... George was blowing his whole wad on it... He said, 'It's like a pimp with just enough money to either buy an apartment or a Cadillac. He buys the Cadillac, and he sleeps in the Cadillac. Saves money one way but he got the flashy car he can ride around in, make the hoes think he's got a place, so he can make the hoes work and then spend that.' I said, 'That makes good sense'."

George was aware of the competition and knew he had to come up with something much bigger than a few spangled codpieces. The sky couldn't even be the limit, just as he had fiercely resisted Bogart wanting to call the last album *Landing In The Ghetto*, recalling, "I said, 'No, no, ghetto is a cool place by now. You're late with that shit! People ready to build up the ghettos and keep 'em! So that ain't gonna shock nobody.' It was Parliament again, so if we're gonna go back to costumes we got to go way deeper, couldn't come back looking like Earth, Wind & Fire or Ohio Players. We gotta come back lookin' like we're *steppin'*."

Scripted by George, the P-Funk Earth Tour employed the talents of Broadway designer Jules Fisher (who had designed the lighting and production for both Bowie and the Stones), Kiss haberdasher Larry LeGaspi, an 80-strong touring party that included over 40 musicians, 35 crew members (including riggers from *Disney On Ice*) and four semi-trucks, three buses and a Winnebago camper to transport everything. It cost $500,000, with the Mothership alone accounting for $275,000.

Dress rehearsals started in summer 1976 at the Kiss rehearsal space in a former air force hangar at the public/military Stewart Airport, Newburgh, 60 miles north of midtown Manhattan. The first two weeks were spent making sure the Mothership worked, along with the inflatable Rolls Royce to be stripped down by car thieves, a skull smoking a huge joint and floppy pyramid for the band to make their entrance from. For once the chaos was choreographed on a set designed for maximum impact.

Starting in New Orleans on October 27, the Earth Tour rolled around the country playing to nearly a million punters in cities including Baton Rouge, Jackson, Houston, Denver, San Antonio, Dallas, Tulsa, Shreveport, Nashville, Baltimore, Pittsburgh, Charlotte, Greensboro, Birmingham, Columbus, Jacksonville, Miami, Philly, Atlanta and Madison Square Garden again on December 17. The following year, the tour cranked up again as the Flashlight Tour to reach cities including Washington, LA, Oakland, Memphis, Kansas, Las Vegas and another Madison Square Garden that December.

James Jackson's introduction ended with him sticking a six-foot spliff into the mouth of the Funkadelic skull and lighting it with a five-foot Bic lighter, as the band appeared from the pyramid through the smoke and George made his entrance in a pimpmobile constructed out of silver pillows on a wire frame. There was a stroboscopic Bop Gun wielded by 'Starchild' Garry attached to a harness, bombs and pyros; and later giant birds and other silliness joined the massed troupe sporting an array of outrageous costumes ranging from silver space creations to Egyptian robes. The huge 'Funk Trunk' was stuffed with props and costumes, through which the band would rummage to find something suitable for that night's show. Apparently, the almighty whiff which went up when the trunk was opened was also not of this planet. Sometimes, George still favoured the sheet or tablecloth with a hole cut out for his head, extravagantly accessorised with platform boots and a long blonde wig.

The ex-J.B. musicians found it hard to adjust from shiny shoes and tuxedos to outrageous fancy dress, so they just kept it casual. "George didn't care what you wore though," recalled Maceo. "His motto was, 'Come as you are, life ain't nothing but a party', and he meant it. Half the time, he didn't have anything on under the giant white fur coat he wore everywhere."

Amid mounting crowd uproar, the huge venues would plunge into darkness while Glenn Goins gazed into the distance shielding his eyes and drawing from his gospel grounding to declare 'I think I hear the Mothership coming, I think I see the Mothership coming', while the crowd sang 'Swing down sweet chariot stop and let me ride'. Sparks started flying at the rear of the arena as a small spaceship on a wire descended overhead, making its way towards the stage before an explosive cavalcade of smoke and noise heralded the gargantuan silver Mothership itself landing almost on top of Bigfoot. With smoke billowing, lights blinking and engines roaring, the hatch opened to reveal George as Dr Funkenstein, swaggering and pimp-rolling down the staircase in shades, huge white hat, long blond wig and white ermine coat with cane; arrived from outer space to show Earth what the funk was all about.

Unlike his freewheeling bandmates rolling around the stage Bigfoot was tethered to his drum stool for the duration, keeping the essential pulse up no matter what insanity was happening around him and sounding as big as a planet's heartbeat. "I got cooled off because everything landed on top of me," he recalls. "All the foam and everything landed right on the drum riser so it was shhhhh – relief! When the thing landed in front of me you couldn't see me for the about five minutes. It would land there on top of the drums and they would bring up the stairwell in front of me but it was cool. I would complain 'When that thing land I can't be seen!' When you're young you're thinking 'How come I can't be seen?'"

The resolutely teetotal and lifelong drug-free Maceo, who became musical director, stage manager and MC, tried to inject some order into the onstage chaos by steering musicians on and off stage. "The first time I saw the Mothership land onstage and watched George emerge from that thing was every bit as impressive and awe-inspiring as any of James [Brown]'s electrifying spins, twirls and splits," he observed.

"That moment where the Mothership gets ready to come down and George gets ready to come out, I would say that's probably my greatest thrill," said Parlet mainstay Jeanette Washington. "You're not looking at the audience because you're facing George to give them this effect, 'Dr Funkenstein is here.' But to hear those people just go out of their minds…"

As Parliament toured throughout 1976, their support bands included Bootsy's Rubber Band, Hugh Masekela's Nigerian group and original inspiration Sly Stone, who'd fallen on hard coke-wrecked times since his late sixties peak. This new Family Stone, led by Sly and Cynthia Robinson, included 17-year-old Dawn Silva from Sacramento, California and Sly's cousin Lynn Mabry as backing singers. After the Family Stone played the guest spot between Bootsy's Rubber Band and Parliament/Funkadelic in November 1976, the girls were whisked onto the Mothership after George asked them to sing on projects being worked on at the time, including albums by the Horny Horns and Eddie Hazel, before they joined the touring chorale.

Dawn shared everyone's amazement when she witnessed the live P-Funk spectacle for the first time, recounting, "It was the most bizarre thing that I ever saw. I'd never seen men with make-up on. They were incredible entertainers, massively powerful voices, sarcastic lyrics. Just like a little kid going to the circus for the first time, I was in such awe. Sly loved 'em."

Suffering from acute stage fright Sly appeared on the tour for a month. Then, having difficulty dealing with the changing world of funk, he headed for his lengthy drug-accompanied sabbatical, giving his blessing for the girls to join up with George. "I went to the school of funk," recalled Dawn. "George one day came up, gave me a little silver button. He says, 'This is your funk badge. You just graduated." The following year, the pair would be unveiled as the magnificent Brides Of Funkenstein. "I've always wanted to be in the audience when the Mothership came down," she added. "I felt that same emotion every night, night after night, wondering what they were experiencing. Because it was dark, all you could see was this spaceship, and I can feel the audience roaring and screaming, and couldn't see them. Thousands and thousands of people. The vibrations would literally go right through me."

"The audience is as much a part of the opera as we are," said George. "The entire arena is part of the event, even the parking lot attendants. When they come to the show, they can get into it from wherever they please. That's how it is designed." At one show, the pyrotechnics guy packed too much explosive into the charges and the blasts shattered all the windows in the building, cutting some of the crowd with broken glass. Maceo recalls being shocked at how the injured were proudly "wearing their cuts like badges of honour". He also revealed "It's no secret that George and a lot of the guys in Parliament used to be into some heavy stuff on a pretty regular basis, but even when they were messed up those guys could play well."

Former Invictus producer Ron Dunbar, who helmed Freda Payne's 'Band Of Gold' and often kept United Sound running around the clock for any band members who might be around to put something down, remembered, "I went on the road with them, and that's when I got really impressed, because I had no idea they were that huge. I just thought it was another group out there with a bunch of guitars, just trying to get over. But it was beyond my imagination, because George had these semis full of equipment, he had this spaceship. Then I saw the crowds. You're talking about 15, 20 thousand people being packed in."

George landed the Mothership in Times Square at daybreak and in front of the United Nations building on First Avenue the following afternoon. "All of that, we knew it was history when we was doing it," stated George. "I mean, when I decide to spend half a million dollars on a show – $275,000 on the spaceship, and then all the stuff that went with it... Since we'd had to come out of the hippie vibe of the sixties and do something new, it was time to be glitter again. With the Mothership and the glitter and looking like money, I knew what we were doing. I knew that it was gonna be Broadway play, movies… historical."

James Brown's father, Joe, made a sharp observation concerning the US black music industry in Gerri Hirshey's history of soul, *Nowhere To Run*, "White folks, some white young folks, run *away* from America. They ashamed. Black folks, they run all over, up North, everywhere, tryin' to get *into* America." George bypassed that issue by simply *taking* America, black and white. Like Alan Freed attracting 25,000 teenagers to his mixed bill Moondog Dance at the Cleveland Arena in 1952, Clinton's demolition of inter-musical segregation with the P-Funk tours of the late seventies remains one of his greatest achievements.

But there was discontent brewing within the P-ranks as the distance between George and original Parliaments Davis, Haskins, Simon and Thomas widened way past staying in separate hotels on tour. The last straw was reported to be contracts of employment they were presented with for George's new Parliafunkadelicment Thang Company, of which he was sole president.

It was perhaps inevitable that members fled the nest as P-Funk continued to grow and 1976 saw the original quartet's last recording sessions before leaving the following June. This sparked some crossover chaos when two Funkadelic albums emerged within a month of each other, caused by George signing a deal with Warner Brothers, which released *Hardcore Jollies* in October (although it wasn't released in the UK until two years later), while still owing Westbound an album. Boladian was given *Tales Of Kidd Funkadelic*, released the previous month. In theory George kept the more commercial tracks for the major debut, seeing the new deal as a step towards the greater success and wider audiences he was enjoying with Parliament over at Casablanca.

Bigfoot played on both album sessions, recalling "*Hardcore Jollies* came out when he got the deal with Warner Brothers. It wasn't at all distinctive like if we'd been doing these tracks for Warner Brothers and these tracks for Westbound. Like when 'Field Manoeuvres' was done we were doing the tracks that went on *Hardcore Jollies*; 'If You Got Funk

You Got Style' and all those things... We were doing tracks at that time but some didn't come out till years later on the *Uncle Jam* record."

Tales Of Kidd Funkadelic was constructed out of *Hardcore Jollies* off-cuts handed over by George after he'd signed to Warners. Or, as Pedro Bell's cover credit puts it, "This album was conceived from basic atomic particles of funkasonical protons, combined with chemical products of rubberious fleshy membranes that go 'squish!' in the night and consequently produced by the Main Mangustian of the PARLIAFUNKADELICMENT THANG: George Clinton." Pedro's cover plants the nervous looking Kidd among the usual flotilla of weird space beings and P-Funkers.

The 'Funkadelic Main Invasion Force' was extensively name-checked as 'Bernie da Vinci', Jerome 'Blastifying' Brailey, Garry 'Doo-wop' Shider, Fuzzy, Sting Ray, Calvin 'Coolcumber' Simon, 'Shady' Grady Thomas, Boogie, 'Mangusta' Mike Hampton, Worrell, Nelson and Glenn 'Slumgouster' Goins, joined by 'Maggotusi Vocal Choir' of Jessica Cleaves, Cynthia Davis, Donna Davis, Debbie Edwards, Taka Khan, Pamela Vincent and Debbie Wright, plus the 'Spastic Funkadelic Alumni'; Eddie Hazel, Billy Bass, Bootsy and Ron Bykowski. George's parting shot to Armen Boladian in the thanks is 'P-Funk's Gonna Git Yo Mama!'.

The same roster could now just as easily create a Parliament album as the styles and line-ups of the two outfits became almost interchangeable. Outstanding tracks on the album include the Bernie-driven proto-prog squiggle-pulses of 'Butt To Butt Resuscitation', the quintessential mid-period Funkadelic positive rocker 'Let's Take It To The People' (later sampled by A Tribe Called Quest on *The Low End Theory*'s 'Everything Is Fair') and the Bootsy-bassed sci-fi grind of 'Undisco Kidd', which took a shot at how disco was magnetising increasing numbers of funk brothers to its accelerating bandwagon. Co-credited to Bootsy and Bernie, the track's expressive semi-rap gets into its well-known 'move your sexy body' refrain (which could easily have come from a Parliament album). The storming 'Take Your Dead Ass Home' is the strongest funk track, with Clinton utilising nursery rhyme abuse a-plenty, including his favourite 'There once was a man from Peru, who went to sleep in his

231

canoe, while dreaming of Venus, he took out his penis and woke up with a hand full of goo'.

Glenn soars on 'I'm Never Gonna Tell It', an understated vamp backed with delicious harmonies. (The song would be redone for Philippé Wynne's *Uncle Jam* solo album). 'How Do Yeaw View You' looks at narcissism as addressed by George, Garry and Mudbone. Bernie's 13-minute title track could at first sound a bit noodling compared to the rest of the album but, taken as a stand–alone piece, is another prime example of his relentlessly questing spirit as he pushes around doomy synth tones underpinned by only percolating congas; the closest thing to the original Funkadelic spirit of aural astral travel on the last album before the original contained group concept unravelled following this final release on the record label which launched them. The band had actually been reluctant to part with the label that had given them their start, Calvin Simon declaring "We didn't want to leave Armen. It was George's idea, more or less. He said Armen couldn't afford to do what we wanted to have done. Warner Brothers would spend the money. That's basically what it came down to. At least that's what George was telling us."

Released on October 29, *Hardcore Jollies* was received poorly by fans and press but, despite the lack of a central theme, hit the funk quotient and boasts several gems. For their major debut Pedro 'Blastoid Blaster' Bell's garish sleeve depiction of the album's loose theme of debauchery is hardly a bow to the mainstream, with boggle-eyed mutants, topless women, liberal white globules and references to Funkadelic's past including an 'I Call My Baby Pussy' T-shirt-sporting P-Funk warrior. Side one was originally called 'Osmosis Phase 1' flipped by 'Terribitus Phase 2'.

Dedicated to 'the guitar players of the world' the album boasts some unaccredited Eddie Hazel guitar, and featured duets with Michael Hampton on the scathing title track based on the riff from Parliament's 'Livin' The Life'. Eddie's runs are reminiscent of Jimi's Band of Gypsys period. In fact, 'Comin' Round The Mountain' boasts their former drummer Buddy Miles on percussion. Any long-time Hendrix fan will tell you that the emotion being transmitted from Jimi's soul through his fingers was as important as the technique he could turn on at will. Eddie's style had evolved since the earlier albums, dispensing with effects, in favour of a little Echoplex and phaser on his black Les Paul. On 'Comin' Round the Mountain' his guitar has gained a deeper resonance, dive-bombed by groin-churning swoops and dazzling runs.

'Smokey' is George and Garry on a lust-quivering slow-burner draped in hallucinogenic gospel and embellished with another of the ground-breaking electronic loops being pioneered by Bernie round then. Bootsy co-write 'If You Got Funk, You Got Style' steps out friskily, 'Soul Mate' is a lightweight love ditty co-credited to Eddie's Grace Cook nom de funk. There's also a remake of 'Cosmic Slop' with Hampton in Hazel's role, captured at the hangar rehearsals for the Earth Tour. These sessions appeared in 1995 as a Japan-only album called *Mothership Connection, Newburgh Session* on the P-Vine label.

The album's requisite soul ballad is the cracked, caterwauling plea of the addictive 'You Scared The Lovin' Out Of Me' (with hilarious vocal acrobatics going on in the background), while 'Adolescent Funk' marks Hampton's first composing credit in Bernie's traditional closing statement which here takes the form of a pastoral synth instrumental. The album charted six weeks after *Tales Of...*, reaching number 12 during its 14-week run.

With both groups on major labels now it could really get to be neck and neck in the popularity stakes between Parliament and the revived Funkadelic, although the distinctions between the two outfits had all but disappeared. But not before the Dr Funkenstein space opera reached an interplanetary climax worthy of Godzilla's greatest battles and the hits really started coming.

Chapter Eleven

Don't Fake The Funk Or Your Nose Will Grow

"I use all the styles. I ain't impartial to nothing. If I do disco, it would still be funk because it's that attitude and not the music. I don't dig one-dimensional funk or one-dimensional disco."

George Clinton

"Eddie was the closest thing to Jimi in all the guitar players."

Jerome 'Bigfoot' Brailey

Disco. A despicable death ray for The Funk. Repetitive meathead clump with mirror-ball testicles. The Anti-Funk.

And so on. By the late seventies, disco was a dirtier word than Funk had ever been and is still met by derision when mentioned in some quarters today (including esteemed sources related to P-Funk). The party line is that disco arrived to starch the soul out of black music with its incessant thump, after being hijacked by the corporations as the latest trend and turned into the weapon of mass destruction that claimed soul and anything in its path. As with any major movement from hippie to punk, there were appalling bandwagon jumpers, but disco's early evolution and ethos (before it was neutered and destroyed) is strikingly similar to that of funk. Disco just rode a different groove to become the biggest social movement of the seventies, along with punk, and encountered just as much opposition.

Of course, the P-Funk crew saw disco as a threat and watering down of black music's essence and said so in their inimitable fashion. But after sending it up on 'The Undisco Kidd' and targeting it as the 'Placebo Syndrome', Parliament were actually inventing a new strain of electronic disco-funk on the same album with 'Flash Light'. 1978's global dance-floor smash 'One Nation Under A Groove' saw disco's original unifying spirit recast in the P-Funk vat without going the way of James Brown whoring himself as The Original Disco Man the following year.

No matter what happened after the A&R departments and Rod Stewart got hold of it, P-Funk's most successful period was when disco was in full swing. After hordes of white lunkhead jocks held a Disco Demolition Night to ceremonially burn a mountain of black music during a football game at Chicago's Comiskey Park in 1979, they and many others found themselves bereft of hits from then on as the industry moved on to another fad it could milk dry.

The genre attracted hordes of dodgy imitators, sporting increasingly ludicrous fashions, but its deeper ramifications are often overlooked. This was a new form of party music that attracted white and black, and gay and straight, to the same dance floor, under the same groove. For the first time, many women felt unthreatened dancing without partners. By the time Larry Levan's Paradise Garage was busting down colour and sexual barriers towards the end of the decade in the most flagrant demonstration of dance-floor unity to date, disco could be seen fulfilling many of the civil rights aspirations espoused during the previous decade, simply by bringing all strains of human life together for one giant party.

When disco producers started referencing their P-Funk adolescence in the eighties, black music got even more wigged-out and fun. However, in hindsight, it's not hard to see how the huge success of *Saturday Night Fever* and its Bee Gees-led soundtrack stigmatised the genre and outraged musical purists, but funk and disco were a lot closer than many like to admit (and not just because of the man in the moon and his coke spoon hanging over the Studio 54 dance floor, who often seemed the real ruler of that particular time).

In the sixties, the mixed acid-fuelled parties at David Mancuso's Loft, Francis Grasso's Salvation, Nicky Siano's Gallery and Larry Levan's Paradise Garage would have been unthinkable. Now all can be seen as defiant, triumphant celebrations directly descended from the struggles for integration and personal liberation that raged throughout that pivotal decade. As a strain of black dance music, P-Funk was often lumped in with disco. For instance, Vince Aletti's Disco File column in *Record World* magazine, which charted black music's development through his reviews and charts between 1973–78, lists Parliament's 'Bop Gun' as a number one record at a Brooklyn club called the Guest House in the week of November 26, 1977, reigning over the likes of Isaac Hayes, Donna Summer and Roy Ayers. Vince described the "pumping, delightfully spacey" tune as "their strongest disco entry in years". This acceptance in the dance clubs was totally natural to those with more open minds about where rapidly evolving black music was going.

With George always keeping an eye on latest music business developments, Parliament and their marketing men happily took advantage of the new 12-inch single format that had been stumbled upon in late 1975 by disco producer Tom Moulton when he needed an acetate of his latest edit and the engineer had run out of seven-inch lacquers. Tom asked him to try spreading it over the grooves on a larger slate. The improvement in sound was so remarkable that the first 'giant singles' were being sent to DJs by the following spring. The first commercially available 12-inch was New York DJ-producer Walter Gibbons' pounding rework of Double Exposure's symphonic Philly Soul on 'Ten Per Cent' in June 1976. Thanks to disco, DJs now had a fresh electronic weapon suited to the powerful new sound systems. Francis Grasso had the first DJ sound mixer, which meant the art of mixing records was also now under way. This would also be central to the hip-hop scene then starting to gestate up in the South Bronx.

The rock mainstream soon caught on to the concepts born in New York's disco underground, hiring producers to make their music more accessible to this new audience. It wouldn't be long before the Rolling Stones were releasing their new disco-flavoured single 'Miss You' on 12 inches of pink vinyl with a club mix. But away from the media-fuelled furore that caused, the likes of Gibbons, Moulton and Levan were hitting the unblinkered party crowds, who were also getting into P-Funk. This new breed of producer were black music innovators working to develop the form with sonic breakthroughs while crucially elevating their music above the bandwagon jumpers by injecting the rare spiritual soul and emotion that often got overlooked amid the hackles being raised by ignorant disco haters. It's now obvious how much disco actually scared the establishment by uniting previously disparate social groups such as gays and blacks. The oppression and derision heaped on the genre in 1979 uncannily resembled George's fun-stomping Sir Nose D'Voidoffunk character.

Until 'Flash Light' P-Funk had been a slow-hump beast rarely clocking in above 90 beats per minute. This key song changed all that, coming as a major turning point as George unleashed P-Funk's take on the electronic dance sound being pioneered by the likes of Giorgio Moroder and took the funk into the future. After being developed (and rejected for his album) by Bootsy, it was ignited by Bernie's synthesized bass and handclaps, which created the walloping new electronic P-Funk groove that would become a key element in his sound until the present day. It would also heavily influence danceable pop, disco's next incarnation as boogie and even Detroit techno, while giving Prince a blueprint to take to world stardom.

While P-Funk was enjoying its 1977–78 peak of success, Chic were the world's other hottest-selling black group. They were also perhaps the most woefully misrepresented black music act of that time. There were many parallels between the two camps not least former Black Panther Nile Rodgers and Bernard Edwards coming up through similar formative scuffles as the P-Funkers, such as the former backing Screaming Jay Hawkins at the Apollo and finding himself opening for Parliament-Funkadelic in 1973 while playing with New York City of 'I'm Doin' Fine Right Now' fame.

Chic broke through the disco stereotype that had emerged after the original Philly Soul templates had been corrupted into stomping conveyor-belt fluff, wielding sublimely funked grooves, wittily sensual lyrics, universal choruses, Nile's skittering guitar, Bernard's life-pulsing bass and heavenly embellishments like glacial strings. Chic are one of the funkiest groups of all time and the earliest hip-hop block parties were fuelled by their music as groove breaks. My old partner-in-punk Danny Baker hit the nail on the head when he declared in *NME* that "Chic are that James Brown riff in modern times."

Obviously Chic's sleek Afrocentric elegance and exquisite productions were a designer-suited contrast to George's intergalactic filth squad, but between 1977 and 1979 these representatives of cutting-edge black music were reaping huge success within the top echelons of the music industry. While 1977 saw George intensify the P-Funk empire building that had started the previous year with Bootsy, Nile and Bernard launched their Chic Organisation with hits such as 'Dance, Dance, Dance (Yowsah, Yowsah, Yowsah)' and 'Everybody Dance' before taking their sophisticated urban majesty to Sister Sledge and a string of landmark productions for the likes of Diana Ross. Among the glorious escapism their music provided, every Chic song carried what they called, 'a deep hidden meaning' ('Le Freak' started life as "aah, fuck off" after Studio 54 denied them entry while their records were being played in the club). Chic's 'Good Times' was their 'One Nation Under A Groove' and got the same euphoric response whenever and wherever I played them from the eighties onwards. By then the vitriol had subsided, so nobody cared what category these anthems had been consigned to. Apart from revolutionising the music industry, disco opened up the dance floors and the charts to make black music an industry in itself, and George and Chic had been right there in the front line.

But in 1977, it was still Mothership versus mirrorball as the Earth Tour continued its marauding path around the country (although the Horny Horns and Glenn Goins found time to appear on blues legend Albert King's *King Albert* album).

The Mothership now chimed even more resonantly with the times after George Lucas' first film in the blockbuster *Star Wars* series opened in May to kick off one of the most successful franchises in movie history. This would be followed in November by the colossal mothership of Steven Spielberg's *Close Encounters Of The Third Kind* reinforcing the trend for a new breed of big-budget sci-fi movie drenched in state-of-the-art effects and a generous dose of philosophy. It was a good time for George to be emerging from a giant Mothership every night on stage.

While Westbound recouped some of its early faith and financial outlay with 1977's *Best Of The Early Years* compilation, Phonogram acquired a 50 per cent stake in Casablanca. This essentially meant George was now signed to two major labels.

Money and success were in the air when Parliament's hastily assembled double album *Live/P-Funk Earth Tour* was released in May as a much-requested tour souvenir, complete with poster of a fur-bedecked Dr Funkenstein clutching a spaceship and an iron–on T-shirt transfer emblazoned with the legend 'Take Funk To Heaven In '77'. The set was promoted with a 'Promotional 4-Track Disco Sampler' led by 'P-Funk (Wants To Get Fucked Up)', Parliament's first venture into the world of the "giant disc" (although 'Flash Light' was already being given a 10-minute version for its own 12-incher). "I always knew I had the best band in the world, but I never really considered a live album," said George at the time. "The demand was so great we just had to do it. So here it is!"

The set was drawn from shows the previous January at LA's Forum and Oakland Coliseum, mixing songs from both groups' catalogues centred around a sequence called 'The Landing Of The Holy Mothership' (which, along with 'This Is The Way We Funk With You' and the old Parliaments-reworking 'Fantasy Is Reality', were recorded at Hollywood Sound and United Sound studios). Elsewhere were crucial cuts in the Mothership saga, sometimes frustratingly edited and jumbled, including 'P. Funk (Wants To Get Funked Up)', 'Dr Funkenstein's Supergroovalisticprosifunkstication Medley' (including 'Let's Take It To The Stage' and 'Take Your Dead Ass Home'), 'Do That Stuff', 'The Undisco Kidd', 'Children Of Production' , 'Mothership Connection', 'Swing Down, Sweet Chariot', 'Dr Funkenstein', 'Gamin' On Ya!', 'Tear The Roof Off The Sucker Medley' featuring 'Give Up The Funk' and 'Get Off Your Ass And Jam' and 'Night of The Thumpasaurus Peoples'.

While welcoming back Eddie Hazel, the album marked the last recording by the original Parliaments singers before they departed after the LA Coliseum show on June 4. Fuzzy, Calvin, Grady and Ray were dissatisfied with the haphazard payments and the manner in which their original barbershop nucleus was being edged out by the constantly increasing size of the band. Also, Neil Bogart had promised George his financial backing if he assumed the frontman role to give the group a star figure. This started in earnest with George alone appearing on the cover of *Mothership Connection*. "I guess, business-wise, it was up to George to keep hisself together and maybe not worry so much about friendship," said Grady Thomas. "I started feeling like, 'Well, you know, he moved on somewhere else.'"

Fuzzy was the first member of the P-Funk clan to break away and get his own solo deal (and only one of the Parliaments). "Things were happening within the group," he recalled. "Money, bickering, things like this, jockeying for position. Because a lot of people started coming into the group, where the five of us started originally... a lot of the attention was shifted to George, and it started a lot of confusion and conflict. I wasn't really being satisfied, and then I left."

By then, Fuzzy had already released his first solo album, *A Whole Nother Thang* on Westbound. It was not part of George's empire and so it became the first P-Funk spin-off not produced by Clinton. Every song bears Fuzzy's writing credit, while no specific musicians are named apart from Bernie, who also handled the string and brass arrangements. However, the lavish gatefold sleeve is plastered with gushing thanks to Bootsy, Richard Becker, Tiki Fulwood and Ron Bykowski, while his Parliaments homeboys can be clearly heard lending support. Boogie gets a co-composing credit on loping funk instrumental 'The Fuzz And Da Boog' and is an obvious presence throughout.

Jerome Brailey isn't mentioned anywhere apart from the potted P-Funk history in Fuzzy's liner notes where he's mis-credited as 'Jerome Bradley'. Bigfoot remembers the recording sessions that provided the material: "Any time we were in Detroit and had some days off, Armen

(Boladian) would come by and grab me, Garry, Glenn and Boogie and we'd go over to this studio that was in a garage and lay down tracks for Fuzzy's record. We did those during the time we were with P-Funk."

The album's mix of funk, rock and speciality soulful ballads went fairly unnoticed, although it included Fuzzy's humping version of the lascivious long-time Funkadelic live favourite 'Cookie Jar', which would soon be re-recorded by Parlet and later Prince. Two tracks seemed aimed in the direction of Dr Funkenstein – the anti hard drugs blues of 'Mr Junk Man', and 'Which Way Do I Disco''s tough J.B. groove floating lines such as 'the Mothership just got disconnected'. 'I'll Be Loving You' boasts one of those dramatic 'All Your Goodies' dark gospel choruses that is loaded with the passion and presence Fuzzy brought to Funkadelic and would be missed within the overall band dynamic.

Bootsy unveiled another killer for his second Rubber Band album – *Ahh… The Name Is Bootsy, Baby*. One of the key P-Funk releases of this era, it instantly starts stoking the bassist's burgeoning mythos with the opening 'We Want Bootsy' crowd-noise intro and some of Bootsy's meanest bass-driven funk lolloping into the fuzz-cranked 'Auld Lang Syne' coda that harks back to Hendrix's New Year's Eve 1969 Band Of Gypsys performance. There are Horny Horns, loose chants and vocals percolating, but Bootsy towers over everything with his bass and an evidently increased confidence in his persona.

Abnormally funky, 'The Pinocchio Theory' introduces the villain on the next Parliament album, Sir Nose D'Voidoffunk, with its 'Don't fake the funk or your nose will grow' exclamations among the Rubber Band and Funkateers references. The Bootsy Ballad form is further elevated by 'What's A Telephone Bill?' (Mudbone uncurling around phone innuendos that are set against Bootsy's love talk and slap soloing). The sweet, sticky metaphors of 'Munchies For Your Love' hump on for nearly 10 minutes in a masterpiece of subtlety that steadily builds into Bootsy's orgasmic fuzz bass solo. Heard in its original vinyl form, the album was a small but perfectly formed masterwork, balancing the up-tempo funk emissions with dreamy, sensual horns.

★

December 1977 saw Parliament's *Funkentelechy Vs The Placebo Syndrome* provide another candidate for the greatest P-Funk album of all time. Its seismic, scenic funk bubble boasted George's most ambitious foray into the Dr Funkenstein/Starchild saga yet, using it to lampoon modern society and complacency while introducing new characters.

The album's story goes that after Dr Funkenstein turned the funk gene loose on the planet via his Clones to go viral in true Jes Grew fashion, the Earth turned out to be devoid of funk – like the Unfunky UFO in the song – because of the actions of Nixon, the government and big business. Sir Nose D'Voidoffunk represented greed, consumerism, oppression, grey conservatism and unfunkiness, declaring 'I have always been D'Void of Funk, I shall continue to be D'Void of funk'. His strategies included 'sucking [the people's] brains until their ability to think was amputated... simplifying their instincts until they were fat, horny and strung out.' As George put it "The very source of life energies on Earth have become the castrated target of anile bamboozelry from homo sapiens' rabid attempts to manipulate the omnipotent forces of nature."

Consumerism (and to many, disco) was lambasted as the shallow 'Placebo Syndrome', whose cheap imitations were disintegrating all around. 'When the syndrome is around don't let your guard down,' came the advice. 'All you got to do is go on a bump.' Saving the day, Starchild shoots Sir Nose with funkatising rays from his Bop Gun (the live shows saw Garry brandishing a strobe attached to a space rifle and flying over the crowds in his diaper 'chasing the Noses away'). Sir Nose was forced to 'give up the funk' and dance.

"Dr Funkenstein knew that 'cool' would get in the way of being totally funky," explained George. "But at the same time people liked 'cool'. So we invented Dr Funkenstein and Sir Nose D'Voidoffunk. Sir Nose represented the concept, 'I'm cool up to here. I got my suit on and I don't wanna wrinkle it, I don't sweat, I don't make love and I don't dance!' Dr Funkenstein said, 'Well since that is attractive to a lot of people we won't want them to get strung out on being cool to that extent where you have no fun'. He cloned Starchild, who was totally funky and cool and he would shoot Sir Nose with the Bop Gun and the

Flash Light and make him dance – not to hurt him, but to loosen him up a little bit."

Miraculously, George had fashioned the album from two years of the groove graft going on in the P-lab. Opening track 'Bop Gun (Endangered Species)' leads in with a titanic bass, and some punchy horns from the Hornies joined by Clay Lawrey, Darryl Dixon, Valerie Drayton and Danny Cortez. Against another astonishingly passionate Goins vocal, the Brides Of Funkenstein unveil their trademark sexy squeals on the counter lines, while the guitars of Michael Hampton, Catfish, Glenn and Garry are kept to a clipped rhythm, and are all the more lethal for it. There were more singers than ever on this album including regulars George, Ray, Glenn, Garry, Bootsy, the Brides, Debbie Wright, Jeanette Washington and Boogie. They were joined by 'Extra-extra terrestrial funk bearing alumni-Strokers, Chokers, Clappers and Chanters': Catfish, Frank Waddy, Rick Gilmore, Mudbone, P-Nut, Billy 'Bass', Ron Ford, Lou Goldman, Joel Johnson, Rubber Band, Parlet and Horny Horns. Sting Ray was back, too – drawn by the financial promise of the Warner Brothers deal.

After a scene-setting distorted vocal intro, 'Sir Nose D'Voidoffunk' steams in with one of Bootsy's classic stealth bass lines; sliding, grunting and popping around the core riff and Bigfoot's sinuous pulse. George appears as Starchild – the nemesis of Sir Nose, who gets ribbed by the massed chorale reprising the twisted nursery rhyme routine with 'Three Blind Mice' ('They all ran after the farmer's wife/Turned on the fun with the water pipe on') and 'Baa Baa Black Sheep' ('yes sir, yes sir, a nickel bag full!'), Mr Jinx's 'I hate those meeces to pieces' from the *Pixie And Dixie* cartoon is joined by the horns playing the *Looney Tunes* theme and extracts from commercials of the day, as Sir Nose squeaks and splutters his indignation.

'Wizard Of Finance' is the album's ballad, with George's old-school soul croon likening romance to Wall Street, as Bernie's angular synth laid another template for the following decade. The 11-minute 'Funkentelechy' sees George on top vocal, arranging, and lyrical form, dealing with the system's control over freedom, fun (and therefore funk), while attacking consumerism. He represents The Funk as a way out, which again parallels punk at a time when it was carrying a similar message to disaffected kids in the UK. Of the original Parliaments, Sting Ray's basso boom was the most unmistakable sound, so it's good to hear him in there with Fred's increasingly complex horn mosaics and another Bootsy/Bigfoot groove behemoth. Bigfoot says it's the first song he wrote with Bootsy and George. 'Placebo Syndrome' also lays into complacency and how easy it is to lazily drift into acceptance of the norm and received modes of behaviour. Co-written by George and a briefly returning Billy Nelson (who also plays) it's the lightest track, with the sort of breezy harmonies which would grace Prince's 'Diamonds And Pearls' era.

The album closes with 'Flash Light', which became P-Funk's first R&B chart number one the following year. Bernie's window-rattling keyboard bass groove would be so inestimably influential on the music of the next decade that it changed the bottom end forever. Special mention also has to be made of Catfish's abrasive rhythm guitar metronome, which glues the track together as its crucial lynchpin and human counterpart to Bernie's robo-whale flatulence. The 'la-da-dee' hook was taken from a Jewish Bar Mitzvah chant (later providing De La Soul's breakthrough hit 'Me, Myself And I'). It's the final battle between the Bop Gun-toting Starchild and Sir Nose, George declaring 'There's nothing that the proper attitude won't render funkable' as he grooves to victory.

Writing in his *Village Voice* Consumer's Guide, Robert Christgau gave the album a maximum A. Remarking on its subtly insidious power he declared "...never before has George Clinton dealt so coherently with his familiar message, in which the forces of life – autonomous intelligence, a childlike openness, sexual energy, and humour – defeat those of death: by seduction if possible, by force if necessary."

I got my copy (complete with Sir Nose poster and eight-page Overton Lloyd comic book explaining the album's concept) at a record shop in Soho when punk rock was breaking out and stuck it most ravingly among the new wave records I was reviewing in my *Zigzag* magazine. The way I saw it, this was a new wave of black music, flinging open the gates so anything could happen in the spirit of proper funk anarchy.

The success of this raggedy-ass gang from the outer galaxies of the ghetto was a mighty victory for their awe-inspiring music that carried a message still basically the same as *Free Your Mind ... And Your Ass Will Follow*. There was something deliciously punk-like in the way the P-Funk crew had traversed their own chaos-strewn path, often off their P-bollocks, shocking or upsetting a procession of institutions and the old guard along the way. Punk had sparked another revolution in the dive bars of New York City and London, setting a rocket under the rock music dinosaur, which by 1976 had been in danger of disappearing up its own drum solo. Considering the similarly seismic effects George's earlier antics had on black music, I had no hesitation including an early P-Funk track on a compilation I put together called *Dirty Water: The Birth Of Punk Attitude*. What was P-Funk if not a chaotic DIY operation that horrified the establishments of both music and society?

Although cut from the same rebel flag as punk, George always stressed he used the Funk and his self-created world as a more peace-loving statement against the normal one outside explaining, "We make it satirical or funny, not point blank aggressive, like maybe the punks. You know why? 'Cause we are the direct descendants of the 'You're fucking up' society. This is us. But that's a dangerous one to play with because the fact still remains you will get popular. And if you get popular you might believe it. And if you believe it then you'll live and you'll die being a pawn for real. So I have to play with it because when I come offstage I wanna tuck it away somewhere. It's too intense otherwise... Once you believe your part, once you can't step back from being what they want you to be, it's all over."

With the ongoing success of Parliament, Funkadelic and the Rubber Band, George was hot. In a fertile industry looking for a slice of P-Funk magic he started creating different projects for the ever-expanding Mothership crew, which he sold to different record companies for a hefty advance. A classic case was the Horny Horns. George dreamed of forming and overseeing a stable of acts backed by the same core musicians while creating stars out of the different talents whose vocals or musicianship were planted on the tracks they were churning out.

Once again the record company that George had first tried to make it with was a major influence. "I looked at Motown as a group. Not as a company with a lot of producers, but as one big group... It was so many combinations of talent there that whenever an artist start getting cold, they just shift to the next set of producers and get him a fresh sound. So I started treating Parliament/Funkadelic like that... I could just keep mixin' 'em up."

He also continued to be inspired by James Brown. In terms of record sales and gig attendances George had sailed past the Godfather as an outlaw funk-rocker who was also managing to crash the white market. Earlier in the decade, Brown had clinched a deal with Polydor to release his new label People Records, requiring several albums a year by himself and other artists under his wing. People had gone on to release albums by Lyn Collins, Hank Ballard, Maceo & the Macks and Fred Wesley with the J.B.'s – his 'first family of Soul'. Like Motown, all Brown's acts were released through the same major label, but George was farming his acts out to assorted labels for different advances. Ultimately this would be his undoing as he wove a web bound to freefall into clashes and logistical disaster.

Next came Eddie Hazel with his one and only solo album, *Games, Dames And Guitar Thangs*. Deleted soon after release by Warner Brothers, it became one of the most sought-after items in the P–Funk catalogue, so I was ecstatic to pick one up for two dollars on a downtown New York street in 1986. It was so rare that a 1994 episode of *Homicide: Life On The Streets* concerned a character who shot the guy who had wrecked their copy.

The cover text reads, 'Produced, Pronounced, Professed and Prophesised by George Clinton and Eddie Hazel'. It seems like Eddie was given full rein on the album as it's a strong showcase for his guitar playing (backed up by Bigfoot, Tiki, Bootsy, Michael, Glenn, Garry, Bernie, Boogie, Mudbone and the Brides). His genius was obviously being recognised somewhere as he was let out of jail to record it, as Bigfoot remembers: "When I got with Funkadelic, Eddie was doing a little time because he'd bit the stewardess on a flight. He'd been smoking some wacky tobaccy. Something went down so he was incarcerated in California. The managers had told Warner Brothers they had to release him so he got out of prison just before we done the album so we did the *Games, Dames And Guitar Thangs* album. The two of us were tight."

Although rendered in the all-action Pedro Bell style, the cover's striking collage of photos and dollars is credited to Lou Beach. Eddie is depicted astride a red-eyed horse holding a black Les Paul in one hand and a scimitar in the other. The album kicks off with his sublime version of the Mamas and the Papas' 'California Dreamin'', the 1967 west coast summer of love anthem which takes on a darker hue in this setting sung with a soul-tearing passion by Eddie, backed up by the Brides. It's the only track to showcase his often overlooked voice, as Bernie's languid piano provides a cool counterpart to his reverbed-up guitar flickering. The track was released as a single with an instrumental version on the flip. 'Frantic Moment' is a George/Bootsy/Bernie song said to have been meant for the first Brides album, and it sounds like it – with their haunting chorale over which Eddie's guitar snakes the convoluted arrangement.

'What About it?', which rides a Jimi-type riff with quicksilver chording, popped up as 'Clone Commando' credited to Funkadelic on volume three of the *George Clinton Family Series*. In that disc's liner notes, George explains how the song was Funkadelic's first giveaway single at gigs: "We gave them away cause we was probably feeling guilty cause we were taking so much money in from the hood. We was doin' pretty good back then. And 'Clone Commando' was one of the first. One of our gifts."

Eddie's album wasn't recorded as a complete project, instead it was compiled from existing tracks he'd played on, plus some out-takes and covers. This could have easily fallen flat but where this guitarist is concerned every note he played should be available to be devoured. 'I Want You (She's So Heavy)' is Eddie's take on the Beatles song from *Abbey Road*, inspiring him to uncork the album's most stratospheric soloing over the main descending riff, which the Beatles could have cribbed from Hendrix's '1983'. Eddie still seems to be building up an unbelievable head of steam as the track fades after nine minutes.

An instrumental version of Bootsy's 'Physical Love' is the third cover version, and could well have been a backing track from the first Bootsy album with the guitar turned up.

In 2004 Rhino Records reissued the album with the material recorded between 1975 and 1977, which made up another album called *Jams From The Heart*: 'Smedley Smorganoff', 'Lampoc Boogie' (a searing instrumental based on Crosby Stills and Nash's 'Carry On' from *Deja Vu*), 'From The Bottom of My Soul' –12 minutes of 'Maggot Brain' desolation topped with Eddie's imploring vocal. Another hard-to-find collection called *Rest In P* appeared on Japanese P-Vine featuring these and further ceiling-scorching instrumentals.

1977 also saw the Horny Horns release their lush update of 'Up For The Down Stroke' as a single on Atlantic followed by *A Blow For Me, A Toot To You*. Produced by George and Bootsy, it seemed like a proper P-family affair with the front line of Fred, Maceo, Rick Gardner and Kush backed by a hefty squad. But George was actually ingeniously recycling already recorded tracks with the Horny Horns overdubbed. Fred was subsequently pretty disparaging about the album, describing it as "a joke… a collection of discarded George and Bootsy tracks with the horns up in the mix. Maceo and I had put in no real time, consideration or input, but I was promised that the next one would be different."

When *Mojo*'s Lloyd Bradley asked George about these charges in 2006 he replied that he "Don't know about any problem like that", before adding, "Like anybody else in P-Funk the Horny Horns was free to do exactly what they wanted to do. Truth is, I was against what they did! I agreed with Fred that it didn't have to be as commercial as we were, because they wanted to do a jazzy-type thing, then I let them go on it because it had to be. Nobody wanted it to sound too much like Bootsy or Parliament or anything, and it didn't." The album isn't as bad as Fred claims, providing a pleasant diversion for P-Funkers and even J.B. fans, while unlikely to win new converts. It made number 31 in the *Billboard* soul album charts and 181 on the pop charts.

Maybe George was trying to woo disenchanted old fans of the Godfather, whose own career had gone off the boil in recent years with falling show attendances and IRS problems bringing down his People empire. By 1977 Brown had lost his omnipotence, having failed to score an R&B chart hit since 'Get Up Offa That Thing'. The simplest explanation is that he hadn't moved with the times and was now being marginalised by disco and the unstoppable power of P-Funk. Calling his album *The Original Disco Man* didn't provide the answer.

George now had his old band, status and sales, which were set to shoot even higher the following year, although more mutiny was brewing in the ranks…

Chapter Twelve

The Empire Strikes Black

"Everybody on the One, the whole world on the same pulse."

George Clinton

The year 1978 started with 'Flash Light' scoring Parliament their first R&B chart number one and ended with Funkadelic gaining their first million-selling single with 'One Nation Under A Groove'. In between, Bootsy snatched the pole position for himself with his volcanic monster jam 'Bootzilla' – his self-proclaimed 'stereophonic funk-producing, disco-inducing, twin magnetic rump receptors' perfectly describing all three songs.

These became key tracks in the electronic revolution about to grip post-disco dance music. In the fallout from 'Flash Light' hitting the Top 20 and spending three weeks at the top of the *Billboard* Soul chart, funk bands started stacking up Moog bass tones on their tracks as the seeds were planted for a machine-driven new musical strain later called electro, while Detroit's future techno innovators were inspired to start planning the sound which would rock the next decade.

Spending six weeks at the top of the soul charts at the end of the year, but mysteriously only making 28 in the Hot 100, 'One Nation Under A Groove' took its title from the Pledge of Allegiance's 'One nation under God' and became one of the most life-affirming club anthems of the decade – the nearest thing Funkadelic got to a signature song. Through the track's sheer newness, invincible vitality and George's microcosmic subtlety in arranging its different elements, Funkadelic had recast disco in their own image (although he had originally meant the song for Parliament). Club crowds regularly went bananas at the first grunt of Bernie's belching electronic disco bassline and heavyweight clap-track, letting the hauntingly sensual harmonies and vocals ooze into the collective soul as a call to arms and declaration of defiance: 'Nothing can stop us now'. The song caused 'Jes Grew'-style mass dancing, through cutting loose ingrained constraints to open the mind and shake the rump. It was a more ebullient declaration of the 'Free Your Mind And Your Ass Will Follow' philosophy except, according to George, "Now they're gonna pledge groovallegiance to the United Funk of Funkadelica."

"Funkadelic is an attitude to whatever it takes," explained George. "You can get away with so much when you haven't got to think about structures or constructions and can leave yourself to your instincts and know that it's cool and all the musicians know it that way. Then the possibilities are unlimited... We've learned how to relax and play and be inspired by one another, and by being crazy all along we don't have to play by no rules."

Both the song and its parent album were bolstered by the arrival of former Ohio Players singer and keyboards wiz Junie Morrison, who had quite an effect on arrangements and songwriting, with his talent for building orchestral musical layers while his own brand of quirky sleaze infected his vocals.

Growing up the oldest child in a poor family in Dayton, Ohio, Junie ran away from home at the age of 14, eventually hooking up with the local musicians who would form the Ohio Untouchables. The group had toiled around the area since 1959 (including a stint backing the Falcons, who were fronted by Wilson Pickett). After Leroy 'Sugarfoot' Bonner replaced singer-guitarist Robert Ward in 1965, the group changed their name to the Ohio Players and, after a one-album stint at Capitol, joined Funkadelic at Westbound in 1970. They developed their urgent, steamy funk across a series of Westbound albums (*Pain*, *Pleasure*, *Ecstasy* and *Climax*), which also drew attention on account of striking cover model Pat Evans' provocative leather-and-chain clad poses. The Players made their name with a skin-tight funk and unusual time signatures, fluidly imbuing their music with blues, jazz and rock in often complex arrangements. In 1973 Junie's 'Funky Worm' became an R&B chart topper and Top 20 hit, its keening synth squeals later inspiring west coast G-Funk productions such as NWA's 'Gangsta Gangsta'.

The band then signed to Mercury, debuting with 1974's marvellous *Skin Tight*, featuring the jazzy aural clacker-valve of its strutting title track. However, Junie had stayed behind on Westbound, striking out solo on three symphonic weird soul albums (*When We Do*, *Freeze* and *Suzie Super Groupie*). While the Ohio Players were enjoying enormous success with singles such as US number ones 'Fire' and 'Love Rollercoaster' and a string of other hits that included 'Sweet Sticky Thing' and 'Who'd She Coo?', Junie hooked up with George for a couple of highly productive years (also producing spin-off projects under his 'J.S. Theracon' pseudonym).

Bootsy's unstoppable rise continued with the groin-rattling 'Wiiiiiind me up!' stomp of 'Bootzilla' knocking Parliament from the top of the R&B charts and his third album, *Bootsy? Player Of The Year*, showed the Rubber Band evolving as rapidly as their leader's increasingly cartoon-like character. Thanks to the stellar playing (particularly from Catfish) and the telepathy between the engine room and Horny Horns, everything fits right in the pocket for maximum funkage. This time, the funky jams and ballads were mixed, rather than being divided onto separate sides of the disc. The album included ferociously chomping gems such as the crazed lollop of long-time live favourite 'What's The Name Of This Town', which opened shows on the 1978 tour (with Maceo funking on flute before Bootsy fuzzes into 'America The Beautiful'). 'Hollywood Squares' is another choppy, slab-chord rampage ('Of course I've got a cartoon mind') and the lustrous ballad 'May The Force Be With you' shows how *Star Wars* had infiltrated the Mothership. Apart from the scandalous title track, 'Roto-Rooter' is the other bomb here – a groove-gouging, flame-snorting beast that portrays Bootsy as the plumber come to unclog constipated minds, his bass cranking up into a nuclear funk plunger until it all ends with a flush. The whole album crackles with the rare energy coursing through the road-seasoned band at this time. Bootsy introduces two characters – Bootzilla and his Player persona who's the musician, lover and superstar. Many consider this to be his best album.

The success of 'Flash Light' meant that Parliament were now selling 3,000 little torches every night on the eponymous tour that ran on from the epic Earth Tour as the year commenced. They were still playing to anything up to 20,000 punters a night, supported by combinations of Bootsy's Rubber Band, the Brides, Parlet, Cameo, and the Bar Kays. Madison Square Garden was becoming a second home.

New bassist Rodney 'Skeet' Curtis had joined up the previous year to become a dominant figure in the live set, and steered the band into the next song to the point where even George described him as 'arrogant'.

Playing packed stadiums while Parliament albums were shifting in their thousands prompted some of the musicians to protest about how few of those dollars came their way. This had recently contributed to the departure of the original Parliaments singers, followed by some of the band going on strike during the tour. This led to the departure of Glenn Goins, and then Jerome Brailey.

"There would be people as far as you could see but something was wrong," bristles Bigfoot. "One day we were in LA and George had to go back to Detroit for something, so he stopped by and he had these jeans or something he wanted me to put in the dry cleaners for him. I said 'All right'. So I went to take them to the cleaners. When I picked up the pants a plastic bag fell out the pockets. In the pocket were three wrinkled $100 bills, which I immediately put in my pocket. In the plastic bag there was a round ball of cocaine. I was like 'Wow!' so I told Garry and Glenn. We were the three hotheads so all we did was lick the joint – it was still solid. I made the mistake of telling Bernie. Bernie was older than us and he used to be the spy. You didn't say anything around Bernie because he would run back and tell George. I gave Bernie some and he told George and all he did was laugh: 'Aha ha – they got me!

253

They got me!' Glenn would say 'Don't say anything around Bernie or he'll go back and tell George'.

"I would talk to Glenn about this. They would tell us that everybody was broke because there was no money. One day when we were checking into the hotel there were two representatives from Casablanca there and talking about how *Funkentelechy* had done 750,000 already. It was a platinum record. Glenn and myself heard the representatives talking and we were like 'Why they telling us we're broke?'

"George would never stay with the band in the hotel any more. They always snuck him somewhere else, so whenever we needed to get with George we had to like catch him. He would come in for a soundcheck then he was gone. We wouldn't see him until show time. He'd come offstage after a show, sit around for a minute then he'd be gone. You couldn't say 'Yo George, I need some money' because he'd be gone. We never rehearsed. We only did soundchecks. We had people travelling with us going 'There's no money around'. I had to go through the managers to get money so I got tight with the managers. Once I saw what was going on I said 'I'm going to get tight with the managers'. The guys that were setting up the Mothership and the sound engineers were making more money than we were.

"Everybody was different. George would give certain band members something. You could get paid in cash or you could get paid in drugs. Certain guys would take the drugs. I'm not calling out any names!"

Trombonist Greg Boyer, who joined the tour in the absence of the Horny Horns, verifies that "People were getting paid with narcotics. Some people were getting paid with equipment. Sometimes they got paid with money, and sometimes they got promised a gig 'cause maybe they weren't on tour [with us] at the time. There were all kinds of way to barter your war around a session, and it didn't always involve money."

It is slightly puzzling how such a monumental talent as Glenn Goins could be fired instead of paid, especially as he had recently contributed such epic tracks as 'Bop Gun'. Jerome is evidently still perplexed, especially as Glenn's story took a tragic twist after he went back to Detroit and started working with Quazar, which included his brother Kevin on guitar.

"Glenn was the bomb!" roars Bigfoot. "Believe me, he could have replaced George. He knew how to do that whole personality and whole stage thing. He would say crazy stuff. He could be just as wild. He had that whole thing. We went to LA and Frank Zappa was trying to take him away. He was told he could make $500 a week. We told him, 'You're only making $200 a week with George, you could sleep with all the white women you want but you'll still be a backup musician for Zappa. If you stay here and learn from George you could be your own star, just learn.'

"George knew about it. He said to our manager, 'We got to do something about it. Frank is about to take Glenn. I don't want to lose Glenn. Robert was like, 'What you want me to do? You want me to give him more money?' Then George was like 'No, don't give him any more money. Let's talk him into staying!' He was adamant about not giving him any more money.

"Me and Glenn had talked about leaving. We had asked him for our back royalties but George used to tell most of us in the band he didn't want us to make all the money because we would get bigheaded. We were like, 'Nobody's bigheaded, just pay us when we need to be paid' but his whole concept was he didn't want to give us any money because it would affect our minds. We were in the studio and we did everything, vocals and everything. He just put the names on the record. We just said, 'We need our back money.' One of the managers put a notice on the bus notice board saying 'There'll be no back royalties paid.' We were on our way to a gig in Pittsburgh so we just stopped the bus driver, Joe Miller, and said we wanted to get off. So me, Glenn, Mike Hampton, Skeet and the horn players we had at the time with Darryl Dixon all got off the bus and walked on back to the hotel. We said, 'We're not doing the show, we got to make some money'. When Skeet got back to the hotel he was like, 'I don't wanna go through this, I'm gonna catch a bus back to Baltimore' but he actually caught a cab and did the gig. When they came back they fired the horn players, fired Glenn and put me and Mike on a three-gig suspension. So that's how that happened.

"After the third gig I got suspended from I met up with them on the road in Greenville. One of the road managers told me that actually I was fired too. I said 'Why did you have me come here, I've got me a room?' He said, 'George just decided he wants you to play with the girl groups'. I said, 'What girl groups?' I said, 'No I'm not playing with the girl groups.' So then Bernie got a whiff of it, then some of the band got a whiff of it. He had Frankie Kash out, he had Tyrone Lampkin out and he had some guy named Nate who used to play with James Brown. So he had three drummers when I went back. Bernie and them said 'We got to get J back' so George said, 'All right, but I'm gonna keep those other drummers'.

"Glenn was calling me every night at the hotel to let me know he's got a group he's recording," says Bigfoot. "He went to Detroit and recorded a band for Armen Boladian under the name of Eclipse. Then he went to New York because Clive Davis had got him a deal under Quazar but it was the same record. Glenn was calling to let me know he had some things happening. When the tour was over I decided to go back and see what Glenn had going on so we started on Quazar but we couldn't use all the tracks because he had already recorded with Armen and tried to steal the album from the studio, but Armen caught him at the airport with the duffle bag.

"I was dating Glenn's sister at the time. She used to always ask me 'How's Glenn doing?' and I was like, 'He seems fine' but right after we had left I went to Texas and came back. Glenn had shrunk a whole body size. You see a person then you see 'em again and it's like 'Whoah!' It looked like he was shrinking. Billy Bass told me Glenn knew he had the cancer when he was in high school. It had gone into remission. He had mentioned to Billy he was joining P-Funk and Billy had told him, 'Don't go with George, it'll kill you. You're a great vocalist, you had the church, you're definitely going to be a star anyway'. He said, 'Don't deal with George'. That lifestyle brought everything on that more quickly because he was tooting and drinking and everything.

"He got sick one Friday. On the Monday we were supposed to have a meeting with Clive Davis about Mutiny being signed. He got sick that Friday and they took him in. He couldn't walk. This roadie we had at the time had to put him in the car. That Saturday, I went by to see him in the hospital up in Jersey. He had this look on his face that he was scared and stuff. He said they couldn't find anything despite sticking loads of needles in him and stuff. I had to go back to Richmond to get some more clothes. By the time I got home my mum had called me to say my friend Glenn had passed. He just went so quick. Then they found out a couple of weeks later that it was the cancer that came back. At first the doctors didn't know what was wrong. He was 34."

Jerome resolved to finish the album he had started with his friend and saw it released later that year. "Everything was done up, like the artwork," he says. "I just finished the record, I didn't think where it was gonna go. I just finished it up. I played on 'Funk With The Bigfoot', 'Funk With A Capitol G', 'Your Loving Is Easy', 'Saving Your Love For A Rainy Day'; seven or eight tracks. Me and Glenn wrote 'Funk 'N' Roll (Dancin' In The 'Funkshine')' together. The album turned out to be a classic. Glenn had that P-Funk stuff down. He could do Bootsy. He had *all* the sound down, it was so rare."

For decades, the Quazar album was another lost treasure until it was released in 2013. It now stands as a rip-roaring valediction of Glenn's unearthly talent, with its mix of funk, soul and rock riffs underpinned by Bigfoot's distinctive drum patterns. Darryl Dixon (who played the sax on 'Flash Light') lets rip on the hectic 'Working On The Building', alongside the dreamy Bootsy-ish ballads, potential hit singles and behemoth funkers – all brought home as a final tribute from Bigfoot.

Pedro Bell added a dedication to Glenn inside the gatefold cover of *One Nation Under A Groove*: 'In Memory of a Funkateer: Glenn Goins (1954–1978) This Funk Shall Ever Roll On with son Kasette.' He was the first P-Funker to fall and one of its greatest talents, but he was driven out of the group in a scenario that now seems more akin to James Brown's cynical policy of hiring and firing.

One Nation Under A Groove was not so much a concept album as a declaration of independence for a funky new way of life. It became George's most commercially successful and critically acclaimed album, hitting platinum status after being released that September. Many rate it as P-Funk's finest and most coherent long-player, mainly on account of the incredibly high trajectory it achieved with its title track (now one of the Rock and Roll Hall Of Fame's 500 Songs That Shaped Rock'n'Roll and *Rolling Stone*'s 500 Greatest Songs Of All Time).

Although he joins George and Junie on vocals, funk purist Garry later dismissed the song as "too bubblegum for me" while protesting that Funkadelic were supposed to be a rock band. He recalls the day he was sitting around United Sound with Junie and Bernie waiting for inspiration to strike. Bootsy sat behind the drum kit and started playing over a click track, joined by Garry playing some old changes he remembered from his United Soul days: "The change is basically gospel... I can't remember where I got it from... But then that was totally just jamming. I started the jam off, and everybody joined in. You can hear the vibe in our music. You can hear that we're all in it together." George heard what they were cooking up and came out with his usual yelps of encouragement at the monster now unfolding, recalling: "Junie was one of the most phenomenal musicians you'll ever see. I remember his first day with the group in the studio was 'One Nation Under A Groove'. We opened up brand new boxes of Yamaha equipment for him and Bernie... Garry started 'One Nation' and they just fell in behind it. There was so much vibe with Junie. He came with a full stack." George has since revealed how, "I gave 'One Nation Under A Groove' to Funkadelic when it was really more like a Parliament song because, although Funkadelic sold millions of albums, they hadn't had too many hits and that song was always gonna be a sure-fire smash. I wanted Funkadelic to have that because they always meant more to me."

The rest of the album maintained its momentum with Michael Hampton's guitar-savaging 'Who Says A Funk Band Can't Play Rock?' ably illustrating the record's theme of busting down musical and social barriers. The slow-burning 'Grooveallegiance' pledges to the 'United Funk of Funkadelica' with heaving bass solo, while Bootsy propels 'Cholly (Funk Getting Ready To Roll)'. Scatological stoned hilarity runs amok on the back alley serenading of 'Promentalshitbackwashpsychosis Enema Squad (The Doo Doo Chasers)', in which the world is a toll-free toilet and 'Fried ice cream is a reality'. The magnificent basso tones of sole returning Parliaments singer Ray Davis get a rare turn at lead on 'Into You''s declaration of separation from society's malignant decline. Initial pressings came with a bonus seven-inch single coupling the axe-driven 'Lunchmeat phobia (Think! It Ain't Illegal Yet!)' with Michael Hampton's searing take on 'Maggot Brain'.

While Funkadelic were still basking in their huge hit, Parliament struck again with the aquatic funk masterpiece of *Motor Booty Affair* – turning the Mothership into a submarine to take The Funk to a groove-hungry Atlantis. George announced the album at a press conference at New York's Americana Inn near Times Square, appearing naked to appease early followers. It's the last and most extravagantly epic of George's concept albums (originally intended as a soundtrack for a P-Funk film which never happened called *Music From The Deep*). George explained, "I was on a yacht and really fucked up. I saw dolphins and they were saying, 'We want to funk too'."

Essentially created by the same crew, plus the Horny Horns (and an unaccredited Eddie Hazel), the new sub-aquatic theme ingeniously teleported Parliament from the skies to the depths of an undersea realm unaffected by the world's problems. It opened up a whole 'nother world of thematic possibilities on a stronger album than even the most recent Funkadelic set. *Motor Booty Affair* is the most surreally hilarious P-Funk concept, taking full advantage of its huge cast, while much of the credit must to go to Junie for his warped sense of humour and expansive musical vision. The new nautical cast of characters in George's "underwater *Star Wars*" included Queen Freakoleen, A Mouth Named Jaws, Moby Dicked, Octapussy and Howard Codsell.

After opening with the supremely silly deep-sea boogie of new Clinton creation 'Mr Wiggles' ('I can do my thing underwater') our gurgling submariners traverse a gamut of pulsating oceanic funk splash-downs including George and Bootsy's 'Rumpofsteelskin' and the bass-synth surfing 'Aqua Boogie (A Psychoalphadiscobetabioaquadoloop)'. The album also features one of the greatest P-Funk ballads in the shape of Garry's gorgeous '(You're A Fish And I'm A) Water Sign'. 'Deep' attaches the One to a trunks-detonating, disco-appropriating groove with Poseidon-pounding bass, shoals of vocals and lyrics that aim a cackling torpedo at landlocked views on race and government.

'One Of Those Funky Things' and the Mudbone-sung 'Liquid Sunshine' navigate Parliament's multi-layered chorales, giving their growling undertow new depth and a gleaming coat of storm-resistant paint that protected it from anything else going on above the surface. The album excels on every front, from horns and groove, to its politically prescient lyrics, which climax with another victory by Starchild over Sir Nose D'Voidoffunk, who is thwarted in his attempts to blow up Atlantis.

George's production is widescreen and multi-layered throughout, intricately weaving in nautical jokes, sound effects and musical subtleties as if heard from the kind of ocean's bed where eels wear Day-Glo jockstraps and party hats. But beneath the goofiness, this remains the most towering realisation of P-Funk's bottomless potential – which unfortunately would never be plumbed so effectively again.

Also issued on picture disc, the original release was an elaborate gatefold affair based around Overton Lloyd's suitably themed artwork featuring a pop-up Atlantis and cut-out figures. The whale-milking electronic slap of 'Aqua Boogie' was reeled in to provide yet another R&B chart number one and marked Bernie's last composing credit on a P-Funk album.

Bernie subsequently expressed his admiration for the way in which, "George was the first person to work out how to have involvement with different record labels whereas, for the most part you only do one thing and that's it. He was the first one to be about diversity into different entities within the business."

Eventually, this would prove to be his undoing, as George didn't have the time or the discipline to invest in the acts that he was grabbing deals for with different labels. This was in contrast to Motown, which had all its artists under the same roof, benefiting from the label's super efficient marketing system. One of George's dreams was to produce a classic girl-group for the new age of Funk, so the Brides of Funkenstein and Parlet were temporarily close to his heart at that time.

Parlet were formed out of a Detroit band led by studio backing singer Debbie Wright and her drummer brother James. George got Debbie in the P-Funk choir, first in the studio then on the Earth Tour. He then brought in the 19-year-old Jeanette Washington to start shaping a female answer to Parliament, which he completed with the addition of old friend and funk scout Mallia Franklin. To this end, the Parlettes, who had been around in name since the early sixties, became one of the first P-Funk acts to get a deal, signing to Casablanca. The first line-up consisted of Jeanette Washington, Debbie Wright and Mallia Franklin (who George hadn't seen for a couple of years and was then singing in LA clubs). The girls simply recorded new vocals over existing tracks.

"Sensual satisfaction guaranteed, that's what this group is about," declared George in their promotional blurb. "I've been grooving on the girl group thang for a while, but I need three girls with the right amount of sex and soul. We put it all together at the P-Funk labs [United Sound Studios] and now we're ready to woo you."

Or at least, they would have done if the album had been thrust more firmly into the public consciousness. Parlet are the most glaring example of George's offshoot projects not being seen through, from the grab-bag creation of the album using George's funk-trove of already recorded grooves, to slapdash marketing and patchy radio play. The usual suspects are strongly in evidence, including Bernie's major presence across the whole album, with Glenn Goins on guitars, and also featuring Billy Bass and the Horny Horns.

Their first single, 'Pleasure Principle', reached number 66 on the R&B chart, which would be the sum total of Parlet's commercial success. The album now stands as another lost P-Funk classic, starting with the title track that established the girls' distinctive unison vocals, 'deedly-dee' flapper scatting, and their uncanny female replication of George's low-level croon over its breezy string-embroidered disco-funk mutant backdrop. Bassist Skeet is on excellent form, popping and humping under the fiery horn aerobics. Other highlights include 'Love Amnesia''s languorous stealth-funk and their yelping vamp through Fuzzy's 'Cookie Jar', whose piano-hammering glomp echoes the Stones 'Lovin' Cup'. The songs are long and episodic, as opposed to the punchy sex-killers that might have made more people sit up and take notice. If the girls had bust out singing solo a little more on 'Cookie Jar' it could have risen above being merely an archetypical P-Funk sex-chant. 'Are You Dreaming?' provides a rare chance to hear Bernie stretching out on piano to inject the track with jazz spirit and gospel momentum. Soft-focus Carpenters-smooth ballad 'Mr Melody Man' prompted Mudbone to declare "They did such a beautiful job with that song."

After the album was finished, Debbie suffered a nervous breakdown that was exacerbated by the growing drug habit which sent her to the psychiatric ward. She never recorded or toured with Parlet again and was replaced by Shirley Hayden when they played P-Funk's summer 1978 Funk Festivals and the three-week European tour at the end of the year. Mallia walked out after the Paris Olympia date, where Parlet had once again endured harsh working conditions to open for the Brides Of Funkenstein and Parliament/Funkadelic, to be replaced by Janice Evans. Mallia then embarked on a proposed P-Funk offshoot with her bassist beau Donnie Sterling called Sterling Silver Spaceship. George rated Donnie highly, but gave him the new project instead of admission to the ranks of Funkadelic, explaining, "Donnie's a good musician. Straight out. He would have been a Funkadelic if Skeet hadn't shown up just in time to be Funkadelic's bass player." Mallia later observed that George saw Parlet as LaBelle (the space-suited female trio who hit with 'Lady Marmalade') and the Brides Of Funkenstein as the Supremes.

Bride Of Funkenstien Dawn Silva agrees that Parlet seemed lower on George's totem pole than the Brides, who released their *Funk Or Walk* debut album that September: "I think we were George's ... I don't want to say 'favourites' – I felt bad sometimes because our sister group Parlet would come out onstage and they'd be wearing Danskins or tights. We had these outrageous costumes that cost thousands and thousands of dollars, and I used to feel bad. I wished that Parlet was wearing the same thing."

Lynn Mabry and Dawn Silva were another of the first P-Funk spin-offs to come together as a parallel act and seemed to get much more attention than Parlet. Signing them to Atlantic, George's game plan for the duo was to contrast heavy funk workouts with sensual ballads, again using grooves already churned out for Parliament or the Rubber Band. George also seemed to regard the Brides as something of a vanity project, as he subtly projected the notion that they came from his intergalactic P-Funk harem. "In the beginning George took care of Lynn and I very much," says Dawn. "We were basically kind of spoiled. All the parties, the autograph sessions – and the whole concept of the bigamist George Clinton. A lot of people actually thought we were married, and that George had two wives. People come and ask me, 'You don't have a problem sharing George with another woman?' I was like, 'Oh no, not at all.' I really started to believe and be a part of it."

The first song they recorded was the slinkily melodic sweet soul ditty 'Love Is Something', written by studio engineer Jim Callon with Eddie Hazel. Also featuring Bernie, Billy, Tiki, with Eddie singing and playing guitar, the track was conceived as far back as 1971: "One of the last records the original Funkadelics played," says George. Although mixed in April 1977, it wouldn't see the light of day until Volume Three of the *Family Series* in 1993.

George explained how the tune never saw release at the time because this kind of love song didn't fit the P-Funk scheme of things in 1977: "At that time, even though we all knew it was one of the best songs we had ever heard, everybody in the groups said the same thing. But it was at a time when we was doin' so good, the Mothership was flying all over the place. And everybody had started fallin' in love, out of love. One thing I hate to do in records is like pimp, you know, that love and break-up thing. I mean, it is easy to get a hit record with that but... I felt uncomfortable and this record was so good in that direction of being sad and makin' sad seem like a positive thing. I don't know, I was scared of it.

"This was the beginning... Everybody was in love with everybody. And everybody was breaking up including myself. Let's leave things, everybody was happy. Let's not put something out that's gonna be bittersweet all over the place. Let's just fly a Mothership."

Released in September, *Funk Or Walk* featured Catfish, Daryl, Michael Hampton, Bernie and Joel Johnson on keyboards, with Bootsy and Skeet on bass, various drummers and the Horny Horns (mysteriously unaccredited despite being on the same label at that time).

I still remember the day in September, 1978 when the album turned up as a Warner Brothers promo complete with sleeve depicting the two girls as bionic women. I knew nothing of P-Funk politics then, but the album didn't leave the turntable for two days after the first blast of the opening 'Disco To Go' (which was originally intended as the title track for *Aah... The Name Is Bootsy, Baby*). The song's convoluted soul revue brass–drum intro still pops up in the live show today. George wrote the words as a means of mocking disco (using barnyard references), but the trademark squeals and skin-tight Bootsy groove ensured a barrel of fun and provided a gold record. Elsewhere, they straddled outer-space ditties, ragtime send-ups, weighty guitar groovers, the feisty funk of 'Amorous' and my personal favourite P-ballad in 'Just Like You'. George allowed the song to massage its romantic magic for over nine minutes.

By now, Fuzzy Haskins was squarely out of the Mothership's orbit but retained his faithful old homeboys to release his second album, *Radio Active*, that year. A bit slim at 35 minutes, the album was produced by Fuzzy, who, sang and wrote all eight songs apart from Glenn's 'This Situation'. He's joined by old bandmates Bigfoot, Boogie, Bernie, Garry and Glenn, plus the delightful Brandye (aka Talika Hopkins and Joyce Vincent) on another enjoyable mix of dirty funk and sprightly soulful ballads.* 'Not Yet' boasts the immortal line 'If you let me play in your garden, then I'll let you play in my stash', while 'Thangs We Used To Do' is a discofied funky Brides-style diamond, adorned with some amazing drumming. Interestingly, 'Woman' was mixed by prolific disco supremo Tom Moulton taking a rare excursion into pure funk at Sigma Sound Studios. Further highlights see Fuzzy letting fly like a lunatic on 'Cinderella' and some prime early Funkadelic-style acid psych-hump

---

* Special mention for Brandye, Millie Jackson backing singers who only released one album in 1978's *Crossover To Brandye* but could have easily joined the girls in George's girl group stable if it wasn't already too crowded.

on the Boogie-enhanced 'Silent Day'. At that time it was possible to say 'They don't make 'em like that any more'.

Finally, Bernie released his first solo album *All The Woo In The World*. It's a solid enough P-Funk release, containing more previously recorded tracks and some input from Junie, while Bernie sings throughout. There is still the nagging feeling that, with all the panoramic influences and flavours he'd been slipping into P-Funk, a Bernie Worrell solo album might have launched further into the unknown to explore his avant-classical side rather than making a proficient P-Funk set with no real concept. Every spin-off album seemed to contain at least one stone killer. Here it's the 12-minute 'Insurance Man For The Funk': a densely populated *Mothership Connection*-style loping steamer with testicular bass frequencies and a brazen chant. The raw old-school piano grind of 'Much Thrust' sounds like Funkadelic if they'd been transported back to a sweating sixties juke joint.

Untypically going back to his roots to take his music back to the streets, early October saw George stripping down his live operation to play what he called an "anti-tour" with no Mothership, extravagant glamour, or cast of thousands. Starting in Memphis, the jaunt took in two nights at Washington's Howard Theatre, Philly's Tower Ballroom, Berkeley Community Centre (where Hendrix played one of his greatest concerts) and New York's Palladium on 14th Street (where I had the unforgettable pleasure of witnessing the P-Funk All Stars the following decade and can vouch for its funky intimacy).

The three-hour show was almost like an old-school revue, opening with the Brides before funk comedian James Jackson did his warm-up turn getting opposing halves of the theatre to chant 'Loose booty' and 'Loose butt' while doing a moonwalk smoking a spliff. He then brought on a Funkadelic comprising the Rubber Band minus Bootsy and Catfish, sporting olive paramilitary urban guerrilla clobber and pledging allegiance to the One Nation flag (although Garry refused to cover his diaper and George still sported his favourite long blond wig). The set reverted back to pre-Mothership times with 'I Got A Thing You Got A Thing Everybody's Got a Thing', '(If You Ain't Gonna Get

It On) Take Your Dead Ass Home', 'Get Off Your Ass And Jam' and 'Cosmic Slop'.

"The wrong way is to go out and riot and make yourself mad when you ain't really doing nothing but diverting your energy with a little blowing up," explained George. "The new way of looking at it is 'Screw it, we won't pay it no attention one way or the other.' It's always all right 'cause we ain't gonna deal with 'it's all wrong'. Yes, there's still the ghettos but we're looking at it different now and we're feeling more positive about what's happening. That way we can do more about it."

George added that "get up and party music" is "just black America's way of expressing that we got a raise and that we're being more like what white success looks like... violins, big productions, disco, the Teddy Pendergrasses, it all sounds like white pop music of the fifties. A lot of it is cool, but it's still just a rehash of what white America did. Give 'em time, it'll gradually change."

And it would the following year when disco was systematically squashed by a fearful music industry, ironically opening the door for black music to become the most fertile area of discovery and massive success during the next decade.

Chapter Thirteen

Invasion Of The Booty Snatchers

"What goes up must come down and it was time for us to take a break."

Garry Shider

Perhaps one of the hardest things in the world to imagine is Bootsy with a serious face, but that's what he presented one afternoon in 1990 when recalling the burnout he experienced towards the end of P-Funk's golden run. Clouds seemed to descend behind the famous star glasses and that cool singsong voice took on a darker tone. Placing his elbows on the table in the New York piano bar we were sitting in, Bootsy almost seemed to start welling up while remembering the time he thought he was going to buckle under the superhuman workload and pressure of being Bootzilla 24 hours a day.

Bootsy was caught in the whirlwind of Parliament/Funkadelic projects and spin-offs after George's label-hopping shenanigans intensified following the success of 'Flash Light' and *One Nation Under A Groove*. Demand was also sky high for his Rubber Band. With his larger than life persona, he now had the most recognisable image of the whole crew and was even more likely to get stopped in the street than George.

"It was too much," he sighed. "It just kept on building; a deal here, a deal there with George and myself trying to be on every one. It was too much but you couldn't tell us that then! I think back and realise I was trying to figure out, 'Oh God, how we doing all that crap?' One thing right after another. George and I was winning so tough and everything was so easy that we stopped being really creative after a while. We'd stopped reaching because we were thinking about so many things. It's called burnout.

"That's what made me wanna stop doing everything. By 1979 I got to the point where I didn't know who I was. I had to be Bootsy so much I didn't have time to sit down and just cool out. You can tell if you listen to *This Boot Is Made For Fonk-N*. That's when it hit me because things were just so… I couldn't go out the door without getting attacked. It was like, 'Wow, can I just take these glasses off and walk down to the store and people don't say anything to me?' I had such a hard time with that one and I couldn't do it. I couldn't go on like that.

"I just made up my mind. That just made me go, 'Oh man, this is too much monster for me. This is too much monkey on my back.' So I just told George I gotta quit. Then he's giving me all the reasons why I shouldn't and what's going to happen etc and what's in it for me doing this. He was just showing me all the things that could happen from doing this so he could be sure that I was making up my mind right. I didn't care because it was so much on. There was so much pressure. I just said, 'I got to give it up'."

It would be another few years before Bootsy got to hang up his star bass in order to take some time to "get my sanity back", as there was simply too much going on. By now, much of the P-Funk organisation was running on Peruvian marching powder, which can be perilous creatively when a group is desperately trying to hold on to the lofty status that can disappear overnight. Although the P-Funk albums released during 1979–80 still boasted their share of killer tracks there was little of the cohesion and sense of epoch-making greatness that had permeated *Mothership Connection*, *Funkentelechy* and *One Nation Under A Groove*. The mind-blowing funk-rock excursions of the early Funkadelic now seemed like another band.

Listening to *This Boot Is Made For Fonk-N* next to 1978's *Player Of The Year* illustrates Bootsy's plight and stands as an accurate representation of the state of the P-Funk nation at that time. That's not to say it's bad, just not as *baad*, as numbers such as 'Under The Influence Of A Groove' and 'Bootsy Get Live' displayed a form of funk autopilot that meant much-loved elements were present and correct, but that rare vitality that booted his previous album into realms of intensity became diminished. The album was hastily banged out amid growing inter-band tensions to satisfy demand and sometimes sounds like it. There's not even one of his classic ballads, only the pleasant 'Oh Boy, Gorl'. *Village Voice* columnist Robert Christgau described Bootsy as sounding "like a kiddie show host at the end of his tether".

Of course, even when coasting the Rubber Band still grooved like no other. 'Under The Influence' features the highly flammable combination of Bootsy funking at bass level and the sumptuous harmonies going on between Mudbone, P-Nut and the Brides. Despite Bootsy's cartoon vocal acrobatics and the Bridal screeches, it sometimes sounds more like they were going through the party-starting motions. Having said that, 'Bootsy Get Live' packs a punch (including a cheeky guitar lift from James Brown's 'The Payback'), 'Chug-A-Lug (The Bun Patrol)' is fun with puns, and 'Jam Fan (Hot)' cooks up a mesmerising slab of densely layered hoodoo with Parlet, the Brides and Horny Horns all caught in the moment. The song provided the album's title by referencing Nancy Sinatra's 'These Boots Are Made For Walking'.

'Jam Fan (Hot]' was the album's biggest single and has been credited with inspiring Talking Heads' only US Top 10 hit, 'Burning Down The House', released in 1983 as the first single off their fifth album, *Speaking In Tongues* – by which time Bernie Worrell was playing keyboards for them.

"Tina and I went to see the Parliament-Funkadelic thang at Madison Square Garden in the early eighties," recalls drummer Chris Frantz now. "At some point during the show George Clinton began chanting 'Burn down the house! Burn down the house!' with full audience participation. It was the crazy wild show with the Mothership when P-Funk was at the peak of their popularity and fame.

"Shortly after that, we were writing songs based on jam sessions in our Long Island City loft. That was how we always did it up until *Little Creatures*. Remembering the P-Funk show, I started chanting 'Burn down the house' over the drum beat I was playing. This evolved into the chorus of 'Burning Down The House' and became one of our most popular songs."

Meanwhile, George was faced with the tall order of following *One Nation Under A Groove*. He did this by expanding on the military metaphors which accompanied the album cover's appropriation of the World War Two South Pacific flag-raising image to come up with *Uncle Jam Wants You*. This subverted another American icon by heisting the old 'Uncle Sam Wants You!' posters. Instead of the usual Pedro Bell painting, George is pictured striking a Huey Newton pose in military gear on a mission to 'rescue dance music from the blahs'. But his main weapon was the 13-minute '(Not Just) Knee Deep', which further crystallised P-Funk's new electronic boogie-funk sound (with Bootsy on drums). The single, which featured an even longer 12-inch mix highlighted by Michael Hampton's fabulous guitar solo, took them to the top of the R&B charts for the last time. Sung by Garry and George, with scatting from new Funkadelic member Philippé Wynne of Spinners fame (who also croons the title track), it was another new electronic disco workout, which caused a storm in the clubs with its hypnotic 'something about the music' middle stretch. De La Soul sampled groove and choir to great effect on their breakthrough hit 'Me Myself And I'. The songwriting credit to George Clinton Junior prompted the story that dad gave his son the song as a graduation present. Garry Shider once said that Junie provided the music and they just went and sang it. When I interviewed Junie in 1990 he growled, "Yeah I did all the music and George didn't even put my fuckin' name on it. It's not the money but the way they recreated my music."

The song featured backing vocals from Jessica Cleaves, the operatic former Earth Wind & Fire and Friends Of Distinction singer who George credits with "one of the most beautiful voices I've ever heard". He recalls how Funkadelic "scared the hell out of her" with their use of backwards tapes. "She thought, 'This must be the Devil' so ran out of the session… She did 'Knee Deep' with us; that's that beautiful voice. Jessica was one of my favourite artists… Jessica, the Brides, Bootsy was like *it* for me." George and Junie recorded several tracks with Jessica that didn't get released at the time, including a Tyrone Lampkin slow jam called 'Send A Gram'.

The rest of *Uncle Jam* ranged from the intoxicatingly complex title track's militarising of *One Nation*'s Funk Wars concept to nightclub piano ballad 'Holly Wants To Go To California', which pushed George upfront to sound unusually vulnerable and all the better for it. Eddie Hazel returned again to splatter his magic across marching band throwaway 'Foot Soldiers (Star Spangled Funky)' while other old faces such as Ray Davis, Tiki Fulwood and Billy Bass pop up elsewhere on the album.

With this militant attitude it wouldn't have been unreasonable to expect musical fireworks to match, but no arrangers such as Bernie, Bootsy or Junie were present for the project – which could explain the occasional lack of unifying spark. Plus, new recruits such as DeWayne 'Blackbyrd' McKnight and drummer Dennis Chambers had started to acquit themselves well but, as with any incoming new members, needed more guidance now that the intuitive free-for-alls of the seventies were a thing of the past.

In part, George dealt with the pressures building through 1979 by buying a farm outside Detroit and announcing he planned to cut back on touring to concentrate on production once his label was under way. I've still got the bit of paper he scribbled the address on some time in the nineties with an invite to visit if I was in the area. His rural pile was situated next to the Michigan Raceway with a home studio and 4,000 acre lake to accommodate George's love of fishing. He even subdivided about 90 acres of the land for locals to plant wheat or other crops. They called him 'Farmer Funkenstein'.

George was starting to get a grip on the realities of business. "Most musicians don't want to think about money," he asserted. "They are programmed by their managers who say they'll take care of everything. I figured I was too busy to check on all this money I thought I had in my pocket. Then it was gone, so I figured maybe I wasn't that busy. And I stopped taking 'ludes."

He seemed semi-serious about taking a back seat on gigging while overseeing proceedings from backstage (and making the odd cameo appearance) when "George Clinton's Production of Popsicle Stick starring Parliament/Funkadelic" played a stretch at Harlem's Apollo Theatre between October 10–21, followed by 12 more gigs in February. During his stay, George was put in an unusual interview situation by *New York Rocker*, the city's downtown underground music magazine which had covered the punk scene from day one. I'd been their UK correspondent since 1976 thanks to their late publisher, Alan Betrock, and we also had a nifty arrangement trading features with my own *Zigzag* magazine. It was great to see them focusing on George at a time he was supposed to be slipping, putting him on the cover with post-punk sax-blasting jazz rebel James Chance to trailer a meeting between the two and downtown dynamo Anya Phillips. The conversation is fascinating, mutual respect in evidence after Chance had caught George's Apollo show the previous night, along with James Brown who George says "sat me down and gave me some fatherly advice last night. Every time I see him he sits me down and talks to me for half an hour and goes over things with me. I told him to come out on the stage and give it."

George expected some negative reactions to *Uncle Jam*, but 'Knee Deep' was like a final force 10 blast of defiant funk before the following year's troubles kicked in, as he explained: "I feel our attention span is being tested right now. Like with a car, once the novelty wears off, you're susceptible to buying a new one. I think that's what's happening with us right now, because we've had a lot of hit records. After a string of hits they'll be looking for the next group to come and kick your ass. That's when reports start coming out that you're dead, or gone gay. Reviews start to come up negative, because it's not cool to write about this guy that's been good for three years.

"We feel we have to do something before that happens to keep it interesting. We give them something new to reactivate ourselves. 'Knee Deep' was the shot in the arm that was needed, plus the fact that Funkadelic had the hit. It was to make people say, 'Them again? We thought we

e late Eddie Hazel in full flight. ALDO MAURO

Renegades Of Funk, including George, Afrika Bambaataa and Ice-T. P-FUNK ARCHIVES

Wonder, George and the author, Echoes office July 11, 1991.

George and Denise Johnson get a little funky at Primal Scream's MTV recording, NYC 1994. GRANT FLEMING

Atomic Dog returns to *Creem*, July 1983. P-FUNK ARCHIVES

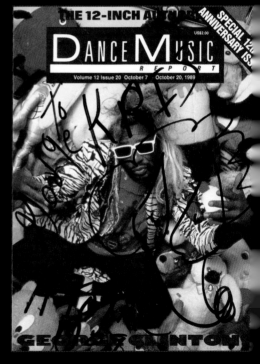

George signed the piece that started this book: *Dance Music Report*, October 1989. KRIS NEEDS ARCHIVES

eorge and Bobby Gillespie, backstage at Brixton, April 9, 1994. GRANT FLEMING

orge holds court with unreleased barbershop gems, MTV New York 1994. GRANT FLEMING

Old friends: Bernie & Bootsy guffaw in the studio. JUDIE WORRELL

Daddy's home: Marshall & Garry Shider, Washington DC 1992.
SERGE DODWELL

Serge primes Bootsy's Star Bass. PHOTO COURTESY OF SERGE DODWELL

Happy birthday George! SERGE DODWELL

eorge & Sly on the hog 2012. CARLON THOMPSON

orge's favourite dog Buddy rules Farmer Funkenstein's Michigan back garden 1993. SERGE PODWELL

knew them!' We sold a million records and didn't even get off the R&B chart yet… 'Knee Deep' is number one on the *Billboard* R&B charts for the past three weeks. Haven't seen it on the pop charts yet!"

George expounded on Funkadelic's live shows, recent hit singles and onstage sporting of army fatigues: "That was because we'd had so many hits with Parliament. And with the Casablanca hype, it was easy to get tagged, so I said that the only way to seriously make a dent is for Funkadelic to get a hit. That's why we gave them 'One Nation Under A Groove' and 'Knee Deep'. It's unlikely for Funkadelic to get a hit, so it meant more for them to get a hit than Parliament. With Funkadelic you got that sort of dark vibe, so we put on the fatigues – y'know that's terrorist, but we put roller skates on to take the edge off it. We know not to push the system into a corner 'cause they will react against that. We go, 'We're revolutionary, we're crazy, but we ain't gonna push you too far.' 'Cause that's when they'll destroy you. That way they won't feel threatened, and we'll be able to grow. Because if we do, we'll take over what disco is now. It's basic for us, dance music."

When Anya asked George how he dealt with the cut-throat modern music business his whole philosophy came tumbling out: "Keep getting a lot of deals, keep cutting a lot of stuff, and don't let them get nothing exclusive. And don't be partial to a certain name or using certain musicians, or being on a particular company. You can add more people to your thing, but the more you do the hassle is to make sure all of them know what it's for. A lot of people can't wait for their individual thing to happen, while I'm working on the whole thing. All my people that leave me, I say, 'I know the pressure that's driving you away, but you can always come back and nobody's gonna say I told you so, because I know what's happening.' But you've got to have a lot of deals going – that way all the companies can't get together to stop you, because each one wants to make their own money. The more deals you got, the safer you are, if you can keep it all under your one thing. With me it happened as an accident, but once I realised the advantage, I said I'll never be without it again."

Finally the much-missed Anya (who was Debbie Harry's best friend in the seventies and succumbed to cancer in 1981) asked George how he looked so fit at 40. "I guess I've been lucky," he replied, adding to the calm-before-the-storm nature of the conversation. "But it was so much a dream for me that I never wasted energy wondering if it would work or not. I knew it would work, and didn't care if it didn't work. 'Cause it was working just doing it. I've never spent no energy worrying about whether I should commit suicide or get a job. I thought it was laziness at one time but it was really my ability to say 'Funk it' when things didn't go right or fast enough."

While George was touring the radio stations promoting *Uncle Jam* he became aware of another recently released album called *Mutiny On The Mamaship* by a band called Mutiny, which Jerome 'Bigfoot' Brailey had planned to form with Glenn Goins before the young singer passed away the previous year.

"Boogie Mosson told me that George had every DJ throw my record in the trash at every radio station where they went to promote their *Uncle Jam* record," recalls Bigfoot. "He said 'George told them mugs to throw your record away'. It slipped through the cracks and everything but he tried to sabotage it. Then George was going round telling people, 'It's a great record, it should have been on my Uncle Jam label'!"

The pair started plotting the Mutiny concept as they got close to completing Glenn's Quazar album. "Then after it was finished my manager, Robert Mittleman, was like 'What do you want to do?' I said 'I guess put some group together and do the Mutiny thing,'" recalls Bigfoot, who formed a band which still operates around the drummer under that name today. "I wanted all my rights and all my publishing," he affirms. "I had a high royalty rate. I wanted the kind of deal where I own everything. I wanted my own shit." Mutiny lined up as lead guitarist Lenny Holmes, guitarist Skitch Lovett, bassist Raymond 'Bro' Carter, keyboardist Nat Lee and a brass section fronted by former P-Funk saxophonist Darryl Dixon, which also included Marvin Daniels and Melvin El.

Mutiny On The Mamaship unleashed a vengeful style of rocked-up heavyweight funk with Bigfoot's lyrics taking pot shots at his old boss, noticeably on 'Lump' (his nickname for George). Although the album

was well-received, Bigfoot didn't know the rules of payola then ruling
black music, which stifled the album's promotion and sales, while its
hybrid style also confused the record company. With its sleeve shot of
Bigfoot in pirate gear making George walk the plank, there's little doubt
he has an axe to grind, pulling no punches in his self-sung lyrics over a
sound recalling the elemental power of early seventies Funkadelic. This
is further amped up by Bigfoot's mastery of lunging the One beat into
the uptempo tracks. Songs such as 'Go Away From Here' and 'Funk
And Bop' are aflame with reckless energy, multi-tiered vocals and the
latent power of men on a mission.

"The critics loved it," he recalls. "We just had problems with CBS.
The A&R pop department loved it but the R&B department, who had
all these pictures on their wall of themselves with gold chains around
their necks, didn't know what they had. We were young and stuff so
didn't know that what you had to do was pay them guys under the table
and they would make sure you had a hit. I just couldn't fathom that we
got to pay the guys who work at the record label! CBS was involved
with all that payola. If we'd have given them 20 grand or something we
would have had a hit. Now we know!

"Then the A&R pop department couldn't do anything because it
wasn't a pop record and it was also a funk record so the guys over on
the R&B side didn't know what to do with it. We were like 'It's a
Funkadelic type record, that's what you do with it!'"

Having got the George-baiting out of its system, Mutiny followed
this bomb with 1980's equally hefty *Funk Plus The One* (with Cordell
Mosson guesting) and 1983's *A Night Out With The Boys*.

Less effective among the rebel P-Funk missions was the renegade
album recorded by Fuzzy, Calvin Simon and Grady Thomas under the
name Funkadelic, which was released in Germany in 1980 under the title
42.9% and the following year in the US as *Connections & Disconnections*.
'This album does not include any performances or creations by George
Clinton' disclaimed the sleeve – and it showed. From the opening
'Phunklords' to its closer, 'Who's A Funkadelic?', it's pretty weak, the
trio backed by a bunch of funkless session musicians. Their use of the
Funkadelic name led to a bitter legal battle between them and George

which only served to dilute its legend, while hastening the demise of the P-Funk empire.

The Horny Horns were about to move on too. Fred Wesley was unhappy that George had denied his request for residual royalties on songs he'd played a major part in creating, especially on *Mothership Connection* (although he was shocked to discover the horn players were getting three times as much as the others for gigs). After completing the Earth Tour, the Horny Horns were expecting to go straight out with Bootsy's Rubber Band on their first major headlining jaunt, but this was cancelled at the eleventh hour. The reason given was that Bootsy had gone down with shingles.

This ended Fred and Maceo's time playing with P-Funk but they still had a second Horny Horns album released in August 1979 called *Say Blow By Blow Backwards*. Once again Fred, Maceo, Rick Gardner and Richard Griffiths found themselves mainly playing over a grab-bag of grooves and backing tracks with the vocals removed, such as that gorgeous Brides ballad 'Just Like You' and Parlet's 'Mr Melody Man'. 'We Came To Funk Ya' is a slinky rump-referencing P-style chant with Bootsy popping and dipping into 'Bootzilla' while 'Half A Man' is a welcome burst of Billy Bass-led throb action that could have sat proudly on any of the P-Funk flagship releases of the time. Sadly that would be it for Fred and Maceo with the P-Funk. It's a shame the pair couldn't have realised more of the potential they had shown within the ranks after bringing their original funk class and magic to the party.

Parlet were not happy bunnies either. "It felt like George had lost interest in us," insisted the group's only constant presence, Jeanette Washington. "I don't know if we were a tax write-off for the record label, or a way for George to pocket a recording advance, but none of us ever felt we got his attention, or our chance at success."

1979's *Invasion of The Booty Snatchers* referenced disco with its title track flying close enough to the mirror ball to get Funkadelic purists spluttering into their bugle, but Parlet also carried enough verve to fire up quintessential P-funkers such as 'No Rump To Bump' and the 'Three Little Pigs'-inspired lolloper 'Huff-N-Puff'. Although disco's soon-to-be-exterminated success attracted the most ridiculous bandwagon jumping, its real spirit was pure, hedonistic and craved little more than dancing all night on the right drugs. So what was different apart from the beat?

Co-produced by P–Funk newcomer Ron Dunbar, the album goes against the P–grain with specially tailored songs performed by specifically assigned musicians, including guitarists Gordon Carlton and Jerome Ali, his bassist bro' Jimmy on bass and drummer Kenny Colton. The record also heralded the first appearance by new P-Funk horns Bennie Cowan, Greg Thomas and Greg Boyer. Parlet would follow this album with 1980's *Play Me Or Trade Me*, which unfortunately became buried in the collapse of the P-Funk empire. This was a shame because it's another great set, with its orchestra-sized Horny Horns-led brass section and corkers such as 'Wolf Tickets' coming on a like sinuous sequel to 'Cookie Jar'.

After the interchangeable nature of the material which provided the first Brides Of Funkenstein album, November's robust *Never Buy Texas From A Cowboy* saw more songs created especially for them. The pregnant Lynn Mabry been replaced by new lead singers Sheila Horn and Jeanette McGruder, while their touring band provided the sessions' core musicians in future P-Funk mainstays 'Blackbyrd' McKnight, drummer Dennis Chambers, bassist Jeff Bunn and keyboardist Gary Hodgkins. Produced by Clinton working closely with Ron Dunbar, the girls were also joined by Bootsy, Eddie and even George (singing on the rambunctious 'Smoke Signals'), making for a fine-tuned all-round set which earned them a *Cashbox* Rhythm & Blues Award in 1981 for Best Female Group, while an edited version of the ultra-funky 15-minute title track became a hit in the Midwest, Europe and Asia.

Once again, this period saw George trying to sharpen up his spin-off projects. Here he did it to the extent that the album ended up superior to anything released by Funkadelic or Parliament that year in terms of originality, funk energy and performances – which were among the best on any P-Funk record. A definite victory for the ladies which prompted Christgau to make the point that, "It's good to hear women asserting themselves in what has always been a sexist setup". In 2001 *Rolling Stone* rated the album among its 50 coolest albums of all time.

Parliament's eighth album, *Gloryhallastoopid* (or *Pin The Tail On The Funky)*, was released the same month, but the cracks were showing despite its rich concept that The Funk was responsible for the creation of the universe. George's Starchild scene-setting on the title track was promising but this wasn't really followed through. The set might have worked better if that tantalising theme had been explored beyond attempts to find another dance hit such as 'The Big Bang Theory', 'The Freeze' and the unashamed four-to-the-floor disco pump of 12-inch single candidate 'Party People'. The most fun track is 'Theme From The Black Hole' where Sir Nose makes another attempt to conquer The Funk, but explodes in the process. The album's gritty funk standout 'Colour Me Funky' sees George delivering a rare full vocal that declares, 'Nothing has changed, even the bang remains the same' as he reinforces his loyalty to The Funk.

The album is notable for the absence of many P-Funk veterans, with minimal contributions from those who remained. This meant that much of the music was supplied by the younger musicians, who had no qualms about dipping into disco. Although pretty much dismissed over the years, the album proved popular with later generations who hadn't grown up with the P – much to George's surprise: "For *Gloryhallastoopid* I really thought it was time for us to go sit down. So I just put some songs together that I liked... when I think we're in trouble we make the best records. I said, 'I think we've had too many hit records, they gonna shaft us upside the head for this motherfucker, no matter *what* the record sounds like.' 'Cause you know our planned obsolescence period come into effect. I don't care how good it is, it's like get the fuck *outta* here! And I thought *Gloryhallastoopid* should have been that one. But when it came out... it was like really fuckin' happenin!"

George's title track declaration about 'silliness as a positive force' seemed to provide a more accurate picture of his *modus operandi* as he introduced a new, backward-speaking character named 'Wellington Wigout'. George had always revelled in the ridiculous, was proud to be potty and defiantly showed solidarity for the stupid. In 1979's close-to-the-edge days when drug use was inevitably contributing to the comedown, he tried to explain, "A lot of folks feel our group and our songs are silly, ridiculous and stupid. While they might expect me to get upset, I just laugh and consider even the negative things they say as highly complimentary – that's how stupid I am. As a matter of fact, I wrote a song for Funkadelic a few years ago called 'Super Stupid' and I guess it applies even more today. People just have to realise that in the unlogical world we live in today, logic has gone completely out to lunch. I mean, I'm lunchin' too, but we're just eating at different counters."

1980 started promisingly enough for George, when CBS offered him a multi-million dollar distribution deal to start his own record label. Now he could realise his long-held ambition of running another Motown. Called Uncle Jam Records, he even persuaded his old buddy Sidney Barnes to uproot from LA and move to Detroit to help run the label with manager Archie Ivy.

Uncle Jam's first two albums were released at the end of 1980 – Bootsy's *Sweat Band* and Philippé Wynne's *Wynne Jammin'*. The latter was a major break for the former Spinners singer and although graced by Bernie and other P-Funkers, its sublime contemporary soul is a departure from what might be expected, but it remains a total delight. Wynne's jumping 12-minute tear-up on 'Never Gonna Tell It' is one of the best P-Funk covers.

Incredibly, Bootsy's Rubber Band had been royally shafted by a lawsuit over their name from a folk group resulting in them owing Warner Brothers $275,000. Bootsy's next few albums would go towards paying off the debt, including *Ultra Wave,* scheduled to be released in November 1980 under his own name (to ignite the usual 'Zilla funk griddle with stonkers like 'Mug Push'). Over at Uncle Jam, George decided to release the album that would be called *Sweat Band* (to avoid further legal complications) that same week. He would effectively be in competition with his own album!

Sweat Band (graced by a cover depicting just that) was put together from old Bootsy, Rubber Band and general P-Funk jam sessions which had been gathering dust on various studio shelves over the years. No Bootzilla out front or smooch-fests, just solid grooves with the odd chant and the cool, Chuck Mangione-style jazz of George and Maceo's 'Love Munch'.

In a typically perverse move, George's scheduling of Bootsy's album came a month before the release of the final Parliament on Casablanca, Trombipulation just before the label met its doom and his band's name was cast into legal limbo. George pulled out all the stops, and for the first time he had a close-up of his face adorning the sleeve, albeit wild-eyed and gurning behind his elongated plastic elephant's trunk.

Awash with disco strings, horns and backing vocals, it's one of George's most widescreen productions, although some tracks were almost entirely played by Bootsy – who co-produced tracks with George along with Ron Dunbar, Junie and Ron Ford. The album concludes the Sir Nose saga after his son pledges to keep The Funk after dad finds out his people were its original keepers, the Cro-Nasal Sapiens. The title track refers to using the hooter to pick up things like an elephant (which, by all accounts, was chemically the case by that time). The classical strings and dense chorale on 'Long Way Around' forge a brave departure into orchestral soul, while the crunching 'Let's Play House' is one of the great overlooked P-Funk tracks (as heisted by P-Funk worshipping west coast hip hoppers Digital Underground on 'The Humpty Dance').

Sometimes the album seems to be all wired bluster riding a wall of sound reaching back to Sly-style soul hootenanny, but songs such as the subsequent single 'Crush It' and 'Doo Doo Chasers' are a taste of where George planned to take the convoluted Parliament saga next. As a snapshot of our hero staring impending disaster in the face, it deserves a higher profile in the catalogue and is the other album from this period to have been picked up by newer fans. Now sounding like a defiantly twisted last gasp from a beleaguered cult, it later built a following after being lambasted for years. George hit the nail on the head on why *Trombipulation* and *Gloryhallastoopid* are the most popular P-Funk albums when he observed, "But only because *now* we been away from that sound so long that you can appreciate it… that's *all* they sampled, those records. That's their favourite two. We might've been movin' too fast at the time… I never would have thought that anybody would ever *think* about buyin' 'The Agony Of Defeet'!"

While *Trombipulation* raised questions concerning the whereabouts of original crew members such as Garry Shider and Bernie Worrell, Junie

Morrison was already planning his departure from the ranks, signing to Columbia and releasing a solo album called *Bread Alone* in 1980. Junie played all the instruments himself, pre-empting Prince to a startling extent on quirky pop-funk workouts such as 'Love Has Taken Me Over (Be My Baby)' and 'Seaman First Class (Jock Rock)'.

The demise of Casablanca in 1980 could be seen as a symbolic farewell to seventies-style excess. First, Donna Summer left the label after clashes about her future musical direction (the Queen of Disco had become a born-again Christian). Then Neil Bogart's lifestyle caught up with him. He was renowned for his extravagant spending on parties, events and promotion and while this often resulted in hit records, profits inevitably took a dive. PolyGram, which already owned 50 per cent of the label, was not impressed when it saw how much Bogart was splashing out on entertainment, so it made an offer to buy his half of Casablanca. After accepting, Bogart was told his services were no longer required and paid off, while his label was absorbed into Mercury Records. I can recall sitting in a Swiss Cottage hotel room with former Runaway Joan Jett and her telling me she'd just signed to a new label Neil was starting, called Boardwalk. This was news as he'd always seemed inextricably linked to Parliament, but sadly Neil wouldn't live to see his first signing ascend to stardom after he succumbed to cancer in 1982. Along with bringing down the curtain on Parliament, these events nixed plans George also had in the works to start yet another label through Casablanca called Choza Negra.

George had also become uneasy about his increasingly fractious relationship with Warner Brothers, despite bringing the label two million-selling Funkadelic albums in a row. Perhaps starting a label with another record company while his other group was signed to Casablanca made Warners uneasy, or maybe it was just having this maverick wildman tossing his latest outrageous schemes around its nice office while in constant financial chaos. George wanted to make the next Funkadelic a double but Warners wouldn't wear it, claiming that it would be too expensive. He also expressed plans to start yet another label through the company to be called Park Place.

The final straw which broke the record company relationship, Funkadelic and even the P-Funk empire came from George and Bootsy helping a young singer from Ohio called Roger Troutman, who had a band called Zapp with his three brothers and was an early exponent of the talkbox. Zapp knew the Collins brothers Catfish and Bootsy from Ohio, the latter inviting them to United Sound in 1978 to record some demos, which Catfish produced. George was impressed with their song 'More Bounce To The Ounce' and suggested playing it to Warner Brothers, which signed them in early 1979. Zapp's Bootsy-produced, self-titled debut album was released in July 1980, followed by the electro and G-Funk-influencing single 'More Bounce To The Ounce', which reached number two on the R&B chart.

In the middle of all this, George had tried to pull off the old Parliament/Funkadelic wheeze of signing Troutman to Uncle Jam under another name, getting CBS to fund demos of his solo album *The Many Facets Of Roger*, which included a 10-minute version of Marvin Gaye's 'I Heard It Through The Grapevine' (which, rather strangely, I have on 12-inch released by hip-hop label Sugarhill). After getting the Uncle Jam advance through CBS, Troutman sold the album to Warner Brothers, which single-handedly poleaxed the Uncle Jam label project with CBS. Some say it also prompted Warner Brothers to drop Funkadelic, although news stories at the time had George suing the company with three separate lawsuits for breach of contract claiming total damages of a hundred million dollars. Either way, Warners dropped its support of Funkadelic, while keeping their name on the company books. Meanwhile, separate litigation was on the horizon with the renegade outfit formed by the old Parliaments singers.

"Roger took the tapes and the exact same liner notes and pictures from CBS and then gave them to Warner Brothers," recalled George. "So (Warner Brothers) thought that I did it. They thought I was in cahoots with him." George admitted in the *Oral History*. "That's one of the only fallouts from the whole thing that I have to admit I got peeved at… It cost about five million dollars and a lot of people's jobs and what we consider as the empire falling."

In April, Warners sneaked out *The Electric Spanking Of War Babies*, its title inspired by the Vietnam War, having rejected Pedro Bell's original cover of a woman being spanked by a giant cock-and-balls space machine. George had reluctantly consented to this censorship, although he made sure the new sleeve contained subtle messages such as, 'The cover that *they* were too scared to print'.

The album featured newer crew members such as Blackbyrd, Ron Dunbar, Ron Ford, Donnie Sterling and bassist Lige Curry, alongside familiar names such as Hampton and Lampkin. Sly Stone rasps a few lines on the early Funkadelic-recalling 'Funk Gets Stronger's second hard-rocking version, which also features Eddie Hazel on guitar. At that time, new Funkadelic member Sly was firmly ensconced in the hardcore cocaine addiction that he brought to the Funk Mob when he joined their touring party for an ill-fated stretch.

The Junie-driven title track (which was also the single) comes on like a spikier 'Knee Deep', commenting on the baby boomer generation over a metallic bounce. 'Electro-Cuties' coins a new musical term and George's X-rated rap on 'Icka Prick' predates hardcore gangsta with Blowfly-style humour ('You ain't seen obscene yet!... doing push-ups with his clit... Graffilthy! Suck my mind!') 'Brettino's Bounce' is a unique Funkadelic diversion consisting of nothing more than percussive dialogue.

The whole album is a trip back to the experimental nature of the early Funkadelic, letting ideas run riot. Had it been a double, which could have been stretching it a tad, it would have included tracks such as 'Mayday', 'I, Angle' and a little thing called 'Atomic Dog'.

Parliament/Funkadelic played their last show under those names in Detroit in June, 1981, fittingly retiring the names in the city where all the madness had started. With his plans for a world-conquering stable in ruins, George licked his wounds and moved quickly and smoothly onto his next phase. It seemed a logical move to go out under his own name as a solo artist. He now found himself increasingly in the position of revered pioneer with a new generation to corrupt with The Funk. The mission was far from over...

Chapter Fourteen

Old Dog New Tricks

"I'll never holler. 'Cause to me, without humps there'd be no getting over.'
George Clinton

June 1989, the Warner Bros Building, 75 Rockafella Plaza, New York. It's a relatively cool afternoon in the city for mid-summer but George is warming up rapidly as he gleefully revisits his vast back catalogue, gushes about the new album he's just done with Prince and expounds with gratitude about the hip-hop movement which has hauled him out of the post-P-Funk doldrums with a renewed profile as Godfather of Funk and now hip-hop.

It's this writer's first time interviewing him and, as one piece resulting from our meeting began, "Right now I'm having a job convincing myself that it is really George Clinton sitting opposite me…" As a maggot-brained devotee for the previous 18 years it was a little hard to believe that the genial giggling wise man with multi-hued explosion-in-a-mattress-factory hair extensions sitting here in a Warner Bros boardroom is Dr Funkenstein himself; the cosmic pimp responsible for some of my favourite records of all time. As mentioned earlier in this book, a pile of my beloved P-vinyl is sitting in front of him, which he scrawls and doodles on as he lets fly with his memories and theories radiating all the stoked, soiled charisma that could be hoped for. Open and articulate with a wicked sense of humour, there's no burnt-out super-fry here, just a long-time musical hero sitting at a glass coffee table in all his extraterrestrial splendour dishing out the refreshments he's thoughtfully brought along.

The previous night George's current P-Funk All Stars had rocked New York's Palladium on 14th Street for over two classics-stacked hours. It was opening night of annual music business schmooze-fest the New Music Seminar, where George was announcing his upcoming comeback album *The Cinderella Theory* on Prince's Paisley Park label. I was officially there in my capacity as assistant editor of Tommy Boy Records' Dance Music Report tip-sheet, which was letting me do a George special with him on the cover. Inside I was fulfilling a lifetime's dream of finally seeing George and his Funk Mob in their onstage element. To sit in a room with him for around the same amount of time as his set was unreal at first but we soon settled down. It was also pretty surreal getting a cassette of George's new single and letter on headed writing paper from Paisley Park's Vice President, Alan Leeds, thanking me for the feature.

The main subject on George's mind that day was the hip-hop revolution which had given his music a new lease of life. After a quarter of a century wielding a sonic machete through the stifling conventions of the music biz he started seeing his creations being turned into hits for other people. Some, like Public Enemy and De La Soul, gave him due credit and paid for their sampling in financial terms. I was working at Tommy Boy's First Avenue HQ then and seen these three shy teenagers from Long Island edge into the office one afternoon and sign to the label as De La Soul. Then it was immensely enjoyable experiencing the mounting excitement as their *3 Feet High And Rising* debut album and breakthrough single 'Me Myself And I' started taking off earlier that year, each radio add or chart rise announced over the intercom to rousing cheers. This was in the free-for-all time just before sampling litigation started spreading like a tenement blaze.*

---

* The first action came from sixties group the Turtles suing De La Soul over the use of their track 'You Showed Me' in the 'Transmitting Live From Mars' interlude on *3 Feet High*.

'Me Myself And I' was 'Knee Deep' with D.A.I.S.Y. age rapping. Tommy Boy had also signed the Digital Underground who'd plundered *Trombipulation* and *Motor Booty Affair* for their P-homaging *Sex Packets* debut. At first it had been James Brown, but George was now the second Most Sampled Man in Showbusiness and rapidly overtaking as Schoolly D, EPMD and LL Cool J dipped into the catalogue.

I wondered how George felt gaining this ripe new crowd through hip-hop.

George smiled, eyes twinkling behind his big screen shades, and stopped scrawling Atomic Dogs on my copy of *Maggot Brain* for a moment. "There is a brand new audience," he reflected. "Public Enemy and De La Soul took it to the top. They're proud of the fact that they listened to P-Funk. And there's a whole lot of other groups. Digital Underground make it and they intend to take it wherever it's ready to go. They're the ones that's really ready to go. Tone Loc said 'Don't everybody listen to P-Funk?'

"Rap has really saved The Funk but it's the DNA for hip-hop. We put our own DJs on the records and that was like the birth of hip-hop. DJs would talk over records in the clubs, that's how they kept you on the dance floor. Chuck and Flavor listened to the Parliament live LP from beginning to end and they've said that. They said I'm their mentor and that came at a good time because I was giving up. Now I feel so good.

"I saw what was going on with James Brown. I knew who'd be second. I said by the time they get to me I want to have learnt what the concept is with this shit. Public Enemy are the epitome of rap. I learned how I had to have respect in the rap world then I learned a couple of Public Enemy songs. Once I got those two together it was easy from there. Public Enemy are my favourite group. They're saying something, they get through.

"I don't mind if they sample me because I get back more than they do. Like De La Soul. They used 'Knee Deep' and they paid but I get paid in a different way because I know how to appreciate the fact that they used the music. If they're hot with the kids and the kids like them then they'll like me. There was a lot of kids at the Palladium show last night. They knew all the words. Black and white kids, it doesn't matter. We had such a ball in that place. Everyone's into the One Nation Under A Groove concept. So I'm glad they sample the shit. Now if I took 'Knee Deep' to the radio stations they'd tell me it sounds like De La Soul!"

George traced a direct link between funk and rapping both using "the talk you talk in your natural environment" rather than fake sex shock-pop or drippy MTV fantasies. He'd been talking the language of the streets since 'Music For My Mother' and saw P.E. doing their own take. 1988's *It Takes A Nation Of Millions To Hold Us Back* had turned hip–hop upside down the previous year with their P-Funk upbringing evident in 'Bring The Noise's loop from 'Get Off Your Ass And Jam' onwards. Ironically a chunk of the money George obtained from sampling went to record companies he was at loggerheads with, but now his legend was swelling in a new light.

When the P-Funk empire collapsed in the early eighties hip-hop had just started its inexorable rise to becoming the most popular musical form in the world. It's hard to convey the excitement which greeted new movements such as psychedelia, punk and acid house when they first appeared, but hip-hop seemed so alien and fresh that one of the only reference points to hang it on was what P-Funk had been doing since the first Funkadelic album. The press has always loved convenient boxes suggesting one or two pioneers had an idea then everybody followed, and now millions more were running with what they'd soon turn into a formula, waiting to be branded and the record companies to steam in.

First reports of this new strain of black music which had gestated in the South Bronx were fascinating. Regular visits to Groove Records in Soho to snarf up the latest hip-hop imports on labels such as Enjoy and Sugarhill revealed a new form of black DIY ghetto punk evolving before the world with every innovative new missive. Hip-hop was a new form of primal artistic expression from kids with nothing to lose, looking for escape and a few minutes of self-earned glory rather than the big dollars which inevitably came later.

The South Bronx of the seventies was one of New York's worst symbols of abandoned urban decay. The poverty and neglect from city authorities created an environment where an underground scene could incubate away from the eyes of the world, media and even the rest of the city. The (often Pedro Bell-influenced) graffiti appearing on subway trains were the only messages from this forgotten world.

Like the Funk owes its origins to the trio of James Brown, Sly Stone and George, hip-hop had its own big three prime movers in DJ Kool Herc, Grandmaster Flash and Afrika Bambaataa. According to legend, hip-hop was born in 1973 in the South Bronx housing project recreation room where Herc started homing in on the breaks sections in his records. He then started setting setting up his Jamaican-strength sound system in parks powered by hot-wired street lights inspiring others to take to the decks and rap over the breaks. Teenage electronics boffin Joseph Saddler constructed a primitive double-deck setup, developing his "quick mix" technique which would lead to the turntables' art of cutting, back-spins and scratching. By the following September, the newly named Grandmaster Flash could fill uptown venues with breakdancers and budding rappers. Rapping, turntablism and breakdancing evolved for another five years before the first recorded evidence took the world's charts by storm in the shape of the Sugarhill Gang's 'Rapper's Delight' – albeit something of a novelty record which heisted Chic's 'Good Times' as its vehicle. Apart from George's proto rapping, P-Funk was littered with ripe beats and riffs for producers to plunder as the new sampling technology started making its presence felt in the mid-eighties, while rappers were inspired by George's call-and-response catchphrases and early seventies proto-rhyming. As Bootsy told me, "Rap is the new funk. It's funkin' by mouth."

P-Funk also encouraged black singers and players to bust out of the norm in the way they looked, notable examples including the Jonzun Crew, who proclaimed 'Space Is The Place' in 1983, and Afrika Bambaataa and the Soul Sonic Force, who went for the whole inter-galactic superhero look and started creating a sci-fi theology that saw The Funk as the saviour of mankind. Their now legendary Hammersmith Palais show in 1985 saw them taking the stage like Mothership-era Parliament in their space warrior comic-book costumes. Bambaataa's album sleeves thanked the P-Funk, Sly and James Brown; at that time not considered the cool move it would be the following decade.

Musically tracks such as 'Planet Rock' and 'Renegades Of Funk' were heavily influenced by late period P-Funk, keeping the chain going by revolutionising hip-hop and providing a template for electro. George repaid the compliment on 'Loopzilla' bellowing "like 'Planet Rock' it just don't stop, gonna drive you nuts".

When I interviewed Afrika Bambaataa the day after the show he spoke about how like George he escaped gang culture to concentrate on music. In 1974, inspired by the film *Zulu*, he formed the Universal Zulu Nation, a worldwide network offering the message he coined when he teamed up with James Brown in 1984 for a single called 'Unity' – peace, unity, love and having fun. Bam also pioneered working with past heroes before it became de rigueur.

In person, Bambaataa's calmly authoritative leader-demeanour and quietly imposing charisma reminded me of George (without the craziness) as he explained, "We came with that whole Parliament-Funkadelic look because most rap groups looked like the Temptations. I said, 'I'm coming out like George Clinton', wearing all kinds of shit."

At different times both George and Bambaataa had voiced their disdain for musical boxes. Bam put this into action as a DJ in the seventies, telling me his own take on the original P-Funk philosophy, "When I first started I was playing heavy metal, funk rock and new wave. Everyone wanted to know who was this young black guy playing heavy metal to all-black audiences. I used to play the Rolling Stones, Grand Funk, Clash and Blondie and everyone would bug out! It all depends on how I mix it and when I play it. There's funk'n'rock, rock'n'roll, jam roll... music is music, y'know what I'm sayin'?"

The ceremonial burning of disco records by cheering meatheads in 1979 and the movement's subsequent lethal injection by the paranoid music biz unintentionally wiped the slate and left the farm gate open for a new strain of electronically driven dance music hugely inspired by Bernie Worrell's synthesized basslines with P-Funk in the late seventies. The first half of the eighties saw synthesizers take over but George was already in the thick of it as funk gained a new makeover and steely sheen. The pulsating bastard child of disco was called boogie (soon to morph into electro, then acid house), which inevitably seeped into hip-hop as it gained steam with stark social comment appearing in epoch-making statements such as Grandmaster Flash's 'The Message'.

Somehow, George managed to place himself at the forefront of this revolution which would reshape music in the eighties before the new sampling technology brought him back in touch with the impact of his earlier endeavours. Ass before face, maybe, but George would never argue with the wisdom of the butt. After the Parliament-Funkadelic Mothership came crashing down he continued undaunted, stripping down operations to record under his own name because both his groups were bogged down in legal problems.

Although George would later confess to 30 years spent pursuing the illusive nirvana of his first cocaine high, the only time he sat back and let it become his only fixation to the exclusion of his relentless work ethic was his "lost weekend" in LA after the fall of the P-Funk empire. He was reported as being busted for possession while in the company of Sly Stone, although the charges were later dropped, telling *Rolling Stone*'s Michael Goldberg in 1983, "I got frustrated. I came to LA and spent three or four months in the Beverly Comstock Hotel and didn't have nothing to do but get high. I didn't look at it as no frustration; it was just something to do while I couldn't get any records out. But I wasn't going to feel frustrated cause that wouldn't have helped me get back at all. 'Cause then you would do drugs with another attitude. Then you do drugs to totally escape, and with freebasing, it makes it easy 'cause it takes all your time. I wasn't into it like that. I was into it just like I'm into any other drug – I liked it. I tell you, it could have worked out the other way, 'cause I think I took a chance. I was being rather cocky. I really was having a ball. I don't want anybody thinking I'm bragging that I had fun, but I did. I mean, it got scary, but drugs are like that."

While George was on the pipe, his managers and legal team were negotiating a new record deal with Capitol Records under his own name. George said he got an advance of $300,000, which seems to have been achieved against all odds as Warners came out of the woodwork to claim he was signed to that label and CBS voiced similar objections. Faced with all this chaos, Capitol got cold feet and told George he could have the album he'd sold the label back if he returned the advance, but his dogged manager, Archie Ivy, squeezed it through and forced its release under threat of the money never being returned. "They were scared to death," said George.

In 1982 it wasn't that major a step for George to emerge under his own name fronting his latest take on the sound he'd pioneered. Rather than crawl out shrouded in the agony of defeat he came bounding back on a major label he hadn't yet tapped, signing to Capitol under his own name. 1982's *Computer Games* brought his old concepts bang up to date in the modern age.

The album, which included tracks held over from the original *Electric Spanking Of War Babies* double album, was an immediate success after the buzz which started when a 12-inch blank orange-labelled promo appeared with just a white sticker announcing 'George Clinton – Loopzilla'. He was back to bring the P-Funk to modern dance floors, planting his radio DJ patter and snatches of his old hits over juddering boogie-funk, biting the new with Bambaataa's 'Planet Rock' ('Like Planet Rock, you just don't stop, gonna drive you nuts') and Zapp's 'More Bounce To The Ounce' with a smattering of the old with the Four Tops' 'I Can't Help Myself' and Supremes' 'Baby Love'. George added his own 'Don't touch that radio, don't touch that dial, don't touch that knob' as main hook. The tangled confusion of those last Parliafunkadelicment days had been stripped away and replaced with a slavering turbo-funk monster with bass croak not unlike the Japanese movie monster's heaving bowel movement. To make sure the track kicked off on the right foot George namechecked New York's three major black music radio stations – WBLS, KISS and KTU. At the time all three were leading the field in breaking tunes and turning the 'mastermix' editing concept into the art form which would go on to influence the acid house generation.

George's return was compounded by the appearance of 'Atomic Dog' in December, 1982. No tree, club or sane human being was safe from its demented war-bark. Cleverly grafting traditional P-style word play onto a panting beast of an electronic groove, the track struck an erogenous public nerve which plunged the world's clubs into a leg-humping, tail-chasing, tongue-slobbering canine frenzy with its 'Bow wow wow, yippee yo yippee yay' chant (including when I played it at Goth birthplace the Batcave). Using the backwards loops on the drums which would soon be adopted by Detroit's techno militia, P-Funk had created a massively influential new dance sound which sent shockwaves through the burgeoning hip-hop movement. After weeks waiting outside the back door 'Atomic Dog' managed to topple Jacko's 'Billie Jean' off the top of the US R&B charts on April 16, 1983, staying there for four weeks.

"George proved that from a creative perspective he is a master genius, because he came out with 'Atomic Dog'," Ron Dunbar told the *Oral History*. "Zoom, right up the charts. And without the name Parliament-Funkadelic, George Clinton was still showing that he is the genius of this whole movement."

Recently recruited keyboards player David Spradley spent five hours building 'Atomic Dog's backing track over five hours on a snowy night at United Sound. As the studio filled up it came time for George to do his vocals so Garry Shider went to grab him from the hotel over the road. Speaking in the *Oral History* he recalled, "George came running in there, thinking his career was over.... 'Gimme a track, gimme a track!' And we had 'Atomic Dog' up, with no drums. All we had was all this backward shit in it. George put on the headphones. First time he heard it, you could see his expression: 'Oh Lord, I don't understand this music!'"

David Spradley adds, "He had just gotten through really wearing out the blow or whatever he was doing at the time. He couldn't find the downbeat. He couldn't find the microphone either; we had to show him where the mike was, then he went ahead and did it. But that's why his rhythms are the way they are. George laid the lyrics down as you hear them on the record. Then Garry threw a couple of the backgrounds – 'A-to-mic dooog'..."

When George returned next day asking for his part to be fixed Garry said the track was finished, telling him, "We done sang all over you!" After the initial trauma George quickly came to love the way he'd been inadvertently plonked at the forefront of a cutting-edge movement, revisiting 'Atomic Dog' the following year as a rap version with the

K-9 Corp Featuring Pretty C (with manager Archie Ivy given his day). George happily made a glitzy video surrounded by hip young things and TV screens (along with a show-stopping appearance on British TV show *The Tube* with little left to the imagination in his knacker-swinging one-piece.

Computer Games saw George stepping out of the Mothership into a modern world where his original sci-fi visions were coming to life in the way technology had started its inexorable rise into today's all-encompassing obsession. Before the soul-sucking escapism of the next century's Xbox and mobile phone obsessions birthed the zomboid tech-addict so, while happy to modernise his sound, George made a stand for the human element, todger power and pursuit of doggy-style carnal fun. "I want to get it both futuristic and primal," explained George.

Along with Spradley, he brought in many of his old crew to add bass, drums, guitars, horns and massed voices to this new digital funk. P-alumni on board included Garry (who co-wrote and produced 'Atomic Dog' and 'Loopzilla'), Eddie, Junie, Bootsy, Bernie, Mallia Franklin, Michael 'Clip' Payne, P-Nut Johnson, Mudbone, Ray Davis, Dawn Silva, Lynn Mabry, Ron Ford, Jessica Cleaves and the Horny Horns. Bootsy, Junie and Garry are credited as co-producers on some tracks, many of which date back to the projected *Electric Spanking* double album.

Bootsy co-wrote thwacking opener 'Get Dressed''s uproarious web of animated vocal interplay on a road song which continued the theme of 'No Head, No Backstage Pass'. The title track stars a computer vampire booming 'Monster Mash' style over clicks, whirrs and strident guitar while George boasts he can "out-Donald a duck", "out Woody a woodpecker" and "out wiggle a worm". 'Pot Sharing Tots' is a lightweight ditty about babies sharing potties while 'One Fun At A Time' is a jaunty ode to... fun. These three were co-written with Junie. Three other tracks are distinguished by the return of the duck call – obviously George's favourite noise during the sessions. Speaking as a duck-call veteran it's not hard to imagine one quack suspending operations for several minutes while the assembled collapse laughing. George also had to be cackling when the album, which was essentially the other half of *Electric Spanking* rejected by Warners, hit number 40 in the charts and three on the R&B lists.

The musical climate had changed dramatically by the time George and a stripped-down band of old reliables and new faces set off on the Atomic Dog tour. The Reagan-ruled eighties inflicted a major decline in already struggling black communities as deregulation of companies hit the working classes so jobs disappeared, welfare benefits were slashed and the homeless problem mushroomed. Crack cocaine joined the heroin infesting the ghettoes; essentially a dirty new style of freebasing where the user becomes obsessed with chasing the impact of the first hit.

Grandmaster Flash & the Furious Five were on the button message-wise and musically when they released 'White Lines' in 1983. With its graphic lyrics and glistening electro backdrop (shamelessly hijacked from a downtown band called Liquid Liquid) the song was an anthem for the eighties and consummate example of the digital revolution spreading through hip-hop, black pop and machine-beleaguered funk. Michael Jackson was on his way to becoming the highest-selling artist in the world with *Thriller* but Prince from Minneapolis had evolved from late seventies sleaze-rock outings such as 'Soft And Wet' and 1980's horny masterpiece *Dirty Mind* (which made his name with black audiences) to arrive at the apocalyptically sensual allure of *1999* and *Purple Rain*. He then became the most fascinating and influential new star of the whole decade, playing everything himself and invoking the excitement of James Brown at his gigs. Jacko and Prince both managed to break into the previously whites-only MTV video channel, which boosted their success and unleashed the lavish video scourge of the next few decades.

From Prince's home city also came the motoring naked funk of the Time and a 'Minneapolis Sound', but their effect on the rest of the country resulted in a rash of unsexy synthesized disco-funk cash-ins from the likes of Slave while Kool & the Gang went electronic pop. Meanwhile, bands such as Cameo, the Gap Band and Bar-Kays took the new P-Funk-derived sound through the decade with an element of class and energy.

1983 also saw George manage to revive his Uncle Jam imprint

through Columbia to release the first album under the P-Funk All Stars banner. Familiar names such as Bootsy, Garry, the Horny Horns and Eddie appeared on 1983's *Urban Dancefloor Guerillas,* which featured a different line-up and often production combination on each track. Sly Stone collaborates on 'Catch A Keeper' and the robo-scrotum jiggle of 'Hydraulic Pump', the duck call again becomes focal point of Princey retro-ballad 'One Of Those Summers' and 'Copy Cat' is the feline's answer to 'Atomic Dog'. Garry's butt-detonating 'Pumpin' It Up' [with its arcing Eddie guitar solo] caught fire in Britain but its fate in the US illustrated George's all but blacklisted position in his home country, as he told *Spin* magazine in 1985: "The record was selling like a motherfucker, bustin' out in Dallas, Houston, Chicago, LA and CBS acted like it wasn't even theirs."

George returned to military metaphors on the sleeve to recommence his mission to rescue dance music from the blahs declaring, "And now as the war cries of 'WOOF' are being shouted from every club and concert dance floor across the ONE NATION, the people most affected by the system's onslaught of repetitious mindnumbing cow-like moosick are now totally stirred up against such trash. Most of all they need the FUNK, and nothing but the P." Now all George's previous troops fight under the banner of the US Funk Mob and it's up to "Uncle Jam's Army's division of Dancing-Terrorists" to "Gorilla your way to the true groove, for only the P-Funk can pump it up". Recent years have seen this previously overlooked album reappraised as a dance classic.

George's Capitol stint saw three more albums. The complex wit and mainstream mutations of *You Shouldn't-Nuf Bit Fish* was released simultaneously with *Urban Dancefloor Guerillas* in December 1983, his name only appearing in the composing credits on 'Nubian Nut' (which saw his first stab at adapting the current rapping style to The Funk) although he's again supported by Eddie, Bootsy and Junie. The anti-nuke title track is notable for its percolating electro-voodoo pulse and synth acrobatics – complete with inexplicably hilarious command "Lord bless this fish". *Rolling Stone* described the tracks as like "tiny, funny little musicals". This time they only reached number 102 in the pop charts.

★

Bootsy had been keeping busy around his George activities, producing and playing on Cincinnati trio Godmoma's *Godmoma Here* album for Elektra in 1981. Harking back to the Brides' feisty style and jumping Rubber Band energy while updated with rapping and bolstered by the Horny Horns and Catfish, it's a bit of a lost funk classic. 1982's 'Body Slam' single was credited to Bootsy's Rubber Band but only keyboardist Joel Johnson remained from the original line-up. It showed Bootsy delving into electronic funk with worryingly little bass action but shades of Hendrix in his vocal delivery and distinct Prince feel.

That April also saw Bootsy's last album for Warner Brothers, *The One Giveth, The Count Taketh Away*. George only pops up co-writing the opening 'Shine-O-Myte (Rag Popping)' as Bootsy produces himself with a gaggle of old muckers such as the Hornies and less expected characters including synth-funkers Midnight Star. Although again sporting contemporary electronic production elements, Bootsy still manages to pack in enough bass and funk essence on tracks such as 'Number One Funkateer' and 'Landshark' at a time when the One needed all the help it could get.

In the Presidential election year of 1984 Bootsy teamed up with Talking Heads' keyboard player Jerry Harrison as Bonzo Goes To Washington for one of the era's most infamous spoof tracks. Released on tiny New York hip-hop label Sleeping Bag, 'Five Minutes' used the proto-sampling cut-up technique developed by Double Dee and Steinski to work Ronald Reagan's joke microphone-testing announcement that bombing would commence on Russia in five minutes into a spiky funk groove. The name refers to the doddering old cowboy's 1951 *Bedtime For Bonzo* chimp movie. Bootsy wouldn't surface again until 1988's comeback album *What's Bootsy Doin'?* on Columbia, rejoined by the 'Still' Horny Horns and Mudbone, with help from producer Bill Laswell who was going to be a major force in reinstating P-Funk in the next decade. It was good to hear the star bass popping under the man's inimitable Jimi-cool drawl and 'wiiiind me up' again as lead track 'Party On Plastic' wreaked damage in the clubs.

George was alleged to have declared himself bankrupt in 1984 when besieged by huge tax bills dating from the seventies. He had another

Capitol solo album out in 1985 called *Some Of My Best Jokes Are Friends*; all booming drum machines and period synth riffing courtesy of collaborators including 'She Blinded Me With Science' boffin Thomas Dolby and Slave's Steve Washington plus old hands including Garry, Junie, Bootsy, Eddie, Blackbyrd and George's son Tracey (who contributed the balladic 'Bangladesh'). Also lending support is bassist Doug Wimbish from industrial hip-hop heavyweights Tackhead – previously the original Sugarhill session band also comprising drummer Keith LeBlanc and guitarist Skip MacDonald – who were then working with Adrian Sherwood's conscious On-U Sound crew in London. Pedro Bell, who designed the sleeves of all the Capitol albums, described Tackhead as "the P-Funk of the eighties, they are what P-Funk should have been doing now".

The period clatter cloaks some of George's most seriously political lyrics as he tackles nuclear war, poverty and violent crime on one of his most socially conscious but abrasive-sounding albums to date. "I don't want your war" goes the chorus on 'Bullet Proof' while the title (and best) track sees George as serious as he gets talking about "basic training in the ghetto". The flute duelling with reversed bass clanks on 'Pleasures of Exhaustion (Do It Till I Drop)' show his production values still circling his own creative cowpat rather than the bland mainstream vat this sort of stuff could so easily fall into.

That didn't sell too well although May 1986's final Capitol album, *R&B Skeletons In The Closet,* made it to 81 in the album chart. Led by irresistible single 'Do Fries Go With That Shake' the album tackled how black music's traditions were being ignored and core audiences lost in the face of desperate attempts to cross over to lucrative white audiences. George backs up his message with a smaller unit of Garry, Bootsy, Blackbyrd, Fred and Maceo plus Slave's Steve Washington pitching in on songwriting (and former Miss America Vanessa Williams acquitting herself well on contagious mega-bass second single 'Hey Good Lookin'', after she'd been disgraced when old nude pictures appeared in *Penthouse*). 'Intense' and 'Electric Pygmies' drape those big electronic drums with exotic surface ephemera while 'Mix-Master Suite' is George's slightly oblique comment on hip-hop with classical and western themes. Remaining unreissued this is now one of the rarest Clinton albums and, in its eighties way, one of his most overlooked or wrongly derided works.

In 1985, George was picked by the then little-known Red Hot Chili Peppers to produce their second album, *Freaky Styley*. The band were huge P-Funk fans. They formed out of Hollywood's eighties maelstrom of rampant drug abuse and had seen their self-titled debut album (produced by the Gang Of Four's Andy Gill) flop in 1984. After rejecting potential producer Malcolm McLaren's typically sweeping suggestions they piped up that they wanted George to produce their sophomore effort. Flea and manager Lindy Goetz travelled to Detroit to meet him, armed with the first album and demos. George accepted $25,000 to do the job at United Sound that May, suggesting the band spend a month with him to bond and work up ideas for the remaining songs they needed. Before renting a house of their own, they stayed at George's farm in the village of Brooklyn outside Detroit for a week. As soon as they moved in singer Anthony Kiedis started experiencing acute heroin withdrawal. All George could offer was coke, which only exacerbates and increases the intensity of cold turkey. After a few days he subsided into battered normality and joined the rest of the band in falling in thrall to George's relentless charisma and story-spinning.

Then-drummer Cliff Martinez recalled, "George had a party atmosphere in the studio all the time, but a productive party atmosphere. You took care of business, but he made sure you had a lot of fun doing it." The bugle was flowing and the band dived in with gusto – apart from Kiedis, who laid off for two weeks while he recorded his vocals, which he compared in his autobiography to "deciding to be celibate when you're living in a brothel".

Kiedis told *Mojo*'s Sylvie Simmons that George "was insane and a bit dysfunctional, but he was so smart and so creative and so loving and non-judgemental. He wasn't like the great super-genius who was above us, he was the great super-genius that was right in there teaching and cheerleading and pushing and being part of the band."

The title track – based on a popular eighties saying for anything a bit out there – was going to be an instrumental but George wrote vocals and lyrics. The One-driven funk groove of 'Yertle The Turtle' features George's dealer reading lines from Dr Seuss in lieu of his unpaid drug debt. George also got in some of the P-firm to sing backing vocals, including P-Nut, Pat Lewis, Garry, Michael 'Clip' Payne and Andre Williams.

Flea had been listening to New Orleans' syncopated gumbo funkers the Meters and wanted to cover one of their songs. George suggested using them to dedicate a song to Hollywood – "What if you did the song 'Africa' but had Anthony do a rewrite so it's no longer Africa but it's your 'Africa', which is Hollywood?" Retitling the song 'Hollywood (Africa)' George helped with the vocal arrangements and added lines of his own. He also suggested covering Sly's 'If You Want Me To Stay' from *Fresh* (bringing in the Horny Horns).

The album is compelling as a bunch of barely controllable LA junkie punks under the direction of a master producer then careering through his own drug-fuelled demonscape. Tracks such as the rocked-up Ike Hayes vamp of 'Blackeyed Blonde' are the funkiest they ever got. It was critically well received, *Rolling Stone*'s Ira Robbins calling it "rougher, wilder, funnier and funkier" than their debut, adding "the Chili Peppers are taking advantage of the current crossover free-for-all to universalise funk by expanding its limits and incorporating new ingredients without diluting the basic bump. Fed up with the empty calories of effete high-tech dance records? *Freaky Styley* is stick-to-the-ribs rock that puts meat back in the motion."

Freaky Styley didn't trouble the Hot 100 but has sold since the group shot to fame after 1991's Rick Rubin-produced *Blood Sugar Sex Magik*. At that time it was the funkiest album around, white or black (including most P-Funk as it boasted real drums).

There was another revolution brewing in Detroit by the middle of the eighties, which, like artists and movements it had previously nurtured reflected what was going on in the Motor City at the time. By then the auto industry had pretty much evaporated, white flight had swept away its willing participants to the safer suburbs and much of the city had been left to rot. The desolate blocks, dangerous streets and colossal ruins of the old automobile plants inspired three black teenagers called Juan Atkins, Derrick May and Kevin Saunderson to start producing a new form of electronic inner-city blues which became known as techno. Derrick once described it as being "a complete mistake... like George Clinton and Kraftwerk caught in an elevator, with only a sequencer to keep them company". Now it's one of the biggest musical movements in the world, one of the few where emotion and creativity can mate to get thousands dancing their asses off.

Raised in north west Detroit, Juan had got into gang-related trouble as a teenager so ended up in a suburb west of the city called Belleville. Like many other Detroit music fans he first heard Parliament-Funkadelic on Charles 'The Electrifying Mojo' Johnson's Midnight Funk Association radio shows which ran from 1977 until the mid-eighties. Emblazoned in advertisements as 'The Landing of the Mothership', Mojo's programme mixed P-Funk and Kraftwerk plus anyone from Hendrix and Prince to new wave bands such as the B-52's.

When I interviewed Juan in 1992 he was still speaking of the shows in hushed tones and over 20 years later still credits hearing Parliament-Funkadelic on them as the epiphany which got him trying to play funk on synthesizers like Bernie Worrell. "'Flash Light' was the one," the now renowned originator recalled over a coffee in a London café. "That was the track which took me right over the edge and changed everything. By then Parliament and Funkadelic were using synths on a lot of their tracks and I was right along there with them. Then came 'One Nation Under A Groove', 'Knee Deep'... This was what I was listening to in high school and it changed my life."

Even if George's chart status had dipped by the mid-eighties, his influence was at an all-time high when Juan formed Cybotron with a Vietnam veteran called Rick Davis, recording seminal electronic instrumental 'Clear' in 1983. This morphed into his Model 500, which brought in electro beats and space sensibilities derived from Afrika Bambaataa's Soul Sonic Force and George's Mothership on 1985's 'No UFOs' – arguably the first techno track. Juan started his Metroplex label while by 1989 his school friends May and Saunderson had formed their Transmat and KMS imprints, after being profoundly influenced by the anarchic disco mutation called house music going on in nearby Chicago. Detroit had a new musical underground which seemed to echo the ghosts of the vanished auto plant machines with piledriving beats washed in unearthly synth melodies. These heart-freezing soul symphonies created on primitive electronic tackle inspired many more Detroit kids – including Underground Resistance, Robert Hood and Carl Craig – to find their own creative outlets through the machines. All have credited P-Funk's part in the music which became a global phenomenon because, as is always stressed, what sets Detroit techno apart from the countless copyists is it never loses The Funk. By the nineties a more aggressive, bass-driven electronic strain called Ghetto Tech had emerged from the Motor City through producers such as DJ Assault. Here George's influence showed up in another way as songs with titles like 'Ass 'N' Titties' reflected any number of ribald seventies P-ditties.

Ironically, now George was the one following current sounds by building his tracks on drum machines and synthesized bass. Along with a crew including Garry, Eddie, Blackbyrd, Donnie Sterling, David Spradley and recently joined keyboard player Amp Fiddler, he recorded an album under the Funkadelic name called *By Way Of The Drum*, for MCA. It was rejected with a curt letter saying, "We would like to inform you that we will not be releasing the album by your 'so-called' concept group, Funkadelic" before the master tapes went missing. I was sent the title track as a promo 12-inch in 1989 while at *Dance Music Report* and remember being quite shocked by the eighties production excess with jump cuts, big synth slashes and vocal histrionics plastered over booming electro beats and even proto-house riffs. George was now following instead of leading, even if it was still quite a glorious racket.

The rest of the album leant further back into the rock direction than anything George put out in the eighties, tracks such as 'Nose Bleed' fired with gritty riffs and guitar solos with unison vocals rather than cartoon asides and snappy sound-bites, although 'Primal Instinct' harks back to the Funkadelic of the seventies with its gospel chants and shuffling groove. Other tracks included 'Beware Of Freaks Bearing Gifts', Tracey Lewis's rewrite of Slick Rick's 'La-Di-Da-Di' into 'Yadadada', 'All Eyes Right', 'Jugular', 'Some Fresh Delic', 'Intuition' and Michael Hampton's party piece on Cream's 'Sunshine Of Your Love'. Happily for incorrigible P-Funk completists the album was finally released in 2007 by Hip-O-Select.

So George was in a pickle with a rejected Funkadelic album, no solo deal and a mound of debts dominated by the freedom-threatening IRS. In the *Oral History* he says he called Prince up in 1988 and said, "Yo, bro. We need to get some funk out there." Elsewhere it's been said Prince called George to be on his label (which had also just signed the venerable Mavis Staples). However it transpired, Prince was repaying some of the debt he owed George, from the inspiration he got from P-Funk shows and Bernie's synthesized funk to former Funkadelics joining his eighties touring band.

When I asked George about signing to Paisley Park he started remembering Prince sitting on the side of the stage at seventies gigs then declared, "I'm on Paisley Park because Prince gave me the break I needed. Most record companies aren't prepared to take that chance. After the Palladium show last night the record company got really excited but I was trying to tell 'em that before. That gig proved that people are starving for some funk. Prince had input as far as putting the right attitude in and pulling my coat to things. Prince is one funky motherfucker!"

George released *The Cinderella Theory* in August 1989 trailered by a 12-inch called 'Why Should I Dog U Out?' – a sequel to 'Atomic Dog'. The beat was still drum machines but pure funky drummer hip-hop countered by live playing. George sampled himself for the 'dawg' stabs, got the girls singing "How much is that doggie in the window" and weighed in on the canine tip again while busting a new catchphrase, "Not to be confused with".*

This boded well, but then came the album. A lot sounded like Prince's discarded backing tracks but apparently some of the album was originally

---

* I've still got the badge Paisley Park sent out.

intended to be the Brides Of Funkenstein's third album, *The Shadows On The Wall Shaped Like The Hat You Wore*. Public Enemy's Flavor Flav and Chuck D acknowledged their own debt to P-Funk by guesting on 'Tweakin'' but much of the album is spoiled by the drum machine bucket beats, a lack of original P-Funkers apart from an inaudible Bootsy and the distinct feeling that low-in-the-mix George is on a leash for the first time. '(She Got It) Goin' On' is one of the few tracks where the Prince hookup lives up to its potential and the Paisley sound invokes the funk. It's also the most live-sounding track with George finally cutting loose. The version of 'The Banana Boat Song' is not one of his finest moments.

One of the album's main plus points was recently joined keyboard player Joseph 'Amp' Fiddler stepping up to provide some inspired performances. Hailing from Detroit, he had come up with the doo-wop influenced Enchantment before hitching up with George in the mid-eighties. "Ain't he fabulous?" asked George while talking to *Soul Underground* magazine's Jasper the Vinyl Junkie at the time. "He did the whole keyboard part on the album. He's our new Bernie all right, but without copying Bernie's style. He's young, but he's been around and he's classically trained, but not as deeply as Bernie was."

I asked George what the Cinderella Theory was. "It's like a concept: how I love the pop-star philosophy, all the high marketing and publicity... then after 12 o'clock I turn into the funky nasty dude. I'm on a mission. I agree to be the pop star for publicity reasons. But after midnight I turn into a nasty dog."

Which is where we came in. I wouldn't say George was pulling any pop-star behaviour that afternoon in the Warner Bros. office. In fact, by the time we wound up he seemed to have brought the clock forward a few hours to turn into the funky nasty dude. That's nasty as in good.

Chapter Fifteen

Give Out But Don't Give Up

"Everybody's 'Where's the funk? What about the samples? Is the funk dead? Yo man, smell my finger! 'How do I know where your finger's been?' I say 'You don't'."

George Clinton

"George said 'Those guys can be on the Mothership'. 'That's the best thing anybody's ever said to me.'"

Bobby Gillespie

November 25, 1989, Apollo Theatre, Harlem:

For the last two hours George and the P-Funk Allstars have been giving up The Funk on the stage which probably figures higher in his early history than any other stage in the world. It was to here George used to sneak from school to catch doo-wop acts of the day over 30 years earlier, and on these very boards the Parliaments suffered the humiliating debacle of their first headlining gig in 1967.

This is one of George's first times back at the now landmark-status building since the P-Funk empire imploded at the start of the decade, but even the arrival of a Fully Operational Mothership couldn't have elicited a more fervent reaction from a crowd which boasts its own formidable legend. The theatre reeks of history and is selling the Apollo T-shirts to honour it, but tonight George is celebrating his own illustrious past with some of the P-Funk diehards who've weathered the storms of the last few years and beaten the incoming digital invasion which threatened to engulf George on his previous few albums. It seems more like Sun Ra's Arkestra than ever as George directs his exotically attired ensemble through 'Let's Take It To The Stage', 'Cosmic Slop', 'Maggot Brain' and other classics which pump the crowd to further heights; one hand directing the band behind him while the other whips up the baying throng at the front of the stage.

George's power in front of a homecoming crowd was quite awesome to behold but 18 months later I watched him do it all over again at Brixton Academy for his devoted British funkateers. With old inspiration James Brown fallen on hard times since the previous decade with angel dust, domestic violence, prison and parole problems, George was the last black cultural icon still standing from the seismic sixties but, on the day of the Brixton show, he told me, "I try my best to stay clear of even thinking that I would use any kind of power. I don't need the headache. I'll say what I want to say in the records but at the same time I ain't no guru or preacher.

"I'm just running thoughts through my head in songs. If you think whatever you decide that's up to you but here's a thought, here's something to think about. Thinking itself will do much more for us, but you can only go so far with this 10 per cent of brain power we've been allotted. They said we only use 10 per cent of our brain. Whoever issued out the brain power needs to come back and give us some more! We're peaking with this 10!" Elsewhere he has said he tells fans, "I'm not your guru, because I'm trying to get some pussy, you'll catch me trying to get some dope... ."

That day George also proved he had the power to stop traffic as we made our way through London's West End to the offices of *Echoes*, the long-running soul publication I was writing for at the time. It was amazing the effect he had on that scorching summer afternoon, even attired quite conservatively for him in T-shirt, loud shorts and big sneakers topped with multi-coloured barnet. Workers hung out of office windows to gawp, disbelieving fans ran up to grab an autograph or just to shake his hand. At one point he decided to check out the David Clulow optician's shop on Oxford Street to try on their most flamboyantly framed specs, charming assistants like he did everyone else that day. Photographer Ray Burmiston had the dream assignment as George gurned and swung around the lamp posts.

Once ensconced with ice lollies in the *Echoes* office George posed again for my little camera then got in interview mode. He'd been his silly self for much of the afternoon – that finely honed weapon behind which lurks a wealth of knowledge and philosophical wisdom extending into personal politics and conspiracy theories. Today the latter include James Brown's imprisonment ("not only because he's black but because he's a powerful threat on a cultural level") although the monster-bowel bass croak on 'Loopzilla' got the same secretive sideways glance ("That was a good one!"). George could expound on American politics at the slightest opportunity, revelling in scandalous sex stories but concerned to hear the FBI was infiltrating street gangs to cause internal friction in the same way the Black Panthers had been set against each other. He also revealed plans to make a $30 million "black sci-fi" P-Funk film with the Hudlin brothers (of *House Party* fame) involving the whole Mothership crew in a warped "*Star Trek* meets *Beetlejuice*" scenario: "the P-Funk Nation versus the New World Odor". It's a shame what sounded like George's own take on Sun Ra's *Space Is The Place* went the way of other projects which failed to land.

Last time we'd met George was punting *The Cinderella Theory*, which had been poorly received and not sold well, but now he was excited about the second Paisley Park album he'd got lined up, then called *Is The Funk Dead? Yo Man, Smell My Finger*. He recounted how His Purpleness contributed to a couple of tracks (including co-producing and co-composing George's first excursion into house music on 'The Big Pump') but on the same level as Bill Laswell or his son Tracey, who co-wrote a couple. "He told me my stuff was sacred to him and he wouldn't take it away and mess with it, just like I would never go off and remix Sly. Prince only came in on the music when I invited him, which is why I could trust him."

George explained how "the new theme is Maximum Is-ness," pointing out the punctuation although it would change to one word by the time the album was finally released in 1993 as *Hey Man – Smell My Finger*. Try this for size: "As it is, so shall it be. If being is what it's about I is! So we just being. Human being. *Funk* being. We just into being this time. Maximum Is-ness is all that you can be. Funkentelechy was reaching your maximum potential. This is maxing out human style."

Getting even more buzzed up he went on "Bootsy's on, there with the big old bass and he hasn't played like this in years! I did one called 'Rhythm And Motherfuckin' Rhymes' which was actually written by a kid from here called JC001, a hell of a fine writer. He's gonna be one to reckon with. He's the only one I know who's in the league with Rakim (George's favourite rapper). But it's hard to understand what he's saying because he's really fast. Not being British it's hard to understand but when I first heard that shit I said 'What the fuck is this?'"

Since our previous chat George had overtaken James Brown as most sampled man in showbiz. He started talking again about the ongoing career boost he was continuing to get from having his old songs so widely plundered. "Rap has really saved The Funk. Chuck and Flavor said I'm their mentor. They're proud of the fact they listened to P-Funk and that came at a good time because I was giving up. Now I feel so good. I'm glad they sample the shit. I get back more than they do.

"That's the way people are tipping back into The Funk. There's so many people in funk rehab that the next batch of funkers is being cautious. They don't want to get no funk habits. They have to go and join funk anonymous. So you get more samples of funk but funk is like potato chips – taste one, you got to have some more!"

In the face of P-Funk going viral in hip-hop George was on a more serious mission to reclaim some of his music. Apart from the more conventional avenues he came up with the novel idea of releasing an album of ready-to-bite P-Funk clips called *Sample Some Of Disc, Sample Some Of DAT*, first released in 1993 on the independent imprint Music Of Life before appearing on other labels.

This was partly prodded by P-Funk's overwhelming recent presence in west coast hip-hop. It had started with Digital Underground (whose roadie and dancer was future rap superstar fatality Tupac Shakur). If their *Sex Packets* debut used P-Funk grooves and cartoon alter-egos, 1991's *Sons Of The P* proclaimed the Oakland group as sons of the "Father of Funk". George himself pops up on the title track, as remembered by Greg Jacobs, aka Humpty Hump, in Rickey Vincent's *Funk*: "George blew our minds when we was working with him in terms of how to hear things and how to play things and how to just kind of let it happen... just to let it flow out of us. He led me onto a theory that we're just conveyors... the people that are directing the energy in the funk, but he seems to feel like it's a collective spirit that comes from the whole rhythm of the world, the rhythm of people. Brothers seem to have a rhythm with everything they do. One of the things George was about was capturing that in the studio."

South Central LA gangsta troop N.W.A. took hip-hop to hard-hitting new levels as they reflected life in the 'hood, relentless police brutality and the constant struggle to get over in a sampladelic barrage of triple-X lyrics. N.W.A. first replicated Bernie Worrell's sine-wave synth sound on 1991's 'Alwayz Into Somethin'' before P-Funk provided the well-spring for the already disintegrated group's solo spin-offs such as Ice Cube's 'Bop Gun' (with George appearing in the video). Dr Dre built his Gangsta-Funk template on P-Funk, going as far as matching the 'Mothership Connection (Star Child)'-derived chorus of 'Let Me Ride' on 1992's genre-defining *The Chronic* album with a video containing seventies Mothership landing footage. The song won a Grammy for Best Rap Solo Performance in 1994 while the album's blunted hump and ultra-violent lyrics realigned hip-hop in a mellow but menacing new direction. This was the most flagrant – but acknowledged and paid for – use of P-Funk so far. 'Fuck Wit Dre Day (And Everybody's Celebratin')' alone drew from 'Atomic Dog', 'Knee Deep', 'Funkentelechy', 'The Big Bang Theory' and 'Aquaboogie'.

The album let lazily laconic stoner Snoop Dogg out into the world to become one of hip-hop's biggest-selling rappers after 1993's *Doggystyle* cocked its leg on the G-Funk and further established the new style.

Producer Dre built Snoop's multi-million-selling debut single, 'Who
Am I? (What's My Name)', on elements from 'Knee Deep', 'Atomic
Dog' and 'Give Up The Funk (Tear The Roof Off The Sucker)'. George
appeared in the composing credits and appeared on the album's later-
released title track. Sharing a mutual interest in dynamically enhanced
vegetation, the collaboration cemented a friendship which continues to
this day as George regularly appears on Snoop's GGN TV chat show
where exotic strains of weed are often sampled.

Hey Man… Smell My Finger was delayed for various business-related
reasons (including commercial potential), finally emerging in October
1993 after George worked on tracks with new jack swing producers
Kerry Gordy and William Bryant III, who suggested getting some of
his admirers in the hip-hop community to rap on a 'Chocolate City'
sequel about government racism called 'Paint The White House Black'.
When the track was released as a single George posed on the sleeve in
old-school white wig and War of Independence redcoat uniform.

Thus the album became George's own hip-hop statement when
released at the height of G-Funk led by first single 'Martial Law'
promo'd as a green and red double-pack (now a collectors item).
The track launched the album on safe ground with its 'Atomic Dog'
backing track and splices of 'Flash Light' and other hits. The album
was dominated by big synthetic beats and guest rappers countered by
George's innate P-Funk production sensibilities. Old faces such as
Garry, Bernie, Bootsy, Maceo and Fred Wesley were present alongside
high-calibre guests including Herbie Hancock, Dr Dre, Ice Cube, Bill
Laswell and the Red Hot Chili Peppers plus the biggest roll-call of
singers and musicians ever seen on a P-related album. One hip-hop
roll follows another but there are standouts such as the mellower funk
created by George and Bill Laswell with Herbie Hancock to frame
'Maximumisness'. 'Kickback' also trades beats for funk and mentions Jes
Grew over the horn hook from Bootsy's 'Under The Influence Of A
Groove', while 'Hollywood' skewers Funkadelic's 'Holly Wants To Go
To California' to attack Tinsel Town fakeness.

George previewed tracks from the album among P-Funk classics at
that night's Brixton show, bringing on the "world's fastest rapper",

JC001, to let fly with his motormouth prattle on 'Rhythm And Rhymes'. George conducted proceedings in flowing white robe with an eternal funk sign on his fingers and catchphrase never far from his lips. Churning out One-sodden grooves there was no glitzing up or synthing down of the essential funk essence, philosophy and attitude.

After the show the party continued at the Shepherd's Bush Hilton with George floating around the bar and various rooms obviously on a different planet to the one I'd met him on earlier. The only slight bummer was the Academy being half full because the show was booked at the last minute and New York art-house trio Deee-Lite, then hot with their *World Clique* album, had sold out the next two nights. This was quite ironic as their 1990 UK number one breakthrough single, 'Groove Is In The Heart', featured vocal interjections from none other than Bootsy (who didn't play bass on the track as it was sampled from Herbie Hancock's 'Bring Down The Birds').

The song's psychedelic D.A.I.S.Y. age video was the first exposure for many to the P-Funk ethos which obviously ran wild in the group, Bootsy bringing The Funk into many UK front rooms for the first time. The video considerably raised his profile and the Rubber Band appeared as Deee-Lite's backing group on their world tour.

Since 1988's *'What's Bootsy Doin'?* the bassist had hitched up with Bill Laswell to start a relationship which reunited the Rubber Band on 1990's *Jungle Bass* EP. Released on Island Records offshoot 4th & Broadway, the 12-inch EP kicked off with the 13-minute Jungle One/ Long Form version blending traditional Bootzilla wobble vocals and murderous star bass exclamation marks over an exotic panoply of Horny Horns blending Miles Davis' 'In A Silent Way' with soul-revue tattoos, Bernie Worrell's soundtrack synth flotation and – audaciously for those of a sensitive disposition – a percolating four on the floor house groove. Bootsy had never sounded so riotously widescreen.

"There's a lot of different things in there," Bootsy told me shortly before the EP's release. "The first piece is different for me cause it's like a dance-house type thang. That was Chris Blackwell's idea. I'm into taking chances. I pretty much know what the fans *want* – the P, the whole P and nothing but the P. So I had to decide whether I was going to do this because of that P-Funk religion. I thought if I did this I was gonna have certain fans who might be through with me but then all I would have to do is come back and deliver a serious P-Funk record. I figured I would take this chance and do these thangs. I might even get some different airplay and pick up some new ears and introduce them to the real funk. So I made the decision to do it. I figured I've been in this so long I'm going to take the criticism and everything that comes with it but I had to weigh up going against the rules. I want to keep my old fans but I want some new fans too! It was about trying something new. I had to make up my mind if I would make that sacrifice and maybe let down some people here.

"I used all the original Rubber Band on there because I wanted to put that package together. That's why I cut this record. We were all doing different sessions – Bernie, myself and the horns – but then we got together and it was 'Wow, this is a good opportunity; let's cut a record with Bootsy's Rubber Band and take it on a tour'. We all want to go back on the road and bitch a little. I talked to George yesterday. He came down when we were doing the video 'cause he couldn't miss that and jumped right in the video."

'Jungle Bass' was packed with the startling production twists which established Laswell as one of America's most vital producers of the eighties. Growing up in Michigan, he had played bass in Detroit funk bands and witnessed the Stooges-Funkadelic double bills which ignited his disdain for compartmentalising musical styles. After moving to New York in the late seventies Laswell formed Material and became in-house producer for the eclectic Celluloid label, specialising in "musical collisions" between wildly disparate artists such as Afrika Bambaataa and John Lydon on their incendiary Time Zone duet 'World Destruction' (predating 1986's Run DMC-Aerosmith collaboration 'Walk This Way' by two years). His breakthrough production had already been Herbie Hancock's *Future Shock* in 1983, which included 'Rockit', whose game-changing electro-hip-hop broke new ground when Grand Mixer D. ST brought live scratching to record for the first time. Laswell used his new found status to fund his esoteric projects by taking on albums by the likes of the Ramones, Motörhead, PiL and Iggy Pop. 1990 was his watershed year, as he started working in his Greenpoint studio in Brooklyn and was invited to start his Axiom label by Island supremo Chris Blackwell. Flying under his "Nothing is true, everything is permitted" banner he used P-Funkers such as Bootsy and Bernie on many projects including his experimental funk-metal outfit Praxis (which released its *Transmutation [Mutatis Mutandis]* debut album in 1992).

Along with the Deee-Lite exposure 'Jungle Bass' can be seen as a turning point for Bootsy, and also for Laswell as he was introduced into the world of P-Funk. Soon many more of Bootsy's old bandmates would be drawn to the multi-cultural funk alchemy going on in Greenpoint Studios.

The next white rock'n'roll band George worked with after the Chili Peppers came in the form of Primal Scream, then a notorious walking demolition squad who had managed to combine crystallising the late eighties ecstasy revolution with being the UK's last proper punk band on 1991's epoch-making *Screamadelica* (whose title alone was a clue to where one of their greatest musical influences lay). Having been in the front line of both punk and acid house I welcomed the Scream as a nineties manifestation of the Clash's fearlessly ever-questing attitude and George's approach to using different musicians from outside the band to make beautiful music. I'd got to know the Primals through *Screamadelica* producer Andrew Weatherall, becoming their DJ for several tours in the nineties. On first meeting singer Bobby Gillespie it was immediately obvious that, beneath the last gang in town having a riot of their own, lay a voracious musical appetite which could take the group's sound anywhere through the magic of inspired collaboration with the core band, which then also included guitarist-studio dynamo Andrew Innes, guitarist Robert 'Throb' Young and keyboardist Martin Duffy. As Bobby told me in 1991, "Our whole thing is we just want to make beautiful music. Whatever it takes to do that, we'll do it. By any means necessary. We can do all sorts of stuff but if we think someone can do a great piece of work for us then we'll do it. The great bands have always done that."

The success of *Screamadelica* on Creation Records meant the Scream now had a licence to live out their musical fantasies when trying to construct the follow-up amid the unfettered hedonism and drug abuse which mushroomed during the fallout. The creation of the album which became *Give Out But Don't Give Up* had been convoluted and tortuous after starting in a sea of heroin at a Camden Town studio.

In an attempt to ignite their creative spark, operations moved to Memphis' world-renowned Ardent Studios, where they worked with veteran soul producer Tom Dowd and crack session legends including pianist Jim Dickinson, bassist David Hood, drummer Roger Hawkins and the Memphis Horns. They worked on rockers, spiritual soul ballads and a loose semi-instrumental called 'Funky Jam', along with two slowies called 'Give Out But Don't Give Up' and 'Free'. Never one to hog the mike if it's for the good of the song, Bobby sent for Manchester-based singer Denise Johnson to lend her soulful tones to the tracks.

To rescue 'Funky Jam' they called in the "Father of the Funk". P now stood for Primal as George was commissioned to remix the three problem tracks. "I can tell the difference between some oldie-but-goodie vibe and something that's new," George said later. "It's like what the Stones or Clapton did with the blues or what Funkadelic and Parliament did with gospel or doo-wop. Those boys are just picking up on the same vibe and doin' their own thing."

Like with the Chili Peppers, George didn't just do a perfunctory job, whack his name on it and run off with the dosh. As he had repeatedly proved, any project worth doing had to aspire to greatness to avoid sinking into workmanlike oblivion. And who'd want to employ him in future if he didn't pull off something special? So he pumped 'Funky Jam' into a brass-boosted climax, added his own vocals to Denise's on the title track and kept her gorgeous performance on 'Free' stark and slightly glazed.

George later told me he "had a ball" working and partying with the Scream while cheerfully admitting he'd had some trouble understanding Bobby's Glaswegian accent. "I'm sitting next to him for about five minutes," he smiled later in an MTV interview. "I agreed with everything he said whatever that was.... He's a real intelligent dude but the real fun part of it is to be able to make music and not even know what he's doing and he don't know what I'm doing and it gels. We had a good time doing that stuff. They sent me tapes to remix and they were ballads. I'm used to remixing dance songs but how do you remix a ballad? So I just went and did it. They must have been confident I can do something."

In January 1994 on the eve of the album's release, I happened to be in New York and, coincidentally, so were Primal Scream, recording a live MTV slot with George at the Manhattan studios. It was the first time the Scream team had actually met him and, within minutes, the two parties were getting on like one of their hotel rooms on fire as George trotted out barbershop stories and played unreleased tapes including an astonishing doo-wop album which still remains in the vaults. The band were filmed playing three songs including 'Funky Jam' with George, who couldn't contain himself and also joined in with 'Rocks', the album's stomping lead single.

Reflecting in 2014 on this surreal but magical collaboration Bobby says, "Working with George was a total joy. He taught us a lot. He gave us funk lessons in Chicago. I'll never forget it. He made us aware of the power of space in music; that is the power you can create by being quiet and listening to the other players, playing when you need to and then shutting up. It's all about respect for the song. George is a true shaman. Super intelligent, politicised. Although he was and is a total hero of mine and the band I just went with the energy of being around him. He makes you feel welcome, makes you feel good. He's a great guy. Sometimes I had to check myself that it was all actually happening.

"George is one of the greats. In my opinion he's up there with Sly Stone, James Brown and Sun Ra as a composer and band leader. From the early Motown-inspired Parliaments singles like 'I Wanna Testify' to the deranged psychedelic soul of the first Funkadelic albums through the interstellar space funk of Parliament he took us on a trip through Funkadelic galaxies that changed us forever. Listening to his music for the first time is like taking LSD; you're never the same after it."

Next time we saw George was at the now legendary all-night double-header at Brixton which saw Primal Scream sharing the bill with the P-Funk All Stars; an inevitable result of the new bond which had formed between the two camps. It was the first time I'd witnessed the Funk Mob backstage as they mingled with the band sharing smiles, stories and drugs. There were about 15 people in George's band with the P-Funk girls taking over three dressing rooms alone. It was hilarious watching the touring party line up behind George as he dished out a pre-show livener on a flight case; cathartic when the P-Funk All Stars turned in a two-hour masterclass in tearing the roof off the sucker, and nerve-shredding playing my funk set between one of my all-time heroes and my favourite British band. I watched the Scream do their set from the wings next to George, who looked round and bellowed, "That's the damn funkiest shit I've seen for years!" Certainly the damn funkiest night of my life.

"Scream/Funkadelic – wow!" recalls Bobby. "I went down to watch the soundcheck and walked onstage to say hello and welcome to London to George. While we were talking Garry Shider began playing the opening guitar riff to 'Maggot Brain' and then the rest of the band joined in. It sounded beautiful. I was in heaven. Such a great memory."

Primal Scream returned the compliment by collaborating with George on the bluesy funk chant of 'Lost Dog', which appeared on the double white vinyl UK version of his 1993 album *Dope Dogs*. Bobby delighted in recalling the session where George placed his hands on Martin Duffy's shoulder and told him to "go to church" with his piano playing, which he proceeded to do. The rest of the 1994 album, which was first released on Japan's P-Vine imprint before UK then US issues, thrusts forth some of George's most provocative word play and abrasive funk of that decade. In perhaps the most thought-through then fantasised manifestation of George's conspiracy theorising, the theme is based around US customs sniffer dogs getting hooked on the dope they encounter. Titles such as 'US Custom Coast Guard Dope Dog' and 'Help Scottie, Help (I'm Tweakin' And I Can't Beam Up!)' are George at his most hilariously subversive, with a full funk squad to back him up as he accuses George W. Bush of trafficking the drugs they're supposed to be at war against ("Old Mac Uncle had some drugs, CIA I-O"). Pedro Bell similarly goes to town against Bush and cronies on the cover.

George also released two volumes of *Dope Dogs* on his own Detroit-area One Nation label which was sold at gigs and consisted mainly of remixes and versions of 'Dope Dog' (which he'd sung a capella at gigs in the late eighties). New titles include 'G-Man Dawg', 'Niggerish' and 'Kibbles & Bits'.

At the 1993 Grammies, although he'd never won a trophy himself, George performed 'Funky Dollar Bill' with winners the Red Hot Chili Peppers. "We had two days rehearsal with them for the Grammies, and they taught us our songs!" George once said. It was another indication of the way George was finding himself being embraced by new white audiences. In America a new generation of "alternative" college kid lapped up the All Stars when they were booked to play truncated hour-long sets on that year's Lollapalooza jaunt around the US with the Beastie Boys, Smashing Pumpkins and A Tribe Called Quest. Meanwhile the four-hour sets they played in the clubs started drawing Grateful Dead fans who were all at sea after the death of mainstay Jerry Garcia in August 1995. George was also invited to play President Bill Clinton's inaugural ball in 1993. When asked to consider that the previous three American presidents bore some form of his names, George told Ireland's *Hot Press,* "Oh yeah, that's pretty weird. The Bush smoke bush, snort coke and the Clinton don't inhale, he get head. So all in all, it seems to be all right."

The back of Primal Scream's *Give Out But Don't Give Up* album featured an image of Eddie Hazel's face blown up from the inner sleeve photo on the first Funkadelic album – their tribute after Eddie had passed away from internal bleeding and liver failure on December 23, 1992. Recent years had seen the guitarist in and out of the hospital under strict orders not to drink or take drugs. Old Plainfield buddy Sammy Campbell has recalled how he would go on fishing trips with Eddie whenever he was in New Jersey but frequently spotted him prowling the local corner drug spots. On what turned out to be their last outing, Eddie ate a spicy sausage sandwich which set off his problem and sent him back to hospital for the last time.

"I remember taking him to the airport in Dayton when he couldn't take the road no more," recalled Garry in the *Oral History*. "The last thing he said is, 'Be careful, man. And hang in there.' And I remember my son saying, 'Dad I don't think we're gonna see him no more.' Eddie was the sweetest mug in the world... he just had to stop drinking. He drank himself to death. And I guess he felt he got beat in the industry, but all he had to do was just hang around, because you're gonna get what is due to you."

Bill Laswell has said an album was being planned featuring Eddie, Billy, Bernie and Bigfoot after the guitarist had showed up at his studio sober and focused but the recording kept getting pushed back."

Since his seventies supernova guitar blitzkreigs Eddie had been less prominently heard on the P-related tracks he did appear on, although he could still plug in and bring an audience to tears on 'Maggot Brain'. Talking to John Corbett in 1993 George said, "Mr Maggot Brain. His music will be here forever. His was a ball of sensitivity. He just felt everything. He'll be here for a *long* time."

Billy 'Bass' Nelson was still living in LA when Eddie passed but, shortly afterwards, recorded his only solo album and dedicated it to his childhood friend after driving back to New Jersey. Working under the name O.G. Funk, Billy recorded *Out Of The Dark* with Bill Laswell for his Black Arc series. The album's robust blend of funk and balls-out rock riffing was forged by Billy and a line-up including Bigfoot, Bernie and Mudbone, making it the closest thing to the album they'd talked about doing with Eddie. While Billy leaves no doubt about his own legacy with tracks such as 'Funkadelic Groupie' and a heaving take on his old band's 'I Wanna Know If It's Good For Ya Baby', the most poignant track is his devastating eight-minute guitar instrumental 'Music For My Brother'.

By 1994 Billy was living with his girlfriend in Pittsburgh and jammed with the P-Funk All Stars when they came to town. About a month later George's daughter Barbarella called and asked him to join the P-Funk All Stars for five dates in Japan as a trial return to the fold (which has lasted until the present).

Bootsy paid tribute to his late musical sparring partner on his 1993 CD *Blasters Of The Universe,* with 'Good Night Eddie' poignantly wishing,

"I wish you could have stayed a little while longer" over its 'All Along The Watchtower'-like riff. The album also featured Eddie's explosive performance on 'Blasters', one of the last tracks he recorded (complete with 'Voodoo Chile [Slight Return]' and 'Star Spangled Banner' lifts plus Bootsy in spaced Jimi vocal mode).

Having become something of an ultimate bass icon, Bootsy has increasingly seen himself on a continuing mission since this time, telling me in 2002, "It's now about keeping The Funk alive. When you're doing stuff, you don't know how people are gonna react. That's how it was when we started with P-Funk. We didn't care whether you liked it or not, though hopefully you would. Now it's about taking The Funk to the next generations and keeping it alive. Get the Mothership out of the pawn shop, patch it up and she'll be ready to fly."

Nothing had been heard of Tawl Ross, another of Eddie's old Funkadelic comrades, since he took one trip too many in 1971 and had to depart the band, ending up back in his native North Carolina. In 1995 he released his first and only solo album, *Giant Shirley*, under the name 'Tal Ross aka Detrimental Vasoline'. Even held up against the wigged out P-Funk pantheon it's one of the strangest albums of all, but also one of the most beautiful with dense guitar layers intertwining under his racked, fragile vocals, which sometimes recall Ronald Isley or Curtis Mayfield at his most sensitive. Riffed-up rockers such as 'Get So Mad' are full of unexpected chord changes and unusual guitar textures but the luminescent ballads inhabit a gorgeously melancholic world of their own – 'Forget Her' and 'Cry And Show Me' charting deep seams of ghostly soul-baring. 'It Was' remakes Funkadelic's 'Wars Of Armageddon' to wind up one of the great lost P-related masterpieces.

While guitars hover and curl like supernatural vapour trails, songs are anchored by old mucker Jerome Brailey's sympathetic but solid drums. Bigfoot recalled how this unexpected project came about: "That was a crazy thing. [Producer] Pete Wetherbee answered an ad for a record label in Miami called Coconut Grove. He used to work with Bill Laswell. They hired him so he went down there with another artist they wanted to do but that never happened and he got something on Tawl Ross' record.

"I did the drums last on that album. They'd already done the whole record then he called me and said, 'Man, can you come up to Quad studios?' – that's the Manhattan studio where Tupac got shot in the lobby. He said, 'Can you play on the record, we got to finish it? I want you to play on it but it's kind of strange.' When I heard it I'm like, 'Where's the time on this joint?' He said, 'That's what we got'. I said I'd see what I could do.

"That album is a classic. I played it for my brother and he said, 'That album is a killer but I don't know what he's singing about'. I thought, 'I know, but you can't understand!' Tawl did a bad trip. When we played Boston Sugar Shack one time I walked over to the park across the street from the hotel and he was sitting there on a bench. He'd just gone over there, spaced out. He's still kind of crazy. He's not all the way back yet."

After the Mutiny period Bigfoot played countless sessions for the likes of Keith Richards, Snoop Dogg, Lucky Peterson, Dave Stewart and expat P-Funkers. He became a favourite of Bill Laswell, playing on acclaimed fusion outing *Blues From The East*, Jah Wobble's *Heaven And Earth* with Pharoah Sanders and Axiom Funk's *Necronomicon*, along with being introduced to James Blood Ulmer and Buckethead. "Laswell was the one that turned me on to Buckethead, who I played with on their *Giant Robots* album. And he was the one to really bring Bootsy back to the forefront. I went back to P-Funk in '93 for about six months when I was doing the Dave Stewart record [*Greetings From The Gutter*]. I was playing some of those records on the bus one night. Blackbyrd and all them are like 'Turn that trash off!' I'm like 'You don't know 'cause you don't expand your minds'. They don't like the stuff I did with Laswell. I'm like 'That's all right'."

By the middle of the decade Laswell's work with P-Funk refugees was thriving and throwing up fascinatingly esoteric collaborations such as the Last Poets' *Holy Terror* in 1995, which saw Bernie and Bootsy beefing up funk beneath original hardcore rappers Umar Bin Hassan and Abiodun Oyewole.* Tracks such as 'Black Rage' show Hassan and

---

* At the same time founder Jalal Nuriddin and Suliaman El Hadi also claimed the Last Poets name to release a single called 'Scatterrap'.

Oyewole had lost none of their fire and penchant for graphic imagery. George lends vocal support to the 12-minute 'Black And Strong'.

That same year Laswell put together *Funkronomicon* by Axiom Funk which brought together P-Funkers including George, Bootsy, Bernie, Blackbyrd and Bigfoot with the likes of Sly and Robbie for a two-CD delight including Bootsy's version of Jimi's 'If Six Was Nine', a new 'Cosmic Slop' and last recordings by Eddie Hazel on 'Orbitron Attack' and 'Sacred To The Pain' (where his guitar meditation is joined by Bernie and Umar Bin Hassan's impassioned prayer poem). The P-Funk connection is cemented by one of Pedro Bell's last creations.

The P-Funk All Stars continued to make periodic sorties to the UK throughout the nineties. The July 1995 show at London stronghold the Clapham Grand saw George's son Shawn rapping and Pedro Bell onstage scribbling messages in felt-tip pen then throwing them into the howling capacity crowd. George now compared his All Stars to the orchestras of Duke Ellington or Count Basie, with a solid core of veterans and many revolving-door sidemen. He once confessed that sometimes, if the invariably super-tight band was really starting to lock in tight, he wasn't averse to throwing them a curve "that'll fuck it up" by suddenly signalling them to stop; "Now they've got to wake up… It makes it alive again… It's order and chaos at the same time."

George marked the 20th anniversary of the Mothership's first appearance by landing a newly constructed aluminium model onstage at a July 4 show in New York's Central Park (which is now being donated to the Smithsonian Institute). That November he released *T.A.P.O.A.F.O.M. (The Awesome Power Of A Fully Operational Mothership).* First released as a double, the concept, said George, also included S.E.A.A.I.C. – Socially Engineered And Anarchically Induced Chaos – but it was almost a statement of closure as old band members rallied round with a lush new cosmic sound retaining recent hip-hop flavours in the single 'If Anybody's Gonna Get Funked Up' but tempered with snaky G-Funk pulses, bulbous bass and crisp beats. It was as deep as *Motor Booty Affair* but replaced cartoon elements with modern R&B

slink (although 'Flatman And Bobbin' dates back to the 1972 Toronto sessions which had produced *America Eats Its Young*).

The multi-tiered vocal arrangements and sultry harmonies on tracks such as skinny-dipping floater 'Summer Swim' and 'Let's Get Funky' exhaled sinuous R&B female chorales contrasted by George just below the surface muttering about booty, and bent on pinging their bikini bottoms. On 'Hard As Steel' he's got "a heavy metal hard-on". These and dirt-slow choral humps such as 'Underground Angel' and 'Sloppy Seconds' made for George's sexiest album that decade, while the swirling title track is almost a eulogy for the much travelled Mothership about to fly away until well into the next century.

In 1997 George finally achieved mainstream music industry recognition when Prince inducted him and the Funk Mob into the Rock and Roll Hall of Fame. "I'm here to testify about Parliament-Funkadelic tonight," declared the purple-suited one from behind his shades. After describing funk as "the force which tore the roof off the sucker that is modern music and changed the world" Prince recounts how George once sent him a tape with the instructions: "You pee on it and send it back to me and I'll pee on it and we'll see what we got" before recalling when he witnessed a 14-strong Funkadelic choir singing 'Knee Deep' at a gig then went home and wrote 'Erotic City'.

The tall, dinner-jacketed figure of Jerome Brailey took the stand first before the P-Funk massive took it in turns to step up to the microphone to accept their awards and voice their thanks: Garry, Fuzzy, Calvin Simon, Sting Ray on booming form, Eddie Hazel's widow, Brenda, Boogie in a huge rude hat, Bernie, "Shady" Grady Thomas, Bootsy a vision in red spangles, Junie, Tiki Fulwood's daughter, Billy and finally George in huge blond do and cloak proclaiming that "without all of us together it could not have been done". Glenn Goins was also among the fallen comrades honoured.

This was the last time many of these modern folk heroes would be together on the same stage or even in the same building. It was a profoundly moving sight for their legions of fans.

★

Seeing these old soldiers who had fought the Funk Wars under, and sometimes even against, George across the decades stood as proof of the indestructible unity of the P-Funk, and the intangible allure of Dr. Funkenstein himself. There is no doubt that George Clinton is the essence of that Funk, the nasty dog who created his own universe and illuminated it with this unique cluster of stars to put a whole planet under the groove.

Epilogue

"That funk, we just played it. We lived it. We slept it. We ate it. We fucked it. We stole it. We sold it. We done everything we could possibly do with it. And that's why we just never could let go."

Cordell 'Boogie' Mosson

George's profile has never been higher. Since getting off the major label treadmill following 1996's *T.A.P.O.A.F.O.M.*, he has only released two new studio albums under his own name. With nothing left to prove, George Clinton has become an in-demand king of the cameo, popping up anywhere from cutting-edge hip-hop and college comedy movies to cartoons, commercials and computer games.

The post-G-Funk career boost saw George appear on albums including Tupac Shakur's breakthrough *All Eyez On Me* and Outkast's *Aquemini* in 1998 through to dogging Wu Tang's *8 Diagrams* and puff mate Snoop's *The Blue Carpet Treatment* in 2007. He appeared spinning 'Loopzilla' as radio DJ the Funktipus on video game *Grand Theft Auto: San Andreas*. George's movie appearances have included 1994 jock comedy *PCU* and 1997's Nickelodeon fast food spin-off *Good Burger* as a mental hospital inmate called Dancing Crazy. He has also popped up on surreal animated talk-show parody *Space Ghost Coast To Coast* and appeared in CBS sitcom *How I Met Your Mother*. George is currently embarking on an Osbournes-style reality TV show called *The Clintons*, built around his extended family.

With George's music, characters and catchphrases continuing to feed into American culture and daily life, he has appeared in ads for Nike, Apple and Rio MP3 players. Meanwhile, his ongoing schedule of four-hour shows continues to satisfy demand for the stretched-out party previously provided by the Grateful Dead. George likes to call it "'Hoodstock". P-Funk shows now attract anyone from "old-school black folks" seeking nostalgia to hip young white kids discovering a funky alternative to limp modern warblings.

In 2005 I found myself DJing for the P-Funk All Stars again, this time at London's Forum which they indeed held in a magical funk-like grip for several hours as Primal Scream watched from the balcony. Little seemed to have changed in the overall set since Brixton Academy over 10 years earlier apart from some musicians in the ranks. Garry was still leading the band in his diaper, there was a guy dressed as Sir Nose D'Voidoffunk and George had sprouted more multi-coloured hair and assumed even more of a messianic appearance conducting proceedings in his robes. Sadly it would be my last encounter with Garry, the ultimate embodiment of the P-Funk. He told me that night that he and the others watched George's right foot to see where the music was going. If they watched the left they could end up anywhere. To stagger offstage after my set to bump straight into a grinning Dr Funkenstein remains another favourite moment, especially when he gave me his thumbs up.

It would be nine years since his previous album that George established his The C Kunspyruhzy record label and released an epic 148-minute double album compiled from this period called *How Late Do U Have 2BB4UR Absent?* in September, 2005. "One of the best records we've ever done," he said of the album's lushly carpeted excursions into *Abbey Road*-era Beatles, futuristic doo-wop and even whimsical Wings/ELO-style AOR. These stylistic diversions are offset by welcome blasts of axe-strangling Funkadelic ghetto metal like 'Viagra', low-flying funk such as 'Something Stank' and the deliciously grimy 'Paradigm', another collaboration with Prince. Female tour singers Belita Woods and Kendra Foster get showcased on several tracks and son Tracey also has a strong presence.

Even old press ally Robert Christgau, who'd been reviewing George's albums since Funkadelic's first, described it as "Two and a half hours that confound my capacity for quantification", bemoaning "standard issue ass-bounce" funk, slowies that "run down" and "too much throwaway, experiment, and crap" but praised the Prince track and "stripper shit-talk" of 'I Can Dance'.

Discounting last year's Sly teamup on Lord Buckley's 'The Naz' (music by Right Said Fred's old guitarist!), George's last studio project was 2008's *George Clinton And His Gangsters Of Love* – the kind of retrospective covers album most artists indulge in at some point in their career. Bolstered by star mate guests, it was back to the barbershop as he tackled chestnuts such as the Impressions' 'Gypsy Woman' with Carlos Santana, 'Let The Good Times Roll' with the Red Hot Chili Peppers and 'Ain't That Peculiar' with Sly. He also throws in a duet with gospel singer Kim Burrell on his own sprawling Prince-like ballad 'Mathematics Of Love' and the Parliaments' 'Heart Trouble'. George's voice is pretty shot but this only adds to the reflective, wistful ambience (and it is fascinating hearing George tackle Barry White's 'Never Gonna Give You Up').

Following the Rock and Roll Hall of Fame induction (which George has since declared he tried to get the P-Funk All Stars included in), awards have come thick and fast, including the North Carolina Music Hall Of Fame in 2009 and 2012's Honorary Doctorate at Boston's Berklee College of Music, where he donned ceremonial robes and led a "P-Funk orchestra" in a career-straddling selection. On May 20, 2010 George received a proclamation from Mayor Sharon Robinson-Briggs of Plainfield at a fundraiser for the city's Barack Obama Green Charter High School, to which he has pledged a percentage of Warner Bros.-era Funkadelic earnings.

George entered his seventies beating his long-term crack addiction, telling *The Guardian* how he spent 30 years chasing the first "bustin' a nut" high: "It never happened again and, after the first time, you're always reaching for that again and it never happens. I thought I'd found acid again and it took me 30 years to realise that it ain't acid. It ain't even cocaine."

He also ditched the cosmic pimp robes and hair extensions, revisiting the New Jersey tailors of his youth for a new wardrobe of smart suits and hats. These moves were partly born out of his ongoing mission to fight the plundering of his illustrious back catalogue by corporate record companies, which has seen him sitting on panels and saying it loud wherever he can that he has been royally ripped off. George will no doubt provide the gory details in the autobiography he coincidentally announced while I was doing this book but the goodwill towards sampling he expressed in that Warner Bros. boardroom 25 years ago has turned into a bitter fight to reclaim his own music. Suffice to say it's an ugly scenario led by ignorant courts, greedy lawyers and even what George now claims was a falsely concocted bankruptcy back in the eighties. He told *Uncut* magazine he has written to Barack Obama for help as he seems like a funky President with the "one nation" references in his speeches and love of Al Green (this in itself is a situation George could never have imagined when he was recording *Chocolate City* nearly 40 years ago). He added that he's planning court document T-shirts and underwear ("legal briefs!").

Most recently, George took over London's Metropolis studio for the weekend of January 31, 2014*. The purpose was a pledge event to fund a live Parliament Funkadelic CD and DVD for which punters were able to buy tiered tickets, going up to £750 for the gold box with waiter service. For this they could witness a live set, meet George, be on the album and hear original multi-tracks of P-Funk classics. This was George cutting out the record labels (even cutting an album straight to vinyl on a lathe for a limited edition), turning his funk into a cottage industry. In a way like going back to the barbershop.

July 2014 will see George turn 73, no doubt with his annual Motor Booty Affair party near his Florida homestead. Footage of his recent studio extravaganza and other activities he got up to in London, such as hooking up with Last Poet Jalal at the Jazz Cafe, show him more larger than life than ever and busting out more energy than in the previous decade; now a force of nature fighting for his achievements with renewed vigour. I wish him all the luck in the world in these new wars of Armageddon plus an outhouse full of thanks for The Funk.

---

* Coincidentally the deadline for finishing this book so I couldn't go.

Where Are They Now?

The singers, musicians, managers and funkateers who have brushed George's orbit over the last seven decades could literally amount to a cast of thousands. Instead, I'm listing those who emerged as major players in this story. Sadly, many are no longer here.

ARMEN BOLADIAN
The Westbound founder and Bridgeport Music boss is currently one of George's main opponents in his ongoing catalogue wars.

SIDNEY BARNES
George's Jobete colleague and Geo-Si-Mik partner has carried on writing, recording and performing, now finding his sixties releases selling for astronomical amounts on the Northern Soul collectors market. He recently published his autobiography, *Standing On Solid Ground*, and keeps in touch with George.

PEDRO BELL
The artist who dreamed up, drew and defined much of P-Funk's look, language and lore was last heard of living in near-blindness and poverty in Chicago.

JEROME 'BIGFOOT' BRAILEY

After Mutiny Bigfoot became an in-demand sessions drummer for names including Keith Richards, Snoop Dogg, Lucky Peterson and Dave Stewart while becoming a favourite of Bill Laswell, playing on albums such as acclaimed fusion outing *Blues From The East*, Jah Wobble's *Heaven And Earth* with Pharoah Sanders and Axiom Funk's *Necronomicon*. Bigfoot was one of the P-Funkers inducted into the Rock And Roll Hall Of Fame in 1997. In 2013 he revived the Mutiny name for *Funk Road*, a powerhouse smorgasbord of nuclear funk-rock, blistering JB rhythm and 21st century production suss, crystallising the musical strain he calls 'Neo Funk'. Along with revisiting 'Lump', the album includes fully-formed songs, such as sleazy casting couch ditty 'Lights Camera Action' and defiant single 'We're Keeping Our Thang'. The P connection continues with Bernie Worrell appearing on rap-outing 'Something Better To Do' and 'Prayer For The Living' while the thunderous Bigfoot groove on 'Rome Dog Roaming!!' is his gift to the samplers.

DENNIS CHAMBERS

Joining Parliament-Funkadelic at 18 in 1978, Dennis stayed with George until 1985 before moving on to jazz fusion with the likes of John Scofield, George Duke, John McLaughlin and, most recently, Maceo Parker and Carlos Santana. Jason Bonham named him as the drummer he would choose to take his dad's drum stool in the Led Zeppelin reunion if he hadn't.

BOOTSY COLLINS

In 2014, Bootsy remains the highest-profile P-Funker next to George, still stalking the world's boards with his star bass and immersing himself in a relentless array of projects while his persona inspires characters in TV sitcoms and movies. After his Laswell-stoked nineties, which also included an album called *Third Eye Open* with the Hardware trio he formed with ex-Band Of Gypsys drummer Buddy Miles and guitarist Stevie Salas, diverse ventures have included forming bluegrass-funk outfit the GrooveGrass Boyz with legends Doc Watson, Del McCoury and

Mac Wiseman, 2000's star-studded Motorola commercial, collaborations with UK big-beat titan Fatboy Slim and Snoop Dogg, even a self-titled restaurant in Cincinnati. Bootsy also released the first P-Funk seasonal album, *Christmas Is 4 Ever*. His current 'space bass' was custom built in 1998 by Manny Salvador of GuitarCraft. In 2010, Warwick started producing a signature 'Infinity Bass' while 'Professor' Bootsy launched his online bass school, Funk University ('Funk U'), covering theory and history on a virtual campus.

PHELPS 'CATFISH' COLLINS
During P-Funk's golden age, Bootsy's brother Catfish was rarely far from his side as the ultimate funk rhythm guitar player. Both were recognised by the Rock And Roll Hall Of Fame in 1997. In 2007 the two brothers got together with Bernie and J.B. alumni Clyde Stubblefield and 'Jabo' Sparks for the soundtrack to Judd Apatow's comedy *Superbad*. That December they took part in the first tribute concert remembering James Brown, who died on December 25, 2006. Catfish succumbed to cancer on August 6, 2010. Bootsy's statement said his brother wanted partying instead of mourning – "Just celebrate my life the way I celebrated my life, having fun and bringing the joy... I want to be roasted, toasted and have people drinking and having a good time in my name, no other name but the Catfish."

GARY 'MUDBONE' COOPER
Rubber Band co-founder Bone stayed with George until 1995, scoring parallel pop success as Sly Fox in 1986, also working with Prince, Laswell and Dave Stewart on 2006's radio-friendly voodoo pop-blues masterwork Fresh Mud. He's now back singing with Bootsy again.

LIGE CURRY
Michael Hampton's cousin, Lige became a long-term P-Funk All Star after impressing George with his Electric Sparks Band at an after-show party in 1978, studying under Bootsy and co before a bass slot arose.

RODNEY 'SKEET' CURTIS
The bass titan who joined up in 1977 continues to exercise his low-end funk in P-related places.

RAY DAVIS
From doo-wop beginnings to furthest-out space shanties, Sting Ray's low-down bass vocal was a major element in anchoring P-Funk to its street-corner tradition. In 1995 Ray briefly replaced Melvin Franklin in the Temptations, appearing on 1995's *For Lovers Only* album. After being inducted into the Rock And Roll Hall Of Fame in 1997 he joined Fuzzy, Calvin and Grady the following year in a reunion under the name Original P, releasing *What Dat Shakin'* and 2001's *Hyped Up Westbound Soljaz* (revisiting classics, both on Westbound). On July 5, 2005 Ray died of respiratory problems in New Brunswick, New Jersey.

AMP FIDDLER
While still in P-Funk Amp recorded 1990's *With Respect* album with bassist brother Bubz and worked with the likes of Moodymann, Jamiroquai, Prince and Corinne Bailey Rae. He recorded his first solo album, *Waltz Of A Ghetto Fly,* in 2004.

MALLIA FRANKLIN
After quitting Parlet in 1979, George's Detroit-based "funk scout" formed Silver Sterling Spaceship with bassist Donnie Sterling, going on to appear in Prince's *Rainbow Bridge* in 1990. In 1994 Mallia released her only solo album, *Funken Tersepter,* on Japan's P-Vine, comprising material recorded between 1982–86 with Junie Morrison and Eddie Hazel. Sadly, the Queen Of Funk passed away on February 5, 2010.

RAMON 'TIKI' FULWOOD
Although fired by George over his heroin addiction in 1973, original Funkadelic Tiki returned at different times, also briefly playing with Miles Davis. He died of stomach cancer on October 29, 1979, his

Rock and Roll Hall Of Fame award accepted by daughter Stuff Nicole Cleague.

GLENN GOINS

After quitting P-Funk in 1977, Glenn started the *Quazar* album which was finished by Bigfoot after he succumbed to Hodgkins lymphoma on July 29, 1978. One of P-Funk's most formidable talents, Glenn was posthumously honoured by the Rock And Roll Hall of Fame in 1997.

MICHAEL 'KIDD FUNKADELIC' HAMPTON

Another Hall Of Fame inductee, Michael's been a P-Funk guitarist since replacing Eddie Hazel in 1974, also appearing with Mudbone on Slave Master duo Islam Shabazz and Bill McKinney's heavy-duty *Under The 6* set released in 1993 as part of Laswell's Black Arc series. In 1998 Michael released his solo debut, *Heavy Metal Funkason*. His unearthly 'Maggot Brain' is still a highpoint of the Parliament-Funkadelic set.

FUZZY HASKINS

After quitting P-Funk and releasing two solo albums by 1978, Fuzzy joined the other ex-pat Parliaments on 1980's saggy *Connections & Disconnections* and in 1998's Original P reunion, the year after he was inducted into the Hall Of Fame. Recent years have seen him return to the church as vociferous funked-up preacher.

EDDIE HAZEL

As already reported, Eddie passed away on December 23, 1992. Finally he seems to be getting recognised as one of the greatest guitarists of all time.

ROBERT 'P-NUT' JOHNSON

P-Funk vocal fixture since joining the Rubber Band in 1976, all the way to 2008's *Gangsters Of Love*.

TYRONE LAMPKIN

The great drummer passed away in 1987.

PAT LEWIS
In 1989 George's former partner and early vocal support became backing singer co-ordinator for UK producer Ian Levine's Motorcity Records, where former Motown artists recorded new material. Along with hundreds of arrangements, Pat recorded more than 50 tracks herself ('Separation' released as a single in 1991). After Motorcity's 1992 demise she continued working with Levine on Northern Soul classics and K-Tel gospel albums. Pat now works for a small North Carolina rental company.

TRACEY LEWIS
George's son, aka Trey Lewd, has been with the P-Funk All Stars since 1990, releasing his *Drop The Line* album in 1992, titles such as 'Yank My Doodle' showing a chip off the old block.

LYNN MABRY
After leaving the Brides in 1979 to have a baby, Lynn returned to carve her name as a respected backing singer, touring with the likes of Stevie Nicks and George Michael, and joining Talking Heads on *Stop Making Sense*. She's a business partner with Latin-percussion dynamo Sheila E.

DEWAYNE 'BLACKBYRD' MCKNIGHT
After joining Parliament-Funkadelic in 1978, Blackbyrd became an incendiary guitar presence for the next 30 years. He stood in after Chili Peppers guitarist Hillel Slovak died in 1988 and released his first solo album, *Bout Funkin' Time,* in 2009. Its incandescent instrumentals syphoning Jimi's spiritual guitar catharsis gained much acclaim from lovers of the early Funkadelic sound. Blackbyrd also plays with the Trulio Disgracias jam band with various Fishbones, Chili Peppers and P-Funkers.

WALTER 'JUNIE' MORRISON
After his fertile stretch with Funkadelic Junie released three solo albums (1980's *Bread Alone*, 1981's *Junie 5* and 1984's *Evacuate Your Seats*) while continuing to contribute to P-related projects until 1996. He was

inducted into the Rock And Hall Of Fame the following year. 2004 saw Junie release *When The City* on his Juniefunk imprint.

CORDELL 'BOOGIE' MOSSON

Hall Of Famer Boogie, one of the longest-serving P-Funkers, sadly passed away on April 18, 2013 while I was writing this book. Boogie continued performing until hospitalised with an undisclosed illness in July 2011. On George's website current Parliament-Funkadelic keyboardist Danny Bedrosian called him "the ultimate funk theologian" and "one of P-Funk's most pivotal and vital musicians... Boog's knowledge and understanding of rhythm, the One, the Pocket and the Feel of P-Funk was unmatched."

THE MOTHERSHIP

Although the full-blown original ended up on a Maryland scrap-heap in 1982 the aluminium replica built in the mid-nineties has been donated to the Smithsonian Institute for a black history exhibition being put together for 2015.

BILLY 'BASS' NELSON

After becoming first Funkadelic to quit over dosh in 1971, Billy went on to play with the Temptations, Commodores, Chairmen Of The Board, Smokey Robinson and Fishbone. He briefly returned to Funkadelic in 1975, playing on 'Better By The Pound' on *Let's Take It To The Stage* and releasing his *Out Of The Dark* album as O.G. Funk in 1994. He rejoined Parliament-Funkadelic the same year.

MACEO PARKER

After his P-Funk stint, Maceo rejoined James Brown between 1984–88 (and appeared on Keith Richards' *Talk Is Cheap* solo album in 1988 among dozens of sessions, including P-related projects) before beginning a solo career with albums such as 1990's *Roots Revisited*, 1993's *Life On Planet Groove* and 1998's *Funk Overlord*. Maceo started contributing to Prince's activities for 10 years in the late nineties, including the 21 nights at the O2 stretch. He homaged Ray Charles on 2007's *Roots & Grooves* set, standards on 2012's *Soul Classics* and continues touring European jazz festivals.

MICHAEL 'CLIP' PAYNE

Detroit-born Clip, aka 'The Man In The Box', has sung on over 20 P-related albums since 1977. Based in Woodstock, NY, he founded WEFUNK International Records and Filmworks in the late eighties to release projects such as DRUGS, Cadillac Heights, the 420 Funk Mob and Cacophonic FM. He also sings on a lost P-Funk gem called *United State Of...Mind*, released by Detroit's Enemy Squad in 1998 on Tufamerica. Complete with Pedro Bell sleeve it harked back to early Funkadelic with screaming guitar section including Blackbyrd underpinned by beefed-up drummer Gabe 'Undisco Kidd' Gonzalez. Belita Woods and George joined the barnstorming choir on scabrous titles such as 'Return Of The Swamp Thang'. Clip also contributed to Daniel Bedrosian's *Som'n Fierce* and *Muzzle Moosick* sets along with Garry Shider and Lige Curry.

LUCIUS 'TAWL' ROSS

After vanishing back to North Carolina for nearly a quarter century after his horrendous acid-guzzling marathon, Tawl reappeared with the enigmatic shimmer of 1995's *Giant Shirley* (boasting Jerome Brailey on drums).

GARRY SHIDER

For nearly 40 years Garry was the devoted embodiment of P-Funk's anarchic, stanky ghetto essence and George's right-hand man (inducted into the RARHOF in '97).

Although appearing on outside projects such as releasing a Prince-like electronic dance 12-inch called 'Beautiful' in 1988 and appearing on the Black Crowes' *Three Snakes And One Charm* album in 1996, Garry's first allegiance was always to George and P-Funk. Working with wife, Linda, he released *Diaper Man*, *The Second Coming* and *Diaperman Goes Starchild* in 2002. In early 2010 it emerged he was fighting brain and lung cancer but he insisted on doing one last P-Funk All Stars tour before losing his battle that June 16 at home in Great Upper Marlboro, Maryland.

While George had lost one of his most faithful lieutenants, The Funk had been deprived of one of its most colourful characters. "Garry was the heart of the group... always about making the whole ship better, and finding new ways to make it consistently run," commented George. "No creature in this world or any other can replace Garry Shider. He is virtually un-clonable."

DAWN SILVA

After the Brides, Dawn toured and recorded four albums with the Gap Band and soundtrack songs with Eurythmics, other sessions including Ice Cube, Roy Ayers, Snoop and Parliament-Funkadelic. She released her first and only album, *All My Funky Friends*, in 2000 in Europe, its quality selection of funky R&B and those sultry vocals produced by new school funker D' LaVance. Parlet sister Jeanette Washington returned after 20 years' absence to lend vocal support.

CALVIN SIMON

After joining the post-1977 ex-Parliaments activities through bogus Funkadelic to Original P, Hall Of Famer Calvin turned to gospel in the 21st century, setting up his Simon Says Records. 2004's *Share The News* album reached number 32 in the Top Gospel Album charts.

DAVID LEE SPRADLEY

Undersung keyboard mainstay from the late seventies to *Gangsters Of Love,* David has also worked with Anita Baker, Roy Ayers and a raft of rappers.

GRADY THOMAS

Hall of Famer 'Shady' Grady also followed the post-1977 ex-Parliaments route, now residing in Stone Mountain, Georgia.

FRED WESLEY

Fred, who published his excellent autobiography, *Hit Me, Fred: Recollections Of A Sideman,* in 2002, embarked on a solo jazz-based career after leaving P-Funk in the late seventies. 1988's *To Someone* was his first album as leader, followed by sets including 1990's *New Friends* and 1994's *Amalgamation*. The nineties also saw him touring with Maceo in the JB Horns and Maceo Parker Band, forming his own Fred Wesley and the New JBs in 1996. He also played with and arranged for the likes of Ray Charles, Randy Crawford, Van Morrison and De La Soul. Fred also works as a visiting musician around US schools while continuing to release albums such as 2003's *Wuda Cuda Shuda*, 2008's *Funk For Your Ass* and 2010's *With A Little Help From My Friends*.

BELITA WOODS

After making her name in Detroit disco outfit Brainstorm, Belita sang for the P-Funk All Stars for two decades after joining in 1992, elevating albums of this time and shows. Sadly, this overlooked Motor City soul goddess died of heart failure on May 14, 2012, at the age of 63.

BERNIE WORRELL

After his innovatory P-Funk presence lessened by the early eighties, Bernie released solo albums up to 2011's *Standards* including 1981's *Funk Of Ages*, 1993's *Blacktronic Science* and 1997's *Free Agent: A Spaced Odyssey*. He also played a crucial role in Talking Heads until the band disbanded in 1992, appearing on 1982's *The Name Of This Band Is Talking Heads*, 1983's *Speaking In Tongues* and 1984's *Stop Making Sense*. Much of Bernie's nineties studio work was with Bill Laswell, including projects such as Praxis, Sly and Robbie's Rhythm Killers and Fela Kuti's Army Arrangement. Bernie has also recorded with former Cream bassist Jack Bruce, joined rock band Black Jack Johnson with Mos Def, Doug Wimbish and Dr Know and formed Colonel Claypool's Bucket Of Brains with guitarist Buckethead, bassist Les Claypool and drummer Bryan Mantia. Bernie's Baby Elephant project with Stetsasonic's Prince Paul and Don Newkirk released their *Turn My Teeth Up!* album in 2007, guests including George, Shock G, Yellowman, David Byrne and Nona Hendryx. 2009 saw him join up with Blackbyrd, bassist Melvin Gibbs and drummer J.T. Lewis to form the hard-rocking SociaLybrium, releasing an album called *For You/For Us/For All*. The 21st century has seen Bernie touring with his Woo Warriors and Orchestra.

PHILIPPE WYNNE

Former Spinners singer Philippé joined Parliament-Funkadelic in 1979 and released the sublime *Wynne Jammin'* on George's Uncle Jam Records. After the crash-landing Mothership disgorged its occupants he appeared on rap outfit Treacherous Three's 'Whip It' before releasing his own album on Sugarhill in 1984. On July 13 that year Philippé suffered a heart attack while performing at Ivey's nightclub in Oakland, California and died next morning.

Acknowledgements

Wﾑhen I started this book a year ago I knew I was in for a monumental white-knuckle ride to the outer limits but not even 40 years as an obsessed fan could have prepared me for the sheer magnitude of the ups, downs, triumphs and tragedies in store. The book swiftly took on a life of its own as a Funkenstein's monster, sprawling like a nascent P-Funk track or Pedro Bell album cover before gradually morphing into shape as this astonishing story unfolded.

Firstly, doing this book led me to my soul mate Helen Donlon, who was behind the project from the start and ended up taking it to the finishing line with me during the tortuous final weeks against a mushrooming P-Funk love story. Helen became my muse and sounding board as she helped steer my outpourings during marathon Funk chats, painstakingly corrected them and calmed my increasingly frazzled brow (even in the face of the three broken ribs I sustained in the final stages). She also steered the picture sections into realms surpassing anything I could have hoped for. Thank you angel (and Jack the Atomic Dog). *Gangsters Of Love* made perfect sense in Ibiza.

Of course, I have to thank George Clinton for providing the inspiration for this tome after that first encounter for Dance Music Report in 1989 when he talked his way through my P-Funk record collection, brilliant meetings since from further interviews to DJ engagements and, most of all, some of the most amazing music ever created. George's freewheeling Funk devotion is the essence of this story.

As I've said, this whole work is motivated by my undying love for that Funk. Interviews conducted with the supercool and larger-than-life Bootsy, which appeared in *Echoes*, the *New York Review Of Records* and *DJ Mag*, also proved invaluable. Jerome 'Bigfoot' Brailey is the ultimate funky drummer and so this tale didn't just come out like a load of starry-eyed gush, I spoke to him about his time in the P-Funk engine room and why he left to start the Mutiny project with Glenn Goins. Jerome was funny, frank and excited about his latest Mutiny album so still flying the flag. I would have interviewed Glenn too but sadly, like many names here, he is no longer with us. Luckily I was fortunate enough to meet and speak to Garry Shider, the soul of Parliament-Funkadelic, when they played with Primal Scream at that memorable all-nighter at Brixton Academy in 1994, along with Cordell 'Boogie' Mosson.

I'd like to thank Primal Scream's singer, Bobby Gillespie, for his eloquently heartfelt tribute to George, Talking Heads' Chris Frantz for telling how a P-Funk show inspired their biggest hit and Brendan Greaves at the wonderful Paradise of Bachelors label for his vivid description of the North Carolina country where George sprang into the world.

Interviews I've done which proved useful include pivotal P-Funker Junie Morrison for *Echoes* in 1990; Afrika Bambaataa and Jalal Nuriddin of the Last Poets at different meetings for *Zigzag* in the mid-eighties; late MC5 singer Rob Tyner and cultural guru John Sinclair bolstering the Detroit angle in *Zigzag* in 1977; 'Voice of Woodstock' Chip Monck talking for my *Record Collector* piece celebrating the festival's 30th anniversary in 2009; Fugs mainstay Ed Sanders for *Record Collector* in 2008; 'Godfather of Techno' Juan Atkins relating in 1992 how P-Funk helped birth Detroit's machine music.

Thanks also to Chris Charlesworth, who had the unenviable task of editing this thang, David Barraclough for letting me do it and the folks at Omnibus. Also a huge shout to Dick Porter and his good lady, Donna, for providing my life-saving pod in their Cornish Mothership, where this was hatched against a background of pet rabbits, cats and Godzilla movies.

Worthy of the highest praise are the photographers and P-Funk inner circle members who were so helpful in supplying the awesome pics: my old friend Serge Dodwell for his particularly intimate selection (including George's favourite dog, Buddy); Tim Kinley for opening up the P-Funk archive; George's manager, Carlon Thompson for the George and Sly photo; Grant Fleming for his gorgeous images from that unforgettable George-Primal Scream hookup; Robert Matheu (whose Clash photos I ran in *Zigzag* over 35 years ago) for Motor City gold; Tav Falco for his classic Sun Ra shot; Caroline Alden for George's undimmed rebel funk spirit in spring 2014; Aldo Mauro for capturing Eddie Hazel's tragic magic, Diem Jones for the Garry Shider butterfly shot; the late Steve Labelle and Edward Colver for the perfect cover photo.

Shouts also go out to those who've offered support, help or fed into this story in some way, including my son Daniel Lee Needs, Wonder, Primal Scream, Jasper the Vinyl Junkie, Crispin Payne, Mitt Gamon, Richard Daws, Angela Reed, Dynamax, Steve Mirkin, David Leifer, Craig Charles, Huey Morgan, Carlton P. Sandercock, Verna Wilson, K-Alexi Shelby, Lois Wilson, Jon Harrington, Chris Wells, Ian McCann, Wayne, Nic and all at the Royal Standard, Gwinear, plus Funkateers and Maggots I've encountered over the last 40 years and those I've inevitably missed out.

Thanks to my *Zigzag* mentor Pete Frame for the pile of late sixties Detroit-era *Creem* magazines, including the early Parliaments front cover from October 1970, which gave an idea of Detroit and underground music at that time. While I was editing *Zigzag*, Pete organised my becoming UK correspondent for *New York Rocker*, whose November 1979 issue included the meeting between George and James Chance in Chapter Thirteen.

There have only been a handful of books dealing with P-Funk but two were particularly inspirational and useful while telling this story. Rickey Vincent's *Funk: The Music, The People & The Rhythm Of The One* is one of the most breathtakingly perfect works I've encountered in six decades of music books, while the rare and elusive *For The Record: George Clinton And P-Funk: An Oral History* was invaluable for insights and quotes.

Bibliography

Other books which fed into or inspired this story include:

Aletti, Vince. *The Disco Files 1973–78: New York's Underground, Week By Week* (DJHistory.com, 2008)

Brown, James. *James Brown: The Godfather Of Soul* (Aurum, 2009)

Brewster, Bill; Broughton, Frank. *Last Night A DJ Saved My Life: The History Of The Disc Jockey* (Headline, 2000)

Carmichael, Stokely. *Ready For Revolution* (Simon & Schuster, 2005)

Chang, Jeff. *Can't Stop Won't Stop* (Ebury Press. New Edition, 2007)

Christgau, Robert. *Rock Albums Of The 70s: A Critical Guide* (Da Capo, 1981)

Corbett, John. *Extended Play: Sounding Off From John Cage To Dr Funkenstein* (Duke University Press, 1994)

Davis, Miles. *The Autobiography* (Picador, 1990)

Doggett, Peter. *There's A Riot Goin' On: Revolutionaries, Rock Stars & The Rise And Fall Of 60s Counter-culture* (Canongate, 2008)

Dury, Graham; Jones, Davey; Thorp, Simon. *Viz Roger's Profanisaurus: The Magna Farta* (Dennis Publishing)

Floyd Jr., Samuel A. *The Power Of Black Music: Interpreting Its History From Africa To The United States* (Oxford University Press, 1996)

George, Nelson. *Death Of Rhythm & Blues* (Penguin, 2008 reprint)

Goines, Donald. *Dopefiend* (Holloway House, 1971)

Gribin, Dr Anthony J & Schiff, Dr Mathew M. *Doo-Wop: Forgotten Third Of Rock 'N' Roll* [Krause, 1992]

Groia, Phillip. *They All Sang On The Corner: A Second Look At New York's Rhythm & Blues Vocal Groups* (Phillie Dee Enterprises, 2001 Revised Edition)

Hershey, Gerri. *Nowhere To Run: The Story Of Soul Music* (Pan Books, 1985)

Himes, Chester. *Cotton Comes To Harlem* (GP Putnam's Sons, 1965)

Iceberg Slim. *Pimp: The Story Of My Life* (Holloway House, 1967)

James, Darius. *That's Blaxploitation: Roots Of The Baadasssss 'Tude* (St Martin's Press, 1995)

James, Etta; Ritz, David. *Rage To Survive: The Etta James Story* (Da Capo, 2003)

Jones, LeRoi. *Blues People* (William Morrow, new edition 1999)

Kaliss, Jeff. *I Want To Take You Higher: The Life And Times Of Sly & The Family Stone* (Backbeat, 2009)

Kiedis, Anthony; Sloman, Larry. *Scar Tissue: The Autobiography* (Sphere, 2005)

Last Poets. *Vibes From The Scribes* (Pluto Press, 1985)

Mailer, Norman. *Miami And The Siege Of Chicago* (Penguin, 1969)

Marsh, Dave (ed.). *For The Record: George Clinton And P-Funk: An Oral History* (Avon Books, 1999)

Miller, Steve. *Detroit Rock City: The Uncensored History Of Rock 'N' Roll In America's Loudest City* (Da Capo Press, 2013)

Murray, Charles Shaar. *Crosstown Traffic: Jimi Hendrix & Post-War Pop* (Faber & Faber, 2005)

Needs, Kris. *The Scream: The Music, Myths & Misbehaviour Of Primal Scream* (Plexus, 2003)

Parker, Maceo. *98% Funk* (Chicago Review Press, 2013)

Reed, Ishmael. *Mumbo Jumbo* (Simon & Schuster, 1996)

Sinclair, John. *Sun Ra* (Headpress, 2010)

Smith, Vern E. *The Jones Men* (Payback Press, 1997)

Szwed, John. *Space Is The Place: The Lives And Times Of Sun Ra* (Da Capo, 2000)

Sullivan, Denise. *Keep On Pushing: Black Power Music From Blues To Hip-hop* (Lawrence Hill, 2011)

Toop, David. *The Rap Attack: African Jive To New York Hip Hop* (Pluto Press, 1984)

Sanders, Ed. *Fug You* (Da Capo, 2012)

Van Peebles, Melvin. *Sweet Sweet Back Baadasssss Song* (SOS Press Free Stock, 1994)

Vincent, Rickey. *Funk: The Music, The People & The Rhythm Of The One* (St Martin's Press, 1996)

Vincent, Rickey. Party Music: *The Inside Story Of The Black Panthers' Band & How Black Power Transformed Soul Music* (Chicago Review Press, 2013)

Weiss, Jason. *Always In Trouble: An Oral History Of ESP-Disk, The Most Outrageous Record Label in America* (Wesleyan University Press, 2012)

Wesley, Fred. *Hit Me, Fred: Recollections Of A Sideman* (Duke University Press, 2002)

Liner notes

Funkadelic reissues on Ace Records by Dean Rudland: *Funkadelic, Free Your Mind ... And Your Ass Will Follow, Maggot Brain, America Eats Its Young, Cosmic Slop, Standing On The Verge Of Getting It On, Let's Take It To The Stage*. Rob Bowman's epic history accompanying *Music For Your Mother. Under A Groove* boxset by Geoff Brown (2003).

Press

Abbey, John. *Blues & Soul* (April 1971)

Bradley, Lloyd. *NME* (December 1982; January 1983), *MOJO* (2006)

Broughton, Frank. *i-D* (February 1994)

Charlesworth, Chris. *Melody Maker* (May 1971)

Goldberg, Michael. *Rolling Stone* (June 1983)

Grabel, Richard. *NME* (December 1979)

Murphy, Peter. *Hot Press* (1996)

Rosen, Steven. *Guitar Player* (December 1977)

Simmons, Sylvie. *MOJO* (July 2004)

Spak, Kara. *Chicago Sun-Times* (November 9, 2009)

Welch, Chris. *Melody Maker* (May 1971)

White, Cliff. *NME* (November 1978)

Various copies of *Creem, Dance Music Report, Disc & Music Echo, Echoes, Hot Press, International Times, Melody Maker, MOJO, NME, OZ, Record Collector, Shindig!, Soul Underground, Uncut, The Wire, Zigzag.*

Websites

The Motherpage.com was a fantastic source of facts and analysis. The definitive P-Funk discography can be found here.

Scot Hacker's incisive essay 'Can You Get To That? The Cosmology of P-Funk' originally appeared in Pagan Kennedy's *Platforms: A Microwaved Cultural Chronicle Of The 70s* (St Martins Press 1994) and can now be found on stuckbetweenstations.com.

Also highly useful were
Rocksbackpages.com
classicurbanharmony.net
solidhitsoul.com/dellarks.html
www.forteantimes.com
www.blaxploitationpride.org

Finally, George's Flashlight2013.com website has been set up to report on his fight against the corporations and record companies he is currently in convoluted litigation with. "I want to be known as the man who brought to the attention of America the copyright issues," says Dr Funkenstein, still battling the Sir Noses at 72. We wish him all our support but hopefully this book shows the massive contribution he's already made to the socio-cultural fabric since the last century. As George still likes to say: "Think – it ain't illegal yet."

Index

A Whole Nother Thang 240–1
Afrofuturism 209–10
Ahh...The Name is Bootsy, Baby 241
All The Woo In The World 265
'All Your Goodies Are Gone (The Losers)'
   62, 138, 194
America Eats Its Young 146–50, 152–5
Apollo Theatre, Harlem 7–8, 13–14, 58–9,
   272, 304–5
Are You Experienced 105–6
Atkins, Juan 80, 300–1
Atkins, Mickey 61, 94, 101, 103
'Atomic Dog' 291–3
Axiom Funk 320
Ayers, Roy 165, 170
Ayler, Albert 36, 84

Babbitt, Bob 42, 101, 103, 118
Bailey, Leslyn 219
Ballard, Hank (& The Midnighters) 80, 90,
   198
Bambaataa, Afrika 288–9
Band of Gypsys 106–7, 108
Bangs, Lester 82, 111
Banks, Darrell 52
Banks, Ron 52
Barnes, J.J. 63

Barnes, Sidney 43–4, 46–7, 52, 137, 225,
   279
Beane, Harold 137, 149
Beatles, The 39, 47, 63–4, 69, 147
Belafonte, Harry 33, 38
Bell, Pedro 163–4, 175–8, 179, 185, 231,
   232, 257, 297
Berry, Chuck 39
Best Of The Early Years 239
Black Merda 182–3
Black Panthers 71, 90, 108
Black Power movement 32, 48–9, 90–1
Blackwell, George 53, 54
Blaxploitation films 164–71
Blue Cheer 65
Bogart, Neil 167, 168, 191–2, 211, 223–4,
   225, 240, 281
Boladian, Armen 95, 96, 137, 175, 256
Bonzo Goes To Washington 296
Bootsy? Player Of The Year 252–3
Bootsy's Rubber Band 214, 215–17,
   219–22, 228, 241, 252–3, 269, 279–80,
   296, 310–11
Bowen, Jeffrey 115, 116, 139–40, 182
Bowie, David 190–1, 209, 224
Boyce, Frankie 55
Boyer, Greg 254, 277

Boykins, Gene 19, 21
Brailey, Jerome 'Bigfoot': early bands 197–8, 202–4; 'Fuzzy' Haskins collaboration 240–1; headhunted by Clinton 204–5; member discontent 253–6; musical influences 201–2; Mutiny recordings 274–5; P-Funk Earth Tour 227; Quazar album 256–7; Tawl Ross collaboration 318–19
Brandye 187, 264
Brecker Brothers, The 197
Brides Of Funkenstein 228–9, 243, 247, 260, 262–3, 277
Brown, Arthur 125
Brown, Eddie 'Bongo' 42, 134
Brown, James 34, 49–51, 90–1, 152, 156–8, 159, 170, 246, 248–9, 272, 286
Brown, Jim 168, 170
Bruce, Lenny 71
By Way Of The Drum 301–2
Bykowski, Ron 172, 179, 192, 240
Byrd, Bobby 50, 156

Campbell, Sammy 25–6, 27, 28, 53, 54–5, 65–6, 316
Captain Beefheart 93
Carmichael, Stokely 49
Casablanca Records 191–2, 223–4, 239, 281
Casalin, Bea 19, 24
Chairmen of the Board 115, 141, 181–2
Chambers, Dennis 271, 277
Chambers Brothers, The 203–4
Chance, James 272
Charles, Ray 42
Chic 237–8
Chocolate City 195–7
'Chocolate City' 196
Chronic, The 308
Chuck D 286, 303
Cinderella Theory, The 302–3
Clapton, Eric 64–5
Cleaves, Jessica 270–1, 293

Clinton, George: anti heroin stance 136–7, 143, 150; 'Anti-tour' 265–6; Apollo Theatre, Harlem 7–8, 272, 304–5; artist spinoff plans 245–6, 260–3, 277; 'assembly line' recording sessions 205–8; audience appeal 120–1, 316; awards 325; band leader 200–1, 206; barbershop career 21–3, 25, 40, 45, 61; birth of 9; Bootsy Collins introduced 159; 'Bootsy' Collins, working with 201, 215–19; Capitol deal 290–1; CBS deal 279; childhood 10–12; *Creem* articles 59, 105, 120–1, 123–4, 128–9; Dr Funkenstein 222, 227, 242–3; drug taking 290; early musical influences 11, 12–13, 15–18; farm purchase 271; *Freaky Styley* production 298–9; The Funk 104–5, 188–90, 245; Funkadelic live 137–9; Funkadelic UK tour 125–8; Geo-Si-Mik productions 46–7, 52, 63; guest appearances 323–4; Hall of Fame entry 321; hip hop, influence on 285–90, 307–9; Jimi Hendrix's influence 66, 102, 105–6; legal disputes 275–6, 279, 282, 290–1, 296, 326; literary influences 168–9, 192–3; management role 93–4, 271–2; member discontent 140–1, 220–1, 230, 232, 240, 248, 253–5, 276; Mothership, concept behind 208–11; Motown acts, impact on 119; music business, future in 272–4, 305–7, 324–6; musical aspirations 31–2, 39–40, 42–3, 45–6; musical influences 92, 147–8; Newark race riots 1967 74–6; Paisley Park recordings 302, 306–7; The Parliaments 19, 21, 23–4, 27, 52, 55, 57–63, 65–7; Pedro Bell's description 179; P-Funk Earth Tour 224–30; Primal Scream collaboration 313–15; Process Church preachings 134–6; psychedelic influences 63–5, 70; psychedelic persona 66–7; radio

station acceptance 187; rapping 210;
renegade Funkadelic 275–6; Roger
Troutman affair 282; Ruth Copeland
collaboration 116–19, 139–40; Sir
Nose D'Voidoffunk 242–3; Sly
Stone, influence of 71, 73–4, 105;
songwriting style 44, 133, 147–8, 152,
172–3, 186; stage antics 65, 67, 89,
122, 137, 200, 214–15; stage props 8,
225, 226–7, 320; Sun Ra, comparison
with 85–6; techno, influence on
300–1; TV appearances 97–8, 120,
293; UFO story 208; Uncle Jam
Records 279; Vietnam War 129, 143,
145–6, 174; Warner Brothers deal
230–1, 281–2; Wellington Wigout
278
Clinton, Julia Keaton 9
Clinton, Robert 19, 129
Clones of Dr Funkenstein, The 222–3
Clovers, The 18
Coasters, The 17
Coffey, Dennis 101, 118, 170
Coleman, Ornette 36
Collins, Phelps 'Catfish' 155–8, 162, 219,
244
Collins, William 'Bootsy': birth of 155;
Bootsy's Rubber Band 215–22,
241, 252–3, 279–80, 296, 310–11;
Brown/Clinton, working with
160–2; burnout 267–9; Clinton,
working relationship 194–5, 201,
206, 215–19; early bands 156; Eddie
Hazel tribute 317–18; 'Five Minutes',
spoof record 296; Funkadelic, return
to 186; George Clinton introduced
159; Godmona 296; House Guests
formed 158; J.B.'s member 156–8;
songwriting style 293; stage antics
218–19; UFO story 208
Coltrane, John 34, 36, 37–8
Computer Games 291–4
Cook, Grace 53
Cooke, Sam 39, 42

'Cookie Jar' 241, 261
Cooper, Alice 123
Cooper, Gary 'Mudbone' 185, 197, 219,
293
Copeland, Ruth 116–17, 118–19, 139
Cosmic Slop 172–6
'Cosmic Slop' 173–4
Cream 64, 92
Creem (magazine) 59, 82, 105, 120–1,
128–9
Crows, The 18
Curry, Lige 283
Curtis, Rodney 'Skeet' 253, 255

Davis, Charles 'Butch' 19, 24
Davis, Clive 72, 184, 256
Davis, Miles 101, 111–12
Davis, Ray 'Sting Ray' 16, 27–8, 29, 114,
150, 179, 243, 293
Davis, Tyrone 61
De La Soul 270, 285
Death 183–4
Debonaires, The 46, 52–3, 151
Deee-Lite 310
Del-Larks, The 25, 26–9, 65–6
Dells, The 19
Digital Underground 106, 286, 308
disco, impact of 234–8
DJ Assault 301
Dolby, Thomas 297
doo-wop groups 15–20, 28
Dope Dogs 315–16
Dr Dre 308, 309
Dunbar, Ron 229, 276–7
Dylan, Bob 38, 147, 152

Earth, Wind & Fire 166, 224–5
Electric Spanking Of War Babies, The 283
Electrifying Mojo, The 300
Ellington, Duke 92

Farrakhan, Louis 47
Fiddler, Joseph 'Amp' 301, 303
Fiestas, The 16, 28

Five Stairsteps, The 202, 203
Flamin' Embers, The 52
'Flash Light' 235, 237, 244, 250
Flav, Flavor 178, 286, 303
Ford, Ron 243, 280, 283, 293
Four Seasons, The 21
Four Tops, The 44, 153
Franklin, Aretha 34, 80, 168
Franklin, Mallia 158–9, 261–2, 293
Frantz, Chris 269
Frazier, Zachary 103, 149
Freaky Styley 298–9
'Free Your Mind And Your Ass Will Follow'
   113
Free Your Mind…And Your Ass Will Follow
   112–15
Freed, Alan 17
Freeman, Bobby 71–3, 133
Fugs, The 70–1, 123
Fulwood, Ramon 'Tiki' 61, 94, 101, 118,
   139, 140, 179, 204
Funk Brothers, The 42, 46
Funk Or Walk 263–4
Funkadelic *see also* Parliament; audience
   appeal 119–21; band development
   92–7, 251; departures and arrivals
   136–8, 140–1, 149–50, 172, 185, 251,
   271, 276, 283; Detroit gigs 84, 88;
   image and stage act 89, 123–4, 273;
   incarnation of 65–8; live recording
   137–9; member discontent 220–1;
   Pedro Bell's artwork 175–7, 179;
   recording deals 72–3, 230; Ruth
   Copeland collaboration 139–40;
   studio recordings 101–5, 112–15,
   129–34, 148–55, 172–6, 178–81, 184–
   7, 231–1, 232–3, 239, 257–8, 270–1,
   283; UK tour 125–9
Funkadelic (renegade) 275–6
Funkadelic 102–5
Funkadelic-Live 137–9
Funkentelechy Vs The Placebo Syndrome
   242–4
'Funky Dollar Bill' 114, 316

Games, Dames and Guitar Thangs 246–8
Gardner, Rick 215, 276
Gaye, Marvin 116, 148, 153, 170
George Clinton And His Gangsters Of Love
   325
Giant Shirley 318–19
Gibbons, Walter 236
Gillespie, Bobby 312, 313–14
Ginsberg, Allen 38
'Give Up The Funk' (Tear The Roof Off
   The Sucker) 16, 205, 212
Gloryhallastoopid 278
Godmoma 296
Goins, Glenn 201, 212, 223, 253,
   254–7
'Good Old Music' 63, 104
'Goose (That Laid The Golden Egg), The
   62, 194
Gordy, Berry 21, 41–2, 43, 44, 79, 89, 94,
   119, 148, 182
Gordy, Raynoma 43, 44–5
gospel music, influence of 13, 33–4
Graham, Larry 71, 72
Grand Funk 182
Grandmaster Flash 288, 294
Grateful Dead 181, 316
Green, Al 148
Grier, Pam 170
Griffith, Richard 'Kush' 198, 219, 276

Hampton, Michael 185, 205, 233,
   255
Hancock, Herbie 171, 309
Handy, Roy 52
Hardcore Jollies 230, 232
Harris, Ernie 45, 47, 62, 114, 153
Harrison, Jerry 296
Haskins, Clarence 'Fuzzy' 29–30, 47, 58,
   59, 66, 150, 151, 179, 240, 264–5,
   275–6
Havens, Richie 99–100
Hawkins, Coleman 35
Hawkins, Screamin' Jay 12, 67
Hayes, Isaac 12, 155, 166–7

Hazel, Eddie: band departure 140–1; birth of 53; death of 316–17; early music career 53–5; Funkadelic line-up 94; guest musician 118–19, 139; jam with Jerome Brailey 204; Jimi Hendrix's influence 106, 130, 232–3; joins Parliaments 60; 'Maggot Brain' 130–1, 138; prison stay 185, 246–7; sensitive personality 132; solo album 246–8; songwriting 179; temporary absence 96; vocal style 179

'Heart Trouble' 52, 175, 223

Heartbeats, The 19

Hendrix, Jimi 34, 57, 64, 66–7, 92, 100, 105–9, 110–11, 112, 124, 130, 131–2, 147

Herc, DJ Kool 288

Hey Man - Smell My Finger 306–7, 309

Himes, Chester 168–9

hip hop 285–9

Holland, Edward & Brian & Dozier, Lamont 115, 116, 181–2

Hooker, John Lee 78, 80

Horny Horns, The 198, 220, 238, 248, 276, 293

House Guests, The 158–9, 216, 218

How Late Do U Have 2BB4UR Absent? 324–5

Hutch, Willie 165, 170

'I Call My Baby Pussycat' 117, 154–5

'(I Wanna) Testify' 57–8, 62, 194

Ice Cube 308, 309

'I'll Bet You' 103–4

independent music labels 18–19, 20, 24–5, 28, 35, 45, 46, 53–4, 58, 80–1, 87, 95, 115

Ink Spots, The 12, 17

Invictus 115–16, 118, 181–2

Iron Butterfly 121

Ivy, Archie 279

Jackson, James Wesley 120, 134, 149, 226, 265

Jackson, Mahalia 38

Jackson, Michael 47, 294

Jackson 5 153

Jagger, Mick 125

James, Etta 107

J.B.'s 156–8, 198–9

JC 001 307, 309–10

Jenkins, Herbie 19, 21

Jethro Tull 92, 148

'Jimmy's Got A Little Bit of Bitch In Him' 180

John, Prakash 149

Johnson, Robert 'Peanut' 219, 293

Jo-Jo & The Admirations 55, 60–1

Jones, LeRoi (Baraka, Amiri) 37

Kapralik, David 72–3

Kennedy, John F. 34, 38

Kennedy, Robert 91

Kerr, George 43–4

Kiedis, Antony 298

King, B.B. 64, 95

King, Martin Luther 38, 90

Kiss 178, 191

'Knee Deep' 270, 272

Knight, Gladys (& The Pips) 44, 168

Kool & The Gang 166, 294

Kramer, Wayne 82, 84, 184

Lampkin, Tyrone 137–8, 149, 151, 179, 256

Larks, The 18

Last Poets, The 108–9, 319–20

Laswell, Bill 84, 296, 309, 311–12, 317, 319–20

Leary, Timothy 68

Lennon, John 123

Let's Take It To The Stage 184–7

'Let's Take It To The Stage' 186

Levan, Larry 234

Lewis, Barbara 47

Lewis, Pat 46, 52, 57, 62, 102, 133

Lewis, Tracey 57, 297, 302, 324

Lincoln, Abbey 35

Lindsay, Theresa 46–7

Live/P-Funk Earth Tour 239–40
Lloyd, Overton 260
'Lonely Island' 24
'Loopzilla' 289
'Loose Booty' 71, 118, 152
Lumpkins, Leon 102
Lymon, Frankie (& The Teenagers) 19–21

Mabry, Lynn 228–9, 262–3, 277, 293
Maggot Brain 129–34
'Maggot Brain' 130–1
Mailer, Norman 83
Manson, Charles 98
'March To The Witch's Castle' 174
May, Derrick 80, 300–1
Mayfield, Curtis 34, 39, 89, 167–8, 202
MC5 81, 82–3, 87, 91, 123, 182
McDonald, Country Joe 99
McGee, Harvey 53, 60, 150
McKnight, DeWayne 'Blackbyrd' 271, 277
'Me, Myself And I' 244, 270, 285–6
Miles, Buddy 109, 232
Miller, Jimmy 24, 118
Mingus, Charles 35
'Mommy, What's A Funkadelic' 101–2, 103
Monck, Chip 99–100
Monette, Ray 101, 118
Moonglows, The 17–18
Moore, Rudy Ray 171
Moroder, Giorgio 224
Morrison, Jim 67, 122–3
Morrison, Junie 158, 251–2, 258, 270, 281, 293
Mosson, Cordell 'Boogie' 132, 149–50, 151, 179, 207
Mosson, Larry 'Cool Pop' 61
Mothership Connection 198, 205, 208–12
'Mothership Connection' 211
Motor Booty Affair 259–60
Motown 41–5, 79, 119, 148, 182
Mott The Hoople 125, 126
Moulton, Tom 236, 264
'Munchies For Your Love' 219, 241
'Music For My Mother' 95–6

Mutiny 274–5
Mutiny On The Mamaship 274–5

Nation of Islam 209–10
Nelson, Billy 'Bass' 53, 54–5, 58, 60, 66, 67–8, 94, 95–6, 103, 118, 139, 140, 185, 256, 271, 276
Newton, Huey 91–2, 152
Nuriddin, Jalauddin Mansur 109–10
N.W.A 252, 308

Obama, Barack 39, 326
Odetta 33, 38
'Oh Lord, Why Lord' 116
Ohio Players, The 251–2
O'Jays, The 58–9, 65, 148
'One Nation Under A Groove' 235, 250–1
One Nation Under A Groove 257–9
Orioles, The 17
Osibisa 128, 168
Osmium 115–18

Pacemakers, The 156
Parker, Maceo 50–1, 198, 199–200, 219, 228, 276
Parlet 158, 241, 260–2, 276–7
Parliafunkadelicment Thang 93–4, 95, 230
Parliament *see also* Funkadelic; departures and arrivals 194–5, 197–8, 201, 240, 253, 281; Detroit gigs 120–1; image and stage act 123–4, 190–1, 214–14; live recordings 239–40; member discontent 220–1, 230, 232, 253–5; P-Funk Earth Tour 224–30, 239–40; recording deals 115, 191, 239; Ruth Copeland collaboration 116–19; studio recordings 115–18, 178, 192–4, 195–8, 205–12, 222–3, 230, 235, 242–4, 259–60, 278–9, 280; US tours 213–15, 253
Parliaments, The: band development 57–63; drug taking 67–8; early gigs 21; formation of 19; image and stage act 27, 59–60, 65–7, 88–9; line-up changes

23–4, 29–30; Motown audition
43–4; Newark race riots 1967 75–6;
recording deals 52, 93–4
Payne, Michael 'Clip' 293
Peel, John 47
Pets, The 47
'P-Funk (Wants To Get Funked Up) 211,
239
P-Funk All Stars 285, 294–5, 320
Phillips, Anya 272–4
Pink Floyd 147
'Poor Willie' 24
Pop, Iggy 84, 88, 124
Presley, Elvis 39
Primal Scream 312–15, 316
Prince 294, 302, 306–7, 321
Process Church of the Final Judgement
134–5
Pryor, Richard 189–90
Public Enemy 285, 286
Pudim, Alafia *see* Nuriddin, Jalauddin
Mansur

Quazar 254, 256–7

R & B Skeletons In The Closet 297–8
race riots 1967 74–8
Radio Active 264–5
Ravens, The 17
Red Hot Chili Peppers 298–9, 309, 316
'Red Hot Mamma' 118, 180–1
Reed, Ishmael 168–9, 192–3
Revilot label 52, 57, 61–2, 93
Richards, Keith 207
Roach, Max 35
Robinson, Smokey 41, 171
Rodgers, Nile 237
Rolling Stones, The 47, 69, 71, 89, 100–1,
147, 224
Rollins, Sonny 35
Ross, Lucius 'Tawl': birth of 61; departure
of 136–7; Funkadelic line-up 94;
guest musician 118–19; joins
Parliaments 61; solo album 318–19

Sanders, Ed 56, 70, 71
Saunderson, Kevin 300–1
Say Brother (TV show) 97–8
Scott-Heron, Gil 164, 180
Scribner, Ron 89, 119–20, 128, 134,
146
Sequence, The 212
Sgt Pepper's Lonely Hearts Club Band 63,
147, 148
'Sex Machine' 156–7
Shaft (film) 166
Shakur, Tupac 308
Shepp, Archie 36
Shider, Garry 'Starchild': 'Atomic Dog' 293;
Eddie Hazel's death 316–17; joins
Funkadelic 132, 149–50; 'One Nation
Under A Groove' 258; United Soul
recordings 150–1; vocal style 179;
vocal training 173–4
Shirelles, The 13, 14
'Silent Boatman, The' 117
Silva, Dawn 228–9, 262–3, 293
Silverman, Tom 143
Simon, Calvin 24, 57, 67, 138–9, 149, 179,
275–6
Simone, Nina 34
Sinclair, John 82, 85, 87, 91
Sly & the Family Stone 72, 100, 228
Snoop Dog 308–9
Solitaires, The 18, 28
Some Of My Best Jokes Are Friends 297
Spaniels, The 16, 18
Sparkman, Herbert J. 95–6, 104
Sparky & the Pimpadelics 96
Spinners, The 158
Spradley, David 292
Standing On The Verge Of Getting It On
178–81
Staple Singers 148, 168
Starr, Edwin 46, 81, 170, 183
Sterling, Donnie 262
Stone, Sly 34, 63, 66, 71–2, 107, 124, 140,
148, 228, 283, 295
Stooges, The 81, 84, 182

Stretchin' Out With Bootsy's Rubber Band 221–2
Strong, Nolan (& The Diablos) 23, 81
Summer, Donna 223–4, 281
Sun Ra 36–7, 83, 85–7, 171, 209
'Super Stupid' 133–4
Superfly (film) 167
Supremes, The 46, 102

Tackhead 297
Tales Of Kidd Funkadelic 231–2
Talking Heads 269–70
T.A.P.O.A.F.O.M. (The Awesome Power Of A Fully Operational Mothership) 320–1
Taylor, Johnnie 58, 212
Taylor, LaBaron 52, 93
Taylor, Ron 25, 26, 29
techno 300–1
Temptations, The 23, 44, 65, 119, 153
Terry, Andrew 'Mike' 46, 62, 94
This Boot Is Made For Funk-N 269
Thomas, Grady 23, 24, 47, 58, 66, 179, 240, 275–6
Tommy (rock opera) 147–8
Tommy Boy Records 285–6
Trombipulation 280
Troutman, Roger 282
Tyner, Rob 82, 83

Uncle Jam Records 279, 294–5
Uncle Jam Wants You 270–1
Unifics, The 197–8, 202
United Soul 26, 150–1
'Up For The Down Stroke' 178, 192
Up For The Down Stroke 192, 193–4

Van de Pitte, David 153
Van Peebles, Melvin 166
Vanilla Fudge 65
Vietnam War, impact of 64, 90, 143–5
Vincent, Rickey 111, 122, 189

Waddy, Frank 'Frankie Kash' 156, 158, 218, 219, 256

'Wars of Armageddon' 134
Washington, Jeanette 228, 243, 261–2
Watson, Wah Wah 202
Wells, Mary 42, 44–5
Wesley, Fred 157–8, 170, 198–9, 200–1, 207–8, 214–15, 219, 220, 248, 276
West Side Story (musical) 40–1
Westbound Records 95, 115, 150–1, 184, 231, 239
'What Is Soul' 98, 104
'Whatever Makes My Baby Feel Good' 94–5, 194
Whitfield, Norman 72, 119
Who, The 58, 147–8
'Who Knows' 106, 181
Williams, Andre 81
Williams, Rose 94, 133
Williams, Vanessa 297
Williamson, Fred 168, 170
Wilson, Jackie 23, 41, 42
Wingate, Ed 46, 52, 94
Winston,, Stanley 47
Womack, Bobby 171
Wonder, Stevie 148, 153
Woodstock Festival 99–100
Worrell, Bernie: band moderator 133; classical training 92; Clinton, working relationship 149, 201; guest musician 118–19, 139, 269; Horny Horns sessions 200; musical abilities 92–3; production projects 150; school performances 26; solo album 265; songwriting highlights 232, 237, 244; studio albums 293; vocal style 179
Wright, Debbie 243, 260–2
Wynne, Philipe 158, 270, 279

X, Malcolm 35–6, 47–8

You Shouldn't-Nuf Bit Fish 295

Zapp 282
Zappa, Frank 126, 212, 255